THE CZECHOSLOVAK ECON(

T0328865

Soviet and East European Studies

Series list continues on p. 317

THE CZECHOSLOVAK ECONOMY 1948–1988

The battle for economic reform

MARTIN MYANT

Department of Economics and Management, Paisley College of Technology

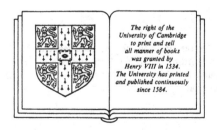

The right of the
University of Cambridge
to print and sell
all manner of books
was granted by
Henry VIII in 1534.
The University has printed
and published continuously
since 1584.

CAMBRIDGE UNIVERSITY PRESS

Cambridge
New York   Port Chester   Melbourne   Sydney

CAMBRIDGE UNIVERSITY PRESS
Cambridge, New York, Melbourne, Madrid, Cape Town, Singapore,
São Paulo, Delhi, Dubai, Tokyo, Mexico City

Cambridge University Press
The Edinburgh Building, Cambridge CB2 8RU, UK

Published in the United States of America by Cambridge University Press, New York

www.cambridge.org
Information on this title: www.cambridge.org/9780521143769

© Cambridge University Press 1989

First published 1989
First paperback printing 2010

A catalogue record for this publication is available from the British Library

Library of Congress Cataloguing in Publication data

Myant, M. R. (Martin R.)
The Czechoslovak economy, 1948–1988: the battle for economic
reform / Martin Myant.
    p.   cm. – (Soviet and East European studies)
Bibliography.
Includes index.
ISBN 0-521-35314-9
1. Czechoslovakia – Economic policy – 1945–
2. Czechoslovakia – Economic conditions – 1945–
I. Title.   II. Series.
HC270.28.M96 1989
338.9437 – dc 19   88-32690 CIP

ISBN 978-0-521-35314-4 Hardback
ISBN 978-0-521-14376-9 Paperback

Contents

Tables

Acknowledgements

This book would have been impossible without help and encouragement from a number of individuals and institutions. My colleagues at Paisley College of Technology enabled me to rearrange teaching and other responsibilities to allow for a four month leave of absence during which much of the final version was written. Visits to Czechoslovakia in 1985 and 1987 were arranged through and financed by the British Academy while one in 1986 was under the auspices of the British Council.

Conversations with many people were helpful, but the knowledge and ideas of a number of Czechoslovak economists have definitely contributed directly to the conclusions in this book. At the Economics Institute of the Czechoslovak Academy of Sciences I learnt a great deal from Jan Klacek, Jaroslav Habr (formerly Halbhuber), Jaromír Vepřek, Michal Mejstřík, Karla Trdlicová, Jaroslav Kutil, Mojmír Hájek, Miroslav Toms, Antonín Kotulan, Kamil Janáček, Hana Rosická, Livia Klausová, and others who took part in a number of discussions. From the recently established Institute of Forecasting I benefited directly from conversations with Karel Dyba, Alena Nešporová, Adolf Suk, Tomáš Ježek and Vladimír Dlouhý. At the Economics Institute of the Slovak Academy of Sciences I was greatly helped by Jozef Vojtko, Viliam Vaškovič, Pavel Hoffmann, Jozef Markuš, Gerhard Brhlovič, Daneš Brzica and Bronislav Prokop. I also had productive meetings with Dušan Štrauch of the Research Institute of Socio-economic Information in Bratislava, Igor Očka of the Research Institute of Engineering Industry Technology and Economics and especially with František Vencovský, Chief Adviser to the Chairman of the State Planning Commission. I would also like to acknowledge the contribution from Jan Pudlák, František Kovář and Eduard Vopička of the High School of Economics in Prague, of Stanislav Grohmann and Juraj Mašláni of the High School of Economics in Bratislava and of Ivan

Kočárník and his colleagues at the Research Institute of the Finance and Credit System attached to the Ministry of Finance. Special mention must also be made of Václav Klaus who recently moved from the State Bank to the Institute of Forecasting.

I have benefited from many contacts during earlier visits to Czechoslovakia in 1967–8, 1969, 1970, 1973, 1975 (under a British Council student exchange) and 1983. Special mention must be made of meetings with Josef Goldmann and, more recently, with Miloš Hájek and Hana Mejdrová.

I used the help of librarians in Glasgow and Edinburgh Universities, in the School of Slavonic and East European Studies in London, in the London School of Economics, the British Library, the Mitchell Library in Glasgow, Paisley College of Technology and the Economics Institute of the Czechoslovak Academy of Sciences.

Some of the material in Chapters 6 and 7 was previously published in articles in *Coexistence*, vols. 19 and 20.

Typing and technical assistance was provided by Linda Hunter, Lyndonne McLeod and Amanda Mullen. A penultimate version was read by Monty Johnstone and Nicholas Anderton, both of whom made a number of helpful comments. I am also grateful for detailed comments from Chris Doubleday of Cambridge University Press and for careful advice on the final version from Alistair Young. It must, of course, be emphasised that all the views expressed and mistakes are entirely my own responsibility.

Abbreviations

ČKD   Českomoravská Kolben Daněk (Prague engineering enterprise)
CMEA   Council for Mutual Economic Assistance
CP   Communist Party
CPSU   Communist Party of the Soviet Union
ČSAV   Československá akademie věd (Czechoslovak Academy of Sciences)
EEC   European Economic Community
HN   *Hospodářské noviny* (Economic Newspaper, weekly published by Communist Party of Czechoslovakia)
HSR   *Historická statistická ročenka* (Historical Statistical Yearbook)
Kčs   Koruny československé (Czechoslovak crowns)
NM   *Nová mysl* (New Thought, Communist Party monthly)
PE   *Politická ekonomie* (Political Economy, monthly of the Economics Institute of the Czechoslovak Academy of Sciences)
PH   *Plánované hospodářství* (Planned Economy, monthly of the State Planning Commission)
RP   *Rudé právo* (Red Right, daily of the Communist Party of Czechoslovakia)
SAV   Slovenská akademie vied (Slovak Academy of Sciences)
SITC   Standard International Trade Classification
SR   *Statistická ročenka Republiky československé*, subsequently *Statistická ročenka ČSSR* (Statistical Yearbook of the Czechoslovak Republic and Statistical Yearbook of the Czechoslovak Socialist Republic)

Introduction

This book is inspired by the fresh wave of interest in economic reform, now encompassed within the even broader term 'restructuring', in the Soviet Union and Eastern Europe. Its aim is to explore the widely held belief that a serious programme for the renewal of socialism is possible only on the basis of a thorough assessment of past experience. Czechoslovakia has a special significance, partly because it was already an industrialised country in 1948 and therefore has 40 years' experience in developing an advanced socialist economy. It was also the scene of the attempt of the late 1960s to combine economic with political reform which must be judged essentially similar to Gorbachov's *perestroika*.

This, then, is not an orthodox economic history of Czechoslovakia. It gives far greater weight to particular key periods during which the economic system was at stake. It explores consistently the three interrelated themes of the development of the system, its relationship to the wider political and international climate and the performance of that system.

Performance over the whole 40 years from 1948 to 1988 must be judged disappointing but not disastrous. Figures on national income per head, which can never be more than an approximate indicator, suggest that economic growth in Czechoslovakia up to 1980 tended to be slightly slower than in neighbouring countries. The absolute level was undoubtedly much higher than the latter in the inter-war period with national income per head nearly 60% above that of Hungary and 70% above that of Poland. Czechoslovakia's economic structure was closer to that of advanced countries of the time with, according to 1930 figures, only 30% of the active population employed in agriculture and 45% in mining and manufacturing. Poland at that time had 67% in agriculture and 18% in industry while the figures for Hungary were 54% and 22% respectively. All have shown a shift towards a more modern structure with a fall in agricultural employment. Czecho-slovakia still leads the way: agriculture in 1980 employed only 13% of the active population compared with 29% in Poland and 20% in Hungary. There is, however, evidence that the gap has closed in national income per head. Figures derived from one method of calculation suggest that by 1980 Czechoslovakia was only 15% above the Hungarian level and a mere 24% ahead of Poland. These are almost certainly low estimates and the margin of error is large.

Comparisons also suggest that Czechoslovakia has grown slightly more slowly than the more successful Western European countries. In 1938 national income per head was about 75% of that of France: the gap was probably as wide in 1980. On reasonable estimates it has been overtaken by Italy, but it has done considerably better than laggards such as Britain.[1] A look at the most recent developments and their likely implications for the future suggests a slightly less inspiring picture as no obvious basis has been created for future success. The economic structure, internal system and set of international relationships created around 1950, which were the basis for that modest success, seem to have outlived their limited usefulness.

The effort to explain this, and to show the obstacles to changing what has frequently been recognised as an obsolete system, starts after the Communist victory of 1948. Considerable coverage is given to the early 1950s as a crucial period for the creation of the system. There is no doubting the close links between economic developments and the political atmosphere at the time with rampant security forces and show trials of real and imagined political opponents. It was also a crucial period for showing the limits of the power of the central authorities over economic processes. In political terms it was a repressive and centralised system, but the accompanying economic system never corresponded to the abstract notion of a 'command economy'.

A central issue for current policy debates has to be the late 1960s. In fact, one of the greatest weaknesses of the thinking behind current economic reform efforts even in the USSR is that their leading proponents are unwilling, uninterested or even forbidden from looking at Czechoslovakia's past. It becomes very clear that there were serious difficulties in 1968, some of which could be avoided if foreseen. There are also serious questions about the whole strategy pursued and the possibly exaggerated expectations which could actually be being repeated again.

The destruction of the Prague Spring brought, in economic terms, what for a time seemed to be a welcome return to stability. It was, however, associated with a failure to confront the economy's long-term weaknesses which were brought back to the forefront of attention at the end of the 1970s. A gradual, persistent decline in competitiveness was shielded for a time by the relationship with the Soviet Union, but ultimately reappeared as the Achilles heel of the Czechoslovak economy.

The analysis of this and other weaknesses is built up by following a number of separable areas as far as possible in a chronological order. Thus investment problems persist throughout the period, but are discussed in greatest detail around the events of 1961–2, 1968 and the early 1980s, those being the periods when they related most immediately to the thinking and policy responses of the time. Similarly the issue of consumer goods shortages was given greatest attention in the late 1960s and recurs, albeit around somewhat different theories, in the 1980s. Hopefully the treatment of these questions brings more life and relevance to the theoretical discussions.

It is impossible to give a detailed and definitive conclusion on how to achieve the economic reform that could overcome the Czechoslovak economy problems. Generalisations exist about combining plan and market, but there are immense practical difficulties that will only be solved during further experience. One point of certainty, however, is that the economic system can never be separated off from political and other considerations. An economic reform cannot succeed as a purely technical matter of changing indicators or economic variables. It requires a comprehensive programme combining economics and politics and involving participation from far beyond the existing centres of power and influence.

1 The end of the Czechoslovak road

The Czechoslovak road

In February 1948 the Communist Party established an effective monopoly of power in Czechoslovakia. It promised to create a more secure, more just and generally wealthier society than would have been possible under any other political leadership. The change in political power would, it was believed, lead to the best possible economic system. Although no official sanction was given to the idea, leading activists were talking optimistically of turning Czechoslovakia into a 'shop window' of socialism that could provide an attractive example for other developed countries in the world.

There undeniably were great gains for large sections of society with the ending of the threat of unemployment, comprehensive national insurance and other changes, but this ultimate ambition was not achieved. In fact, the ruling Communist Party very quickly found itself facing major problems that it was theoretically ill-equipped to solve. Far from finding it easy to change society, it was caught up in a complex web of social conflicts and prejudices that could not be explained or confronted with the familiar concept of the class struggle.

Prior to February 1948, the CP had won 38% of the votes in contested elections and been the dominant force in a broad coalition government which had implemented revolutionary changes in political, social and economic life. The most important for the economy were the nationalisation of 61% of industry, measured by employment, the expulsion of the German minority, which had made up one-fifth of Czechoslovakia's population including the overwhelming majority in Bohemian frontier areas, and an egalitarian land reform.[1] Although there were very clear differences in enthusiasm and in the extent of change advocated by different parties, so that political life always showed signs of dividing into a straight contest between left and right, all legal parties were verbally committed to these measures. There was a conceivable basis there for a distinct model of socialism based around a plurality of political parties and forms of ownership. The CP went less than half-way towards recognising that possibility with the notion, developed in 1946 on the basis of discussions between the Czechoslovak CP leader Klement Gottwald and Stalin, of a specific, Czechoslovak road to socialism. This was to be 'slower' than the Soviet road, avoiding violent repression and civil war, but the final aim was never redefined.

It required winning support not just from the working class, but also from small businessmen (9% of the economically active population and employing another 16%) office workers (26% of the active population) and the 20% that worked in farming. There was considerable mutual distrust between these sections of society with many workers accusing shopkeepers of black marketeering and managers of having collaborated with the Nazis: there was also a deep resentment towards remaining inequalities and privileges in the period of post-war austerity. This was matched by fears from other social groups that further revolutionary changes could only be at their expense.

To hold this alliance together, clear statements about the future were avoided whenever possible, leaving the maximum scope for compromise and pragmatism. There was, however, a continuing, largely unstated assumption that Czechoslovakia would ultimately follow the example of the Soviet Union to become a one-party state with all economic assets collectively owned. There was, then, never any guarantee that the 'specific' road would lead to a 'specific' model of socialism. Nevertheless, the longer a decisive fight for power could be pushed into the future, so the greater the chance would have been of developing new ideas.

There were elements of pluralism[2] in the emerging economic model, most obviously in the plurality of sectors defended by specific interest groups and different political parties. Under the prevailing conditions there was no possibility of creating a single, supreme body with full responsibility for the preparation, formulation and implementation of economic policy. In practice, the Economic Council, an advisory body to the government containing representatives of the different political parties, became the major forum for discussing economic issues. It had no executive power as nationalised enterprises were subordinated to a government minister.

They were also intended to retain considerable independence, and to be able to compete with the remaining private firms as self-financing entities. The principle of one-man management was tempered in the formal structure by a management board – one-third elected from the workers – which could select the director subject only to ministerial approval. Of greater significance in practice was the strength of elected works councils which were often effectively an equal partner with management performing some functions later taken over explicitly by party organisations. The difference in the 1945–48 period was that, even if they were often CP-dominated, the works councils were elected by the whole workforce.

Decentralisation was, however, limited in the conditions of post-war austerity. In fact, the system of economic management had a lot in common with a capitalist war economy where independent units are controlled and restricted by a central selection and enforcement of priorities. This was certainly not Soviet-type planning and neither was it necessarily the basis for adopting the Soviet model. Nevertheless, the CP showed consistently more interest in measures pointing towards centralisation and central planning than the 'specific' elements. Elections of enterprise directors were delayed and given little publicity. Failures were judged against plan targets and frequently blamed on decentralisation. Thus, for example, the investment plan was only two-thirds fulfilled in 1947 and the blame was put on the large private sector – still accounting for 87% of employment in construction – diverting resources away from priority tasks.[3] This was used as an argument for further nationalisation in the construction industry after which it was hoped planning in detail for individual projects with set completion dates, an indication of their importance and clearly recorded costs would eliminate the 'leakage' of capacity into non-priority areas.[4]

The theoretical basis for this approach was, of course, Marxist theory and Soviet practice. There was no interest in recent advances in economic thinking in capitalist countries, although 'Keynesian' ideas had been brought into Czechoslovakia from Sweden in the 1930s. They were taken seriously by some economists in the post-war period who criticised the superficial level of thinking which simply saw a 'plan' as a universal panacea without any real understanding of its meaning.[5] For the CP, however, it was assumed 'that development will lead in the direction of the Soviets'.[6]

They were not pressing for the full adoption of the whole Soviet system, but they were advocating individual aspects selected in a pragmatic way. Thus the nationalisation of industry meant the end to class conflict and they hoped it would unleash workers' initiative: there was even a rather unsuccessful attempt at developing a Stakhanovite movement in coal mines in 1945. They also looked forward to the end of the 'anarchy of production' inherited from capitalism. Soviet industrial organisation was widely seen as an important example:[7] nationalisation could create the scope for following what Soviet economists had called 'the American road' with mass production rationally specialised between factories.[8]

The key element had to be an actual state plan. Very little was known of the detailed practice of Soviet planning. If anything, the first reports emphasised the degree to which it depended on *decentralisation*, individual responsibility and initiative at the lowest levels. It was anyway quite clear that, in view of the lack of reliable data and the shortage of cadres equipped to run a new system of management, the Czechoslovak economy would have to rely very heavily on its own previous experience.

In fact, planning appeared partly as a pragmatic means to cope with immediate problems stemming from the loss of much of the labour force and from war damage. Attempts to quantify that latter element suggest total losses possibly equivalent to the national income produced in six pre-war years. That could be an exaggeration as there had been considerable investment in electricity and heavy engineering and some valuable preparations for a post-war economy. Nevertheless, some sectors were hit very hard and some degree of strategic central coordination seemed logical. This was achieved within the Two Year Plan for 1947 and 1948 which aimed to restore the economy to its pre-war level. For the CP it was also part of a political battle to prove that planning worked and the party put an enormous effort into ensuring that the main targets were met.

Planning then meant primarily the formulation of a more general strategy providing a coherent economic programme for all government organs. It was quite compatible with the expectation of some accompanying revival of the market as wartime difficulties were overcome. The 1945–48 period was no golden age, but the outline of an economic system had taken shape that contained specific elements of the Soviet system set into a pluralist framework and that could stimulate thinking in the future. It could be judged rather successful not only in terms of the pace of reconstruction – the pre-war level of industrial output was achieved in 1948 – but also because economic issues were an arena in which the political parties' representatives could often agree and cooperate.

The coalition interlude ended primarily because of changes in the international situation alongside continuing political rivalries and social tensions. Czechoslovak experience did not confirm Hayek's prediction, which was actually well known and widely discussed at the time, that the concentration of power associated with state control and planning of the economy must lead to dictatorship, totalitarianism and the destruction of political freedom.[9] Neither did the CP's establishment of a monopoly of power in February 1948 lead at once to a complete rejection of past economic policy.

An immediate consequence was a wave of further nationalisations bringing 95% of industry, in terms of employment, within the state sector. There was, however, still a pragmatic acceptance that evolution towards a fully planned economy would take some time. There was still no rigid administrative hierarchy and the priority seemed to be a general strategy with broad objectives rather than the most detailed possible plan. The former was to be provided by the First Five Year Plan which was to take the economy forward in 1949 after completing post-war reconstruction.[10] Initial ideas, which were to form the core of the final version, came from CP economists in mid-1947 and uncontroversially proclaimed an increase in living standards of all sections of the population to be the principal objective. To achieve this they had to start by recognising Czechoslovakia's dependence on trends in the world economy which were felt to create an incontrovertible case for a structural and geographical reorientation.

There was no question of cutting off contact with the West. Trade figures left little doubt that that was the direction of Czechoslovakia's international links both before World War II and, increasingly, after it as the economy recovered from the immediate post-war disruption. The Soviet Union accounted for little over 5% of trade in 1947 while other Eastern European countries accounted for under 7%. There were, however, a number of sources of deep concern. It was proving difficult to win orders in the highly competitive Western market for Czechoslovak exports, especially of textiles, glass and footwear. Moreover, there was a very widespread assumption that the economic history of the inter-war period would be repeated with 'the threatening signs of an economic crisis gathering on the horizon'.[11] Reliance on exporting to the West therefore appeared as a high-risk strategy and it looked particularly dangerous to try to rebuild economic stability around the traditional exports of consumer goods, such as textiles, which had an unstable and limited demand and relied heavily on imported raw materials.

The plan was therefore to continue with the trend, apparent even before the war, for a shift towards exporting heavy engineering products and chemicals. These were sectors that had been sustained under the Nazi occupation and could enjoy a bright future exporting to the developing countries of East and South East Europe, particularly as Germany had 'temporarily vanished as a competitor'.[12] Thanks to political and economic changes throughout Eastern Europe, Czechoslovakia seemed to be ideally placed to benefit from state planning accelerating a structural transformation that had already begun.

If this was to be the core of the plan, then there were three important reservations to a total dependence on structural change. The first was an acceptance of the need to develop the consumer durables sector within the engineering industry. The second was a recognition of the need to invest in and modernise the textiles and leather industries so that they could catch up with the 'world' level and better satisfy domestic needs, even if they were no longer to be the leading export sectors. The third, and most important reservation, which is obviously connected with the previous point, was a recognition of the need for continuing contacts with the capitalist world economy; in the Prime Minister's words in October 1948, 'we will exclude nobody from economic and commercial contacts'.[13] Any alternative view had to be rejected as the emerging socialist bloc simply did not have the full range of raw materials that Czechoslovakia needed. More generally, there seemed as yet no need to abandon, in total, traditional contacts. The structural transformation was therefore to be a long-term and complex process which was only one part, albeit the most important part, of the strategy for Czechoslovakia's economic future.

It was one of the great benefits of the multi-party system in the period before February that these ideas had to be debated with representatives of the other political parties which acted as a control on unrealistic or over-ambitious thinking. There was, however, no alternative in the sense of so comprehensive an economic strategy. The Communists' main opponent, the National Socialists, produced only a set of general observations without any attempt at precise calculations. They clearly disagreed with the international orientation proposed by the Communists, preferring integration into the capitalist world economy with an implied desire to accept Marshall Aid. That did not rule out a structural change although the objective was vaguely presented as 'the example of Switzerland' and an economy based on high-quality specialised products which could be sold around the world.[14] There was no enthusiasm for becoming 'the machinery producer of Eastern Europe' but, after Stalin had vetoed Czechoslovak participation in Marshall Aid in July 1947, some degree of economic reorientation was probably the only option.

It was, however, not a particularly sophisticated plan even allowing for its lack of detail. The general strategy was clear enough, but calculations were rudimentary. An imbalance between the production and consumption of basic raw materials, especially iron ore for the expanding heavy engineering industry, was noticed quite early on, but never eliminated; the hope was to make up the gap by imports. Even such a basic issue as the choice of a growth rate was a fairly arbitrary affair. The development of a planned economy, it was believed 'can and must be at least as fast as the development of capitalist states in their years of boom'.[15] A figure of 11% per annum was therefore chosen on the basis of what was being achieved in Czechoslovakia and Europe at the time. It was actually slightly below Czechoslovakia's performance for 1947–8 which was biased upwards by the recovery after a disastrous harvest in 1947 and, as was admitted, even below the US growth rate 'in the days of war preparation and war effort'.[16]

There was scope for raising the targets while the plan was in preparation; freed from the need to argue a case before political opponents after February 1948, the ruling party could begin to bend to the natural over-confidence of those who seem to have unlimited power. Generally, however, the targets were nearer to reality than to fantasy. The figure for the increase in national income for the whole 1948–53 period was raised from 145% only to 151% by the time the plan became a 'law' in October 1948. Moreover, the target for living standards was actually reduced from 60% to 34%. The original hope had been to reach the level of the most advanced capitalist states by 1953, but signs of serious discontent over restrictions in living standards, discussed in the next section, forced the leadership to make more cautious promises.[17]

Stalin intervenes

This sensible caution was disrupted over the following years by increasingly direct pressure from the Soviet Union. The external influence operated at first through two channels – the Informbureau or 'Cominform' and private discussions between Soviet and Czechoslovak leaders. Stalin's concern at first was the *political* consolidation of his bloc. In 1947 and early 1948, that meant putting pressure on individual Communist Parties to take and consolidate political power. As of June 1948, when Yugoslavia was sensationally condemned by the Informbureau, a new twist was added with the claim that 'specificity' in socialist development was a dangerous deviation. Attempting to apply one's own policy was equated with failing to appreciate the leading role of the Soviet Union and the CPSU. In effect, Yugoslavia was condemned for doubting the need for unquestioning humility towards the USSR. Its excommunication was a clear warning to other leaderships in Eastern Europe that they should accept the Stalinist theory of socialist development, as that now became a necessary gesture of subordination to the Soviet Union.

At the ideological level, Stalin's condemnation of Yugoslavia was accompanied by a reiteration of his vilification of the so-called 'right' in the late 1920s. He pushed again the notion that the class struggle would intensify during socialist construction and that the private sector is continually breeding forces hostile to socialism. The twofold implication was that any problems and conflicts could be explained within the old, familiar categories of class struggle and that the solution was the speediest possible elimination of private enterprise. This carried obvious implications for Czechoslovakia's 'specific road', but the Informbureau's resolutions and Stalin's comments to Czechoslovak leaders were vague enough to allow for considerable delay over the timing of, and flexibility over the form of eliminating private enterprise. The immediate effect was to give a boost to all those who saw no need for any delay while pushing the leadership towards seeking preparations, rather than just quietly accepting that the private sector would ultimately go.

It has been argued that the following years saw continued 'vestiges' of the notion of a Czechoslovak road.[18] There was still a continuing desire within much of the leadership to proceed slowly enough with social change for it to be based at least in part on consent rather than coercion alone, and a clear tendency to base new developments on past Czechoslovak experience. Nevertheless there was no real struggle to *defend* the *general* concept of a specific road. Under the new political conditions it could never now mean the development of new ideas about socialism: it was just a question of how quickly the Soviet model could be reached.

In fact, whenever problems or disappointments were encountered, the reaction was to turn first to Stalin's theoretical propositions and then, increasingly over the following years, to try to apply and copy as closely as possible Soviet experience in all respects. It was, then, not simply a question of bowing to Soviet pressure. It was also a question of how an inexperienced group, holding a monopoly of power and seemingly threatened from several different directions, tried to grapple with complex new problems it had never expected to encounter.

The first clear case was the response to rising working class discontent over the summer of 1948. A drought and appalling harvest in 1947 – with grain production barely reaching 62% of the pre-war level – created food and consumer goods shortages as the latter were exported in exchange for grain. Black market prices rose to five times the official level – the biggest gap recorded[19] – and food rations reached 'the lowest possible level'.[20] If working class living standards were to be maintained then somebody else had to suffer and politically the most acceptable targets were the social groups whose members had been expressing opposition to the government and who could be accused of profiting from the black market and worsening shortages by speculating. Anger was diverted onto a 'class enemy' with a shift towards what became known as the 'sharp course'.

The crucial practical economic element of this was the introduction of 'class rationing' at the start of 1949 alongside a free market in industrial goods and foodstuffs, at prices way above the level for rationed goods. About a fifth of the population, including capitalists, small businessmen and peasants who did not fulfil their delivery quotas, were excluded in total from rationed allocations of industrial goods amidst accusations that these groups as a whole were inciting opposition to the government. Class rationing could have remained a temporary, discriminatory measure to deal with a dire emergency. In fact, rationing for a range of foods was ended during 1949 as the situation eased and a number of free market prices were falling.[21] Had the availability of consumer goods continued to improve it could have been realistic to hope for a final end to the ration system inherited from the Nazi war economy and hence for an end to the more recent discriminatory policy against the regime's alleged enemies.

Such hopes point again to 'vestiges' of the approach of the Czechoslovak road. There frequently were three sides to economic policies in this period. There was a pragmatic, economic rationale, an appeal to prejudices against other social groups from within the working class, and a linked ideological justification based on Stalin's theories. There was a serious discussion in the leadership of how to cope with the inevitable restrictions on somebody's living standards.[22] The solution, however, was justified in public in ideological terms which gave it far greater permanence. Thus, despite some continuing and later hesitations, autumn 1948 marked in social policy the beginning of as big a break as February 1948 did in the Communists' approach towards the political system. From a conception of 'national unity' which had meant seeking social harmony, the regime was now exacerbating social tensions by deliberately encouraging and depending on working class prejudices against other social strata.

There is no doubt that the 'sharp course' was in harmony with the distrustful attitudes of a significant section of the working class.[23] It seemed from resolutions in workplace meetings that sagging morale was raised when tough sentences were handed out for such transgressions as distributing leaflets or spreading rumours.[24] This could never be a reliable measure of public opinion as such meetings were being organised and manipulated to produce precisely the desired results. Nevertheless, successful manipulation did not seem to be difficult and the 'sharp course' did coincide with a temporary lull in visible working class discontent over economic issues. Also many committed Communists *did* see these other social strata as essentially hostile – certainly many lower level activists held and publicly pressed such views. They may also have felt inwardly satisfied that they were applying Stalin's theory of the intensifying class struggle; policy seemed now to be based soundly on Marxist–Leninist ideology rather than on the pragmatic need for uncomfortable compromises that had dominated in the pre-February period. Even if there had been a sudden improvement in the economic situation, it would have been difficult to reverse in total the change that was taking place.

This is the significance of the *interaction* of internal and external causes. There can be little doubt that the Czechoslovak leadership would have complied with Stalin's wishes, but the genuineness of their commitment, and hence the later permanence of elements of the system created in the early 1950s, depended partly on the attractiveness of his theories. The evidence is overwhelming that a major attraction was the apparent popularity of the new approach with a large section of the party's supporters. There were some leading activists counselling caution or even opposing policies they saw as unjust, but the only means of contact the leadership possessed – resolutions sent in from workplace meetings – presented a much harder face. A new theoretical basis for policy was being accepted – based on Stalin's thinking – alongside a new method of maintaining legitimacy. Having eliminated all legal channels for opposition or dissent, the regime could never assess objectively its own social base. Signs of opposition and discontent from the very core of its traditional support led it to rely on engineered demonstrations of support around issues which it was exaggerating into threats to all the post-war achievements: the logic of that was to be the complete elimination of notions of a 'specific road' and ultimately the show trials of the early 1950s.

More immediately, the implication was to seek security in the establishment of 'socialism', the means to which were outlined in the ten points of a 'general line', adopted at the party's Ninth Congress in May 1949. Economic issues naturally figured prominently. The very first point was to fulfil the Five Year Plan and that was to be helped by various changes within the nationalised sector of the economy, which are discussed below and did bring some benefits. Another major objective was 'winning the village for socialism' which was said to mean gaining the confidence of small and middle peasants: large-scale collectivisation could still have been some way off. Capitalist elements in general were to be eliminated, although the fate of smaller businesses was left somewhat vague. Evidently, there was no interest in building from those earlier ideas of specificity towards a distinct model of socialism, but the heat was not really put on the whole private sector until after major changes in economic policy.

Economic integration into the Soviet bloc

The starting point for this was the Soviet assumption that there was a real danger of war in Europe and, according to some accounts, the thought in some quarters that a quick military build up could make it winnable.[25] Pressure was applied following an Inform-bureau resolution in November 1949 with changes to the Five Year Plan in February 1950 immediately increasing the demands on the Czechoslovak economy and exaggerating the structural shift. Up to that time Soviet demands for imports had been adapted to the structure of the Czechoslovak economy. By the end of 1950 the philosophy had very obviously changed to making 'the maximum use of what Czechoslovakia's industrial potential could contribute to the renewal, development and consolidation of the economy of the USSR'.[26]

During 1949 the Czechoslovak leaders had evolved their ideas for an emerging Eastern bloc.[27] At the founding meeting of the CMEA, where other delegates may have had no idea what was intended,[28] Czechoslovakia's representative and party General Secretary Rudolf Slánský took the initiative and argued for an international organisation that would help Czechoslovakia find raw materials and outlets for the products of its light industry: it would work immediately to overcome autarky in industrial structures and 'parallelism' in investment and thereby propagate specialisation and integration wherever possible. In June 1949 the 'Czechoslovak standpoint' was made even more explicit. The aim was tactfully presented as the maximum possible independent self-sufficiency of the socialist bloc, while still recognising the need to expand links with the capitalist world. Czechoslovakia was to build on its existing base of heavy and electrical engineering as part of a *common* industrialisation drive.

As an *immediate* objective this was probably over-optimistic: the other socialist countries were still too backward to act as full partners within such a scheme. Moreover, it was soon to become clear that they had no real understanding of the benefits of integration. Each country tried to develop effectively the same economic structure, with the emphasis on industry and especially heavy industry. The effect was to upset Czechoslovak hopes, incorporated into the original version of the Five Year Plan, that they could sell their consumer goods and cover shortfalls by importing wheat and industrial raw materials from elsewhere in Eastern Europe. Another obstacle, however, was the Soviet decision that the Czechoslovak economy should accept a completely different objective. It seems that Stalin lost interest in the CMEA, with its founding rules that respect national sovereignty of each member and 'preclude integration based on a centralist procedure',[29] and preferred to rely on direct, bilateral contacts. The CMEA was silent until 1954.

Thus, despite initial signs of agreement from other countries with the Czechoslovak conception, the Informbureau's first interventions in economic policy were directed at breaking links with the West. These were already under pressure from the embargo policies implemented by the USA in 1948 and 1949 which aimed to maintain Western military superiority by harming the Soviet economy in any way it could.[30] Trade restrictions were imposed, amid considerable secrecy and with varying degrees of compliance, on all Western countries. Major US targets were advanced technology and easily traceable bulk commodities such as raw materials and steel which were believed to be in short supply in Eastern Europe. It even proved possible to achieve some restrictions on exports from formally neutral Sweden which was a major source of iron ore.

It has been suggested that Stalin may actually have welcomed the policy as 'a most important and almost incontrovertible argument for consolidating the communist bloc'.[31] He certainly referred approvingly to sanctions only strengthening the socialist world market[32] and it is difficult after 1949 to separate out which side was the more active in breaking trade links. Reasonable estimates suggest that the Soviet Union suffered very little from the embargo policy. Any assessment of its impact on Czechoslovakia would be far more complex as it cannot be separated from the enormous changes associated with economic incorporation into the Soviet bloc.

By 1949 trade with capitalists was portrayed as having a clearly *political* character and an Informbureau resolution in September 1949 called for limiting such contacts insisting that CMEA countries should give priority to importing goods from other member states. The full implication of this for the Czechoslovak economy was to be made clear in public in the course of the Slánský trial discussed below.

Czechoslovakia simply could not comply, and that failure was a source of strong criticism over the following months. It was only moderated after clear Czechoslovak reassurances that industrial production and the whole industrial structure were being subordinated to the demands of other members of the CMEA: the following years saw the closure of offices for selling goods in capitalist countries and the loss of many of the export outlets that were still available. Apart from changing the content of economic policy away from the original Five Year Plan, this also implied a shift in *objective* away from a sole concern with raising the living standards of the Czechoslovak people. It was, of course, not expressed in that way at the time. The Czechoslovak–Soviet trade agreement of February 1950 was presented by Foreign Trade Minister Gregor as 'guaranteeing us a free and independent existence', in contrast to 'the trading transactions imposed by Wall Street on the nations of the Marshallised countries'.[33]

It was similarly welcomed when a long-term agreement with the Soviet Union in November 1950 committed Czechoslovakia to the production of machinery and equipment that it had never made before. February 1951 saw a further upward revision of plan targets and an agreement to increase arms production, the implications of which were never incorporated into the plan. Secrecy was maintained, leaving the Western press speculating on whether Czechoslovakia was becoming the arsenal of Eastern Europe but, as arms spending rose from 1% to 10% of gross industrial production taking up 30% of engineering production, it could only create imbalances throughout the economy.[34]

No secret was made of the fact that 'the international situation' was the major reason for changes in the plan. Nevertheless, it was claimed that the faster development of heavy industry would not lead to 'lowering the output of light industry beneath the needs of our population'.[35] Successes with plan fulfilment to that date and the possibilities for non-investment sources of growth from the use of more shifts, the better organisation of work and the initiative released by workers – the realisation that 'they are not working for capitalists but for their own state'[36] – were said to make possible a very substantial rise in living standards.

Much of this was made to sound like wishful thinking. The real point was that firm priorities had been chosen and if resources seemed inadequate then targets elsewhere in the economy would have to be revised during the operational yearly plans.[37] Public promises relating to consumer goods, such as a 70% increase in cotton fabrics, were never as binding as the less public commitments to armaments production.

Various new conceptions appeared at the same time as these shifts in economic policy, but they can hardly be seen as the motive force for change. Thus, in February 1951 Stalin proclaimed Czechoslovakia to be rich in undiscovered raw materials, reversing the original assumption of the Five Year Plan that its economic strategy was constrained precisely by its *shortage* of raw material reserves. Geological surveys subsequently gave very partial confirmation and the plan to become one of Europe's major extractors of iron ore, increasing production fourfold from 1950 to 1955, quickly proved unrealistic: it only increased by 55% alongside a marked decline in quality.[38] The crucial issue was presumably Stalin's insistence that everything possible had to be done to find reserves of iron ore, even at the expense of other sectors and other plan targets.

Figures for Czechoslovak foreign trade show the extent of the economy's reorientation. The socialist countries' share grew from 40% of turnover in 1948 to a peak of 78% in 1953, but it was never possible to cut links with the rest of the world. The geographical reorientation was closely tied in with a shift away from the pre-war structure of exporting consumer goods and even raw materials such as coal towards exporting machinery as is shown in Table 1.1. A semi-

Table 1.1. *Structure of exports and imports in percentages in 1948 and 1953*

	1948	1953
Imports		
Machinery	7.2	14.0
Fuel & raw materials	56.5	54.2
Food	33.4	30.1
Other consumption goods	2.7	1.5
Exports		
Machinery	20.3	42.4
Fuel & raw materials	43.5	36.9
Food	5.6	8.6
Other consumption goods	30.7	12.2

Source: Calculated from *Statistická ročenka Republiky československé 1957*, henceforth *SR* 1957 (Prague, 1957), p. 203.

autarkic economic structure was taking shape with international integration concentrated on a specific range of products and a specific range of countries. The breaking of traditional links and the inadequacy of newly created ones forced Czechoslovakia to rely far more on its own sources of raw materials and to produce as much of its own needs domestically as it possibly could. Published statistics show foreign trade turnover as a percentage of national income falling from 16.0 in 1948–49 to 11.6 in 1950–55. These figures cannot be taken too literally as foreign trade prices are not tied to domestic prices, but they do suggest a trend.

The sources of economic growth

Overall, the new plan targets were unrealistic. The significance of the plan revisions and the final outcome is illustrated by Table 1.2. The hope was to increase the annual average growth rate of industrial output to 20–25%, a figure that seems to have been imposed across much of Eastern Europe. It was actually somewhat below what the countries were already achieving, with the exception of Czechoslovakia. The actual outcome was 14%, itself an apparently remarkable performance, alongside a 10% average growth rate for national income. This was possible despite a very small decline in the absolute numbers in the productive age group: an increase in the female

Table 1.2. *Targets for the First Five Year Plan for selected products as percentages of 1948 output*

	1949 version	1951 version	Actual outcome
Hard coal	118	141	115
Brown coal	136	152	139
Iron ore	100	271	164
Crude steel	135	173	169
Cement	163	213	144
Motor vehicles	182	248	158
Nitrate fertilisers	137	205	120
Cotton fabrics	171	171	124
Beef	163 ⎫		⎧ 129
Pork	215 ⎭	218	⎨ 122

Source: Calculated from *United Nations Economic Survey of Europe*, 1954, p. 43.

participation rate (from 38% of all those in employment in 1948 to 41% by 1955) enabled employment to grow between 1949 and 1953 by just under 2.5% within which industrial employment increased 15%. The key to industry's growth was therefore a substantial increase in the productivity of labour which was twice as large as originally planned. It was, however, not due to uniform causes across all sectors.

The overall picture is indicated in Table 1.3 which suggests at first sight a rapid increase in labour productivity caused by a high level of investment. That, however, is not a valid conclusion. Part of the overall productivity growth was due to structural changes and especially the shift towards industry: part of the high level of investment was directed into agriculture where, for reasons that will be explained, it was often tragically misdirected. Table 1.3 also shows the wide variations between sectors of industry, indicating again a general, but not universal tendency for workers to shift towards more capital-intensive sectors with higher labour productivity. Nevertheless, the reallocation between the 15 sectors within industry referred to in Czechoslovak statistics is not the full explanation for the overall productivity growth. Had the labour force grown at the same rate in all sectors, and had productivity improved at the rate achieved in each sector, a rough calculation suggests that overall productivity would still have risen by exactly the same percentage.[39]

Table 1.3. *Growth in key indicators of the Czechoslovak economy, 1948–1953*

	Production	Employment	Productivity	Investment
All	156 (National Income)	102	155 (Social productivity of labour)	237
Agriculture	116	83	140	626
Construction	227	159	150	516
Industry	193	113	173	188
of which				
Engineering	294	166	195	
Fuel	140	104	132	
Iron & steel	210	140	146	
Glass & ceramics	122	93	134	
Textiles	139	82	170	
Leather & footwear	122	75	159	

Note: 1948 = 100. Employment figures for individual industries are for workers only.
Sources: Calculated from *SR*, 1975, pp. 42–6 and *SR*, 1958, pp. 125 & 128.

The point was that some sectors with *declining* employment also experienced a rapid growth in productivity thanks to enormous gains from rationalisation. Light chemicals, including pharmaceuticals could close down masses of tiny workshops and, using only one-third of the capacity in one-tenth of its factories, still produce more than the poorly organised pre-war industry. Moreover, production could be geared more towards the needs of other sectors of the economy and towards producing a more complete range to satisfy consumer demand.[40] Clearly non-priority sectors, such as wool, were given considerable attention allegedly proving that the party and government were concerned to produce quality consumer goods, but rationalisation also released labour for other sectors.[41]

In the textile industry as a whole the original plan had been for a 68% growth in output and a 15% increase in employment. Instead there was very little investment, and growth in output slowed down from 1951 and was actually falling by 1953, but labour productivity grew in line with the average as the product range was cut from 30 000 kinds of goods to one-tenth that number of standard products and as production was 'regrouped and modernised' so as 'to make it as rational as possible'.[43]

The basis for this success was partly the sheer extent of disruption at the end of the war. Around 40% of the labour force had been of German nationality and left during 1946. Many of the Czech workers were attracted to other, more favoured sectors so that a newer, predominantly female workforce had to be recruited: this must have minimised labour relations problems usually associated with rationalisation and closures. The textile industry in the 1948–53 period was exceptional not only in the small growth of fixed assets but also in its structure. Only 26% took the form of machinery compared with an average figure of 42% for industry as a whole and a figure around 50% for the stock of assets in textiles. New factories often owed their success to the concentration of former production which could even be relocated into previously backward parts of the country.[44]

Food production was concentrated into the best tenth of productive units – for meat only 5% of units remained in 1955 – and the rapid growth in productivity depended almost entirely on the better organisation of existing machinery.[45] In the leather industry, including footwear, the number of factories fell from 353 to 55,[46] and production grew slower than in all other sectors of industry; but, again, productivity increased roughly in line with the average. Published figures suggest that this relative stagnation was compatible with stable domestic consumption. Thus the policy of partial economic autarky could be associated with impressive and cheap productivity gains. The expanding sectors of engineering, iron and steel and mining inevitably had different experiences. In terms of output and productivity, engineering appears as a relative success story as it grew from 15% to 26% of industrial output between 1948 and 1953.

Within that, however, there were some stories of rapid growth alongside other stories of disruption and temporary decline. The shift towards investment goods and industrial equipment, in the desperate bid to meet impossible armaments and heavy machinery targets, often for export to the USSR, inevitably squeezed resources for consumer durables. A clear case was motor vehicle production as shown in Table 1.4.

During the occupation the motor industry had been almost totally converted to producing tanks and aircraft engines plus one type of lorry.[46] It was therefore easy to combine the reconversion to peacetime production with a sharp reduction from the pre-war range, down from 17 and 21 to just three car and five lorry types. Car output

Table 1.4. *Motor vehicle production in the post-war period*

	lorries	buses	cars	motorcycles
1937	1967	57	12634	14116
1945	–	–	–	1800
1948	7221	1122	17971	68007
1950	5984	977	24463	65248
1951	11530	988	17064	69608
1953	13491	555	7300	46369
1956	13449	1215	25068	112023

Source: HSR, p. 289.

grew rapidly to 1950, but high targets even in 1951 were soon revised downwards and mass production effectively ceased in 1952–3 when the Mladá Boleslav factory was used to make Tatra lorries. This unwelcome break was reversed in 1954.

For lorries there was a dramatic expansion of output. The occupation had bequeathed a new model, a Tatra lorry developed in 1943 which was ideal for cold climates and rough terrain. It was to be judged a great invention for many years to come. Nationalisation prevented the restoration of the fragmented structure in which numerous enterprises tried to produce small runs of the same range of model sizes. Unfortunately, expansion brought a new source of disruption and inefficiency as the production of existing models was frequently switched between existing and newly built factories.[47]

Perhaps the most frustrating case was the motorcycle industry. There too production was rationalised, reducing the model range from 15 in 1938 with 15 000 component types to 4 in 1947 with 4 000 components and allocating models to specific factories. Again, there was a splendid heritage in the Jawa range based originally on a model built totally from foreign licences in 1929 but improved with a lot of research during the war. The industry was for the first time seeking and finding export markets and looking even more ambitiously to the future. Unfortunately, indifference from the centre prevented the successful launch of the first motor scooter – the first prototype was ready in 1948 – and left Czechoslovakia with slightly obsolete products unable to compete with the reviving West German industry in the early 1950s. Among major European producers, only the British industry showed a worse ability to adapt to changing demand.[48] The similarity should not be pressed too far. In the Czechoslovak case there was still an understanding of the need to follow and adapt to outside trends. A new product range was waiting for central approval to allow for its launch in the mid-1950s.

In view of these constraints on a substantial part of the industry, priority sections of engineering must have been growing even more rapidly than the aggregate figures suggest. The overall productivity growth of around 100% reflects some rationalisation and specialisation with the absorption of a number of small enterprises and workshops. There was also an enormous investment effort with the completion of 24 new factories, but it is clear that many were little more than copies of older ones. They certainly could not have used the most modern Western technology and there were frequent references to Soviet technical assistance.

The structural transformation inevitably intensified the raw material bottlenecks forcing investment to overcome the shortage of deep-mined coking coal and of iron ore. In the latter case the solution involved re-opening many small and relatively inefficient mines. It was the reverse of the rationalisation process experienced in the least favoured sectors.

Coal suffered from consistent plan underfulfilment with output in 1953 barely above the level planned from 1949 – nowhere near the targets set in the plan revisions of 1950 and 1951. The inevitable consequence was power cuts and an energy shortage throughout the economy. The essential cause lay in wartime and post-war changes. Under the occupation production had risen rapidly but liberation brought an exodus of the Czech forced labour and then the expulsion of the German minority which accounted for around 30% of employment in 1945. The chronic labour shortage could be overcome only by transferring new and inexperienced workers from other sectors and at the expense of a high rate of labour turnover, leaving productivity far below the 1937 level until 1952. An increasingly important instrument throughout the whole of the 1950s was the use of 'voluntary' brigades. In effect, workplaces were obliged to provide a set number of short-term recruits into mining. The hope was that some would be persuaded to stay, but there was considerable hostility from the established workforce with complaints that the very worst workers had been dumped on them: it was suggested on occasion that they could not even produce enough to earn their food.[49]

The result, for industry as a whole, was for productivity to rise relatively slowly in a number of sectors that received substantial investment. Paradoxically, then, Czechoslovak industry in the early

Table 1.5. *Growth in fixed assets and productivity of labour in Czechoslovak industry during the First Five Year Plan*

Industry	All fixed assets	Productivity	Productivity/ Fixed assets
All	128	173	139
Fuel	117	136	116
Energy	130	192	148
Iron & steel	134	145	108
Non-ferrous metals	130	159	122
Chemicals	135	190	140
Engineering	134	201	150
Building materials	127	170	134
Wood	130	174	134
Paper	148	135	118
Glass & ceramics	110	134	122
Textiles	118	171	145
Clothing	117	187	160
Leather	114	166	145
Printing	103	141	137
Food	110	170	154

Note: December 1948 = 100
Source: Calculated from *HSR*, pp. 164–6 & pp. 252–4.

1950s enjoyed a rapid growth in labour productivity, much of which was not due to investment, and a high rate of investment, much of which could even be associated with relatively stagnant labour productivity. It is very difficult to fit that into notions of 'extensive' or 'intensive' growth as both seemed to be taking place in different sectors. Table 1.5 summarises the overall situation which can be compared with later periods in Table 3.8. There clearly is a relationship between growth in fixed assets and labour productivity but there is an abnormal degree of variation between sectors during the First Five Year Plan. Some sectors with high levels of investment were showing a rapid growth in productivity. Energy and chemicals had 62% and 32% of output in 1957 from enterprises built or reconstructed since 1949. On the other hand, fuel and metallurgy, with corresponding figures of 27%, were doing badly while textiles and leather were able to achieve their splendid growth rates in labour productivity with 10% and 3% of output respectively from new or improved enterprises.[50]

Economic crisis and political scapegoats

Alongside the economic subordination to the Soviet Union came pressure for stricter political loyalty ultimately enforced through political trials and the execution of several leading Communists. There is no doubt that the main driving force for this was external pressure which became effectively irresistible after the Informbureau resolution of November 1949 which explicitly referred to the importance of hunting down the 'enemy within'. Its coincidence with the criticism of Czechoslovakia for its continued links with the West is highly suggestive. Questions of economic policy may well have reinforced the conviction in the Soviet hierarchy and elsewhere in Eastern Europe that all was not well in Czechoslovakia. The notion of the 'enemy within' was, however, already becoming a force in its own right as an explanation for disappointments, administrative bungles and policy failures: it was beginning to play the role of universal scapegoat. Soviet pressure was falling on potentially fertile ground especially after the lessons learnt from the handling of discontent in the autumn of 1948.

The security forces often concocted the first suspicions, but decisions to arrest leading officials required the agreement of the Czechoslovak authorities, and especially of Gottwald who became President in 1948. They had no hesitation in making full political use of the arrests and subsequent trials to hide changes of policy and eliminate the possibility of unwelcome reminders of past thinking. Thus Brno party Secretary Ota Šling, arrested in October 1950, was quickly condemned for allegedly maintaining the specificity of Czechoslovakia's conditions: he had actually never expressed divergent views on that issue. The point, however, was that the notion of the Czechoslovak road to socialism was now associated with espionage and treason.

There was, however, a further element in the political exploitation of his arrest. The *original* line of accusations related to methods of inner-party work, and, ironic though it may seem, the arrest of Šling was linked to warnings that party officials would not be allowed to indulge in 'dictatorialism' and 'violations of inner-party democracy'.[51] These phenomena were endemic among officials who no longer needed to fear opposition parties or even their own supporters, but democracy within the party was not an issue of mass concern. Instead, the working class was mostly deeply disturbed by the failure of living standards to rise.

Earlier in 1950 things had been going well. Bread rationing ended and prices on the free market were falling. There obviously was a lot of discontent especially *outside* the working class, over the arbitrary exercise of power and over the policies of repressing and eliminating the private sector, and among some party activists in relation to bureaucratic methods within the party. Neither represented a serious threat and there was no possibility of them coming together as a basis for a coherent opposition.

Later in 1950, however, prices were rising again on the free market and a number of industrial goods had moved out of reach of many employees. In February 1951 chronic bread shortages led to the re-introduction of rations alongside higher prices. In this case Gottwald was very contrite in admitting that the whole party leadership had committed a serious blunder. Bread rationing had been ended without raising the price and as a result wheat was being fed to animals on an unknown scale while the same farmers were buying bread on the free market.[52] It would therefore be wrong to claim at that stage that those in power always pretended to be faultless. This, however, was a pretty costless self-criticism as no opposition, either inside or outside the party, could exploit it and it had no implications for the fundamental concepts on which the regime's policies were based. Moreover, clear admission of a mistake was the most convincing way to generate the feeling that the problem was being put right. As we shall see, however, this was not to be the last word on this particular issue.

Thus the leadership still drew no direct link between supply difficulties and the activities of the 'enemy within'. They did, however, throw in further accusations suggesting for example that Šling had somehow held up the shock worker movement, referred to below, and must have been pleased when his arrest diverted attention from food shortages. The Central Committee meeting of February 1951 was given enormous publicity and four and a half million copies of Gottwald's speech were published.

The line was that Šling was at the centre of a conspiracy to win control of the party and return the state to capitalism. Resolutions from workplace meetings suggested enthusiastic agreement and approval within the party and from wider sections of the working class. That, of course, is not a reliable indicator of public opinion. It is rather an indication of how successfully those opinions that could be voiced were being manipulated. It was, however, the only means left whereby those in power could still assess the public mood and it was clearly pushing the leadership towards still tougher measures. In the words of Central Committee member Gustav Bareš shortly after the February meeting, 'the spirit inside the party and the response to the resolution ... resembles the atmosphere of February 1948'.[53] The leadership was, of course, issuing a virulent condemnation of Šling before any trial had taken place. It had thereby committed its standing and credibility to later establishing his guilt.

It was, however, only a temporary respite. Arresting 'enemies within' did nothing to improve the economic situation which was increasingly influenced by the strains of the higher plan targets. In fact, late in 1951 there were clear signs of an embryonic working class rebellion. Strikes and street demonstrations – involving according to some estimates 10 000 people – took place in Brno on 21 and 22 November. Reports were coming in of passivity and disinterest within the party and even leading officials sometimes came to deliver the protest notes. 800 letters were sent in to the President complaining about the food supply situation without one single indication of satisfaction. In the view of many basic organisations 'we were better off under Hitler than now'.[54] The regime's working class supporters simply could not understand how greater work effort was leading to falling real wages. The principal reason, of course, was in the structural shift in the Czechoslovak economy imposed by Stalin. The regime's supporters, fed on the continual propaganda of success, became increasingly convinced that there must be something wrong at the top. There was an atmosphere of growing distrust towards the whole leadership.

On 23 November the former party General Secretary Rudolf Slánský was arrested, setting the scene for Czechoslovakia to suffer more than any other East European country under Stalin's last purge. A very plausible explanation for this doubtful privilege was the Soviet wish to bury for ever the strong Czechoslovak desire for links with the West.[55] Gottwald's acquiescence in allowing a close colleague of the previous twenty years to meet such an end may never be explained, but once the security forces and their Soviet advisers were hunting for an enemy within they were bound to pick on somebody: there had actually been speculation in the West that Gottwald was likely to be removed, as a one-time advocate of a Czechoslovak road, and replaced by Slánský. Once arrested nobody in the leadership seemed to doubt his guilt. It was suddenly accepted that he had not just been making mistakes, but was undertaking 'deliberately hostile activity'.[56] He was publicly condemned as an agent, an enemy and a traitor

before any trial and thousands of resolutions from workplace meetings came in backing his arrest. To much of the core of Communist
supporters, this was the revelation that could explain away their
worries. There were, however, some reports of level heads expressing
doubts and of a lot of poorly attended meetings.[57]

There were far stronger doubts throughout society. The widespread
use of arbitrary power must have been noticeable as 23 000 people had
already been imprisoned by the State security services in 1949. The
population had seen the effective destruction of the other political
parties and the stage-managed political trials which began in July 1950
around a group largely of former right-wing politicians. Again, mass
manifestations of popular approval had been engineered in the form
of workplace resolutions, but there were plenty of signs of scepticism
at the genuineness of the charges and disquiet at the severity of the
sentences which included the execution of a female former Member of
Parliament. It seemed obvious that far-fetched and exaggerated accusations were being used to discredit and eliminate political rivals.
Many people in later years claimed to have held such feelings, but
there was little chance to give them public expression at the time.
Neither was there very much interest in doing so. There are, of
course, no precise results of opinion polls for this period, but it seems
that attitudes varied from a resigned acceptance that politicians are a
pretty bad lot or an indifferent recognition that Communists were
now turning on each other to, at the other extreme, a firm belief that
the accusations were genuine. There was no particular reason why
anyone unsympathetic to the regime should make any effort to voice
their doubts. The overwhelming effect was therefore further to alien-
ate large sections of the population from anything more than formal
involvement in politics.

The trial of Slánský and thirteen others was based around confessions extracted after prolonged torture. The party leadership ensured
where possible that any issue causing concern was covered and were
particularly punctilious in adding 'economic' crimes after the idea to
do so had been implied in a large number of workplace resolutions.
There were, for example, suggestions that Slánský was responsible
for a decision in 1950 to end workers' Christmas bonuses, without
consulting other party leaders. That point could not actually be
included, as to do so would have implied the possibility of restoring
the bonuses, but quite enough was added to give a general impression
of who was to blame for economic difficulties.

The death sentence was decided on by the party leadership for 11 of the accused and implemented on 3 December 1952. That still left 60 people in prison who were connected with the original accused. These loose ends were tied up with a further series of trials during 1953 which seem not to have involved Soviet advisers and to have continued after the removal from power of Beria in the USSR. They were not public and presumably took place only to avoid having to admit the fallibility of the security organs. In the end, 278 leading officials had been put on trial on the basis of fabricated evidence.

The most immediate effect of the arrests of leading officials, culminating in political trials, was to confirm and justify the closer structural integration of the Czechoslovak economy into the Soviet bloc. More generally, it has been suggested that they played a central role in creating a system of power based around 'unquestioning loyalty'. 'A qualitatively new type of party official' emerged with little need for qualifications or for independence of judgement.[58] Instead, the need was for blind loyalty to a higher organ and a readiness to carry out their every instruction. Complementing this was the unlimited power of central organs, but it was often the very highest officials who were said to embody those dull characteristics. The archetype was Antonín Novotný who became party General Secretary after Gottwald's death in 1953 and President as well in 1957. His prior insignificance borders almost on the incredible as, despite holding important party offices, he is never quoted as having played any role, delivered any substantial speech or even written a brief article prior to his elevation. Exactly how he was chosen, and by whom, remains unclear but the crucial decision must have been taken in Moscow.

This power structure, it should be emphasised, was already taking shape once the rival parties had been suppressed in 1948. Events of the early 1950s only accentuated its most negative features, but on many issues the conception presented above seems highly plausible. It was Gottwald who took the crucial decision for Slánský's arrest, and nobody could then question it. He was responding to a mass of pressures from the security forces, from their Soviet advisers, from the Soviet authorities, and possibly even from workplace resolutions. He did, however, still have some scope to reject at least the pressures from below.

On some other issues, however, the notion of unlimited power is highly misleading. It can only be meaningful where precise, simple and unambiguous orders are possible and where they can then be obeyed. That is definitely not the case in economic management where no central authority can accumulate the necessary information to run a genuine 'command economy'. In practice, unrealisable instructions came to be treated with contempt, and orders were then obeyed in a purely formal manner or evaded by methods that actually required considerable ingenuity and initiative at lower levels in the structure. Thus the striking feature of the emerging system of economic management was the divergence between a simple theory of centralised planning and a somewhat chaotic reality.

2   Towards the Soviet system of management

The evolution towards this concept of a fully planned economy was a gradual process strongly influenced by increasing Soviet pressure. There was a definite shift from applying the general principles and specific elements towards copying the Soviet model as precisely as possible. Sometimes that fitted with the perceived social interests of the working class so that establishing centralised state control appeared as part of the class struggle. Other elements, however, led to latent conflicts between the regime and its working class supporters. In fact, the failure to raise living standards culminated in probably the only real occasion after 1948 when mass working class protest was a possibility. The show trials of 1952 were not specifically intended by their ultimate perpetrators as a means to head off that revolt, but they were used to that end by the Czechoslovak leadership. The repression and lawlessness of the period were an essential element in the development of the system – both in terms of broad state control and of the precise forms of detailed planning – and even more in giving it permanence by generating widespread cynicism towards politics alongside fears of change from those left with guilty consciences at the top of the power structure.

The economy and the working class

Financial instruments were still seen as important in the 1950 statutes for nationalised enterprises which referred to the 'law of value' and set the objective of 'achieving the maximum profit'.[1] Within enterprises too there was a determined effort especially in 1949 to apply more generally the management system developed by Bat'a in the inter-war period. Leading economists did not pretend to be great experts, but the attraction was obvious. Bat'a had been Czechoslovakia's most successful capitalist, building a multi-national

31

company and making Czechoslovakia into the world's leading exporter of shoes. There was a basis here for following Lenin's advice to 'apply much that is scientific and progressive' in systems of work organisation developed under capitalism that had previously appeared as 'enslavement'.[2] Moreover, many of the elements of the system sounded similar to some elements that were believed to exist in the USSR.[3]

The essence was a subdivision of the firm into independent accounting units. If they could cut costs, even by buying from outside the enterprise, then foremen and some selected workers received a 'share in profits'. This system was pushed vigorously throughout industry, but was soon forgotten. Part of the reason may have been the firmer rejection of 'specificity', but there are other possible explanations. The system was based on a very strongly capitalist ethos encouraging a division between those entitled to the profit-sharing bonus and those who were simply expected to work harder. It also assumed a sharing in losses when a workshop did badly. Neither of those elements were likely to receive willing acceptance in the post-war period when the threat of unemployment, ever present in Bat'a's factories, had been eliminated. Neither was the system necessarily appropriate to different production processes and it encountered especially strong resistance from parts of heavy engineering.[4]

The system was anyway developing in a different direction with quantity targets taking on a more important role as strains and shortages forced the continuation of methods from a war economy. By 1951-2 only the products of communal and cooperative enterprises were not allocated from ministry or government level. In effect, the centre was setting priority tasks and ensuring the needs of key customers only. In so far as this system made possible the desired structural transformation of the economy, it must be judged a success. It did not, however, make it possible to fulfil all aspects of the Five Year Plan as non-priority sectors were effectively left as a residual.

Neither can centralisation be explained purely in terms of economic necessity. It also reflected the belief in Marxist theory at the time that an economy can be planned in the same detailed way as a single firm. The Five Year Plan was felt to be weak precisely because much of it had to be worked out in value terms rather than using the allegedly more precise physical quantities.[5] There was, therefore, a firm belief that any problem could be solved by more centralisation and by adopting the methods and ideas of Soviet planning. Czechoslovak economists were clearly behind in planning theory but, in the new political atmosphere, made rapid attempts to catch up with regular journal features on planning methods and publication of the works of Soviet and Polish economists. In fact, the level of theoretical sophistication was low even in the USSR: it was impossible to provide a translation of a basic Soviet textbook because no such work existed, even in Russian.[6] This limitation may have made it easier to believe that stronger central planning would overcome the economy's problems although many that were emerging seem to be the inevitable consequences of highly centralised planning itself.

An example was the excessive level of investment demand from enterprises, which exceeded 50% of national income during the preparations for the 1951 plan.[7] The previous expectation had been that controlling and directing investment would be difficult but not impossible provided it was not left to the private sector. The Chairman of the State Planning Office, Jaromír Dolanský, attributed the problem to unnecessary, ill-prepared projects in which costs had been ignored or understated so as to get the projects accepted. His solution was to 'deepen the planning method' by following the Soviet example and constructing a detailed catalogue of individual projects. Tighter control, he hoped, would also overcome the problem of big projects clarified too late in the plan formulation process.[8] The weakness of this argument, as later experience showed, is that central planners are always ultimately dependent on information from lower levels so that no amount of detail can overcome the tendency to distort information to further the interests of one's own enterprise or sector.

Planning in quantity terms was intended to make this centralised control more effective while financial targets, it was claimed, could be reached without making the precise products needed elsewhere in the economy.[9] The aim for 1951 was to cover 80% of industrial output with 1100 individual tasks in quantity terms. Heavy engineering, for example, was to move from 15 named tasks in physical terms covering 20% of all production in 1949 – and this did not include the most important products – to 70%.

A further justification for this was that it would be easier to motivate workers around quantity targets that they could understand. The belief had been that the February events would lead to an enormous upsurge in workers' initiative and this was encouraged at once by campaigning for and organising 'counter plans' whereby enterprises would take out still higher commitments and thereby complete the Two Year Plan by 28 October 1948, the thirtieth anniversary of the creation of the Czechoslovak state. This obviously required higher labour productivity which it was believed could be stimulated by political activity. With at one time 20% of the total population in its ranks, the CP was expected to 'mobilise party members to fulfil production tasks' as part of its overall 'leading role' in the economy.[10]

So broadly was this defined that there was no longer a clear distinction between the roles of the party, the trade union branch and management. Nothing was *excluded* from the party's competence as it was to 'learn to organise management work in all sections of our economy' while the factory organisation was instructed 'to feel fully responsible for the state of production in the factory'. This, according to Slánský in a major speech to the Central Committee in November 1948, did not mean that party organisations could 'dictate' to the director. The relationship should rather be one of 'cooperation': it is, however, difficult to see a director surviving long without party support, if indeed the party organisation ever really functioned according to Slánský's principles. Moreover, the trade unions definitely were subordinated and given specific tasks such as training new workers[11] or the administration of various voluntary workers' initiatives. Evidently, there was no conception of the need for workers to retain independent representative organs – democratic elements such as works councils and elected directors were quickly forgotten amid the faith in centralisation – or even for the party to avoid too close an identification with management.

Slánský listed the main tasks for the workplace organisation as mobilising the whole workforce to fulfil tasks, organising 'socialist competition', ensuring the best use of equipment, maintaining labour discipline, expanding the piece rate system and improving the workers' social conditions. There is no reason to doubt in this context that a unified political organisation, enjoying a degree of trust from most of the employees, could play an enormous role in finding non-investment sources of economic growth. Backed up with the machinery of state power and the means of mass communication, it could spread ideas for the rationalisation and reorganisation of work practices at an unprecedented rate. The typical method was to take the experience of one factory – be it the whole Bat'a system or signs of workers using their own initiative – and plug the idea vigorously for the whole economy. The contrast with the slow penetration of ideas for scientific management into the British economy is obvious.[12] The conservatism and complacency of management was met head-on and the commitment of a large part of the workforce to party policy should have prevented coherent and unified opposition.

It is, however, obvious from frequent published criticisms that party organisations rarely lived up to expectations: they were often meeting, formally approving Central Committee resolutions and doing no more. In the key mining area of Ostrava-Karviná, it was subsequently claimed that the majority of elected representatives were not involved in economic issues and many hardly ever came to meetings.[13] A great deal of evidence suggests that the expanded role for the party often meant no more than the involvement of a few officials in continual consultation and partnership with the director. This might have been useful, but it could proceed without the involvement or interest of all but a tiny minority of employees.

It seems that party officials had immense power, especially over personnel issues, while ordinary members enjoyed and defended some material privileges, such as a better chance of promotion and better access to housing and holiday facilities.[14] It is very difficult to construct a clear picture of the party's role within the emerging economic system. The leadership and Central Committee had supreme power over major decisions and basic organisations were expected to ensure that those policy decisions were carried out. That meant that a significant section of the workforce was *verbally* committed to supporting government policies, but they often seem to have done little more than go through the motions. Such was the logic of the political power structure especially with the political atmosphere of the early 1950s. The hierarchical structure meant that officials were answerable to higher levels only, so that basic organisations had no real voice with which to point to inadequacies in official policies.

A genuine system of democratic centralism would have allowed open discussion of the appropriateness and weaknesses of aspects of the emerging system of management. A genuine programme for the democratisation of the economy, allowing real participation and initiative in the creation of a new model of socialism, would have included an expanding role for works councils, trade unions, and other representative bodies. In practice, after the elimination of rival parties and Stalin's interventions, the trend was in the opposite direction as independent organs were either dissolved or given very minor roles as 'transmission belts' implementing and administering decisions reached by party bodies.

Meanwhile, the reality of the party's precise role was masked by a great deal of rhetoric which fed the continuing assumption that better party work could *always* lead to higher output. Publicity was given to cases where the management had succumbed to defeatism only to find that, once the alarm bells were sounded, the party and trade union organisations could bring about 'a genuine miracle'.[15] Whether such reports were accurate or not, they helped create the atmosphere within which poor results for some sectors or enterprises in the Two Year Plan were attributed to workplace organisations meeting infrequently[16] or, as in the case of the North Bohemian mines, to poor organisation of work that could have been spotted and acted on by an alert party.[17] The inevitable corollary was a dismissive attitude from the centre towards ubiquitous allusions to objective difficulties. Enterprise managers, however, were learning a different lesson; to them it appeared that the centre was ignorant and indifferent to their problems.

Targets were often set on the basis of neither past achievements nor an objective assessment of possibilities: the key was what was judged essential to the economy.[18] Plans therefore appeared as arbitrary orders from an ignorant centre and were treated with a considerable degree of contempt. In the Vítkovice steel works, a massive workplace within the key sector of the economy which should have been a model for heavy industry, the director apparently became indifferent as to whether it reached 85% or only 75% of its plan target. The management simply informed the party organisation that 'they have sent us some street numbers, but they cannot be achieved'.[19] Apart from seeking salvation in better planning techniques, the central authorities resorted to asserting, in effect, that a good party organisation could achieve anything, which was a difficult claim to refute when none matched the ideal.

They were, in fact, busily accepting elevated targets in counter plans. It always seemed that 'everyone' in the workplace was taking out a collective commitment[20] but then there invariably seemed to be a self-critical reassessment in which disappointments were attributed to the failure to involve more than a narrow circle of officials. On exceptional occasions enterprises were accused of cheating by accepting targets that were really very easy or by fiddling their results to double, or treble-count the output of some workshops.[21] To judge by the methods used by enterprises that were later claiming outstanding results in plan fulfilment,[22] those were probably not uncommon practices. In other cases, however, officials seem to have reacted to pressure from above by accepting extravagant targets, claiming the whole workforce accepted the commitment, and not worrying too much if the results were disappointing. They were faced with essentially impossible instructions – to involve the whole workforce in approving an impossible target – so they complied in the one aspect that was pressed the most strongly. Any view that party officials could perform a controlling function ensuring that managers complied with the interests of the whole of society rather than just their own enterprise or sector is clearly naïve.

Nevertheless, the party's presence as a mass organisation could have eased some problems, especially those concerning employee relations, during the early 1950s. Basic organisations could give support, backed up by media campaigning, to state policies. Thus, for example, the labour shortage for key, expanding sectors of the economy was to be overcome by incorporating state employees, by shifting male workers from other sectors and by shifting 'unproductive' office workers into manual jobs. The deficits created in other sectors would then be made up by recruiting women. There were detailed plans for individual sectors – precision engineering, for example, was to increase the proportion of women from 32% to 40% and internal trade from 33% to 80%[23] – and great publicity was given to women who had made it into high positions in the government, in the party and as directors of industrial enterprises.

There clearly were some such opportunities; within the party itself the Central Committee elected in 1949 was 14% female – compared to one-third of all party members – albeit falling to 11% in 1954 and 9% in 1958.[24] Some women were being trained in unfamiliar roles, such as becoming foremen in the Škoda works,[25] but there was actually little need to combat male prejudice. Instead, the party's 'broadly based consciousness-raising action'[26] was largely aimed at encouraging *women* to come to work in sectors where their presence would encounter little opposition. The implicit official policy was to maintain, and sometimes even create or intensify, a sexual division of labour in terms of particular sectors of the economy.

Far more difficult problems arose from the rationalisation process. The reorganisation of non-favoured sectors partly solved itself as many workers were leaving voluntarily for higher pay in expanding industries, often welcoming the break from extremely unpleasant work on obsolete equipment in decaying buildings. There was still a need for initiative and imagination from management – and there was considerable excitement and optimism at the prospects opened up by nationalisation[27] – but workers' resistance was not a major problem. More complex, however, was the attempt at a more general rationalisation of the labour process and wage system. Some were bound to lose out from the official insistence that 'egalitarianism in wages' was a 'barrier to production',[28] and resistance was inevitable to attempts to divide production into concrete, individual tasks paid on a piece-rate basis. More detail, it was believed, would facilitate a more stable organisation of work and a firm basis for motivation around material incentives.

This had been stated as an objective before February 1948, and the proportion of working time on piece-rates rose from 25% in 1946 to 62% in 1948 and 73% in 1956.[29] This, however, was judged to have made little difference to incentives as, faced with workers' suspicions and even a number of strikes in major engineering factories, piece-rate norms were often made very easy. Tightening them was seen as a secondary issue prior to February 1948 when set alongside the tasks of reconstruction, of building new factories and of winning the political battle against the other parties. By early 1949 the desirability of a transfer towards piece-rates, and of a *toughening* of existing norms, was being pushed more vigorously, but it made little headway until the encouragement of greater voluntary labour through the 'shock worker' movement.

A great deal of publicity was given to the expected emergence of a new, socialist man. 'Workers', it was claimed, 'now realise that they are no longer working for the exploiters'. Instead, 'they are working for themselves, for the working class, for the good of all working people'. There was, then, 'a new relationship to work' whereby it would become 'ever more a conscious, creative activity'.[30] The best way to channel this new 'creative initiative' and to ensure a continual rise in productivity was said to be 'socialist competition', a term that acquired a broad meaning covering a vast range of allegedly voluntary initiatives. The most favoured became the commitment of *individual* workers to raise their output above the level of existing piece-rate norms. To some this could appear as 'a real revolution in thinking and consciousness'. They saw it as distinct from, and clearly superior to, labour rationalisation processes under capitalism because it depended on workers' voluntary initiative. Apart from that there were very obvious similarities as 'shock workers', 'Stakhavonites' and 'improvers' fitted closely with the notion of subdividing work into individual tasks and became the missing link in the pressure to overcome resistance to the revision of piece-rates.

The right to the title 'shock worker' was precisely defined at the trade union congress in December 1949. The workers concerned had to take out, and fulfil, a commitment to surpass a norm over at least a month. They had to use better methods of work organisation, help others to achieve the same and generally behave in an exemplary way.[31] In practice, the administrative tasks – given to the trade unions – proved so immense that all those who surpassed their norms were awarded the title. This was soon felt to be a serious failing and the accompanying privileges were abandoned in 1951.

The movement was of little significance early in 1949, with only 10 000 shock workers. Then they began to enjoy priority in recreation facilities, flats and supplies of meat, chocolate and coffee. Special shops were opened providing goods at affordable prices that were otherwise available only on the free market.[32] By the end of the year there were half a million shock workers. In one factory, the whole workforce had apparently expressed such 'enthusiastic agreement' that every one of them had signed up.[33] This, then, *was* a movement which went beyond 'a handful of officials', but there was always an element of deception in its apparent success and it was hardly creating a new, *socialist* man. The 'best' workers were honoured amid great publicity giving real meaning to 'the cult of the personality' in the sense of an unashamed individualism. Alongside firm denunciations of 'levelling', trade union meetings were used to announce and present outstanding producers while the unions nationally hunted down the best worker in every sector and then those few outstanding individuals who were to receive state honours. The highly plausible suggestion that all this could be disrupting the work collective was dismissed as a 'levelling' view.[34]

There was *always* opposition to this movement. That had been expected on the basis of Soviet experience where both managers and workers could be attached to 'old technical norms'. It seems, however, that many of the piece-rate norms were so easy to surpass that it really did not warrant any publicity; workers could be gaining substantial rewards for belatedly adopting methods used for years in other factories.[35] In other cases, higher output often required substantially greater work effort while the official claim was exemplified by the fulsome praise to a star lathe operator who reached 1200% of his original norm 'with no greater physical effort, but by using your head'.[36]

Suspicions from management centred partly on scepticism as to whether anything was really being achieved and partly on the dangers of excessive work. The directorate of the railways was chastised for indicating that every volunteer shock worker should first undergo an examination of his physical and 'psycho-technical' stamina.[37] From workers, there was a related fear that the intention was simply to intensify the labour process or to cut other workers' wages.

Party leaders found themselves alternately encouraging and trying to dispel such fears. They complained that 'hand in hand with its growth there is no introduction of tougher piece-rate norms'. Instead, 'soft' norms were left untouched due to the lack of courage of party organs: 'After the first unsympathetic response they prefer to run away.'[38] The leadership also stepped back from the most ruthless alternative. Thus Slánský told the typical enough tale of a Comrade Cibulková who had found a means to work on two machines simultaneously. After one week the norm was raised by 50% and she was earning exactly the same as before.[39] The only solution seemed to be a compromise which avoided 'the permanent mechanical revision of piece-rate norms' by leaving that individual with higher earnings 'for a certain period'. Moreover, there was at least a verbal commitment not to change norms without first 'gaining the agreement of the majority of the workers'. Even if this promise were taken seriously, there was still an inevitable source of bitterness when those who thought up new and improved production methods were to be allowed to work on the basis of the old norms for six months. The others somehow accepted new, tougher targets.[40]

Reporting to the Central Committee in February 1950, Josef Frank gave figures that indicate the extent of the lack of interest within the traditional core of the working class. The greatest involvement of shock workers was in the leather industry (62%) while only 32% of those employed in engineering were involved and 17% in the traditional glass industry. He pinpointed key weaknesses in heavy engineering, mining, ceramics, construction and the state sector of agriculture. Figures for participation in socialist competition generally in June 1952 reveal a similar bias towards light industry (71%) and against energy, mining and iron and steel (around 50% of employees).[41] Moreover, women and young people were proving much easier to involve as, in Frank's words, they were 'less burdened by conservatism and prejudices than those workers who worked for decades in our industry under the power of the capitalists'. Party members, according to his figures, were almost as unenthusiastic as non-members.

Frank could have been providing the basis for a partial explanation, but it must also relate to the possibilities opened up by the changes in different industries. Thus in textiles there was enormous scope for productivity gains from the reorganisation of work around the best existing equipment. With this process happening anyway, newer and less prejudiced workers could well have seen more opportunities.

This, then, could help explain the rapid increases in productivity in some sectors.

There is, however, little doubt that official propaganda exaggerated the impact of socialist competition. Whenever a plan was fulfilled in a sector or in a factory it could be attributed to successful competition between factories or workshops, or to a new wages system or to a growing number of shock workers. Such claims were easy to make but never convincingly proven. The only sectors to be given new systems for determining wage differentials were mining and steel, in October and November 1951, and neither were to be outstanding performers after these dates. To the majority of workers the labour process remained totally unchanged by the formal transfer of ownership to the state. They remained unimpressed by boasts of enormous, individual achievements in production and knew enough to be certain that many were phoney.

Their attitudes are probably adequately summarised by a survey of 1200 workers in an engineering factory outside Prague published in a trade union journal in 1947 at a time when discussion and criticism was still possible. It showed 70% either opposed in principle or somehow unhappy about the Stakhanovite movement at that time. Essentially, Stakhanovism was equated either with a greater intensity of labour or with one individual claiming credit for the work of a collective, and that applied even for the 30% who supported the movement. The conclusion was that 'on the whole the workers favour honest and average work from all employees. They reject shirking and also high performances from individuals and excessive talk about work.'[42] They still generally supported their government, but this was one issue on which working class instincts and Communist theory of the period clearly diverged.

In fact, later studies suggest that very little was achieved in terms of rationalising the wage system either. Piece-rates spread, but norms continued to be based on vague estimates and were often over-fulfilled by enormous margins. For the engineering industry, the average was 127% overfulfilment in 1948, rising to 163% in 1951 and 199% in 1953. It was simply impossible to set norms in any other way, as reliable enough information to impose norms on individual workers against their will was not available, and possibly never could be available, for all but the most precisely definable and controllable tasks. The misplaced belief that detailed control over the labour process was possible, leading to the insistence on subdividing work tasks as much as possible, could only accentuate this. Far from giving greater power to norm setters it made their job so complex that they had little choice – especially as management and party organisations gave them minimal backing – but to set norms, as workers wanted, to give them their expected take-home pay after a reasonable day's work.[43] The rapid spread of piece-rates therefore facilitated concessions to strong pressure for high wages in the face of high free market prices. The consequence of this was a wage system which created strong inflationary pressures until rigid controls were imposed on enterprise wage bills in 1952 and which, as elsewhere, retained many arbitrary differentials, between individuals, factories and sectors, but not much conflict at the point of production.

The end of the private sector

The picture was very different in relation to the private sector where the changes imposed led to far more conflict and far worse results. The easiest for the leadership was the elimination of urban businesses which played an important role in some specialised products, in services and especially in retail trade. From September 1948 the party began to take a much greater interest in this sector having previously regarded it as economically of little importance – although the Five Year Plan did originally refer to the value of small businesses in 'repairing productive equipment and means of consumption'; but having regarded it at one time as politically significant in terms of the number of potential voters that ought not to be alienated. Its political significance was now said to be as a source of possible opposition and the only question for economic policy was how quickly it could be eliminated. That meant 'restricting and pushing back' the remnants of the private sector: the problem of small businesses was then solved by their 'voluntary' integration into the state sector as they were hit with restricted allocations of raw materials, labour and credits, by discrimination through the rationing system for consumer goods and in their children's access to education. There must also have been a loss of some services to many customers, but no harm was done to the fulfilment of plan targets in key sectors of the economy. So successful was the policy that, by the end of 1952, only 47 000 small businesses were left, employing just over 50 000 workers, compared with nearly half a million workers in manufacturing workshops alone in 1948.[44]

By early 1950 Gottwald could report to the Central Committee that progress with eliminating the private sector had been most marked in retail trade which was, by then, two-thirds 'socialist', 18% 'capitalist' and 16% in the hands of small businesses. The justification for implementing this transformation was not 'dogmatic reasons of wanting to nationalise every greengrocer and every sales stall'. Rather, he claimed, there was no other means to be certain the goods would get to the strata the government most wanted to help.[45] Liquidation of small private shops was, in fact, associated with the creation of a network of cooperative and factory shops while young people, and especially young men, were to be 'convinced' of the benefits of shifting into industry leaving their former jobs to newly recruited women. The elimination of the urban private sector was therefore fairly straight-forward.

It was motivated in general terms by the belief that socialism meant state control, via ownership, over the whole economy. The urgency of the measure was dictated by the construction of a new, centrally controlled distribution system, around 'class rationing' and by the labour shortage in industry. This, then, had a clear pragmatic logic within the existing economic situation, but imposition of the notion of a class struggle onto very small businesses led to unnecessary elements of inhumanity. Nationalised enterprises were directed to shift the former owner to another workplace and, as František Krajčír, the Minister of Internal Trade, had to acknowledge, this had been applied so strictly as to split up families.[46]

The collectivisation of agriculture was considerably more complicated. To at least as great an extent as in the management system in industry, instructions were internally contradictory so that some degree of deception was required towards those higher up to maintain the appearance that orders were being carried out to the letter. It proceeded in a series of waves based around massive campaigning; as each wave subsided, so the new recruits tended to drift back to individual farming. The timing varied slightly between the East European countries,[47] suggesting that there was no common mastermind, although it was generally associated with the toughening of plan targets.

Soviet pressure only set collectivisation as a general objective which could confirm loyalty to the Stalinist concept of socialist development. Czechoslovakia was one of the last with 'forced collectivisation' as the party was at first very cautious of abandoning commitments made before February 1948, and then around the elections in May of that year, that there was no intention of copying Soviet collectivisation and creating 'kolkhozes'. Gottwald, interviewed by Associated Press in

March 1948, even spoke of the potential for mechanisation of small individual holdings to achieve a 20% increase in output during the Five Year Plan. Later this was raised to the absurdly unrealistic target of a 37% increase in agricultural output.[48]

Collectivisation was finally accepted as the objective in the autumn of 1948 following a meeting with Stalin and similar changes in Hungary and Poland. It was associated with the theory that private enterprise continually breeds capitalism and hence sabotage of the socialist economy. At no time was it based on, or even related to, the immediate needs and potential of Czechoslovak agriculture. It is therefore particularly remarkable that there was no sign at any later period of serious doubts about collectivisation from within the party.

To many in the towns it was quickly accepted as a necessary step for overcoming the periodic difficulties with urban food supplies. Factory workers were often involved in the touchy job of going into villages to secure wheat deliveries. Despite statements of official disapproval, they often carried arms and frequently exerted considerable pressure even on smaller peasants. They were effectively requisitioning agricultural produce which inevitably heightened tension and encouraged hostility on both sides.[49] It was easy for urban workers to point such hostility in a particular direction when, as was frequently pointed out, agriculture remained the last stronghold of private enterprise.

Moreover, apart from the attractions of the Soviet example, collectivisation seemed to follow very logically from all the assumptions of socialist theory. In so far as anything had been written on agriculture in the classical works of Marxism, it all pointed towards the assumption that it was essentially very similar to industry in that large-scale, socialised production would be more efficient. Agricultural specialists backed this up, looking enthusiastically at the new range of tractors, launched and tested in 1948, at the potential gains from 'the appropriate mechanisation of stables' cutting out the hard slog of spreading manure or at the benefits of building suitable milking sheds as 'perhaps no other area of agricultural production could raise the productivity of labour by more'.[50]

At the existing technological level, however, individual private farming was still the most productive form. That was particularly true for looking after animals which required long hours of commitment within a labour process that was inherently extremely difficult to supervise. It was, however, repeatedly and forcefully argued that introducing industrial forms of organisation would raise productivity to the level of industry.[51]

All this could further encourage the view that there was no serious alternative to the Soviet form of collectivisation although Czechoslovak agriculture faced very different problems and was actually at a much higher level of development than Soviet farming: as much as 40% of output was marketed before the war, although the figure fell very slightly in the post-war period when farmers consumed more of their produce. If the objective was to raise this marketed output, then the logical approach should have been not to disrupt what was already an intensive and productive system, but to develop from the existing base by confronting the problems of a desperate shortage of labour – a drop of 36% from 3.3 million to 2.2 million between 1937 and 1949 – and of an inadequate level of mechanisation. There was a very strong case for overcoming the excessive fragmentation of landholdings, but a 1949 law already existed enabling the consolidation of scattered strips into single holdings.

Initially, the regime's policy was in line with this. The Two Year Plan saw a successful switch to domestic tractor production in what were previously armaments factories. The extensive but somewhat chaotic existing system of agricultural cooperatives was rationalised under party control and oriented especially towards providing the means for mechanisation on smaller holdings.

Late 1948 and early 1949 saw the beginnings of the major change, the only immediate effect of which was to block the further development of individual farming. Consolidation of existing farms, which had actually been undertaken by some of the earliest cooperatives,[52] was stopped on the grounds that it could make farming more productive and thereby reduce pressure for full collectivisation.[53] Excessive enthusiasm was, however, tempered especially by Gottwald who saw large-scale, collectivised cooperative production not as an immediate possibility, but as a perspective for two or three years ahead while the immediate policy was for 'restricting' the 'kulaks'.

This term was at first used with some caution; there was no precise Czech or Slovak equivalent and richer farmers were frequently regarded with respect rather than contempt within the villages. In the post-war period there was not really an agricultural proletariat either, as, particularly in Bohemia and Moravia, those with small landholdings typically had a job outside farming. 'Kulaks' therefore had little opportunity to hire the labour of others and their alleged position of economic dominance was often based rather on hiring out machinery.

Therefore it was decided, in February 1949, to enforce the compulsory purchase from richer farmers of all tractors which were to be given to the newly established machine and tractor sections. The measure was paraded as a great success and justified in 'class' terms as protecting smaller farmers from exploitation. In practice, private ownership of tractors was effectively ended during 1949–50. In the changed atmosphere of autumn 1953 government bodies received masses of complaints of equipment compulsorily bought from middle and even poor peasants. In fact, even at the party's Ninth Congress it had been estimated that only about half of heavy machinery was in the hands of the rural rich.[54] For lighter equipment it was far more evenly distributed.[55] Moreover, little had been gained apart from the generation of more bitterness in the countryside as the tractors in private hands were generally obsolete pre-war imports for which there were no spare parts. Sometimes they were even left in the hands of the former owners to avoid unnecessary conflicts around an unpopular policy.[56]

At the same time the first steps were being taken towards creating collective farms under a law passed on 23 February 1949. At first, party officials seem to have thought they faced an easy task and made quite unrealistic promises. The belief was that 'in a countryside like ours with rich cooperative traditions, the organisation of collective farms will not encounter serious difficulties . . . it will proceed quickly and successfully everywhere'.[57] The first approaches were made by sending agitators into villages who, despite their undoubted commitment and enthusiasm, knew very little about agriculture and tried to propagate what was inevitably a very abstract notion of collective farming. Meetings were held in most villages in the spring of 1949, but party officials faced accusations even from party members that their previous policy statements must have been a dishonest trick. Reactions of the whole farming community varied from contemptuous lack of interest to a few cases of violence, including the murders of some party officials.[58]

The first 5–10 member preparatory committees formed at this stage were always initiated by party organs and almost 80% of their members were party members – compared with only 10% of those active in agriculture.[59] Figures provided by Agriculture Minister Ďuriš to the Ninth Congress in May 1949 indicated preparatory committees in 2370 out of the country's 13 000 parishes, but only 208 cases of actually starting cooperative activity.[60] There were very few examples of collective work in the harvest simply because nobody seemed to know how to organise it. The nearest thing was when neighbours helped each other.

There were three responses to these first experiences of collectivisation. The first was to resort to compulsion when over-optimistic hopes seemed to be inexplicably dashed. Criticisms were voiced at the party congress in 1949 of some cases of what was cryptically described as 'violating the principle of voluntariness'.[61] The second was to blame inadequate political preparation, referring partly to the need to overcome the lack of interest of rural party members, but also implying that even more outside agitators would help. That would only have been true if collectivisation had been a logical step for advancing Czechoslovak agriculture. Somehow the truth could not penetrate up to the party leadership who continued to state during that year that the experience of 'workers' excursions into the villages' had shown that they were convincing the peasants.[62]

The third response was to blame the kulaks and seek refuge in the theory of the intensified class struggle. That was to gain greater prominence in later years. For 1949, however, a good harvest led to a 12% increase in marketed output. Collectivisation, the central plank in the regime's agricultural policy, was irrelevant to this success which helped to improve the urban supply situation and thereby reduced the potential for working class discontent. For the meantime party officials could lose interest in agriculture and concentrate more on the issues they felt they understood better. Such hopes for an easy life were rudely disrupted by the shift in economic strategy during 1950 and 1951.

Seemingly impossible targets could be achieved, it was claimed, with the aid of cooperatives and of mechanisation which had always been seen as the key to overcoming agriculture's problems. In practice the machinery manufacturers found that they could not match the rapidly changing and uncertain demands of agriculture: new equipment was often treated with suspicion lying unused or unsold which made it easy to justify switching enterprises to making armaments. Central planners even concluded that investment in farming gave no return. It was therefore better to spend the resources on importing food despite commitments in the Five Year Plan.[63] As research a few years later revealed, mechanisation is more complex and needs more preparation and knowledge of agriculture. There was, however, little serious chance of success for a collectivisation drive which reached its peak in 1952 when, as Table 2.1 shows, the availability of new tractors was almost at its lowest.

Without mechanisation the case for collectivising was very weak. Nevertheless, there was a possible economic logic behind the policy.

Table 2.1. *Production and availability of tractors, 1948–1956*

	Tractors produced	Tractors supplied to Czechoslovak agriculture
1948	9 098	7 176
1949	9 735	5 717
1950	10 455	4 398
1951	9 468	1 797
1952	6 664	1 272
1953	6 518	571
1954	8 256	3 239
1955	12 750	3 705
1956	18 004	8 116

Source: SR, 1957, pp. 86 & 204.

In the view of Soviet writers there was a conscious aim of exploiting agriculture throughout Eastern Europe.[64] This certainly was the outcome although it was never the stated intention of anyone in the party leadership. Collectivisation was associated with raising the share of marketed output from 39% in 1936 to 47% in 1953[65] facilitated by the creation of a separate ministry for agricultural procurements in 1952 and then by the adoption in full of the Soviet method – with fixed supply norms for units of land and higher prices for supplies above the planned level – in 1953.

The 10 000 officials of this apparatus, typically from working class backgrounds and with little understanding of agriculture, were subjected to continual pressure and criticism for not reaching their targets. They faced the seemingly impossible task of allocating and administering production and purchase quotas to individual peasant farmers and, more than anyone else, effectively believed that farmers had to pay their tax towards the development of industry.[66] Cooperatives, even if they made no difference to production methods, could bring agriculture more under state control and systematise this process of exploitation.

They could also help industry in its desperate need to recruit labour but this happened in a very haphazard and ultimately unnecessarily harmful way. Some farmers left voluntarily for better-paid jobs in industry as they feared forced collectivisation or higher delivery quotas.[67] Particularly around industrial centres, one member of a family, usually a woman, would be left as a member of the cooperative while others went to work in industry.[68] Thus the ever rising labour needs of growing industries, especially during 1952, seemed to be eased by collectivisation. Official pronouncements concealed the reality of how this was being done with reassurances that farming was doing so well that 'one of the main advantages' of the new cooperatives was 'the saving of labour power'.[69]

Official propaganda, then, gave no hint of a conscious desire to exploit agriculture and continued to emphasise the inaccurate claim that the first results of collective farms 'were graphically demonstrating to the peasants the advantages of large-scale agricultural production'.[70] There was said to be empirical evidence, based on comparisons between individual and collectivised agriculture in a small sample of villages, showing savings of 50–75% in manual work for some crops.[71] Interestingly, mechanisation was essential to this but the leadership seems later to have forgotten that machinery production was being cut: faith in collectivised agriculture was strong enough for them to become victims of their own propaganda.

This suggests a qualification to the argument in later years that agriculture was given a low priority and its importance underestimated. That was the attitude of some planning officials but among politicians it was certainly not ignored as an enormous effort was put into forcing through collectivisation. In a certain sense, however, the reality of what was happening in agriculture was ignored. In the political atmosphere of the period the leadership was strongly influenced by a lot of misleading information from lower levels which helped it overlook just how bad its policies were.

Lower down in the party there is no sign at all of any awareness of wider economic considerations. The dominant influence became simply 'the hunt for the greatest number of newly created cooperatives'.[72] This was tied in with a toughening of the line against 'kulaks', but collectivisation did not appear to the officials in the villages as primarily a means to eliminate that alleged, potential fifth column. In fact, the kulaks' main crime was said to be their opposition to collectivisation. Attitudes towards them could, however, become a red herring for explaining the slow growth in cooperatives.

The law on cooperatives of 2 February 1949, unlike the procedure in other Eastern European countries, did not exclude them from participating. They were often encouraged, as an example that could help to win other farmers, and they would welcome the 'lower' kind of cooperatives that predominated up to 1950. Under this arrangement, all participants worked together during sowing and ploughing when machinery could be used. They then took the products of their own land. For a wealthy farmer this could help overcome the chronic labour shortage – there were only 60 000 permanent employees in the private sector of agriculture in 1949[73] amounting to less than 3% of the total labour force – and some farmers actually helped initiate such cooperatives. The 'higher' kind of cooperative meant payment according to work and richer peasants obviously had no interest in that.

This was actually to be the basis for accusations that they were 'sabotaging' collectivisation. There were frequent, non-hysterical descriptions of what was happening that leave little doubt that richer farmers joined cooperatives partly to protect themselves against a discriminatory purchase price policy and partly as a means to maintain cultivation of their land. They were simply pursuing their own immediate economic interests. Accusations that they were trying to worm their way into leading positions so as to *destroy* cooperatives typically lacked serious substantiation. Nevertheless, the concept of the intensified class struggle was pushed onto agricultural policy by the party leadership. Slánský in particular insisted at the February 1950 Central Committee meeting and again a year later that collectivisation required a struggle against the village rich; the term 'kulak' was still being avoided. He insisted that they should be ejected from the cooperatives, ironically blaming Šling for ever having allowed them in.

This, however, created an impossible situation for lower officials. There was absolutely no chance of them achieving further collectivisation without compulsion or without the support of the wealthier farmers. Pressures were at their strongest in mid-1952 when the leadership still insisted that collectivisation must be 'voluntary', but admonished lagging areas for not adopting the methods which were apparently bringing outstanding success in the Eastern Slovakian area of Prešov.[74]

Some rural organisations overcame the contradiction by giving 'quiet agreement' to letting 'kulak elements' join.[75] They often found that 'the big farmer will join us in the cooperatives at once' while 'we have to do more convincing with small and middle peasants'.[76] Figures presented in Table 2.2 suggest that the 'big farmers' were not all enthusiastic, but it does seem that, despite explicit and very vigorous instructions to the contrary, 'kulaks' were *never* excluded during the 1952–3 period and many party organisations actively sought their involvement. The official response to this was an almost hysterical insistence that 'we cannot live in peace with the kulaks'.[77]

Table 2.2. *Size distribution of landholdings and collectivisation*

Size (ha)	Percentage of landholdings within size range, early 1949	Percentage of landholdings incorporated into 'higher' forms of cooperative, 1951
under 2	46.1	38.7
2–5	23.3	20.9
5–10	16.9	19.6
10–20	10.6	16.6
over 20 ha	3.1	4.8

Source: Marjinová & Murašková, *Rozorané*, pp. 17 & 304.

They *had* to be driven out because they were class enemies and ruthless exploiters. Moreover, real or fictitious anti-state or terrorist groups were being uncovered while some kulaks confessed in court to joining cooperatives only to cause disruption and, of course, Slánský himself, condemned by then as a traitor, had been giving them support.

This gave encouragement to the alternative means of claiming large numbers of farms collectivised, which was, of course, to use compulsion. That must have seemed closer to the leadership's wishes as collaborating with kulaks met with continual condemnation while there were only occasional reminders to avoid force. Identification of 'kulaks' was admitted to be somewhat problematic[78] but, as one activist was later to admit, 'if we are to conduct a class struggle then we must fight against somebody'.[79]

There may well have been cases of richer farmers causing bitterness among their less wealthy colleagues by how they exploited cooperative property.[80] That, however, was only a minor element in the hunt to find kulaks in every village whose names were put onto a notorious catalogue, formally abandoned in December 1953. Many of those included were not even hostile to the regime, such as one who became a delegate to the 1956 party conference. In other cases condemnations required delving back into events before the war or noting behaviour such as how they treated young girls and stable boys.[81] There must have been plenty of scope for settling personal scores. There were also local officials who quietly refused to go along with this unpopular policy.[82]

The important point, however, was that those named as 'kulaks' could then be victimised with, for example, unrealistic delivery quotas. Once that had brought the farm to the brink of ruin it could be confiscated on the grounds that the farmer was incompetent.[83] 'Kulaks' were often harassed by the police and even held in custody to get their agreement to join a cooperative: judgement was passed on around 80 000 in the 1950s for verbal and economic offences.[84] In effect, they were the example of what could happen to opponents of collectivisation. Many were evicted from their villages and their farms confiscated – a fate which befell 1 077 families up to April 1953.[85] Others were charged with sabotage and imprisoned. Table 2.2 shows how far larger farms tended to be incorporated more frequently into cooperatives.

There was no framework for farmers to express their opposition to government and party policies. The Czech and Slovak Farmers' Unions, their main representative bodies in the post-1945 period, were dissolved by the authorities in 1951.[86] That probably changed very little as 'only one or two party officials' often controlled the whole machinery of local government and of representative organs, such that they could take what decisions they liked without needing to fear outside criticism.[87] Nevertheless, there was plenty of passive non-compliance as peasants were by no means all cowed by the repressive measures used against a minority. By mid-1953 43% of peasant economies were collectivised, with a magnificent 68% in Prešov. That area had a weak party organisation and very disappointing results until June 1952 after which a sudden reversal occurred at the same time as 24 000 people were charged with crimes against the state.[88]

The earliest recruits were in frontier areas where harsh conditions and the desperate shortage of both labour and equipment effectively compelled peasants to do anything that gave a chance of state assistance. The peasants' reasons for not joining elsewhere generally seem to have been extremely sensible and had a strong influence on rural party organisations which were often plunged into a state of inactivity by the unpopularity of the policy. The party chairman in one small village of only 100 inhabitants, for example, was publicly pilloried for explaining his reluctance to press the issue. It would be difficult to found a cooperative, he claimed, because cooperatives in neighbouring villages 'do not work well, and that is not an attraction'.[89] The reporter flatly contradicted this claim, and such reluctance to go out and argue the case was quickly associated with the activities of 'Slánský and his gang';[90] but he was wrong.

Peasants' reluctance was not even a question of an abstract attach-

Table 2.3. *Percentage shares of forms of ownership in agricultural resources and selected indicators of output in 1953*

	Cooperative farms	State farms	Others
Land	30.8	13.9	55.3
Labour	22.1	12.7	65.2
Fixed assets	35.5	36.1	28.4
Gross output	23.7	11.2	65.1
Grain	35.6	9.3	55.1
Meat (without poultry)	20.9	16.7	62.4
Eggs	5.0	1.5	93.5

Source: HSR, pp. 57–87

ment to land ownership – that was too easily broken in later years to be a convincing argument. Instead, they could see that harvests were finished later and that incomes were lower on collective farms. No amount of political campaigning or false promises could alter this reality. Cooperatives were more productive *only* when well organised and mechanised. Figures for the early 1950s show little difference in crop production, but in animal products the private farms were twice as productive.[91]

Table 2.3 shows the full comparison for 1953. The state farms – a relatively unimportant sector including some property nationalised after World War I and a number of farms in under-populated frontier areas – appear as the least productive partly because they often had the worst land but also because they were used quite deliberately to produce what nobody else found profitable. The comparison is slightly harsh on the cooperatives as private plots, usually up to 0.5 ha, are included in their land area but not in their specific output categories.

These disappointing results for cooperatives reflect a wide range of circumstances. Some were 'minority' cooperatives – only encompassing a minority of farms in a village – and could not organise genuine collective work. Membership was often purely formal – one cooperative had 500 members of whom only 25 actually worked on the farm[92] – and in many others nobody knew how to organise things differently from individual peasant farming. The overall performance of the sector must also reflect some cases of gains from the rationalisation of landholdings and elimination of disguised unemployment.

Table 2.4. *Agriculture's performance in the First Five Year Plan*

	1937	1948	1950	1953
Output	100	73.0	86.2	84.4
Output per hectare	100	76.4	91.0	91.0
Output per head	100	107.6	138.1	149.9
Employment (in thousands)	3298	2222	1894	1672

Source: SR, 1975, p. 50

The greatest disappointment was in livestock production which grew by barely 18% compared with a target of 86% during the First Five Year Plan. There was an enormous waste of resources in constructing new buildings which were to remain empty leaving many cooperatives ruinously in debt.[93] Some buildings were inappropriate, but there was a further problem as peasants were especially reluctant to give away their livestock. They were more attached to animals than to land but purely as a source of income, so they often sold their animals first thereby satisfying delivery quotas, but giving the new cooperatives a poor start. There was certainly nothing approaching the mass livestock slaughter associated with Soviet collectivisation in the early 1930s and the 1950 animal populations were quickly restored.

The target of raising output by 37% during the First Five Year Plan was always extremely ambitious. It became quite impossible as the area of cultivated land was reduced – to make way for industry or because of the labour shortage – and as industry itself failed to provide enough chemical fertilisers or the right means of mechanisation. In fact, as Table 2.4 shows, output rose only 17% between 1948 and 1953 and remained some way below the pre-war level.

Something was achieved with the increase in productivity per head, but Czechoslovak agricultural policy in this period must be judged a failure. The essential concept was that agriculture is no different from industry. Cooperative farms were to be run within the state plan and to use Soviet planning methods with the greatest detail in setting tasks. That was believed to be the precondition for agriculture keeping pace with industrial development.[94] Precise and definable tasks, as in industry, were to make possible 'socialist competition' as 'the basic method for increasing production'.[95] Party organisations therefore had a vaguely defined role in encouraging greater effort to reach set targets. This bore very little relationship to the true situation which was characterised by poorly organised and financially precarious cooperative farms based on reluctant or uninterested farmers who knew little of how to organise collective work. The gap between the 1951 revision of the Five Year Plan and what was achieved in 1953 was at its widest in agriculture. The gulf between official propaganda and the reality on the ground was never greater than in early 1953. It was, however, extremely difficult for anybody in a position of power to look objectively at what was happening in the period dominated by arrests and political trials.

Consequences of trials

In general the principal impact of those trials was to make any serious discussion or thinking appear unnecessary. The accused confessed to an extraordinary range of economic 'crimes' thereby explaining away every policy mistake, and every change in policy, as somehow the consequence of the activities of enemy agents. An image was created of a correct, unchanging and unchangeable policy. The accused themselves were obliged to insist that 'the basic conception of the Five Year Plan is absolutely correct'. Frequent changes were required because 'we succeeded in smuggling into the plan a number of sabotage acts'. There was, however, reassuring praise for Gottwald from the mouth of an alleged traitor who admitted that 'thanks to the President of the Republic our acts of sabotage were progressively uncovered . . . especially after the speeches to the February Central Committee meetings of 1950 and 1951'.[96]

Thus Frejka, the leading CP economist who like several others was of German–Jewish origin, had to take the rap for what had seemed to all the leadership to be sensible economic policies when adopted. The aim to keep 60% of Czechoslovakia's trade with the West even in 1953 'proves our hostile intentions'. The proposal to continue investing in traditional light industries was characterised as 'maintaining the pre-war economic structure'. Hopes of exporting 41% of shoe production were ridiculed as were plans for a 128% increase in investment in textiles.

There are three distinct issues here. The first, the suggestion that any mistake was deliberate sabotage, can be dismissed quickly. The second, the question of whether the plan was feasible, is harder to gauge. It is possible that Czechoslovakia would anyway have had trouble exporting such quantities of consumer goods. With the economic division of Europe, and the lack of interest in such products in the USSR, that became a certainty. The third issue relates to how changes in economic policy were handled. It should not be that difficult to admit that the objective circumstances had changed, but it was now proving unnecessary to make even such a mild confession of fallibility. In fact, Frejka pleaded guilty to causing chaos in the bread supply situation in 1950, although Gottwald had previously indicated the leadership's collective responsibility for the mistakes that caused it.

There was a similar approach in relation to mistakes in investment projects. Frejka's testimony, and the evidence of Zdeněk Půček, the 28-year-old Deputy Minister of State Planning who was called in as an expert witness, contained a familiar exposé of investment problems. The only trouble was that they were attributed to sabotage thereby obviating the necessity of a serious analysis. Thus an 'incorrect' policy of holding back investment into heavy industry in 1946–48 led, it was claimed, to an inevitable bunching of new projects in 1950–52. Many were insufficiently prepared and the strain on resources led to delays and an escalation of work-in-progress. There were identifiable mistakes with unnecessary investment, 'gigantomania' and inadequate coordination of projects in the electricity industry which were causing power failures affecting both industrial and domestic users. There were projects that were stopped after a great deal of money had been spent including a factory for an annual output of 20 000 light tractors for which 'no market was assured'. A plan for a factory to produce 50 000 cars per year was abandoned in 1951 because it was 'absolutely unnecessary' and a similar fate befell a tyre factory for which some advanced payment had been made to the USA. In this case an export licence was actually refused as the equipment was being loaded.[97]

These could be seen as investment errors, but they were also a reflection of the changed international situation forcing ever deeper structural changes on the economy. The need to satisfy Czechoslovakia's new customers was made clear by accusations that there had been a refusal to buy tobacco from Bulgaria; instead Czechoslovakia had demanded only industrial raw materials. There had allegedly been a reluctance to give away patents – the second CMEA meeting which took place in August 1949 in Sofia finally agreed that scientific and technical knowledge would be shared without charge[98] – and the Soviet Union had been offered 'various products of our engineering industry' which it did not want and asked in return for 'an excessively large quantity of raw materials which we could obtain or save at home'. That – in a form to satisfy critics in neighbouring countries – is partly a description of the normal behaviour of Eastern European states involved in trade by barter, but it also indicates just how far Czechoslovakia was expected to abandon the thinking of 1949 and fit in with the demands of the rest of the bloc. Půček even claimed that failure to invest in raw material extraction had made it impossible to fulfil foreign trade contracts in heavy engineering. The inconsistency of the original versions of the Five Year Plan was hammered remorselessly and Slánský himself admitted holding up the exploitation of 'comparatively rich' domestic resources as a concrete example of deliberate sabotage aimed at harming the economy.

His other major confession on economic questions was that he had delayed the introduction of Soviet planning methods, and interest in the Bat'a system was condemned as part of that conscious effort:[99] indigenous experience was thereby dismissed. Instead, by the end of 1952 Czechoslovakia was using active involvement of Soviet planning experts in the continuing belief that much greater *detail* would help overcome their difficulties and make it possible to reach high plan targets.[100] The argument for this was embodied in Frejka's testimony which contained a critique of central planning in its Soviet form as much as of the Czechoslovak system of 1952. In the engineering and steel industries enterprises had fulfilled plan quotas in the familiar way. Light products were emphasised at the expense of heavy ones. Small electric motors were made instead of large ones. Weak generators replaced strong ones and thin replaced thick sheet steel. Enough steel was produced, but there was not enough high quality steel. Output targets were reached, but at the expense of excessive raw material consumption. Apparently all this could have been avoided if only Slánský and his accomplices had not 'prevented the utilisation of Soviet planning experiences'. It was still believed that, with rigorous preparation, enough detail could be put into a state plan to prevent these distortions.

These were already familiar complaints among specialists who could see that such weaknesses at the micro level were leading to the wrong assortment and poor quality even of products intended for defence and for export to the USSR.[101] Often the solution was said to lie simply in better organisation and in better preparation around a firm perspective for that sector of industry.[102] This latter theme was soon to become very prominent. During 1952, however, the critique centred more on the organisational structure of the economy.

Part of the argument was that planning was said to be divorced from management.[103] A decentralised structure had been inherited from the pre-1948 period and then supplemented with a central planning authority which simply handed down targets. The only discussion possible was then over enterprises' demands for investment, labour and inputs. The central authority, as it lacked intimate involvement in the process of plan fulfilment, could not check these claims against any objective criteria. Balances were constructed without assessments of real capabilities so that resources were allocated on the basis of 'who shouted the loudest'. The solution was to keep closer control over the plan's progress as a basis for setting next year's target. As part of this, ministries were to set enterprise plans and were to be given individual investment quotas which they could allocate themselves.

This system could bring some improvement as a single central planning body with genuine authority would have more ability to change the plan during the course of a year as parts of it were shown to be unrealistic. Nevertheless, formal changes in the organisational structure could not overcome the inherent inability of any central body to acquire enough reliable information to formulate that perfect plan.

This was even described as a 'decentralisation' of planning and it was hoped that it would eliminate the arbitrary and unattainable targets set from a distant State Planning Office for individual enterprises. In reality, when the new system was introduced at the start of 1953, it involved the final elimination of any element of self-financing of investment and the end to any pretence that workers could be involved at the formulation stage through 'counter plans'. That idea – that workers would take out a higher target – had led only to excessive demands for raw materials or unwanted products upsetting the balance of the plan. Under the new system, involvement would come only at the fulfilment stage. Thus the claim that a plan could balance, even approximately, and yet not be 'dictated from above in anything'[104] was effectively abandoned.

The main message from the Slánský trial for mass consumption was that somebody in power had been playing a deceitful game with the consequence that much of people's efforts had been wasted. No less than 8520 resolutions, letters and telegrams were received by the party leadership and the court between 20 November and 2 December 1952. Along with reports published at the time they leave little doubt that widespread anger and hatred towards Slánský and his fellow accused were being generated. The atmosphere of the period and the detailed nature of the confessions made it difficult to doubt the authenticity of the case and voicing these doubts could lead to the risk of physical assault. There were, however, reports that a lot of people saw the process as a 'naked fraud', as 'a pre-rehearsed comedy' or as an attempt to blame Slánský 'for what all the comrades did together'.[105]

The sort of reaction the authorities liked was expressed by R. Záruba, a foundry worker in a Pardubice factory who was rewarded with good coverage in a national newspaper. In his view people were now 'going to live happier lives and work better, because we know that we are working for ourselves and that nobody can steal the fruits of our labour from us'. He reported the view of workers taking their five-minute tea break as 'that filthy gang sabotaged every sector of the economy. We will show them that we will not be deterred from completing the plan.' So strong was the feeling that some workers had even been coming in to work two hours early and they overfulfilled the plan by 20 to 28% during the period of the trial.[106] No doubt that left them little time or energy for a detailed study of the evidence.

There were, however, ambiguities in the leadership's approach towards the trials in the following months. To blame *all* difficulties on enemy agents would ultimately prove disastrous as it would give no prospect of finding solutions. Speaking at the party's conference on 16 December 1952 Gottwald actually seemed to be presenting a very different explanation. He had to outline what had happened, adopting a rather defensive tone when trying to explain how such a betrayal could have persisted undetected for so long. He blamed the 'conspirators' for *past* damage to the economy, but then, in line with the typical view in economic management, emphasised that 'the common cause' for the majority of industry's problems was 'the inadequacy of state and labour discipline from the top to the bottom'.[107]

Some speakers at the conference reiterated the view that the 'conspirators' had caused, in effect, all the economy's problems and there were attempts to attribute any disappointments to 'the consequences of sabotage by the anti-state centre'.[108] Others, however, effectively dismissed that explanation, warning of the need to recognise 'where the influence of the conspirators ends and where that of negligence, indiscipline and bad work begins'.[109] Others amplified the point with references to fiddled output figures – shifted up above the plan target by counting in components supplied from other factors[110] – or to the sheer inability to identify and act on the causes of poor results. A clear example was the North Bohemian mining area where it had once seemed so easy to blame the party organisation for not finding the means to fulfil the Two Year Plan. Subsequent results had been no better and party officials could not find a clear and agreed answer as to where the root of the difficulties lay. Management blamed absentee-ism and high labour turnover. Miners blamed poor organisation of work and bad transport. The Ministry sent endless investigating commissions, none of which had provided a solution.[111]

The more subtle message, that it was the new planning system rather than just the removal of traitors that would solve the economy's problems, was greeted with even more caution. Deputy Prime Minis-ter Dolanský claimed that the use of balances and technical conditions was a great step forward. If they were calculated accurately it would indeed give factories a better chance of receiving the supplies they needed. Euphemistically, he admitted that the plan was 'not yet at the required level'.[112] In fact, despite the trumpetings about the Soviet panacea it seems that it had generated very little interest. In Vítkovice preparations for the 1953 plan did not begin until November 1952 and then only involved a few managers.[113] In Prague factories 'at most 3–4 economists' were involved and they could only report to party officials that they did not know how the new plan was going to work or how their factories were going to receive necessary inputs.[114] As a further complication, all the initial plan figures were revised following the exposure of 'sabotage in the economy' so that enterprises were left guessing what might be asked of them until well into 1953.[115] The arbitrary setting of targets continued.

The Slánský trial was holding up the development of a serious critique of the evolving planning system but it could not completely prevent a gradual process whereby those working in industrial management were becoming aware of the complexity of their tasks. The typical article in a specialist journal might pay lip service to the trials, but it did not blind the specialists to the problems. The view that better party work alone could solve everything was implicitly being challenged. Some encouragement to this process was given by changes in neighbouring countries following the death of Stalin and by open signs of working-class discontent within Czechoslovakia. That, however, was too weak a protest movement to shake the leadership into a major rethink.

Aggregate figures on living standards are very dangerous owing to the dual market. In fact, precise calculations for the cost of living and hence real wages were stopped in 1951. It seems, however, that average real earnings fell by 12% between 1949 and 1953. Personal

Table 2.5. *Consumption per head of various foods, 1948–1953*

	Meat	Milk	previous year = 100 Eggs	Greens	Grain products
1948	73.2	100.4	150.0	167.6	101.4
1949	114.2	113.5	122.8	82.1	112.6
1950	135.8	108.1	112.1	98.3	108.2
1951	88.2	107.1	112.1	105.5	91.0
1952	106.8	99.1	97.2	84.1	103.3
1953	99.8	86.8	107.0	119.7	99.0

Source: SR, 1975, p. 36.

consumption fell by less, propped up by the higher level of employment,[116] but available figures suggest considerable fluctuations and an overall decline. The available statistics show housing construction running below the pre-war level while the sales of many industrial consumer goods collapsed after 1949 – radios down by 62% by 1953 and bicycles dropping 33% in the same period – alongside fluctuations in food consumption. Meat consumption per head peaked in 1950, then fell by as much as 22% in Slovakia by 1953.[117] The year by year fluctuations are shown in Table 2.5. These uncertainties, periodic supply breakdowns even for basic foods and panic buying were a more important stimulus for widespread discontent than the absolute change in living standards.

Attempts to mask that with the political trials ultimately backfired. Following the execution of Slánský and the others, hundreds of resolutions came in to the party leadership and to Gottwald personally expressing agreement with the outcome but also expressing very deep disquiet. The view was becoming widespread that 'the Central Committee will have something to explain' while some resolutions even insisted that 'it would be necessary to change the whole government' or that 'Comrade Gottwald should conduct a self-criticism'. If leading officials had been so incompetent as to allow enemies and traitors to determine policy then, according to a widely expressed view, ordinary workers should be put in their place.[118]

This intervention from below was not a new phenomenon. The feelings being expressed had already been heard often enough before, but now the distrust and prejudice was being directed back onto the *whole* leadership. There was no repeat of the elation reported after

February, in autumn 1948 or after Šling's arrest. The leadership's ability to manipulate demonstrations of support had finally been exhausted and that could have threatened the regime with a real crisis.

Summarising the overall impact of the period it is natural to look for who had gained and who had lost. Some 200 000 to 300 000 workers were promoted into higher office. Many others benefited materially, particularly in priority sectors of industry. Some families also benefited from greater employment opportunities, higher wages for the very lowest paid and equal pay for women. Kaplan, the prominent Czechoslovak historian who took an enormous wealth of notes from archives to West Germany in 1976, has estimated that around 40% suffered from one form of political persecution or another, irrespective of material conditions. That included 83 000 tried for political offences, including purely 'verbal' ones, over 150 000 interned in labour camps and many more who suffered milder discrimination such as the loss of a job or of promotion prospects on grounds of political or class background or religious beliefs: others were evicted from their flats for being 'politically unreliable'. This was done in the name of a class struggle, but the gainers were not the working class. Political repression created plenty of scope for arbitrary power at all levels, so that confiscated flats were more likely to be allocated to top officials than to those in poverty.[119]

The effect of these changes was to produce and retain a body of enthusiastic support. Among the general public, however, there was a widespread cynicism which did not lead into active opposition. Those who suffered became deeply alienated from public affairs.[120] A very common complaint was that they had actually *never* been anti-socialist; the strongest reaction was to insist on being non-political. There was still a sharp division between those for and those against the system in general, but one common feeling was emerging. Those in power, it seemed, cheat and tell lies, claiming successes that are obviously untrue and blaming each other for their failures. Something was wrong in the exercise of political power, but there was no consensus as to the solution. These signs of a possible developing crisis should therefore not be exaggerated. There was working-class discontent over living standards. There was reluctance to go along with party policy in the workplaces and there was a feeling among party activists that all was not well.

Nevertheless, the regime still had enough sympathy from its working-class supporters, and certainly did not seem to be panicking as it prepared a currency reform aimed at eliminating excess purchasing power, the origins of which lay in the Nazi war economy. Money in circulaticn had risen rapidly without a balancing increase in available consumer goods. The resulting savings were frozen in 1945, but restrictions on the production of consumer goods meant that the essential imbalance persisted through the early 1950s. That created a permanent danger of panic buying and also made it impossible to eliminate the ration system which was preventing the use of the price mechanism as an economic instrument.

Thus the establishment of a market equilibrium with stable prices was still regarded as the essential precondition for the 'economic laws of socialism' to operate. Moreover, there would be a major political benefit as it should later be possible to implement periodic price reductions. First there had to be a currency reform, which entailed political dangers. The measure was worked out with the help of Soviet advisers in the autumn of 1952 and implemented on 1 June 1953 alongside the elimination of rationing and the dual market. The principal effects were to wipe out savings held above a certain level alongside a twofold increase in the price of previously rationed goods. For some the gap to the free market price was even greater, examples being meat and butter. There were some compensating increases in wages and state benefits but, contrary to claims that this was the culmination of the liquidation of the economic power of the bourgeoisie, about 50% of savings were held by workers. The rest were largely held by farmers. Moreover, the elimination of rationing was a severe blow particularly to large families.

This was known to the authorities at the time, but the public was presented with a completely different picture. Zápotocký, the seventy-year-old party and trade union official who had become Prime Minister in 1948, was reportedly interrupted when addressing the Central Committee with frequent 'thunderous applause'. The measure was described as a great success made possible by the doubling of industrial output over the 1937 level. The 'class enemy' would no longer have the means to disrupt supplies to the population, to abuse the free market and to create shortages. There were hints in Zápotocký's speech of a guilty conscience as he indicated the special help that would be given to large families, actually not enough to compensate them fully, and stressed that there had been *no* family allowances in the pre-war republic. He evidently hoped that they would be content with the realisation that the new regime had given them something more than had been available under capitalism.[121]

This, then, was an official account at variance with the reality of what people were experiencing. It could only create bitterness which was further fuelled by a public denial in mid-May that any such currency reform was planned. That had been a response to numerous and renewed bouts of panic buying which need not have reflected inside information: there had been similar rumours several times before. The official media carried reports over the following days of meetings in factories supporting the measure and even claimed unanimous backing from working people for this blow against the remnants of the bourgeoisie.[122]

According to unpublished official reports, however, 129 factories went on strike involving 32 359 workers. In some cases there were major street demonstrations which were crushed by the army. In Plzeň 472 demonstrators were arrested. In several large factories the protests were led by otherwise loyal Communists, but Zápotocký preferred to explain it away as the work of the class enemy taking advantage of the party's mistakes. As a result, two-thirds of the strikers were punished by the loss of some financial benefits.[123] It was, however, a serious warning to the Czechoslovak authorities that reinforced the pressures from other countries discussed in the next chapter. Up to that time they had treated the level of investment and arms production as the priority. Consumption had become a residual. From mid-1953 onwards the need to ensure stability and at least a small increase in living standards always set a limit to the level of investment.

3   A New Course without a new strategy

The New Course

If Czechoslovakia was facing some problems in early 1953 then others in Eastern Europe were doing far worse. The most serious case was the GDR which had switched rather late to a policy of building up its own heavy industry. Forced collectivisation was started only after July 1952, but it did not help provide labour for industry. Instead, thanks to the peculiarity of open borders and a very easy welcome in the expanding economy of West Berlin, farmers and dispossessed small businessmen were simply leaving the country. In April 1953, the East German party leadership asked for urgent help from the USSR but, in the new atmosphere after Stalin's death, were evidently advised to face realities and adopt a softer line. In particular, the suggestion was to cut investment, raise the level of consumption and allow for the restoration of private businesses.[1] The East German leadership seemed to be accepting this in a 'self-criticism' published on 11 June 1953 which called on those who had gone to the West to come back with the reassurance that nobody would be punished for having 'run away'.[2]

The crisis was further complicated by the authorities' determination to toughen labour discipline around piece-rates. The problem was especially acute in construction as the temporary nature of employment there made it very easy for workers to find jobs in West Berlin. Employment was actually declining after 1952 while productivity stagnated; both rose steadily in Czechoslovakia. The attempt to impose a new payment system led to strikes and demonstrations on 16 June which spread to involve more than 5% of the total workforce on the following day. Mass demonstrations erupted in East Berlin and were suppressed with the help of Soviet troops. There was nothing comparable elsewhere in Eastern Europe but, surprised enough by this sudden eruption of discontent, the Soviet leadership pushed more vigorously its notion of what became known as the 'New Course'.

The approach was gradually adopted across the Soviet bloc and there is no sign of representatives of other countries actively participating in its formulation.[3] Its implications differed slightly from one country to another but its broad outline included three interrelated economic objectives. The first was a new start in agriculture; the second was a concentration on overcoming 'imbalances' around basic industries, and in particular the failures in raw material extraction; and the third, possibly most important element was an improvement in living standards. That, it was hoped, would be made possible by lower investment and reduced arms production as the international climate became less tense.

There were to be no changes in the broad outlines of the political system, but there was to be a 'return to lawfulness' – limiting the powers of the secret police – and a restoration of 'collective leadership' with regular meetings for leading bodies. Within the Soviet Union disagreements seemed to centre around some abstract questions in economic theory and in particular Stalin's doctrine of the priority for heavy industry. There was never an explicit change in philosophy, the 1953–4 period rather being described only as a 'regrouping' of the economy. Light industry could therefore have priority for a couple of years but, in late 1954, there were clear signs of a renewed emphasis on the military. At the CPSU Central Committee in February 1955, Malenkov was removed as Premier and the New Course in economic policy was partially reversed. There was a lasting recognition that living standards could not be dismissed as a residual, but defence spending rose in response to the build-up of the West German army and the effects were felt throughout Eastern Europe. During that period the Czechoslovak economy was deeply affected both by an attempt to apply directly the Soviet-inspired policy and by its impact elsewhere in Eastern Europe.

In East Germany the policy seems to have been very successful and was undoubtedly helped by Soviet credits and a relaxation of reparations obligations.[4] Published statistics[5] suggest that agriculture, previously stagnating, could expand rapidly as the labour force grew by 18% between 1952 and 1954. Overall individual consumption rose by 20% in one year reflecting higher real spending on a wide range of foods and industrial consumer goods. Much of this improvement seems to have been due to the renewed expansion of the private sector which accounted for 40% of the growth in national income but only 32% of production. Slower growth in the investment goods sector may have caused some disruption as output dropped for a small number of heavy machinery products. These, however, were still not a major part of the economy. More striking was the rapid growth in cameras and other sophisticated consumer goods: the GDR was already beginning to use its previous industries as the basis for its future economic philosophy.

The potentialities of the New Course were different in Poland which was among the last to follow the change in policy. Over the whole Six Year Plan period (1950–55) there was probably a minimal increase in real wages and little improvement in living standards:[6] 1953 was followed only by a recovery to the previous highest level. The key to this was foreign trade as industrialisation had depended on imported machinery and raw materials paid for by the only available exportable commodities – food and other consumer goods.[7] There is clear evidence in the published statistics of living standards rising again in 1954 and 1955 as investment fell in practically all sectors apart from the iron and steel projects: they were to be completed as soon as possible. The foreign trade structure could then shift back towards importing more food and exporting raw materials. This, however, was only a temporary pause which slowed the pace of industrialisation: there was no change in the overall concept and investment was actually cut harder in the consumer goods sectors.

Hungary's experience was similar with a very rapid and dramatic redirection towards the domestic market quickly restoring consumption to the post-war peak level. Czechoslovakia, however, faced a different situation. The immediate reaction in mid-1953 was to withdraw a harsh new labour code that was very similar to the policy that had just failed in the GDR and to plan a 16% reduction in investment. In practice it fell by very much less and 'recovered' more quickly than intended. As elsewhere, the fuel industry remained a priority accounting for 16% of industrial investment – against 10% of output – in 1954. Unlike Poland, there was a sharp cut for the iron and steel industry which began to reduce its workforce: there was serious consideration of a major shift away from the 'steel' concept for the Czechoslovak economy as nobody seemed interesting in buying its expanded output.

It is far from obvious how this could lead to an immediate rise in living standards. Statistical yearbooks show a 10% growth in real wages and a 14% increase in personal consumption between 1953 and

1954. Unlike other Eastern European countries, that is not reflected in higher consumption across the full range of consumer goods. For most foods there was actually a decline, following a bad harvest in 1954, and housing completions were the lowest since 1951.

Improvements related predominantly to industrial consumer goods, particularly from the engineering industry, which recovered slowly to the previous peak level. Even then, the numbers could be very small: 311 cars or even 14000 refrigerators sold to the public could hardly have assuaged working-class discontent. The most noticeable improvement was probably in the awareness that new products were becoming available, such as televisions, and especially in the stability of the market for basic foods and textiles as, after the currency reform, goods were generally available at the quoted prices.

The distinctive feature of the Czechoslovak economy was the limited scope for transferring resources from investment to consumption. It was possible to import some more food and industrial consumer goods, but higher consumption depended primarily on recovery in light industry which in turn depended on a shift of labour and improvement in raw material supplies. There was, then, no scope for a sudden improvement in the employment situation, as was possible in the GDR, or for a redirection of exports onto the domestic market. In fact, falling orders for machinery and armaments from other CMEA countries accentuated the effects of cuts in domestic investment to cause some disruption in parts of the engineering industry.

Imports still continued, as machinery had previously been sold on credit, but there was no expansion in the food available despite previous long-term agreements as Romania cut its imports from Czechoslovakia by 62%, while Poland, Albania and Hungary also made significant reductions.[8] The output of some machinery collapsed – cement works down to 17% of the 1952 level – but continued investment in some sectors of industry and the successful switch back towards agricultural machinery – growing 350% in two years – and consumer durables must have helped limit the effect. Nevertheless, there was inevitably over-capacity in some sectors.

Table 3.1 shows the changes in the main components of national income in terms of production. The slowdown in growth in 1954 is explained primarily by the poor performance of agriculture. There was also some deceleration in industry and to a slightly greater extent in construction which is a likely consequence of investment cutbacks. The productivity of labour in both of these sectors grew at the slowest annual rate for the whole 1948–56 period: 2.3% in industry and 3.9%

Table 3.1. *Components of national income in terms of production,* *1952–1956*

	Total	Industry	Agriculture	Construction	Others
1952	100	65.3	14.1	9.5	11.2
1953	106.4	68.3	15.2	10.8	12.2
1954	110.2	70.9	13.4	11.1	14.8
1955	121.5	78.1	14.9	12.6	15.9
1956	128.0	84.9	14.5	14.3	14.3

Note: All figures are percentages of national income in 1952, in 1955 prices.
Source: Calculated from *HSR*, p. 88.

in construction as against average figures of 9.4 and 6.0.[9] This suggests some spare capacity, but not a disastrous disruption.

Table 3.2 follows the effects from the expenditure side using the slightly different measure of 'final product'. This is more appropriate than the usual national income which incorporates an arbitrary depreciation rate on fixed assets. Gross investment, a magnitude actually influenced by decisions of central planners, is thus substantially different from the usual 'accumulation', which also includes changes in stocks and work in progress.[10]

The table shows how small the cut in investment was, possibly because, with the productive capacity available, it was impossible to resist demands for its utilisation. Personal consumption grew largely at the expense of reduced stock-building and work-in-progress. The usual explanation for the high level of stocks beforehand was poor organisation leading to unwanted products. Later theories have explained the generally higher level of stocks in socialist economies in terms of enterprises hedging against uncertain deliveries and sudden plan changes. They could therefore be expected to rise in times of shortage and should fall with the investment cutbacks. The continuing growth through 1953 might also indicate some cutbacks in export orders. It appears, however, that the change in the trade balance was very small relative to total national income. By 1956 both the share going in investment and the export surplus were higher than ever alongside a very satisfactory increase in the absolute level of personal consumption.

It would appear, however, that the immediate economic benefits of the New Course were small especially in comparison with East

Table 3.2. *Components of final product in expenditure terms, 1952–1956*

	Total	Personal consumption	Social consumption	Change in stocks	Net exports	Investment
1952	100	51.6	18.4	7.9	0.6	20.4
1953	102.5	49.0	21.7	9.1	0.9	20.7
1954	105.2	56.9	23.4	1.9	0.3	20.2
1955	115.1	61.6	22.1	7.0	0.8	22.0
1956	121.5	66.8	22.2	2.6	1.8	26.7

Note: All figures are percentages of final product in 1952, in 1955 prices. The components do not sum to the total because losses are omitted.
Source: Calculated from *HSR*, pp. 84, 91 & 169, and *SR*, 1957, p. 71.

Germany and Hungary. There was also very little impact on political thinking. Even Rákosi, the Hungarian leader closely associated with Stalin's policies, was hinting at 'the advent of a new era'.[11] In Czechoslovakia it was insisted that the line of the Ninth Congress had been correct. Any mistakes were in its implementation. The Tenth Congress in June 1954 therefore maintained the essence of that line while tacking on references to the general approach of the New Course. This was in harmony with the thinking of party activists very few of whom sought a major revision of policy. Leading figures even still talked of 'the sharpening class struggle' and of the need for strong security organs to 'liquidate the enemies'.[12]

There was, however, one area in which powerful criticisms did emerge. That was the bureaucratic system of economic management. There was a stimulus from the Soviet Union where condemnations were rife of the 'excessive centralism' of the planning system that had so shortly beforehand been presented in Czechoslovakia as a panacea. That might have helped open the door for the flood of criticisms, but there were also the specific problems in Czechoslovakia, which were accentuated when the cuts in investment goods led to a break in the 'chain of orders' between enterprises and hence to growth in unused stocks, in work-in-progress and in unsold finished products. According to Rozsypal, a leading planning official at the time, enterprises responded by demanding that the government should take responsibility for their sales and the result was an element of further centralisation in September 1953.[13]

This, then, was not centralisation to cope with conditions of shortage but rather the opposite. In Rozsypal's view, it demonstrates how the trend towards centralisation reappears in times of 'loss of long-term perspective' and following 'sudden changes in external conditions'.[14] Distinct ideas were already taking shape in Czechoslovakia on the crucial importance of a stable, long-term perspective and work began on such a plan after a Central Committee meeting in December 1953.[15]

There were still a few passing references at the Tenth Congress to how valuable it was to have 'exposed' Šling and his alleged accomplices. Some failures, such as in the iron ore mines, were still put down to 'inadequate work by the regional party organisation',[16] and socialist competition, the delegates were advised, should be modelled on the excellent Soviet example: ironically, Kaganovich, one of the Soviet Deputy Prime Ministers, was soon to refer to 'serious shortcomings in organisation'[17] which contradicted that naïve praise.

Generally, however, the central theme of congress contributions was criticism from the enterprises of inconsistent directives, frequent plan changes and other negative features of over-centralised planning. Just as in 1952, the failure to reach ambitious objectives and to complete projects for export to the USSR – 'arousing doubts about our reliability'[18] – were being blamed on the system of economic management. This was no longer blurred by fabricated accusations against an alleged enemy and neither was there any naïve faith in copying an outside model. It was still presented as correct to have taken 'the most progressive forms and methods of planning and managing the economy',[19] but even that system was said to have 'lagged behind the enormous upsurge in building socialism' so that it did 'not correspond to today's level of economic development'.[20]

There may well have been some exaggeration of the significance of this. Instability and sudden plan changes were partly the result of external events. Nevertheless, failings at the micro level certainly could threaten major policy objectives. Thus it was recognised that a stated intention to keep investment down at the 1954 level for another year required keeping a check on individual investment decisions. The party was told, and certainly not for the last time, of the need not to start any project without adequate preparation and always to check whether higher output could not be gained from existing capacity.[21] Over the following months Soviet leaders became increasingly outspoken in condemning their own system of management: Czechoslovak leaders, echoing many of their criticisms, saw the only remedy in 'consistent decentralisation'.[22] It was unclear what this could mean in practice, but the door was open for new ideas.

Neither could there be any copying of Soviet thinking in agriculture. Khrushchov, looking for a quick increase in food production, pushed the virgin lands project in early 1954. A year later attention shifted to a partial decentralisation of agricultural planning and the replacement of a number of collective farm directors. In Czechoslovakia, the more modest starting point was strong criticism of previous plans for their unreality, but the key policy change was a shift from maximum collectivisation to the maximum output.[23] In view of the insecure state of existing cooperatives, any immediate increase in food production was going to depend largely on individual farming.

This new emphasis was helped by criticisms of the previous use of force. November 1953 saw big personnel changes in Prešov which had been responsible for 40% of all legal cases brought against the 'rural rich', many of which were corrected in the following years.[24] Indicating again the absence of a full self-criticism of past policies, the Prešov party secretary was accused not only of dictatorial methods but of the old error of letting 'kulaks' into leading positions.[25] Nevertheless, the atmosphere in the villages definitely improved with the acceptance that farmers 'did not understand'[26] the policy towards the rural rich: the catalogue of kulaks was ended in December 1953.

The growth in cooperatives had already faltered early in 1953 and was definitely reversed in the autumn, membership falling from a high point of 381 000 to 304 000 in 1954. The decline was stimulated by news of policy 'corrections' in East Germany which began to appear in Czechoslovakia in June and were followed by rumours of the dissolution of Hungarian cooperatives.[27] Then Zápotocký, the new President after Gottwald's death in March 1953, delivered a speech condemning the use of force and compulsion. While advising farmers not to leave the new cooperatives, he added the fateful phrase 'We will not hold you back.'[28] The collapse was most marked where force had been used: only 24 of the previous 233 collective farms were left in the Prešov area.

These political changes left farmers free to respond to their economic interests and the principal reason for leaving was reported to be low incomes in the cooperatives. The currency reform also contributed in a possibly unintended way helping private peasants who could sell their surplus produce alone at high free market prices.[29] There were, however, hints of a more general change in

December 1953 with cuts in compulsory deliveries and improvements in procurement prices: the state machine and tractor stations gave them a little more help than in the previous year.

The evidence from the 1954 harvest was that small private farms could still get the job done faster,[30] but the only long-term perspective for progress was still their elimination. The old rhetoric resurfaced periodically, with references to the need to continue the fight against 'kulaks' tempered only by opposition to their 'premature liquidation'.[31] Khrushchov, speaking of course as much more than just a fraternal delegate, set the scene at the Tenth Congress with the familiar argument that higher output needs mechanisation which is only possible on large, collective farms. That was still an abstract argument when the means for mechanisation were only just becoming available, but it drowned out the cautious reminders not to 'forget the individual farmers in raising agricultural output'.[32]

The 'pause' in collectivisation ended in June 1955 with the start of a new drive based around campaigning by outsiders. It was met with almost total absence of interest. Even party members kept their heads down, especially in the Prešov area. Elsewhere too the overwhelming majority often remained outside the cooperatives. The obvious explanation for the policy shift was the need to ensure urban food supplies and to provide labour for industry again as Soviet policy shifted towards further rearmament. To some extent this was helped by reviving the tough line against kulaks and many of the most successful farmers suffered confiscation of their land and were sent away to work in industry.[33]

Thus ended a unique period in post-war Czechoslovak agriculture when employment actually increased by 83 000. Beyond that, however, the basis for a new approach was always very flimsy. Collectivisation was still an objective, albeit no longer seen as enough in itself to solve agriculture's problems. There was now at least a verbal commitment to provide stable procurement obligations linked to local conditions. There was a recognition of the need to prepare mechanisation more carefully – industry was still providing the wrong products in December 1953 – and of the need to overcome the disastrous labour shortage in some areas.

Unfortunately, it was very difficult to give reality to those promises as agriculture had to fit into a whole economic system of rigid centralised planning. Procurement agencies still had to fulfil their delivery quotas in the full range of foods and investment still had to compete with the demands of other sectors. Thus plans for cooperatives actu-

Table 3.3. *The performance of agriculture during the First Five Year Plan and the New Course*

	1949	1950	1951	1952	1953	1954	1955	1956
Agricultural production	110	106	100	97	100	98	100	104
Employment	96	96	93	96	100	102	102	98
Productivity	116	111	107	101	100	96	108	106
Investment	212	136	161	106	128	96	133	127
% investment in machinery	55	46	35	16	15	30	36	—
Stock of machinery	103	103	103	103	108	107	107	108

Note: Previous year = 100 with exception of investment in machinery.
Sources: SR, 1975, pp. 22, 25 & 32; HSR, p. 162; and Kapitoly, p. 121.

ally became more detailed and targets were raised despite the bad weather conditions of 1954–5. Neither was it possible to raise investment as once hoped to three times the 1951–3 level, although agriculture's overall share certainly did increase. It is very difficult to assess performance over such a short period when weather conditions have so large an influence, but the figures in Table 3.3 at least suggest that more resources were being directed into agriculture and more into machinery rather than unusable buildings, even if the immediate results were disappointing.

1956

Elsewhere in Eastern Europe the limited changes of the New Course were followed by the explosive events of 1956.[34] In Czechoslovakia the Twentieth Congress of the CPSU had far less impact than in Poland or Hungary. That was partly because of the economic situation but above all because the party leadership was fairly united in its desire not to rake over the recent past. No split emerged and that created no focus for popular hopes as happened most obviously in Poland around Gomułka.

The economy was helped by precisely the factor that could cause difficulties elsewhere, i.e. the attempt to renew rapid growth. The production and export of many kinds of machinery rose again and Czechoslovakia even began to penetrate some capitalist markets: arms sales to Egypt earned strong condemnation from British politicians. In exchange for these exports, Czechoslovakia could import cotton, wool and wheat to restore its consumer goods industries. There is no doubt

from published figures that by 1956 living standards had risen notice-
ably with industrial products appearing in quantities way above the
highest previous level: there were already the first signs of the 'consumer society'.

Elsewhere in Eastern Europe there was far more concern over living
standards but Czechoslovakia still faithfully reproduced a Soviet
increase in pensions and reduction in working hours.[35] The leadership were also briefed on how to conduct the discussion after the
Twentieth Congress at a meeting in Moscow on 27 February. The
same procedure was to be followed in all the countries and strict limits
were set on how far the discussions could be allowed to develop. For
Czechoslovakia, the uninspiring framework was an insistence that the
lines of the Ninth and Tenth Congresses had been correct: the errors
had been in their application.[36]

There were soon voices pressing for a deeper criticism. 235 basic
organisations, representing 15 000 party members, called for a special
congress.[37] There was an obvious precedent as the CPSU congress
had been called eight months before it was due. The calls were
rejected and instead a conference, with lower status and no power to
elect a new leadership, was held in June. A writers' congress took
place at the end of April amid great expectations and boasts of what it
could achieve: its final resolution, appropriately enough, was largely
concerned with the role of literature and culture and it provided no
wider conceptions.[38] Some trade unionists complained about how the
party had reduced their role to insignificance, and there were stormy
meetings in some big factories demanding punishments for those
who had used 'Gestapo methods', but it did not develop into a major
working-class protest.[39] Student demonstrations, largely around
academic issues, were kept in check in May by accusing them of
reviving the spirit of capitalism and then encouraging workers to
oppose them. It was even claimed at the party conference that the
working class was 'furious' and that there needed to be a strict
application of 'class' criteria to ensure that students were predominantly from working-class backgrounds.[40]

This, then, was a puny ferment in comparison with Poland or
Hungary. It had, however, disturbed the Soviet leadership enough to
express concerns at the direction and range of the discussion which
was formally ended on 2 May.[41] At the conference itself there were
only a couple of voices complaining at the absence of 'criticism and
self-criticism of members of the Political Bureau, the Central Committee and the government'.[42] The leadership's determination to keep
the skeletons of the early 1950s in the cupboard met with minimal

protests and any thoughts of questioning the political structure from within were further silenced by the events in Hungary in October which could only fill Communist activists with a deep sense of fear.[43] This really did not seem to be the time to risk the luxury of criticising the regime. They should rather be thankful for their country's apparent political stability which suggested that past mistakes could not be all that serious.

This, however, did not mean an end to discussion or to ideas for reform. It rather restricted them to the field of economics and more specifically to management problems within the economy. Within those narrow confines, it appeared to be a very frank and open debate.

The Twentieth Congress of the CPSU, as reported inside Czechoslovakia, called for 'substantially improving the organisation of our whole economy',[44] but there was little detail on how this was to be done. A brief mention was accorded to dividing 'current' from 'perspective' planning with the latter covering several five-year-plan periods for the growth of key sectors of the economy,[45] but the system of management was hardly mentioned. Khruschhov's list of objectives for internal policy were mainly concerned with restoring 'lawfulness' and made no reference to an economic reform. The first hints of the later decentralisation into regional planning authorities, with a reference in a resolution to giving organs at the level of the republic greater economic powers, appeared as an aspect of nationalities rather than one of economic policy.[46] The need for 'priority' to heavy industry as a basis for the expansion of the whole economy was frequently stressed alongside what amounted to smug complacency about the 'impressive strength of Soviet management bestowing inexhaustible possibilities for development'.[47]

'Bureaucratic attitudes' were an obstacle, but largely in relation to weaknesses in socialist competition. The only reservation, to judge from Prime Minister Bulganin's report on letters and comments from below, was the enormous body of concern at the need to improve the material conditions of the workers. That was far less significant in Czechoslovakia and, even in the USSR, it seemed to be used as a pretext to encourage support for ambitious plan targets. Thus, despite Deputy Prime Minister Mikoyan's call for a critical revision of Stalin's theoretical work *Economic Problems of Socialism in the USSR*, the Soviet Union was not providing a lead in new ideas on the precise methods of economic management.

Ideas in Czechoslovakia therefore emerged predominantly from the conflicts and failings visible within its own centralised planning system. It can be observed at two levels with complaints from enterprises and worries from those at the centre with overall responsibility for the performance of the economy. There were only the beginnings of a more theoretical critique of over-centralised planning that could provide a full explanation for the roots of visible problems.

Perhaps surprisingly, there was not so comprehensive a statement of the problems as there had been in the Slánský trial when difficulties could be discussed maybe because they could be explained away so conveniently. Reflecting the actual structure of political power and the position of party organisations within it, the emphasis was on raising individual, local complaints. It was as if party organisations, forbidden to link together to create a more general theoretical position, performed only a 'trade union' function representing sectional interests. Thus, although the pre-conference discussion and the conference itself produced suggestions covering a very wide range of economic issues, a lot related to individual workplaces and were referred back to be dealt with there. Others had wider economic significance relating to the management and planning of the economy. The overriding impression from published comments was of exasperation with the apparent incompetence and insensitivity of central planning bodies.

The conference became a platform for recounting a barrage of past complaints which had met with varying degrees of indifference from higher levels in the economic and political apparatus, causing offence to managers and workers alike. Thus the Kladno steel works had acquired a bad reputation for failing to reach its plan targets but the real blame, so its delegates thought, lay with the system which had prevented action on workers' suggestions to raise productivity. Another delegate spoke of the plan targets for Brno engineering factories being impossibly high: this was apparently obvious to the majority of workers, but even the Minister had said he could do nothing about it. A delegate from a neighbouring area pinpointed the absurdity: 'To accept verbally that there are mistakes in the plan and then not to change it, that is a strange way to carry on.'[48]

This was only one half of a full criticism of centralised planning. It covered complaints from below at the behaviour of the centre. It was left to a subsequent Central Committee meeting to even up the balance criticising some of the comments from the floor at the conference and drawing attention to apparent irresponsibility. They pointed, for example, to some regional organs supporting exaggerated demands for additional investment to create employment in areas still experiencing some labour surplus and effectively accused them of complicity in understating project costs.[49] This, then, was the reply from central planners who were exasperated by lower levels concealing capacity or biasing output to satisfy plan targets set in terms of particular measures of quantity. They seemed to be forcing the centre to become increasingly bogged down in the operational management of the economy rather than working on genuine long-term planning. Ideas for improvements in the planning system embodied a possible solution to the problems faced at both levels of the system.

There was too much paperwork in planning, so there should be a cut in the number of plan indicators. Precise plans were proving unreal and suffering from continual changes, so the centre should not get involved in work at too detailed a level. Above all the problem was said to be the absence of 'reliable perspective plans' covering a two- to three-year period.[50] If that weakness could be overcome then, so it was argued, the centre's task could be greatly eased and enterprises too would begin to look further into the future. One benefit, which was beginning to gain a lot of attention, would be a new incentive for enterprises to undertake major long-term research efforts which could improve the country's international competitiveness.

There was one, major obstacle to overcoming the lack of a stable perspective. As Prime Minister Široký argued in his concluding speech at the conference, the principal problems in the key engineering industry – the sector that worried him the most – were the high level of dependence on foreign trade and the 'frequent changes' in military technology.[51] This suggests a possible vicious circle. To improve international competitiveness, the disappointing quality of products exported to both East and West being recognised as a problem, depended on an improved system of economic management based around greater stability. That, however, inevitably depended on international trade which was inherently hard to predict. Široký therefore gave an understandably enthusiastic welcome to the agreement to coordinate plans within the CMEA and on specialisation in some sectors of industry and agriculture.[52]

This, however, was a very rudimentary form of coordination. Five Year Plans were at least to run concurrently, but they were to be compared only after formulation. That did show up some inconsistencies in particular categories of machinery, but the benefits of that were anyway greatly reduced following the economic disruption after the Hungarian events and as individual countries' plans were themselves subject to frequent revision.[53] Czechoslovakia did benefit by giving credits for the development of extractive industries which were to be repaid with the raw materials produced, such as sulphur and coal from Poland.[54] That did not overcome the semi-autarkic nature of the Eastern European economies and neither could it prevent manufacturing industries being built up without any certainty that markets would be found.

The low level of international specialisation was obviously a handicap, but attention naturally focused on what the Czechoslovak authorities could influence. 'Subjective' weaknesses were, in Široký's view 'not of secondary importance'[55] and, taking the same general conceptions that permeated much of post-Stalin thinking in the USSR and throughout Eastern Europe, criticism was directed onto 'rigid centralisation'. That was then linked to a conscious deviation from Soviet experience. According to Široký, the 'centralist system' was a 'historically necessary stage' enabling the learning of the basic principles of planning.[56] Complaints from below now seemed to confirm that, at the level of development of 1956, it had become an obstacle to developing creative initiative and revealing hidden reserves. Others went further in criticising the 'mechanical adoption of organisational forms' which had been successful in the different situation of the USSR.[57] Both arguments could lead to the same conclusion that power should be decentralised in economic as in political life towards enterprise directors, ministries and local government bodies. This was the theoretical basis for an economic reform the broad principles of which were outlined in the conference resolution.

The Rozsypal reform

The 1956 party conference was quickly followed by the formulation of a new system of management of the economy. For the first time, specialist economists worked together with managers in the economic apparatus. The package they produced gave an appearance of theoretical sophistication and many of its ideas were to be resurrected in the 1970s and 1980s. It was, however, logically inadequate and probably had no significant impact on the performance and behaviour of the Czechoslovak economy.

There was a clear verbal recognition of the need to seek specifically Czechoslovak solutions for what were believed to be specifically Czechoslovak problems. This, then, was not a model that anybody was trying to present for wider adoption throughout Eastern Europe. Neither was it lifted from the experience of others, which was worth studying 'only for generating the main common features of the social- ist system of organisation'. Beyond that, the need was to examine one's own 'concrete conditions' and especially 'natural resources and the level of development of the productive relations'.[58] This is already a somewhat cautious and narrow view of what is specific. There is never a clear statement that Czechoslovakia is a small, industrialised country heavily dependent on international trade. Specificity could mean, to judge from some of the comments justifying the reform, little more than a reference to the dominance of 'socialist' ownership forms.

There was criticism of the past adoption of the Soviet planning system. It was said to have been right in 1951–2 to bring the whole economy under a single economic plan, but wrong to adopt specific elements allegedly linked to the peculiarities of Soviet political and economic development. All this was just providing the background for criticisms of 'a relatively rigid centralised system of management' which could now be altered to take account of Czechoslovakia's *own* experience.[59]

There was certainly no retreat from a conception of socialism based on the initial assumption of collective ownership. Neither was there any retreat from the view that planning can and will work. Even the replacement of 'administrative' with 'economic' management was explicitly rejected, just as Široký at the party conference had con- demned some unnamed proponents of an 'anarcho-syndicalist' pos- ition.[60] This, then, was to be no copy of Yugoslav experience, nor did it derive anything from Polish reform ideas which were bound up with an ultimately unsuccessful struggle around a conception of democrat- isation of the economy. Enterprise independence was given an absol- utely central position alongside workers' councils and an Economic Council to oversee government policy.[61] In Czechoslovakia there was no coherent pressure for general democratisation, no suggestion of reviving works councils or other ideas from the 1945–48 period and the leadership was very soon conducting a 'ruthless struggle against any signs of revisionism'.[62] Economic reforms too were to be pro- tected against 'various incorrect and revisionist conceptions':[63] the effect of this was to confine them as an issue between managers and central planners.

Leading economists, some of whose careers had benefited from the earlier show trials, seemed happy with this cautious approach.

Moreover, the absence of a major influence from outside the economic apparatus meant that criticisms of excessive centralism were always half-hearted and over-generalised. 'The directive organisation of the development of the economy from one centre', the reform document proclaimed without reservation, 'is under socialism, the necessary form of management.'[64] To support this apparent conservatism, critical comments about over-centralisation were tempered with references to the 'tempestuous upswing of the economy' proving the success of and the high level of economic management 'built above all on proven Soviet experience'. Alongside some strongly critical comments, then, were reassurances that basic principles were sound and that problems related to 'partial unfavourable phenomena'[65] proving the existence of substantial further reserves. This complacency was in line with the general approach of the regime's supporters. There might be strong criticisms of individual failures within the bureaucratic system, but there had been no coherent pressure for any major change.

Following on from ideas that had been developing since the start of the 1950s, the key to improving planning was said to be ensuring stability of plans by taking a longer view. Excessive centralisation was again related to the instability of Five Year Plans forcing the centre to set precise and detailed tasks both for the whole economy and for individual enterprises.

The solution was better 'perspective' planning, covering the 10–15 year periods required for major structural changes, and better Five Year Plans which would set the economy's productive capacity. These should be 'maximally stable',[66] although the inevitability of some flexibility was recognised. It was obviously assumed that that would not disrupt their function as a fairly 'permanent and reliable guide' for enterprises which could then be given far more responsibility for their own operational one-year plans. Rather than attempting to balance everything out in the State Planning Office, suppliers and customers could negotiate together and enter into long-term contractual links. The centre would 'only' have to check that these were conducted in line with the aims of longer-term planning and with society's interests.[67]

Decentralisation in Czechoslovakia, then, meant only a proper demarcation of power to different levels in the hierarchy with the centre taking responsibility for long-term planning. It depended crucially on a reasonably stable central plan which in turn depended partly on external factors. On this basis links at lower levels were to be stabilised and to facilitate that it was said to be necessary to cut down on 'the large number of often very small enterprises' that create immense organisational problems for centralised planning. The solution was to simplify relations by centralisation into associations. These multi-enterprise bodies stood as a level of authority between the ministries and the enterprises and took some powers from the former. There was no hint of a fear that they might use their monopoly positions to pursue their own, sectional interests. Instead, the hope was to 'eliminate the danger of anarchy and unhealthy competition'.

It was also intended to 'use' the 'law of value' so as to simplify administrative tasks. As explained at the time, that did not mean the market influencing the allocation of resources but rather a more systematic approach to material incentives in the hope that choosing the right success indicators and setting them as cunningly as possible would eliminate the distortions of the past. Thus the gross output indicator was to be dropped, following criticisms that it led inevitably to the production of unwanted goods.[68] Instead, profit was to be the target. Enterprises would be rewarded for the maximum over-fulfilment of their target and punished financially for failure, but the tendency to seek a low target by actively concealing reserves was to be countered by comparing performance with previous years' actual results. That showed an awareness of the problem but was hardly a solution: enterprises could quickly learn to conceal reserves by never going too far above a plan target.

Another striking difference from ideas of the late 1960s was the absolute insistence on inflexible prices: 'We cannot allow the spontaneous operation of the law of value and permit prices to be formed from supply and demand.'[69] Instead, this planning system needed the maximum stability in enterprises' environment and that was taken to include prices changing only about once every five years, even if that meant growing deviations from genuine costs of production. It was recognised that this would lead to unequal levels of profitability and maybe a reluctance to manufacture loss-making products. No real solution to this problem was offered as it was accepted that some direct controls over enterprises might still be needed. It all depends, of course, on the degree of irrationality of the price system but it could easily be large enough to compel a reversal of the planned decentralisation.

The 'subjective' element in economic activity seemed now to be accorded a very minor role. Decentralisation was, according to the Central Committee, a basic precondition for increased participation and hence for 'deepening socialist democracy'. The proposals for the new system of management concentrated rather on the harmonisation of interests, after which trade unions might be encouraged to participate more. The emphasis, however, was on more narrowly economic questions. In particular, the wages structure was to be rationalised, ensuring the same pay for the same job in different sectors of the economy: this was already being done but, as we shall see, was never completely successful. There was also concern at 'levelling' with the hope that qualified work would be better rewarded. That too was to be a recurrent theme and much of the solution related to the incentive structure. Managers were to be paid bonuses related to enterprises' profits while workers' wages were to rise on the basis of improved productivity. There was an additional point here as, in the past, any means of measuring productivity (i.e. against gross output, net output or sales) could lead to a biased result. Managers, concerned with higher profits, would now have an incentive not to connive in that practice and could therefore be expected to resist one of the major sources of manual workers' wage drift.

A potentially even more important element of the reform package was the attempt to overcome problems with the planning of investment. Up to then it had been based on yearly plans and annual contracts with construction firms. As it was centrally financed, the enterprise's sole interest was to ensure that projects were started. It could not know for certain how they were to be completed and therefore had no means to ensure that they were fully prepared. It had no need to either as it could get finance 'practically irrespective of its economic results'.[70] The solution was to decentralise both the decision to invest and the financing of that decision. Only part of investment was to remain centrally financed when it set 'the proportions, the decisive direction and tempo of development'.[71] In practice 50% of heavy engineering investment was to be planned and financed within associations meaning that they could choose for themselves between expansion, modernisation or replacement.

Previously there had actually been an annual plan for repair which meant minimal incentive for enterprises to care for their own equipment. Enterprises were now to be provided, following estimates for 1955 of individual repair costs,[72] with enough to meet their differing expenses. They would be encouraged to take a longer view because funds could be carried forward into the following year. The only non-financial restriction was the need to prove the availability of materials before proceeding with a project. This, then, looked like an

Table 3.4. *Indicators of industry's performance before and after the 1958 reform*

	1955–58	1958–61
Growth in wages/growth in productivity	0.866	0.885
Growth in output/growth in assets	1.178	1.123
Growth in output/growth in machinery	1.117	1.075
Growth in productivity/growth in assets	1.065	1.018
Growth in productivity/growth in machinery	1.010	0.974

Source: Calculated from figures in *HSR*, pp. 161–2, 241, 251 & 253.

investment system that could switch attention away from building evermore new and expensive factories towards the smaller changes that were seen as the key to modern technological progress.

It was a system intended to allow a switch from 'extensive' to 'intensive' growth and, if successful, it could reasonably have been expected to achieve greater stability in growth, less investment per unit increase in output and a slower growth in wages relative to productivity. In fact, a comparison between the 1955–58 and 1958–61 periods suggests that, during that short time when the new system operated, there was no substantial improvement at all. It is impossible to assess seriously the stability of plans over this short period. The only real issue was the effect of the incentive system. Wages grew slower than productivity in both periods, but the ratio between the two growth rates worsened slightly after the reform. Every conceivable measure for the use of fixed assets reveals a similar trend. Moreover, this applies across all sectors of industry with the consistent exceptions of chemicals and paper. There is evidence of better use of machinery in a very few sectors, but the general trend is clear from the selection of indicators in Table 3.4. It would seem, then, that any success claimed for the end of the 1950s owed nothing to the reform of the system of management.

This is hardly surprising as actually no essential change was made. The new system of management was introduced over the following years without much fanfare. In April 1958, Novotný announced the reorganisation of ministries and enterprises but, despite claims from some specialist economists that the new system differed 'in essence from previous partial reorganisations',[73] the party leadership seemed uninterested. Those first steps were to be followed in the second half of the plan with the concrete preparations for all changes in planning, incentives, rewards and relations between economic units. Novotný claimed that the first results were good, but his evidence was thin because it was based on the achievement of plan targets, which largely depends on how high those targets are.

It is clear from complaints throughout the late 1950s that many enterprises still felt the weight of 'the cumbersome planning system' and found it impossible to implement ideas for technical progress because of the enormous delays and political battles.[74] Nothing seemed to have changed for them. The fundamental point was that profit targets were set for each individual enterprise with the clear intention that they should take account of notional investment and wage costs. Some targets were more flexible than others but ultimately they all depended on the same method of bargaining between levels in the hierarchy.[75] Moreover, the bargaining was really still over familiar quantities such as wages and investment. The link between bonuses and profitability was therefore ultimately an illusion.

A plan that worked

The development of ideas for the new system of management coincided with the preparations for and beginning of the Second Five Year Plan. The general philosophy, as outlined at the 1956 party conference, was for priority to heavy industry and especially engineering. According to Široký that did not mean pushing consumer goods into the background; rather it was the unavoidable precondition for a lasting improvement in the material and cultural level of the population.[76] That familiar old argument is questionable in the specific case of Czechoslovakia where so much heavy engineering output was exported. It was, perhaps, more reasonable for Široký to claim that natural and economic conditions were favourable for iron and steel, engineering and mining. Most iron ore had to be imported – two-thirds of domestic consumption during the 1956–80 period – but there was even a surplus of coking coal for export. Only in later years were the dangers of this industrial structure to become apparent.

Unlike the early 1950s there was a very serious effort to make the plan realistic. Široký accepted the desirability of more investment especially in housing and education, but pointed to the need for restraint if the chosen priorities were to remain. Industrial output was set to rise by 50%, with producers' goods growing 57% and consumers' goods by 40%. Textiles, food and leather were to grow much

Table 3.5. *Performance of Czechoslovak industry during the Second Five Year Plan compared with earlier periods measured by average annual growth rates*

	1949–53	1954–55	1956–60
Output	14.1	7.5	10.7
Employment	2.4	2.6	3.1
Productivity of labour	11.5	5.3	7.0
Investment	13.5	−1.1	16.8
Productivity of assets	9.7	5.9	5.4
Productivity per unit of machinery	7.7	4.6	3.3

Source: SR, 1975, pp. 22, 25, 26 & 28.

Table 3.6. *The structure of investment during the Second Five Year Plan compared with earlier periods*

	Percentage of total investment		
	1948–53	1954–55	1956–60
Non-productive	39.83	43.10	34.26
Productive	60.17	56.90	65.74
of which			
agriculture	8.88	12.23	16.08
industry	41.81	35.17	38.16

Source: Calculated from *HSR*, p. 170.

Table 3.7. *Investment in selected sectors of industry during the Second Five Year Plan compared with earlier periods*

	Percentage of total investment		
	1948–53	1954–55	1956–60
Fuel	10.33	15.95	19.03
Energy	12.52	17.82	15.45
Iron & steel	15.43	15.34	12.95
Chemicals	10.29	9.40	7.12
Engineering	19.29	13.62	15.65
Textiles	4.52	2.22	2.84
Leather	0.83	0.19	0.69
Food	6.07	4.10	4.44
Glass & ceramics	1.09	1.03	1.19

Source: Calculated from *HSR*, pp. 179–80.

more slowly than the average while energy, chemicals, steel and some metal products were set to grow the fastest. These were achievable targets. The only lasting element of unreality was the expectation, again, of a 30% rise in agricultural output. This, then, was essentially a return to the structural strategy of the early 1950s with a clear commitment again to the 'steel' conception. There was no longer the absurd over-ambition, but neither was there the potential for large productivity gains in traditional industries. That was reflected in the results. Tables 3.5, 3.6 and 3.7 suggest a more 'extensive' growth in industry than ever before and also a greater commitment in practice to the basic industries of fuel and energy – the greatest in any Five Year Plan period – and away from consumer goods.

There was still the hope that rationalisation would bring productivity gains and the Rozsypal reforms certainly could have helped. The key elements here were the reorganisation, allowing for the specialisation of products between enterprises and factories, and flexibility in the use of investment resources. Thus in the engineering industry many cases had been found of similar products based on very different technologies and hence widely divergent costs.[77] The new organisational structure should make it easier for the 'better' technology to prevail.

Reorganisation was, however, only one step towards 'a deepening of the specialisation of production in individual enterprises'. Ultimately, it depended on managers and workers seeing and responding to the new opportunities and this they were slow to do.[78] By the early 1960s specific plans had been worked out for narrowing the range of products in some parts of heavy engineering, but a closer look suggested that other enterprises were broadening their range of products. It seemed that greater specialisation was not 'substantial', was not coming as the result of conscious policy and did 'not correspond to our potential'.[79] Even the formulation of plans within enterprises for full modernisation to allow for a switch towards mass production was very slow and seemed to be confined within heavy engineering.[80]

In less favoured sectors scope was far more limited because of the lack of resources. In textiles, hope rested again on minor improvements with existing equipment which had brought such good results in the past. There was, however, a clear awareness that the industry could not stand up internationally without substantial further investment in new machinery.[81] Thus the picture across practically all sectors was now the same: a change in organisational structure could lead to greater specialisation between enterprises, but that could only

Table 3.8. *Ratios of growth in productivity to growth in fixed assets in Czechoslovak industry, 1948–1973*

	1948–52	1952–56	1956–60	1960–65	1965–69	1969–73
All industry	1.39	1.10	1.08	0.94	1.04	1.05
Fuel	1.19	0.94	1.07	0.90	1.26	1.03
Energy	1.55	1.00	1.13	0.97	1.11	0.97
Iron & steel	1.04	1.05	0.96	0.75	1.01	1.10
Non-ferrous metals	1.14	1.09	0.75	0.78	1.11	0.98
Chemicals	1.32	1.10	1.10	1.04	0.99	1.03
Engineering	1.43	1.09	1.13	0.92	1.10	1.09
Building materials	1.36	1.05	1.21	0.96	0.98	0.94
Wood	1.29	1.17	1.01	0.84	1.01	0.91
Paper	1.18	0.93	0.93	0.90	1.00	1.00
Glass	1.22	1.20	1.12	0.88	0.81	1.00
Textiles	1.61	1.17	1.14	1.11	1.04	1.00
Garments	1.52	1.06	1.08	0.73	0.97	0.98
Leather	1.32	1.22	1.02	0.96	1.01	0.97
Print	1.27	1.21	1.05	1.08	1.23	0.84
Food	1.46	1.14	1.10	1.02	0.97	0.98

Source: Calculated from *HSR*, pp. 164–6 & 253–4.

bring benefits in the context of substantial further investment. Table 3.8 gives support to the view that sources of productivity growth independent of investment were steadily diminishing after the post-1948 reorganisation. Annual changes for individual sectors confirm that there is a gradual, steady decline from 1950 into the late 1960s. The only deviations from the trend are exceptionally bad years in 1954 and 1962–4. For some sectors the decline was really insignificant, such as the iron and steel industry, which never made gains from rationalisation in the early 1950s. For others it was very sharp after 1952 which is consistent with the view that rationalisation there brought immediate benefits which were quickly exhausted. It is therefore not surprising that the late 1950s brought the first public expressions of regret over low investment resources in non-priority sectors.

In fact, the successes of the 1956–60 period were not that remarkable. The main contrast with earlier periods was the economy's stability. Living standards increased slowly but steadily – real wages up 17% and real incomes up 26% which was little more than in the three-year period 1953–55 – and the regime could boast about approximate equilibrium on the consumer goods market. They could even continue with some price reductions, claiming an annual average 1.8% fall in the cost of living. It was the kind of stability that discouraged discontent and reassured the authorities that they were in control.

It was claimed that the priority to heavy industry had facilitated the rise in consumer goods output. There was, according to Minister of State Planning Otakar Šimůnek in 1960, no need to prove this with figures. Shops were visibly full of goods as wages were rising. He could confidently assert that consumers were happy and that economic results were showing the superiority of socialism.[82] The time seemed to be right for Novotný to promise to solve the housing problem by 1970, starting with half a million flats over the following five years.[83]

Any fears there might have been about a repetition of the Hungarian, or even the Polish events had been proven quite unfounded. There were still attacks on 'revisionism' which caused several dozen persons to suffer and a policy of careful and quiet repression of outspoken opponents.[84] This was nothing to match the hysteria and lawlessness of the early 1950s and neither was there any sign of mass discontent. The leadership was judging the atmosphere by letters, resolutions, individual contributions at meetings, and participation in elections and the public discussions around a new constitution. The impression, for example from almost 200 000 letters received by central offices during 1962, was of a lot of concern at administrative malpractices but little general hostility to the system.[85]

4 From confidence to crisis

Thus, the dominant feeling towards the end of the Second Five Year Plan was one of success. This was also the impression of outside observers. The UN Survey for 1958 suggested that the country's 'diversified production and export structure' had enabled it to recover after the 1953–54 period better than, for example, the seemingly vulnerable East German economy.[1] The 'efficient light engineering industry', developed before the war, seemed to some to be increasingly able to compete with the West, with machine tools doing particularly well.[2] That, as we shall see, was to prove too optimistic.

Within Czechoslovakia the most obvious source of confidence was simply the fact that targets were being achieved. In 1959, industry grew by 11% which was fully 2% more than planned. The target for the whole five-year period was obviously going to be over-fulfilled: it was actually completed by March 1960 and the success was 'remarkably even'[3] across sectors so that there seemed every prospect of overcoming specific bottlenecks. Moreover, as Novotný could boast, the regime had just achieved a string of successes in rationalising the wages and prices systems, reorganising industry, collectivising agriculture and developing new ideas in the education system. All this must have encouraged his conviction that unspecified 'new reserves' would soon be revealed. He therefore announced, in July 1960, that the targets for the next Five Year Plan would be raised from 50.8% to over 56% growth in industry and from 21.4% to 22.8% in agriculture.[4]

A second, and more ideological, source of optimism was the atmosphere in the Soviet Union where Khrushchov was talking confidently of 'catching up with and overtaking' the capitalist world. By 1965, the socialist countries would account for half the world's industrial output and be able to compete with *any* advanced capitalist country. This optimism was based on figures for output of particular basic products, such as steel, and paid no attention to many important and expanding sectors of modern industry. Nevertheless, the Twenty-Second Congress in 1962, where Khrushchov presented the new party programme, struck a chord in Czechoslovakia. So, for example, believing the 'material base for communism' to be near at hand, the rising Slovak party official Alexander Dubček was already predicting a 'tempestuous development of the forces of production'.[5]

Already at the Eleventh Party Congress in April 1958 the completion of socialism, meaning the final elimination of private enterprise, was presented as the principal objective for the immediate future. Raising the level of technology and 'deepening socialist democracy' were subsidiary to this. The priority reflected that enduring belief that the complete 'victory' for 'socialist ownership relations' would have some particular significance for economic success. By 1960 Czechoslovakia was said to be creating a 'mature socialist society'. A new constitution added the word 'socialist' to the country's title asserting that the country was 'gathering strength for the transition to communism ... hand in hand with our great ally, the fraternal Union of Soviet Socialist Republics'.

It is never easy to assess the effect on economic policy of these political and ideological factors, but the optimism dominating leading bodies of the Czechoslovak party around 1960 was so pervasive as to suggest a major impact. Moreover, it could seem to fit with internal political developments after 1956. To some extent optimism ran through the whole of Eastern Europe, but it is plausible that Czechoslovakia was particularly susceptible and hence particularly reluctant to revise policies based on complacency and over-enthusiasm. In Hungary there had just been a painful recovery from 1956 and the 1958–60 period was still set the task of 'liquidating disproportions' in the economy. It was also a period of shifting away from the economic structure built up in the early 1950s with an emphasis less on self-sufficiency and more on a narrow range of products for export including buses, diesel engines and some consumer goods.[6]

Similarly in the GDR there was little cause for boasting. The establishment of the Berlin Wall in 1961 was clear evidence of that. Modesty, however, was to prove a virtue. The previous failure to develop its own heavy industry to a satisfactory level had led the GDR instead to rely on importing finished steel. Around 1955 there was a shift in structural orientation towards sectors less dependent on raw material imports. In the early 1960s the issue was raised again, but the chosen growth strategy gave priority to chemicals and a number of very modern sounding sectors such as optics, precision engineering and microelectronics. From this the GDR could develop a good basis for exports of typewriters, cameras and other goods with a value content high in skilled labour and low in imported raw materials.[7]

Both of these countries did find themselves over-stretched in the early 1960s and both felt obliged to reduce the level of investment, just as Czechoslovakia was to do in 1962. In neither case were the effects throughout the economy so large and national income continued to rise. The difference was partly in the scale of the cuts, although the fall in investment in Hungary in 1961 was substantial.[8] The other difference was the structure of the Czechoslovak economy and its position in an international division of labour which, as in 1953, meant that there was little scope for recovery elsewhere to compensate for a lower output of investment goods. Having had, it seemed, the misfortune to avoid a major political crisis or economic failure, the country stuck to the same old concept of growth based on heavy industry. That left it especially susceptible to both chance and predictable external changes: over-confidence led to an underestimation of the dangers.

Thus little was made in the late 1950s of the failure to achieve targets for agricultural output. In 1960 it was still only 4% above the 1938 level: output in the GDR had grown by 102%. To the party leadership, the slowest growth rate in Eastern Europe could be attributed to the 'highly demanding and complex nature of building socialist forms in agriculture'.[9] It would be more accurate to point explicitly to the resurrection, after the interlude of the New Course, of the mistaken view that agriculture could be left to follow behind the development of industry while collectivisation would almost automatically improve its performance.

There was no questioning of the central position of collectivisation in 1956 which was still seen, despite strong complaints from those familiar with agriculture, as incorporation into rigid centralised planning. A delegate from Jihlava reported 3550 comments which could help explain the peasants' reluctance to join.[10] He pointed, for example, to the need to decentralise investment decisions which had previously been imposed from the centre and often took a form quite inappropriate to local needs. There was also exasperation at delays and excessive checks once construction work had begun, at a bureaucratic procurement system that imposed arbitrary and often unrealistic targets on collective farms and at a system of detailed – and often clearly unrealisable – orders from ministries which 'are still trying to keep a firm grip on all agricultural activity'.[11]

In the late summer of 1957 it finally seemed that the middle peasants in rich farming areas of the Czech interior were joining in substantial numbers. This, however, was associated with a failure to increase output as the level of mechanisation per hectare actually fell. Figures for 1953 showed 37% of arable work on cooperative farms mechanised, rising to 70% in 1957 but then falling back to around 40% in the following years.[12] The reason, of course, was the rapidly increasing land area to be covered by a slowly increasing volume of 'means of mechanisation'. It was explained away with references to 'the development of the productive forces in agriculture lagging behind the great development of socialist productive relations'.[13] The solution might seem to be to delay collectivisation and restore the more natural relationship in which the forces of production would lead. Instead, the policy was to press ahead until in 1960 80% of those active in agriculture worked in state or collective farms.

The consequences for agriculture were serious. Pay on collective farms fell from 65% of industrial earnings in 1955 to 59% in 1960.[14] The exodus of labour continued, reaching a peak of 155 000 in 1959. Over the period 1948–60 agriculture had lost nearly 40% of its labour force and contributed over 60% of the growth in employment in other sectors of the economy. Moreover, the labour force left behind was biased towards women and old people. Those under 19 years old made up 11.5% of the agricultural labour force in 1950 and 4.4% in 1960. By way of contrast, the GDR in 1957 had 8% of its labour force under 18, a much higher proportion of specialists, a far better level of education generally and proportionately higher levels of mechanisation and use of fertilisers.[15] The real difference was that collectivisation there, at least until the very end of the 1950s, was based on a level of mechanisation that could give it some justification. The 'relations of production' were not made to run ahead of the 'forces of production'.

The policy in Czechoslovakia could only make economic sense if the objective were to exploit agriculture for the benefit of industry. As in the early 1950s, that was never the stated aim. Instead, it was made very clear that a big expansion in industry depended on a big expansion in agriculture.[16] The effect in practice was to leave the country very vulnerable to bad weather conditions as a shortfall in domestic food production could easily lead to a hard-currency deficit. Table 4.1 shows the overall performance of agriculture which is compatible with the claims that it was damaged both by the exodus of labour and by the poor use of machinery by the remaining labour force.

Table 4.1. *Performance of Czechoslovak agriculture during the Second Five Year Plan compared with earlier periods, indicated by average annual growth rates*

	1949–53	1954–55	1956–60
Output	2.9	4.2	1.7
Employment	−3.7	2.0	−5.4
Productivity of labour	6.9	2.2	7.4
Investment	44.4	12.9	17.4
Productivity of assets	0.8	7.8	−3.1
Productivity per unit of machinery	−0.4	4.2	−5.5

Source: SR, 1975, pp. 22, 25 & 32.

This weakness in agriculture was aggravated by a number of factors which were coming together to threaten Czechoslovakia's uniquely privileged position as an industrially advanced country within a largely backward socialist bloc. By the late 1950s other CMEA countries had developed their own capacity to produce many of the goods Czechoslovakia had been exporting. Moreover, apart from Czechoslovakia and the GDR, the Eastern European countries proved capable of exporting more to the capitalist world. The obvious example was Romania with its oil. It could then import capital equipment from the West particularly as the embargo was reduced in 1958 to cover mainly goods of an obviously military nature. Romania, in fact, continued to import machinery from Czechoslovakia, but the threat was clear.[17] For the time being it seemed that nothing was wrong, particularly when hopes were aroused around growing trade with China which could again take the form of exchange between an advanced country and an industrialising raw material exporter. It never offered the benefits of specialisation between advanced countries.

The fundamental instability of Czechoslovakia's international situation has been related to 'a deepening disproportion between the dimensions of industrial production and the raw material base'.[18] As Table 4.2 shows, the deficit in raw materials was growing rapidly in the late 1950s, thanks entirely to the growth of heavy industry, but even this could be seen as a healthy development reflecting international specialisation. The real problem was that exports of machinery remained unstable and restricted outside the socialist bloc

Table 4.2. *Trade balance in groups of goods, 1951–1960, in million Kčs, foreign trade prices*

	1951–55	1956–60
Machinery & equipment	+9193	+14234
Materials (excluding food)	−4937	−9889
Food	−6579	−8443
Non-food consumer goods	+4168	+8847

Source: Calculated from *SR*, 1975, pp. 34–5.

by low quality. Exports of consumer goods, such as shoes, were rising but were restricted by the need to satisfy domestic demand and the low level of investment in those sectors. They too could only be sold in the West at very low prices.[19]

Neither was there an easy solution in trade with developing countries. Exported heavy machinery was frequently of a low quality and faced a hard competitive battle. To add to the difficulties for a small country with limited financial strength, other countries were offering credits of up to 25 years compared with a maximum of 12 years for Czechoslovakia[20] leading Novotný to accuse 'the capitalists' of trying to 'displace us from the world market'.[21] There was little scope for a sharp increase in convertible currency earnings here especially as purchasing countries, such as Egypt, often asked for delays in repayment of quite short loans: Czechoslovakia hardly had the strength to insist and anyway felt obliged to show some sympathy for political reasons.[22]

There was, then, very little leeway for importing more food, in the event of a bad harvest, or for importing sophisticated machinery and manufactured goods. Unlike other Eastern European countries, which had scope to export raw materials, Czechoslovakia was specialising in manufactured products that stood little chance of competing on world markets. So great was the reversal since the start of the decade that it had the lowest share of its trade with advanced capitalist countries of any CMEA member[23] and the structure of its exports probably left it the most vulnerable to a recession.[24]

Rather than emphasising these longer-term, structural factors, the Czechoslovak authorities identified their economic difficulties largely in terms of failures to reach specific plan targets. The overall strategy and the specific plans themselves were felt to be good. Concern was being expressed publicly over specific failures in steel and heavy engineering during 1959 and 1960 just as the authorities were boasting of their overall success in the Second Five Year Plan. The solution at first was said to be encouraging socialist competition and directing it towards overcoming specific problems: the leadership even added special appeals to the party organisations in the problem sectors of iron and steel and coal.

It is hard to see how that could have made any difference. 'Moral' incentives continued to play a role in economic management but primarily as an indicator of what above-average workers or work groups could achieve. Results from socialist competition were still used for setting targets, albeit far less aggressively than in the early 1950s, but they could not realistically be expected to yield immediate improvements in productivity. The more important measures, which were given no publicity at the time, were 'corrections' to the plan as early as 1960 and imports of rolled steel from the West financed by short-term loans.[25] As far as public statements were concerned, difficulties appeared to be very temporary at the start of the Third Five Year Plan.

Continuing failures in key sectors led towards a slightly deeper analysis blaming the economic reform of 1958 which, it was now suggested, had been 'wrongly implemented' to deprive the centre of the will to intervene in the affairs of lower organs.[26] As a result, the steel and heavy engineering industries were not producing what customers wanted and failing to deliver on time.[27] The obvious solution was to restore greater central control via quarterly and possibly even monthly plans so that output matched up with state plans at a more detailed level. This, it was hoped, would ensure machinery deliveries to key projects.

The results for 1961 showed a 7% rise in national income and almost a 9% rise in industrial output, 99.8% of the planned level. That did not look too bad, but the same sectors were lagging and some important projects were way behind, including a large cement works that was vital for construction throughout the economy. Again, there was an obvious implication when the plan for work on centralised projects was 92% fulfilled, and only 62% for completions, while decentralised projects were 105.7% fulfilled.

The leadership's analysis was essentially that the economy was hitting barriers to growth in basic sectors – such as coking coal, steel and cement – and that the root cause was organisational weaknesses. It still did not believe that the targets were unrealistic. Enterprises were accused of using their greater independence to fulfil the easiest tasks first irrespective of customer demand.[28] The remedy was a degree of recentralisation and the assertion of clear priorities and 1962 saw a return to the operational One Year Plans. With that came a wave of propaganda and publicity for socialist competition as the leadership clutched at the old, familiar hope for raising the economy's performance.

Shortly afterwards, however, the government responded to the developing difficulties with a dramatic cut in the level of investment. The optimism of the late 1950s was finished for good, to be replaced first by a period of questioning and discussion. Even today there is no unanimity on the causes of the economic crisis of 1962–3, although it clearly occupies a central position in any discussion of the economic reform and the economic system in Czechoslovakia.

Causes of the crisis

The nearest to a convincing explanation has been provided by Rozsypal who has pointed to a combination of long-term trends, a sudden external change, chance events and mistakes in domestic policy. The main culprit was 'the unreality of the extent and structure of investment in the Third Five Year Plan' as part of 'the rapid building of the material base for a future communist society'. Its effects were aggravated by changes in relations with China and other socialist countries, by two successive bad harvests and 'the method used to solve [those problems] in the autumn of 1962'.[29]

It is easiest to take these points in reverse order as there is no doubt that the cuts in investment explain a large part of the fall in national income in 1963. Output, productivity (per man and, even more clearly, per unit of machinery) and even employment fell in the construction industry as projects were frozen. The first hit were the so-called 'decentralised' projects where building work was already declining towards the end of 1961. By late 1962 even the major, centrally approved projects were cut, reaching a low point at the beginning of 1963 – 77% of the previous year's level – after which both underwent a gradual recovery.[30] Industry as a whole did less badly with the fall in output explained by some sectors of the investment goods industry plus import-intensive sectors generally. Tables 4.3 and 4.4, showing the components of national income from the production side and final product from the expenditure side, leave no doubt that, this time, the principal change was a cut in investment. Agriculture

Table 4.3. *Components of national income in terms of production, 1960–1964*

	Total	Industry	Agriculture	Construction	Others
1960	100	62.6	13.1	10.7	13.6
1961	106.8	68.7	12.7	11.2	14.1
1962	108.3	72.9	10.5	10.6	14.3
1963	105.9	70.9	12.2	8.9	13.9
1964	106.6	72.0	11.6	10.0	13.0

Note: All figures are percentages of national income in 1960, in 1960 prices.
Source: Calculated from *HSR*, p. 88.

Table 4.4. *Components of final product in terms of expenditure, 1960–1964*

	Total	Personal consumption	Social consumption	Change in stocks	Investment	Net exports
1960	100	56.3	15.4	1.7	24.1	1.2
1961	107.0	58.2	16.6	5.1	25.8	0.3
1962	109.4	59.6	17.5	5.2	25.2	1.1
1963	108.2	60.3	18.1	3.6	22.4	2.3
1964	109.0	62.1	18.8	0.5	25.0	1.3

Note: All figures are percentages of final product in 1960, in 1960 prices. Losses are omitted.
Source: Calculated from *HSR*, pp. 84 & 91, *SR*, 1961, p. 118, and *SR*, 1965, p. 149.

was actually improving by 1963, the one year in which national income fell. Both net exports and personal consumption were helped by an accompanying decline in stocks and work in progress.

Results in agriculture are similarly easy to document. As Table 4.5 shows, output was stagnating in 1961 and fell in 1962. As food consumption continued to rise, there was no option but to increase imports to a higher level than ever before in 1963. That put the squeeze on imports of machinery and of other raw materials from the capitalist states. Not surprisingly, 1963 saw a significant fall in the production of shoes and a number of textile products which depend on imports, but these problems in agriculture alone would certainly not have required so savage a cut in investment.

Table 4.5. *The performance of agriculture in the early 1960s and its consequences*

	1961	1962	1963	1964
Agricultural output	99.9	93.3	99.7	102.7
Productivity per employee	106.3	102.5	111.1	116.8
Agricultural imports	93.6	96.5	112.6	119.8
Imports of other materials	113.7	109.4	111.9	121.4

Note: 1960 = 100
Source: Calculated from *SR*, 1975, pp. 32 & 35.

Difficulties with other socialist countries were very varied. Several were cutting their imports from Czechoslovakia already in 1960 as they moderated their investment projects or, in the case of North Korea, because they had nothing to sell in return. China was altogether a more serious problem. It occupied fourth place among importers of Czechoslovak goods in 1959–60, taking over 6% of the total with a large share going on complete projects for power stations. A long-term trade agreement signed in 1959 seemed to promise steady and expanding trade until it was broken, according to Czechoslovak accounts, from the Chinese side.[31] By 1962 China took only 0.5% of Czechoslovak exports although imports continued at a slightly higher level, presumably repaying past credits. Some of the equipment earmarked for China could be sold elsewhere raising 120m Kčs (foreign trade prices) in socialist countries and 60m Kčs outside the bloc. The loss of imports – largely meat and some raw materials – was made up at the expense of 406m Kčs from non-socialist countries.[32] This more than accounts for the hard-currency deficit of 182m Kčs which appeared only in 1961, although it must be remembered that Czechoslovak statistics show trade only. The balance of payments is never as favourable owing to a deficit on invisibles and possible non-payment by developing countries.

This points to an immediate balance of payments problem aggravated by imports of deficit goods to achieve targets for industry. The contribution of Rozsypal's first point – the unreality of investment projects – could have been felt here in the failure of some expected inputs, such as steel, to appear. In some accounts he accorded this factor a very minor role. In his view, the dangers were already clear enough to justify corrections to the plan in the spring of 1961. Instead, the Central Committee refused 'to retreat in the face of some temporary difficulties'[33] and the correction waited until the autumn of 1962 when 'all the problems of economic equilibrium' were to be solved 'by a radical reduction of the volume of investment construction'.[34] The level of personal consumption and the balance of external payments were, as far as possible, left untouched. Cutting investment left machinery and even steel free for export.

An immediate consequence was 'a chain reaction' of breaks in contracts spreading even into parts of the consumer goods industry,[35] with nobody knowing when postponed projects would be continued. The year 1963 saw a sharp fall in production of investment goods such as foundry equipment (25% down by 1964), generators, agricultural machinery, cranes (28% down by 1963) and electric furnaces. The steel was being exported and much of the demand had evaporated.

Possible reservations to this account relate to a lack of clarity in Rozsypal's various accounts of the relative significance of investment problems, to the ambiguity over what options remained in 1962 and to the evasion of any reference to the economic reform of 1958. Clearly, the plan should have been revised earlier, or better still never adopted, rather than destroyed by a tardy panic measure. Once that chance had been missed, the only alternatives – given the structural weaknesses of the Czechoslovak economy after the growth strategy of the 1950s – were to cut living standards or to run into debt. The first may have been a possibility: there were reports of shortages of some consumer goods and of the need to answer complaints over economic disappointments, but little sign of open discontent.[36] The issue was to re-emerge around the question of whether the country was 'living beyond its means' in the following years.

As the architect of the 1958 reform, Rozsypal could be expected to underplay its negative consequences and in this he differs from the explanation provided at the time by party leaders. The party's Twelfth Congress in December 1962 was inevitably dominated by economic issues and Novotný had to try to explain what had gone wrong as a basis for a possible solution. This, together with a more comprehensive account at a Central Committee meeting in April 1962 which was not published at the time, amounted to the 'official' view of the economic difficulties.[37] Characterising the overall situation as 'an intolerable tension between the resources and needs of society', he put far less blame on 'external' factors, making cryptic references to some unnamed socialist countries that did not keep to their contracts. He admitted that the seriousness of the issue should have been spotted sooner, but did not relate it to any deeper structural weaknesses: there was to be 'no change in the conception of development of our economy'.

Novotný had much more to say about 'internal' influences, although he prudently suggested that the effects of the international situation were so great that they *had* to have a major impact on the domestic economy. He took the view, though, that their impact would have been greatly lessened had there been internal reserves. Moreover, having accepted the previous foreign trade strategy and having dismissed the external influences effectively as a string of unpredictable upsets, any solution would have to be centred *within* the Czechoslovak economy.

The problems there he saw as showing themselves in the failure to complete investment projects, especially in key sectors of the economy, and in disappointments in agriculture. He mentioned additional difficulties caused by the need to switch to higher military spending, by changes in military technology and even by a flu epidemic which affected half a million employees. The central issue remained investment policy which, as Minister of State Planning Alois Indra later argued, held 'the key position in the economy'.[38]

Essentially the same argument was being used elsewhere in Eastern Europe and in the Soviet Union to justify cuts in investment in the early 1960s. In Czechoslovakia, however, the leadership could shift the blame away from their own over-ambitiousness onto the system of economic management. Novotný put this as a final point in his account, but it was the most extensive part of his analysis.

The 'main mistake', in his view, had been a notion that the new system of organisation was to be understood as 'decentralisation' a term which certainly had been used by himself, by other party leaders and in resolutions of leading bodies.[39] He, however, implied that it conflicted with the leadership's decisions and proclaimed that no Central Committee or Congress resolution had contained any word about 'abolishing central management'. Both he and Indra even referred to the economy heading towards 'anarchy'.[40]

There is no sign here of an understanding of the philosophy behind the reform. Indra elaborated enough to suggest the belief that a strong central authority could have enforced production of adequate high quality steel, a redirection of investment towards repair rather than major new projects and a reduction in enterprise stock building. These are precisely the detailed points that are so hard to control. Some planners had previously insisted that centralisation *cannot* overcome the problems[41] while enterprises still complained of unrealistic targets and frequent plan changes.

It is unclear how far detailed control was relaxed – Rozsypal sweepingly insists that 'the relation of state organs towards enterprises was not weakened'[42] – but it is possible that some relaxation made it harder to overcome specific shortages. Just as at previous and subsequent congresses, delegates from industry in 1962 frequently interpreted their local difficulties in terms of poor organisation. That pointed this time towards calls for a stronger central authority that could provide investment, technology and raw materials for whichever sector that delegate happened to represent.[43] Novotný pursued this point, suggesting that steel works had been getting the wrong materials at the wrong time following, he claimed, the weakening of the centre in 1958. The logic of this position was a call for more rigid control over priorities.

The pressure for renewed centralisation therefore cannot be explained with Rozsypal's argument that it was a response to the chaos after the cutback in investment. That came later, in 1963, but the reintroduction of detailed material balances was already in the offing. Nevertheless the 1958 reform was destroyed in the crisis conditions of 1962 as financial resources were linked to planned growth in productivity: under conditions of excess capacity in many sectors of the economy productivity inevitably fell and many enterprises could not pay out wages.[44] As they turned to the government for help so Rozsypal's reform effectively died. There could be no disagreement with the need for more centralisation to overcome the immediate problems. The lesson that the centre could not do everything had been forgotten, for a brief period at least.

The central criticism of the Rozsypal reform, however, related to investment. The decentralisation of more than half the total value of investment into enterprises and local government bodies was blamed for causing excessive investment and hence for the paralysis of major investment projects. As has been argued, this in itself need not have justified the panic response in 1962: only the balance of payments problems could have required such an immediate response. The relationship between these two areas was not clarified at the time possibly because the official policy was to keep quiet about international difficulties in an effort to downplay differences in the international Communist movement. There is evidence that investment problems were a persistent cause for concern and that difficulties in 1961 were not that exceptional: they only received attention in view of the balance of payments crisis. They then become the issue of the greatest public concern within the economic apparatus.

The measure frequently referred to was unfinished investment work which grew gradually from a low point in 1954 to a peak in 1958 and then accelerated to a new high in 1961.[45] It was widely assumed to be an unhealthy feature of the economy reflecting resources tied up. Moreover, a high figure was taken to mean overstretched resources causing excessive delays in completions. The blame for this could now be placed on the new scope for enterprises and local government bodies to start up their own 'decentralised' projects.[46] There were reports of them 'smuggling in' more than resources would allow, despite the clear stipulation that they should not, to satisfy promises to their communities.[47] The point was taken up by Peter Wiles who referred to an 'orgy of investment scatter',[48] but that is a misleading expression. During any sudden upturn in investment activity it is inevitable that a lot of projects will be in an early stage. There is bound to be an increase in work in progress relative to completions. This tendency will be stronger the greater the emphasis towards large projects with long gestation periods. The structure of investment could therefore explain at least a large part of the growth in unfinished investment work although, relative to investment, the figure was actually no higher in 1961 than in 1958.[49]

The crucial issues in blaming the 1958 reform are whether larger projects were actually being delayed more than usual and whether that was due to starvation of resources in favour of smaller, 'decentralised' projects. Novotný, already threatening to freeze decentralised investment in 1960, clearly saw the link as self-evident. Indra too referred to resources scattered over 22 000 unfinished projects and he produced frightening sounding figures on completion times, with investment in several sectors taking almost twice as long as was judged to be necessary.

It is impossible to use aggregate figures from the early 1960s to show a relationship between completion times and the volume of investment. It is possible, however, to relate investment to project completions in a given year and that can usefully be broken down by sector, some sectors having longer gestation periods than others, as in Table 4.6. Unfortunately, published statistics do not provide the ideal measure: the categories of investment and growth in fixed assets contain slightly different elements and are based on fixed prices from different base years. Nevertheless, the results are compatible with resources being tied up in some key sectors of the economy around

Table 4.6. *Ratio of growth in fixed assets to investment in selected sectors of industry relative to the average for the whole 1948–1970 period*

	All	Fuel	Energy	Chemicals	Iron & Steel	Build. matls.	Eng.	Textiles
1956	1.05	0.91	0.71	2.52	0.76	1.58	1.33	0.75
1957	1.08	0.82	0.98	1.70	0.92	0.88	1.20	0.82
1958	0.99	0.86	0.64	1.11	0.45	1.07	1.15	1.10
1959	1.12	0.74	1.61	1.48	0.97	1.05	1.12	0.94
1960	1.07	0.86	1.09	1.14	1.15	0.83	1.06	1.17
1961	0.98	1.24	1.23	0.80	0.82	0.99	0.91	1.41
1962	0.98	1.19	0.91	0.86	0.68	0.89	1.06	0.67
1963	1.07	1.10	0.86	1.08	0.92	0.88	0.98	0.43
1964	1.18	1.00	1.23	0.99	1.36	1.47	1.26	0.63

Source: Calculated from *HSR*, pp. 161, 164–5 & 179–80.

1960, with figures below 1.00 suggesting lower than average completions relative to total investment.

The pattern is far from consistent, with good years for energy in 1959 and 1961, for fuel in 1961 and 1962, for iron and steel in 1960 and for engineering in 1962. Even building materials did reasonably well in 1961. Over industry as a whole the period does not look very bad at all. A slightly different picture emerges from figures on new capacity in key sectors but, using a three-year moving average, 1960 and 1961 were very good years for coal, electricity and the iron industry.[50] It is, then, impossible to prove a general stagnation stemming from excessive investment or to support claims of growing capacity shortages across the range of basic inputs.

Making sense of what was happening requires a deeper look at investment problems. There was, in fact, nothing new in major projects suffering delays nor in the existence of numerous small projects – almost 15 000 in 1958[51] which is the same relative to real investment as the figure quoted by Indra for 1961. By 1959 comparisons were being made showing, for example, a new cement works taking 7–10 years compared with 2–3 years in 'leading industrial states' or coal mines taking twice as long to put into operation as they should.[52] Later comparisons are, if anything, even less favourable and suggest endless hold-ups at every stage of preparation and implementation.[53] Very little of this could have been explained by decentralised projects poaching resources.[54] Construction firms were said to be willingly starting up decentralised projects which were easier to organise, more likely to use standardised materials and hence more likely to progress.[55] They needed this as a hedge against the far greater difficulties they could encounter with bigger projects.

Evidence in earlier periods and some arguments at the time suggest that an 'organisational barrier' was always the biggest problem[56] while in the early 1960s the only specific shortages referred to were steel and reinforced concrete[57] which were more likely to affect the larger projects. The more usual complaints were that the engineering industry was not supplying equipment[58] and, above all, that poor preparation was causing delays across a wide range of sectors.[59] Thus serious discussions of investment difficulties frequently implied that the direction of causation was from long construction periods to high levels of work in progress rather than the converse.[60]

It is quite possible that the total volume of investment was not much beyond the economy's physical resources. Poor preparation often meant idle capacity waiting for detailed instructions on how to proceed. It has, however, been argued that delays were caused by the proposed structural shift towards new sectors, especially chemicals, which placed unfamiliar demands on suppliers.[61] These need not have shown up in the measure used in Table 4.6 if, as is claimed, the projects were still at a very early stage.

These difficulties were exacerbated by behaviour at the micro level. The Rozsypal reform had, as has been argued, changed nothing in the incentive structure or bargaining process over investment. The construction industry's interests naturally led it to connive at understating costs and likely construction periods in the hope of gaining planning approval for as many large projects as possible. This had already been the experience after the attempt to cut investment in 1953.[62] It was a practice that no central authority could check as particularly large projects were usually unique so that costs could only be a vague estimate. It was in the interests of the purchasing enterprise, as it was a means to get a project approved. For the construction firms it was another means to ensure plan fulfilment as it gave the maximum scope for keeping fully employed groups of workers who specialised in the various stages of the construction process: it was a guarantee against poor organisation of work, even giving the enterprises the ability to select out the easiest tasks when problems began to arise. This fits with complaints at the time which referred, for example, to the impossibility of beginning work on a quarter of the 200 new centralised projects in 1962 owing to inadequate documentation.[63] The iron and steel industry had taken on too many new projects without adequate preparation while the chemical industry managed to 'smuggle' a project into the plan despite opposition from heavy engineering.[64]

The evidence suggests that investment difficulties were not much worse than in previous periods: the bunching of new starts could well have been a mistaken policy which might ultimately have delayed completion times, but it was not a valid cause for immediate panic. Moreover, the problem was not decentralisation. Difficulties stemmed from the inability – and even unwillingness in a period of over-confidence – of the centre to control its own 'centralised' projects. There had been plenty of warning as machinery ordered for 1959 and 1960 had already been beyond the scope of the perspective plan for that period.[65]

To summarise, then, the immediate cause of the unprecedented fall in national income in the early 1960s was the centrally imposed cut in investment. It was a blanket measure, leading to disruption throughout much of industry. Maybe the experience after 1953 encouraged the belief that it had to be savage to be effective. It had a short-term justification in relation to a balance of payments crisis, which was the most obvious factor forcing some sort of policy change. The chosen reaction blended in with the official view that the economy was suffering from a more general 'overheating': a sharp cut in some investment projects could then allow for concentration on chosen priorities and enable a resumption of essentially the same growth strategy. The weakness of this strategy was that it understated the international aspects of the problem and took too simple a view of investment difficulties. They were not that exceptional in the early 1960s, although over-optimism may have worsened the situation, and they depended ultimately on poor organisation throughout the economy which could not be overcome by a blanket cut. Nevertheless the door was very soon opened for wider discussion.

The beginnings of an economic debate

The collapse of the Third Five Year Plan coincided with important political changes. Khrushchov strengthened his denunciations of Stalin's crimes and some steps towards rehabilitation of those wrongly convicted penetrated even to Czechoslovakia. Josef Goldmann, imprisoned in 1954 after a trial of leading economists, was allowed to work again in his profession and began to develop an explanation for the crisis of the early 1960s starting from Kalecki's work on economic growth[66] and above all from his view that an 'excessive' rate of investment could bring the economy up against a range of possible 'barriers'. In particular, these were likely to be consumption, manpower, specific raw materials and the ability – or inability – to organise a rapidly changing economy. This, then, was a 'supply-constrained' economy and the first crucial job for the planning authorities was to select an achievable growth rate which then, in effect, determined the broad structure of the economy.

This cannot be understood too rigidly. If there were an inflexible supply constraint, then there would be no scope at all for choosing 'too high' a growth rate. There has to be space for an *attempt* at growth which is beyond the economy's resources, but which only shows itself as such after a period of time. That then must force a cut in investment. Goldmann, possibly harking back to his experience as a leading planning official in the early 1950s, believed that the operative barrier in Czechoslovakia was raw material shortages. Kalecki himself had pointed to the tendency to underfulfil plans in extractive and basic industries, and there were, as we have seen, plenty of complaints about inadequate supplies. The result, according to Goldmann, was 'disproportions and acute difficulties' which could 'only be overcome by slowing down the pace of economic development'. Cutbacks were apparently 'objectively unavoidable'[67] – again a view that was put in the early 1950s.[68]

It is far from clear why this should be inevitable: the most incontrovertible reasons would be mass protests, as threatened in 1953, or a balance of payments crisis forcing a redirection of resources. Avoiding this issue left scope for the misconception that over-investment led directly to declining economic performance. In fact, as has been argued, much of the fall in output is explained by the *fall* in investment and the decline in labour productivity followed from cuts in production with a fairly stable labour force. The logic of Goldmann's argument is that scattering investment over too many projects will delay their completion times and thereby waste resources. The extent of that is, as has been argued, impossible to quantify from published statistics partly because the cutback in investment itself leads to growing delays. Moreover, in so far as the key bottleneck is often at the initial preparation stage, it need not tie up resources in half-finished projects.

In Goldmann's model the negative consequences of trying for too high a growth rate are overcome over time. New projects come on stream and the supply situation improves. The conditions are created for another investment boom. This 'echo effect', recurring it is suggested every 8–10 years, so eases the normal state of shortage as to fill the planning authorities with a naïve sense of optimism. The effect is accentuated by a matching inventory cycle whereby enterprises release or use stocks of previously scarce materials that they have been hoarding.

Thus we have an explanation for the optimism of the late 1950s and for some of the phenomena of the early 1960s. We can also see an obvious means to prevent such setbacks in the future: the centre must avoid being carried away with over-confidence. Writing in the mid-1970s Goldmann could even claim that those factors giving rise to growth cycles had been eliminated and that, especially with many of the same people in high positions in the State Planning Commission, 'the generally satisfactory growth stability of the years 1966–75 can be considered as the result not of chance but of systematic factors'.[69] The necessary lesson seemed to have been learnt.

A number of criticisms have been made of Goldmann's theory suggesting that he too suffered from over-confidence. Although he presented it as a general theory covering other socialist economies, it explains little elsewhere. In Poland, for example, fluctuations in that period were strongest in the consumer goods industries where bad harvests periodically restricted raw material imports.[70] This happened to some extent in Czechoslovakia too but finds no place in his model which relegates foreign trade to the lowly status of an additional 'barrier' to growth: agriculture – the most obviously unstable sector of the economy – is ignored and trade is never the active agent in causing instability. This weakness could be overcome only partially by allowing scope for overstretched resources to cause indebtedness.

Another objection is the narrowly economic focus, omitting political and ideological causes of over-confidence, but 'the most vulnerable point in his whole theory'[71] is the echo effect which can be checked empirically. It did seem to have an obvious plausibility as the rising living standards and economic stability of the late 1950s were often attributed at the time to the completion of major investment projects. Goldmann's figures even showed increments in the flow of new fixed assets going into operation in industry, peaking in 1957, 1959 and 1964. This could fit with the acceleration phase of the cycle and then the post-1963 recovery.

Unfortunately, Goldmann was greatly exaggerating the effect by using *changes* in a rate of growth. The simple rate of growth in industry's fixed assets shows little sign of major fluctuations or of an 8–9 year investment cycle. Completions probably take such widely varying periods of time as to dissipate the echo effect.[72] Even in the extractive and basic industries there is not much sign of Goldmann's cycle: the early 1960s saw more new capacity in power stations, coal mines and steel works than the previous five years.[73]

This objection to the echo effect can be overcome without abandoning the theory of a cycle. The Hungarian economist Tamás Bauer developed a more sophisticated model relying on an analysis of the continuous bargaining between the centre and lower levels.[74] His cycle starts with the centre agreeing to a number of major investment projects. There are at first no major signs of overstrain as lower levels rush in to get their pet projects approved. As investment rises, so the centre responds by shifting resources at the expense of consumption and/or the balance of payments. It is, then, the behaviour at *lower* levels which helps push up the proportion of national income going on investment.

Eventually 'tensions in the utilisation of national income' lead the centre to respond by cutting investment. More projects can then be completed relative to the number started, but any contribution that makes towards restoring macro-economic equilibrium is trivial. There is no substantial place for an echo effect and no particular time-period for a complete cycle. The downturn depends on when the centre decides to respond to signs of overstrain. The upturn is then stimulated by rising pressure on the centre to allow more investment, encouraged by signs of spare capacity. Again, its timing and scale depend on the centre's perception and understanding of what is happening. As Bauer shows, much of this can be fitted to Czechoslovakia in the 1958–62 period.[75]

Obviously, any simple theory of cycles abstracts from a great many other factors. One contemporaneous criticism of Goldmann's theory was that downturns show a suspiciously close relationship with bad harvests. There is, however, no doubting a continuing and permanent pressure for more investment which *could* lead to Bauer's cycle unless consciously held in check. Theories of cycles do not provide an adequate basis for explaining what happened in the early 1960s. They rather formalise and thereby exaggerate certain causal elements which are in themselves real enough and important enough, but should not be seen as the whole story. Goldmann's theory was, however, to have a significant influence on economic policy in the 1960s when combined with new ideas for economic reform.

5   Towards economic reform

An easy victory?

The economic debates of the 1960s centred around two major policy issues. The most important was to become reform of the system of management, but the main debate in the period before the Twelfth Congress centred rather on structural change. Several economists criticised 'the steel conception' looking for an alternative around 'progressive shifts in the structure of our economy'.[1] In its simplest form that meant a shift towards the chemical industry, towards other metals, such as aluminium, and towards the greater use of oil and natural gas as energy sources. The steel industry would be oriented away from mass production and towards smaller quantities of higher quality materials. The engineering industry would become more specialised while concentrating on a substantially different range of products that were less material-intensive.[2]

To some this was always the key to improving the economy's competitiveness, and they got a very good hearing in political circles. Nevertheless, the conception was soon to be attacked as essentially inadequate and professional attention generally shifted towards an exaggerated estimate of the role of the system of management in causing structural problems and hence exaggerated hopes of the benefits of economic reform. The final resolution at the Twelfth Congress contained only the normal woolly platitudes about improving the system of management without pointing towards a market-oriented reform. It was, however, followed by the creation of a government commission in 1963 headed by the newly elected Central Committee member and Director of the Economics Institute of the Academy of Sciences, Ota Šik and including among its members his colleagues Deputy Director Karel Kouba and Otakar Turek.

This was, at least at first, definitely not a free and open discussion of economic problems. Those outside the circles of power were not expected to take part as was discovered by the party organisation in the main Tatra factory in Kopřivnice. They expressed doubts in the discussion period before the Twelfth Congress as to whether they had received the full explanation for the abandonment of the Third Five Year Plan. The reason cited, a failure to reach targets 'for the plan of gross output by a few tenths of a percent', quite rightly struck them as implausible. They even asked further reasonable questions, such as why heavy industry was given such a strong emphasis when Czechoslovakia lacked the necessary raw materials, and were rewarded with the assumption that they must represent 'an anti-state group'. Eleven members were disciplined.[3]

Nevertheless, restricting the discussion to theoreticians could have had its advantages. According to one advocate, the 'abstract' scheme that was worked out 'was all the more intelligible' because 'it ignored tactical details in favour of strategic principles'.[4] It is perhaps more important that it remained unclear how far established assumptions were being abandoned and how specific interests would be threatened, but conflicts still erupted when measures were being implemented.

In the meantime, members of the commission could use their new-found status to ensure publication of their views. Within the prevailing political system that was tantamount to giving them an appearance of official acceptance. The most vigorous advocate was Šik. Although he later claimed to have been convinced of the need for 'radical reform' in 1958,[5] his past was very orthodox and he definitely developed his ideas throughout the 1960s. In a book finished in July 1961,[6] he was already arguing for commodity relations within the state sector of the economy. His theme was that, despite state ownership, conflicts of interest continued and he has some justification in claiming that Czechoslovak theoreticians placed a special emphasis on this area as a key weakness of highly centralised planning.[7] Nevertheless, he continued to see a danger from 'revisionism' and was not yet arguing for 'market socialism'. In fact, he was still close to the theoretical basis of the 1958 reform. He saw no need for competition and the profit motive (although 'various forms of material stimulation' were necessary), because he already saw socialism growing much faster than capitalism. Any shortcomings were 'of a subjective nature in various directing organs'.[8]

He had a sharp polemical style but, true to the spirit of de-Stalinisation, he gave wider significance to the idea of economic reform by linking it to overcoming 'the remnants of dogmatism': those who disagreed were usually 'dogmatic' while any 'true Marxist' was expected to see reform as the principal task.[9] It was a style that was to win a lot of popularity outside the corridors of power while making plenty of enemies within. It was quite different from the more academic approach of other members of the commission who frequently acknowledged reservations about their ideas. Without Šik, however, the political pressure for economic reform would have been far less effective. Nobody before or since has been able to harness the work of a whole research institute in developing a new basis for economic policy.

The starting point, as defined by Šik, was to see 'the cardinal problem of our economic practice' as the significance of commodity relations in a socialist economy. Some, he claimed, saw them as 'alien' while in his opinion they still had a role to play, albeit within an altogether socially planned development. He was, however, fairly open-minded on what this could mean as he called for 'deep thought' and for genuine research based on empirical evidence. The alternative would be 'a half-hearted, compromise solution as in 1958'.[10]

In this early stage economists paid little attention to the 'broad base of world economic literature',[11] but they were aware of the changes in the GDR in 1963 and, above all, of ideas emerging in the Soviet Union. Liberman, developing from the debates in the 1950s on the role of commodity relations under socialism, pushed the idea of a greater emphasis on profitability starting with an article in *Pravda* in September 1962 which was quickly taken up in Czechoslovakia.[12] Profit was to be a 'synthetic' indicator, replacing the existing multiplicity of indicators to give a reasonable summary of overall performance in relation to expanding outputs, cutting inputs and satisfying customers' demands. There was, however, not 'even the hint of a suggestion that the direction of the socialist economy should be decentralised'.[13] In September 1965 the CPSU Central Committee accepted the 'Liberman' reforms and the party congress the following year backed the same approach. That must have reinforced the conviction that change was necessary in Czechoslovakia too, but it was already clear that Czechoslovak thinking had developed further.

Part of the reason was the experience of the late 1950s as the *theoretical* basis for the Soviet reforms was fairly similar to that of Rozsypal's proposals. More important was the different political atmosphere and economic climate. Soviet economists could still boast about fairly rapid growth suggesting a broadly adequate system of management.

In Czechoslovakia the authorities were struggling through 1963 to overcome the disruption caused by the loss of imports, the need to export whatever they could and the sudden cut in investment. Far from speeding up completions, contracts often could not be renegotiated, especially for deliveries from the engineering industry. More goods were being allocated centrally, but equipment often failed to arrive while stocks of metals were building up.[14] All this was despite the abolition of the dual organisation of investment, with centralised and decentralised projects, and the development of 'a degree of central management almost at the level of 1954 to 1955'. For the regulation of projects under construction it exceeded that level.[15] Even with investment concentrated specifically on finishing key projects, it was 1964 before completions approached the planned level.[16]

In fact, as always seems to happen, recovery was hampered by adverse weather – a bad winter in early 1963 and poor harvests in following years. The generally poor level of performance is indicated in Tables 4.3 and 4.4 in Chapter 4 while Tables 5.1 and 5.2 show the hesitant recovery. Only by 1966 could there be much cause for reassurance, but even that was to be tempered by all sorts of doubts.

Against this background of economic failure, ideas that shortly beforehand would have seemed 'outrageous' were being accepted by the group of leading economists. Outright, vocal opposition was non-existent and even those who disagreed with new theoretical ideas put their case very meekly. Rozsypal later blamed this on Šik's abrasive style, backed up by a powerful and prestigious position. His alternative at the time was essentially for another try at the 1958 reform, but with more modest investment targets;[17] however it found little support. He made few further public interventions and even signed a joint statement in September 1968 calling for continuation of the economic reform.[18] Šik was, in fact, soon reporting victory in the battle of ideas, with the commission's proposals being backed by practically all economists and by the majority in leading economic organs.[19] The autumn of 1964 saw their broad acceptance by the party leadership after which concrete proposals were formulated.

This, however, roughly coincided with the major theoretical break which took Czechoslovak thinking decisively beyond Liberman's kind of reform. The crucial influence in mid-1964 was the translation of the important book on economic systems under socialism by the Polish economist Włodzimierz Brus. Up until then the search had been for *individual* measures that could fit into and improve the existing system of management. Brus, however, insisted that there were 'no reasons

Table 5.1. *Components of national income in terms of production 1964–1968*

	Total	Industry	Agriculture	Construction	Others
1964	100.0	62.5	12.0	9.7	15.8
1965	103.4	63.8	10.2	11.0	18.4
1966	112.9	70.4	12.2	13.1	17.2
1967	118.8	73.3	13.4	14.0	18.1
1968	127.4	77.3	14.6	14.7	20.8

Note: All figures are percentages of national income in 1964.
Source: Calculated from *HSR*, p. 88.

Table 5.2. *Components of final product in terms of expenditure, 1964–1968*

	Total	Personal consumption	Social consumption	Change in stocks	Net exports	Investment
1964	100.0	50.6	16.3	0.7	5.1	25.7
1965	100.7	53.2	17.1	0.0	0.7	27.6
1966	112.4	56.0	17.7	4.5	1.0	30.3
1967	117.9	58.0	19.2	5.2	2.4	31.1
1968	125.0	64.2	20.7	4.4	0.4	33.6

Note: All figures are percentages of final product in 1964 measured in 1967 prices. Losses are omitted.
Source: Calculated from *SR*, 1975, pp. 46–7 and *HSR*, pp. 84 & 91.

to believe that there is only one definitive model of operation appropriate to a socialist economy'[20] and even made a distinction between two possible 'models', one 'centralised' and one 'decentralised'. With that, 'one basic taboo' fell and the argument shifted from the question of how commodity relations could improve planning to how they could be combined with planning to create a completely different model.[21]

Brus' views were not accepted in every point of detail. Turek preferred to reword the distinction as one between a 'directive or administrative' model and an 'economic' model, partly because of the excessive and inaccurate use of the term 'decentralisation' in the 1950s.[22] Others were more fundamentally dissatisfied with Brus' definitions because of the power of lower organs even in the ostensibly 'centralised' model to further their own interests by providing distorted information for plan formulation.[23]

They were, however, now opening their eyes to outside ideas and could provide a more systematic critique of the old model. Socialism, it was argued, had been seen as the 'absolute negation' of capitalism. There had been no attempt to separate out those elements which should be maintained: instead, the idea of a plan and regulation of the economy arose in direct opposition to 'spontaneous regulation' in commodity production.[24] Marx, of course, had never really explored these problems but, in so far as the brief comments in his and Engels' works pointed to any definite 'model' of a socialist economy, then it was to be based on calculations in physical terms. By the 1930s the Communist movement definitely assumed that 'the socialist economy is centrally planned not only generally but in all its elements'.[25]

It was a notion that, in the view of one prominent Czech economist, could be derived from Marx's sketchy account of the internal organisation of a factory where 'the iron law' of precise numerical relationships determined the detailed division of labour.[26] It appeared as a purely technical task, never complicated by conflicts of interest. Even if this is true for a single workplace, and the evidence of battles over piece-rates suggests that it often is not, the analogy cannot be valid for a whole economy. There the division of labour has to take account of consumer demand, which is never open to precise prediction. Firms set their inputs partly on the basis of demand for outputs, but even more scope for variation is introduced by possible choices over technology and in developing new products.

The task, then, is not to find the best means to produce a single, defined output. It is far more complicated and therefore cannot be achieved without independent action from lower levels. The final proof of this was seen in the empirical evidence that the attempts to assume away enterprise autonomy had so clearly failed. They continued to act on the basis of their own interests in response to plan targets, and the results did not correspond to society's interests. Thus was constructed an argument that the market was essential as more than an addition to planning. The enterprises had to be 'led by their material interests and compelled by economic pressure which is derived from . . . the market'. There was said to be no 'golden middle way'.[27] This had to be the basic starting point for the new economic model.

An even clearer view was derived by Kouba who followed Brus in looking back at debates in the 1930s about the feasibility of socialism.[28]

He quoted with interest von Mises' view that the value of goods could never be calculated without the reality of market exchange and private ownership of the means of production. The conclusion had been that resource allocation under socialism could never be based on rational calculation and would amount to blundering in the dark.[29]

Hayek developed this towards a less dramatic critique accepting that a perfect plan could, in theory, be constructed if the centre had all the relevant information. Resources would be allocated exactly as in a perfect market. Hayek's point was that, in practical terms, the amount of information needed by the central planners was so immense as to make precise optimal allocation impossible. Planning might not be impossible but it would lead to the overdevelopment of some sectors at the expense of others and hence a lower output than in a market system.[30]

There was no question of accepting the whole of Hayek's argument. Even though he was writing in 1935 he seemed to assume such perfection from the market mechanism that any criticism of planning proved its inherent inferiority. Moreover, the only empirical evidence he adduced was the claim of 'practically all observers' that 'even compared with pre-war Russia the position of the great masses has deteriorated'.[31] That sounded hollow by the 1960s but, even if his theoretical position as a whole was flawed, he was raising some important specific issues. The Polish economist Oskar Lange had proposed a solution with the central planning body calculating and adjusting prices of consumers' goods from the market and then imposing them on lower levels as the basis for decentralised de-cisions. There would, however, be no market for producers' goods exchanged between state enterprises.

This last point depended on the view, accepted on both sides of the debate in the 1930s, that commodity relations were tied to ownership and therefore could not be used between units within a state sector. That had been Stalin's view, but was being challenged from the mid-1950s as just one survival of the old dogmatism. Hayek also found it impossible to conceive of competition without dispersed ownership. As the managers of independent enterprises were not risking their own capital their financial demands would, in his view, have to be checked by the centre with the same rigour 'as if it were actually running the enterprise'.[32] This must be an exaggeration as even large capitalist firms often decentralise responsibility in this way. Nevertheless reference to 'considerable obstacles' to 'pseudo-competition' did point towards a real problem, which was the need to give the enterprise sphere precisely defined independence; however, it was a taboo area for public discussion until 1968.

Kouba, however, went beyond Lange's position and advocated a genuine, functioning market for producers' goods. It was possible, logical in view of the fact that such goods entered into international trade and, above all, necessary in view of the problems of highly centralised planning. Hayek seemed to Kouba to be right about the practical problems facing a central body although wrong to present them as a complete refutation of socialism.

Ultimately even more significant was Kouba's acceptance, following Lange, of the need for 'an objective price structure' as the 'basic axiom of rational economic decisions in socialism'.[33] He was, then, no longer looking for an administrative system improved by adding in a better price system. Instead, the main deficiency of the old model was clearly rooted in the absence of objective prices.[34] The solution was a new notion of planning with prices derived from 'a real, functioning internal market and the influence of the world market'.[35] It was, he admitted, a concept 'at its very inception', which could not be checked against practical experiences; but it meant that he had little time for endless repetitions of the formula whereby 'the plan is and will be the main instrument of management'. That sort of formulation could still have fitted with Šik's theoretically less rigorous work: he wrote of 'planning all economic activity in a purposeful way',[36] although his precise recommendations were far less sweeping. Kouba put a different emphasis wanting the plan's scope to be 'narrowed to the area of macroproportions'.[37]

His theoretical position was accepted, at least in part, at a conference in the State Planning Commission in May 1967. A plan without a market was rejected as was a market 'just as an instrument for implementing the plan'. The relationship was rather of the market as 'a certain complex of economic processes' while the plan was 'a definite programme, a definite subjective will' respecting but also influencing the market.[38] This tortuous formulation concealed some ambiguity. The market would itself inevitably be influenced by decisions from the centre and could therefore not be separated out as a totally 'objective' phenomenon.

Nevertheless, the plan was still to be 'an instrument for perfecting the market', 'enriching its operation' and bringing in 'long-term purposefulness'.[39] In line with the view of a plan predicting a future market, it was 'to accelerate the progressive results of its operation'.[40] It was also somehow to set a 'hierarchical structure of aims' which were to be in a different order from that which would exist if the economy were guided purely by the market. Within this he included 'extra-economic aspects' and the distribution of income.[41]

This conception was later criticised for seeing socialism as no more than an economic system 'broadened by a few humanising aspects, which cannot be realised under capitalism'.[42] It could have meant much more than that. The most serious problem was rather that, working at so high a level of abstraction, it was very hard to see what was being proposed or how it could be achieved. Leading advocates of reform frequently acknowledged that their solutions amounted to little more than 'general principles'.[43] Ultimately, however, they brought three messages: the 'key' to the new system was to derive an 'objective' element from the market; alongside this the centre would somehow exercise far greater authority than seen in any 'planning' under capitalism; and, finally, reform was the precondition for economic success.

For this to be implemented they had to persuade the politicians and the obvious obstacle was the uninspiring President and party leader Novotný who was certainly not a natural advocate of reform. Never able to give any decisive lead, he probably accepted change as inevitable, albeit recognising dangers that could come with it.[44] On specifically economic questions he was probably more receptive than on many other issues because he wanted to be able to claim credit for improving the situation and for that he was undoubtedly aware of the need to seek and use the advice of the best available experts. This was part of the fashionable attempt 'at making scientific the management of the whole of our society'.[45]

Novotný was firm in attacking those who pushed for change from outside the apparatus of power. At the Thirteenth Congress in 1966 he openly attacked 'some cultural journals' for propagating 'anti-party' ideas and his battles with the writers' union are well known.[46] For economists, however, there were only a few warnings from one of his closest colleagues at some wrong ideas and illusions about capitalism that might be creeping in. Generally, it seemed fair to 'attach a high value to the contribution of our economic science'.[47]

He nevertheless stuck to his analysis of economic difficulties in 1962[48] and entered the debate early with an attack on Selucký, an advocate of reform who had referred to 'the cult of the plan'. In Novotný's view this was an attempt to 'impose anarchy and spontaneity onto our economy'.[49] He still believed that 'the basis of all economic activity remains the state plan'[50] and that everything must be derived from that. This led him to interpret reform measures in almost the most conservative way possible.

Some were even less enthusiastic, giving only a grudging accept-ance conditional on 'an unremitting struggle against unprincipled liberalism in practice and theory'.[51] Novotný, however, was for taking 'everything good' from the old system and including new elements. These he saw in very practical terms as a material interest in production, the principle of socialist rewards and of responsibility in work. The key element to achieve these laudable objectives was that enterprises and factories 'would be responsible for their produc-tive activity' and would operate 'within the framework of a fixed plan and fixed prices'.[52] Whether such a combination is really poss-ible must be an open question. If the plan determines what the enterprise is to do, then it is hard to see how the latter can take responsibility.

To Novotný, however, it was wrong to juxtapose the old to the new system as the central need was 'to strengthen the function of the plan'.[53] If he had a clear conception it was that the only change would be in performance indicators. He was, however, not an economist and had little choice but to go along with what the experts were propos-ing. They too were broadly tied to his formulations, as major policy resolutions accepted that 'the basic instrument of organisation . . . is the plan'.[54] Advocates of reform frequently acknowledged the strength of this position making general statements about how their proposals would actually strengthen planning. They were right, in the sense that they aimed for better results compared with those of the centralised model, but the key was to be an end to any attempt at such comprehensive plans.

The principal effect of Novotný's 'conservatism' was to restrict the economic debate both in terms of participation and in terms of its scope. Important theoretical issues were blocked, such as new ideas on the status of the socialist enterprise, and there was a clear antipa-thy towards looking in more than the most general terms at possible alternative models. Support for the Yugoslav method could not be expressed openly: a second 'Yugoslav deviation' had been exposed in theatrical style in 1961. There was, however, some knowledge of that country's experiences – Šik had actually written a stinging reply to a Yugoslav criticism of the Rozsypal reform which was later quoted against him to illustrate the volatility of his opinions[55] – and a lot was written about the Yugoslav reforms of mid-1965. That could have been a veiled form of advocacy.

In more practical terms, despite official acceptance of their work, advocates of reform could never be confident of backing or understanding from the leadership. Whenever proposals had to be made specific, there was frequently a battle with those 'who urged caution and warned against taking risks'.[56]

The first steps

Nevertheless, in January 1965 the Central Committee accepted the need for a 'fundamental change' in the system of management which was judged to have 'fulfilled its historic mission'.[57] The wording was careful enough: it could also appear as 'improving' the system and 'deepening' the leading role of the party. The basic objective, however, was 'an organic union of planning and commodity relations' to give greater powers to enterprises. The centre was to set the basic proportions and sectoral structure, to implement price and wage policies and to influence enterprise behaviour by finance and credit policy. Enterprises would in turn be relieved of 'the great mass of regulations, decrees, intimations, government resolutions, etc.' which had allegedly reached such a volume that directors could no longer remember all the things they were meant to do.[58] Instead, they could work out their own links with suppliers and customers which would replace a lot of the detail in the operational plans. The main success indicator was to be gross income (receipts minus material costs and obligations to the state), encouraging concern with customer satisfaction, and there was to be effectively a tax on fixed assets to encourage economy in their use. As an improvement on the 1958 reform, these financial conditions were to be uniform across all enterprises so that they could be stable and hence a basis for long-term calculations.

This greater emphasis on economic instruments was linked to an attempt to redefine the role of the party. There was far less interest in the 'subjective' element and also a definite shift from the notion of party organisations 'directing every political, economic and cultural activity in factories'[59] or 'having firmly in their hands everything that is going on wherever it is'.[60] The argument now was that, during the economic difficulties of the early 1960s, the central organs had been unable to cope so the party had taken direct responsibility for running the economy.[61] Parallel organs, however, obscure responsibility.[62] The need was therefore for a clearly defined division of labour at all levels. The party was no longer to intervene directly in production and technical processes as that would conflict with managerial responsibility for results.[63]

As in earlier periods, it proved difficult to apply this as the party was still expected to exercise its constitutional position of ultimate authority. Party organisations were sometimes criticised for stepping back completely from economic tasks while it was suggested that they could have played a role in discussions around enterprises' longer-term perspectives.[64] In practice, as indicated by a survey of members in Košice, the party remained as before unresponsive to complaints from its own members[65] and immensely powerful over personnel issues. The change was never intended to mean the abolition of the party's grip through the *nomenklatura* system but rather an end to a chaotic situation in which one hundred organisations had made nominations for one post that was actually for decision by a higher organ and in which even the appointment of bricklayers, cleaners and telephonists was sometimes decided by a party committee. The authority of management was not to be usurped over such trivial issues,[66] but the structure of political power was to remain unchanged and this was one of the main factors devaluing the efforts at reform.

The reform package went beyond the Soviet example only in the introduction of a price system which would leave some fixed, some varying within set limits and some free: in practice nearly all consumer goods prices remained fixed by the centre as even those with limited freedom moved straight to the top limit.[67] Economists, however, viewed these measures as inadequate even before their introduction in January 1966. Turek described it as a 'transitional' model, albeit in inverted commas, which could easily degenerate back into a full centralised-administrative model. He hoped it would bring benefits by finding non-investment sources of growth. Primarily, however, it was only a 'bridge' that still left economic instruments subordinated to the plan.[68] There was a strong body of opinion which, learning from 1958 when the experts finished their work as the new system was introduced, saw the need to look continually for further improvements and countermeasures to problems as they might arise.[69] Minister of State Planning Černík, a highly competent 45-year-old former engineering worker who had worked his way up through the Ostrava mining industry, fully endorsed this view and called for help from 'comrades from the theoretical front'[70] in the incessant and permanent process of improving the system.

Some were, in fact, soon criticising one important element as inconsistent with the spirit of the reform. Following the practice in the

GDR, greater reliance on commodity relations was to be associated with concentration into still bigger self-financing units. No longer would the associations be mere links in an administrative chain. As large units with their own research and marketing departments they could take real responsibility.[71]

The reorganisation, presented as a continuation from 1958, was completed very rapidly, with the number of associations reduced from 254 to 90 by July. Some enterprises were grouped by similarity of product while others were created by vertical integration. There was no suggestion at the time of the need to break up the hierarchical management structure[72] and there were very firm advocates of this reorganisation who argued that technical progress typically required changes transcending the boundaries of a single enterprise, or even of the existing associations. Concentration therefore 'corresponds to the objective tendency of the development of the forces of production'.[73] Examples could even be quoted showing the benefits of linking forestry with woodworking or creating agricultural–industrial complexes.[74]

These could, of course, be specific cases with little general applicability. Others who welcomed this kind of reorganisation had to admit that theoretical work on its significance was very sparse.[75] Nevertheless the suggestion was that concentration would make the economy internationally competitive.[76] There was the hint of a completely different reform strategy – albeit an unrealistic one – which might aim to introduce the market by opening up the economy to pressures of the world economy after an internal organisational improvement, rather than relying on market relations improving performance within an economy still largely isolated from external competition. Perhaps more significant, however, was the place of such concentration within the old model of centralised planning. Higher organs are, of course, unable to cope with the mass of information required and would be happy to be able to decentralise the organisation of supplier–customer relations:[77] reorganisation could therefore make it easier for them to continue in the old way, while not needing to send down quite so many directives.

A few years later the reorganisation was condemned for being 'not fully in accord with the new system of management', because it intensified the trend towards creating monopolies 'under the pretext of specialisation'.[78] That did not mean that enterprises should not merge but, within the logic of a market system, they should do so voluntarily.[79] It certainly seemed that, in the words of the director of the giant Prague engineering enterprise ČKD, 'just the organisational form solves very little'.[80] It still left the same duplication and fragmentation throughout industry with many factories not only small but failing to take advantage of specialisation.[81]

In practice the reorganisation probably made no difference to the performance of the economy and was only a minor issue in debates despite a later claim that it was the key question in 'two fundamentally distinct conceptions of the understanding of economic reform'.[82] To those working in industry the new system was not essentially about 'organisational incorporation' but 'largely about the use of commodity–money relations'.[83] The real division was between those who wanted these introduced slowly and cautiously into essentially the existing model and those who were beginning to push for an accelerated transition towards what was being called 'the target solution'.

One piece of evidence encouraging an exaggerated faith in economic reform was the 'experimental testing' of elements of the new system in 452 enterprises throughout 1965. Regulations varied slightly but good results were being reported almost within weeks.[84] Over the year as a whole it did seem that there was a positive influence on finding 'easily mobilised reserves' contributing to non-investment sources of growth. Above all, they seemed to be better at reducing stocks.[85]

There were a number of important reservations. The first was that most enterprises did do well in 1965 when assessed against reasonably easy plan targets. Those involved in experiments were generally above average – suggested by a greater share of production than of labour – so that a slightly better average performance need prove little. It is particularly suspicious in view of the large variation in results between individual enterprises. Moreover, some were succeeding by manipulating the new success indicators. Prices still bore no necessary relationship to scarcity, so that firms could produce the profitable goods in their range at the expense of those which might be in higher demand while others exploited their monopoly position to get higher prices. Moreover, there was little sign of them using better technology or reducing the demand for labour. That reservation could be brushed aside with the reassurance that a year was too short a time for the benefits to show.[86] In fact, results for the first half-year still depended on supply contracts signed in the previous year which partners continued to operate on the old principles until the start of 1966. The period was therefore too short and the experience too limited to justify any definite conclusions.[87]

Enterprises involved in experiments were anyway the subject of very close scrutiny, reporting excessive visits which could themselves have contributed to some improvement in performance. Above all, they could complain quickly about difficulties with suppliers and expect special treatment. Far from being genuine experiments it seems to have been a political requirement that they should succeed and they received all sorts of advantages to make this possible.[88] Advocates of reform were anyway pressing ahead without waiting for results,[89] but Novotný was persuaded to refer to them as an 'experimental verification' of some of the new system's principles.[90]

System or structure?

Two factors were even more important in the pressure for accelerating the pace of reform. The first was the realisation, following changes in abstract economic thinking, that the package agreed to in January 1965 did not amount to very much. Economic instruments were still 'derived from plan indicators' and there was no easy way to change this because of 'the inadequacy of the price mechanism'.[91] There was a lot of disappointment in the sudden realisation that the new system was really only a very minor improvement and might even be a dangerous hybrid with neither kind of mechanism able to operate.[92] The solution, however, was to 'accelerate' the reform 'as much as possible' if the changes of 1966 were to bring any benefits.

The second factor which helped cement the community of Czechoslovak economists around firm advocacy of acceleration was a theoretical development which again overstated the potential benefits of reform by linking the system more directly to economic performance and structural policy. Šik was at the forefront blaming the 'old directive system of management' for 'the long-term negative effect' of 'extensive' development.[93] There were weaknesses in his argument and important terms were imprecisely defined. Without international comparisons and more sophisticated measures he accepted that he could not state categorically whether Czechoslovakia's post-war development really had been 'extensive' in character.

Nevertheless, the term matched what he believed had been happening. Summarising his argument briefly, expansion rapidly used up reserves of manpower leading to a decline in productivity growth as the most experienced workers were left on old and obsolete equipment while newer workers could not master modern technology. The implication was that 'intensive' growth would mean higher productivity by abandoning the oldest equipment. The obstacle to this was the incentive system encouraging maximum output without regard for costs. By requiring excessive material inputs this created a need for higher raw material output and was therefore at least partially the determinant of sectoral structure.

Šik's analysis ignored external influences and exaggerated the extent to which long-term internal factors were the direct cause of the problems of the early 1960s. He provided evidence of continually declining economic performance which seemed then to have become much worse. His figures could be reinterpreted to show exceptional results in the early 1950s, a sharp drop after 1953 and again after 1962, but only a gentle decline in the later 1950s. Given the specific problems in those two worst periods, it is not valid to attribute the whole of the worsening to the internal effects of the system of management.

Nevertheless, he was presenting an argument with a dramatic political appeal. Its publication coincided with others reaching a similar conclusion from different lines of reasoning and the immediate implications for economic policy came into the open in the approach to the Thirteenth Congress. The discussion document published in December 1965 acknowledged that 'contrary to the original intentions of the Twelfth Congress we have so far not succeeded in restoring economic proportions'.[94] Above all, it warned of the rising share of consumption in national income which 'is beyond the capabilities of the economy' and stood in the way of recovery. It was said to be impossible to continue 'living beyond our means'.[95]

A clear exponent of this position in later years was Rozsypal who blamed the continuing technological backwardness of industry on low investment.[96] The corollary was a need to cut living standards by continuing the trend from 1962 and 1963 when retail prices rose by 1% and 0.6% respectively.[97] This was not stated openly at the time – the leadership was becoming aware of growing complaints about 'persistently rising' prices,[98] an impression possibly helped by more frequent adjustments in an effort to match supply and demand for individual products[99] – and was balanced in party documents by references to the 'system of administrative organisation' as the principal problem. Then an article in the pre-Congress discussion by a new employee at the State Planning Commission brought the issue fully into the open by advocating restrictions on the rate of growth of consumption to below that of national income.[100]

The alternative policy was to maintain living standards and find non-investment sources of growth by a rapid transition to the new system of management. The central figure in this was Goldmann who, with Kouba and other co-workers, based the policy prescription on an extension from his theory of cycles into a theory of long-term growth in socialist economies.[101] It was gradually being recognised, so Kouba wrote, that the problems of the early 1960s were due not just to over-investment but 'to a serious disorder of a structural nature'. Above all, the centralised system was said to be 'the main cause' of the slowdown.[102]

Their evidence started from a comparison of European socialist countries showing, in every case, a gradual deceleration from the mid-1950s through to the early 1960s. It was easy to hypothesise a relationship with the system of management as 'the higher the economic level, the more varied is the pattern of final and intermediate consumption and the more complicated the process of socialist reproduction'.[103] The system could therefore have enabled rapid growth in the early 1950s but subsequently have become a barrier to growth.[104]

The novelty was to try to quantify the impact of the system. Some aspects, such as the stunting of initiative, cannot be measured; others, however, can. In particular the inflexibility of production was a likely explanation for the growth in projects under construction and for the growth in stocks. As far as comparisons were possible, both were higher than in comparable capitalist economies and both were rising during the period of growth deceleration.[105] Much of this, of course, can be explained by short-term factors after 1962, but those difficulties were presented as secondary to a long-term trend. Thus Goldmann could liken an economy to a pipeline: inputs go in at one end but weaknesses in the economic system may allow a lot of 'leakages' reducing the positive benefits that emerge at the other end. The new system was to help stop those leaks.

In fact it seemed obvious that reserves were there. The unrealised potential effect of investment undertaken in the 1962–5 period could lead to an increase in national income of about one-fifth with no addition to productive capacity.[106] This argument was frequently repeated,[107] although there is an obvious danger of exaggerating the potential benefits of reform: a market system would surely lead to the rapid destruction of some fixed assets alongside the possible better use of others. The case was, however, strengthened by a simple extrapolation from the previous rapid decline in growth per unit of investment to suggest a growth rate of −8% by 1970.[108] That could not actually be a serious prediction because the method is based on overstating the importance of the system of management until it becomes the only influence on growth rates. In fact, rapid growth in the early 1950s depended to a great extent on the one-off benefits of rationalisation while the catastrophe of the early 1960s depended heavily on external shocks and policy mistakes.

Nevertheless, the notion of leakages enabled Goldmann and his colleagues to reach clear policy recommendations. The falling share of accumulation in national income was a highly deceptive measure: a closer look, as confirmed in Tables 4.4 and 5.2, showed that the main cut had been in stock-building – a leakage – and not in creation of fixed assets. The fall in accumulation was therefore helping to ease tensions and should be seen as a major contributor to recovery so that there was no need to squeeze consumption. Moreover, to do so would probably lead simply to unused capacity in sectors that were not dependent on imports while consumers might even spend more on food which had a high hard-currency input.[109]

To raise investment could therefore be positively harmful. Signs of recovery in 1966 were attributed to the investment wave from the start of the decade beginning to bear fruit. Acceleration now could cause the problems analysed in Goldmann's theory of cycles: disequilibrium and organisational barriers would leave resources tied up in projects under construction while shortages would escalate with 'socialist speculation' as enterprises hoarded stocks of any scarce inputs.

The attraction for politicians of an economic strategy that rejects the need to cut living standards is obvious. On that point Goldmann's argument was accepted. It is less clear that he was right to place the system of management so unequivocally as the central problem. The alternative, which he attacked, was a 'great structural reconstruction' emphasising the chemical industry. This was seen as an example of 'the habitual outlook of administrative directive management' which seeks to solve problems with 'a new investment cycle'.[110] In his view international comparisons did not suggest major structural problems so that the lack of international competitiveness had to be attributed to weaknesses at the micro level. Moreover, the bias towards extractive and basic industries could itself be due, albeit to an unspecified extent, to the system leading to high demands for inputs. Thus 'the structure is in a certain sense a function of the system of management'.[111] It followed logically that without changing that system 'we will achieve nothing'.[112]

As Table 5.3 shows, international comparisons need not support the Goldmann-Kouba argument when it is remembered that Czecho-

Table 5.3. *The sectoral structure of Czechoslovak industry compared with the UK and West Germany*

	UK (1968–70)		West Germany (1968–70)		Czechoslovakia (1970)	
	output	employ-ment	output	employ-ment	output	employ-ment
Fuel	5.0	4.8	5.6	5.5	6.5	6.6
Metals	7.5	6.9	6.7	6.8	9.8	8.5
Chemicals	14.4	8.6	15.6	9.1	7.8	5.0
Engineering	42.7	40.4	41.3	43.9	36.2	37.6
Textiles & footwear	8.8	13.9	9.2	13.4	10.2	17.0
Food	10.3	9.8	10.1	10.0	14.2	7.7
Other	11.3	15.6	11.5	11.3	15.3	17.6

Source: Calculated from United Nations, Economic Commission for Europe, *Structure and Change in European Industry* (New York, 1977) pp. 103, 105, 242 & 244.

slovakia uses gross output, tending to understate the share of industries at the start of the production chain. A value-added measure could therefore raise the figures for mining and basic metals while halving the figure for food.[113] Figures on the sectoral distribution of labour tend to confirm this. The extent of Czechoslovakia's structural lag must cast doubt on a policy which places all the emphasis on the system of management. The fact that that structure was created within a deliberate policy in the early 1950s suggests still greater reservations. This does not mean that there should have been a reorientation towards a massive investment drive in chemicals – Goldmann's criticisms of that conception must be valid – but it does point towards the need for a strong central policy for reallocating investment.

The 'system' is also partly to blame especially if it is defined in the broadest possible way to bring in international factors. Goldmann and Kouba were beginning to develop methods to show Czechoslovakia's declining international competitiveness and linked this to the elimination of the market mechanism in foreign trade and the isolation of the entire economy from world markets.[114] The philosophy of international integration, as inherited from the early 1950s, was for maximum autarky, with exports necessitated in economic terms by the absence of domestic sources of some raw materials and advanced technology.[115] This conception is fully in harmony with the centralised system. It points to a different notion of structural weakness relating to the minimum of specialisation at every level. The best way to overcome it would be a change in system aiming for more international integration but that aspect, which would obviously raise very sensitive political questions, took second place to the introduction of market relations within the domestic economy. The immediate effect was to give the Fourth Five Year Plan a uniquely vague character.

Another forgotten plan

Rozsypal subsequently tried to present economic policy during the mid and late 1960s as a battle between a trend trying to restore 'the leading role of the party', which to him meant firm direction of the economy, and a trend wanting 'a basic restructuring of the system'.[116] In line with his earlier ideas he stressed the importance of a long-term plan, interest in which was apparently weakened by the advocates of reform. In practice counterposing structural change directed from above to economic reform did prove unhelpful because the transition to a new system was much more difficult than had initially been realised. It is, however, unclear how far a detailed five year plan could have been accurate enough to be of value at a time of structural change.

The economic situation itself also created immense practical difficulties which led to the abandonment of the attempt at a Seven Year Plan – to run from 1964 to 1970 – and then delayed the conclusion of the Fourth Five Year Plan. A further complication then was the growing belief that a new system was the precondition for structural change. Šik had firm views on what was needed and some of his thinking reflected the ideas behind the 1958 reform.[117] He placed strong emphasis on the benefits of a perspective plan and of plan stability enabling firm relationships between lower levels. He then went beyond the old method of planning which, he claimed, was based on such a simple methodology as to amount to setting every sector – and particularly the basic sectors like coal, steel and energy – the maximum realistic target as derived from extrapolating past experience. The inevitable consequence was structural conservatism.

He visualised a new procedure whereby structural change would be worked out at the centre to ensure balance on the basis of investment proposals from enterprises. The key point was that these proposals would not be the old bargaining positions of understated outputs and exaggerated input requirements. Instead, the new system would force

Table 5.4. *Main growth rate targets of the Fourth Five Year Plan*

	planned	achieved
National income	22–24	40
Gross industrial product	30–32	36
Gross agricultural product	20	34
Personal consumption	20	28
Accumulation	20	166

Source: *Czechoslovak Economic Papers*, IX, p. 11 (1967); HSR, pp. 84, 88 & 91.

enterprises to derive them from calculations of future benefits: they would therefore reflect the independent initiative of lower levels constrained by the chosen credit terms.

Rozsypal, then Deputy Minister of State Planning, fundamentally disagreed, still believing that the formulation of a stable Five Year Plan logically precedes allowing scope for commodity relations.[118] Even Novotný, however, agreed that investment was to be determined 'by strict criteria of long-term efficiency',[119] and that depended on a new system of management which was 'not yet' influencing perform-ance.[120] Above all, it depended on a rational price system. Only then could it lead to 'the necessary redistribution of national income and with it structural changes'.[121] The plan therefore remained vague until the Central Committee meeting of October 1966 and was subject to substantial changes in May of the following year.

In practice it set broad aggregates like the proper relationship between consumption and investment. It set structural priorities, targets for basic indicators and the broad directions for investment.[122] Although the plan was soon regarded as irrelevant and the precise figures quickly forgotten, its objectives were some help in guiding general policy measures.

Most indicators grew more rapidly than planned, as Table 5.4 shows, although in the case of accumulation this was judged to be a failing as 20% of national income was seen as the maximum bear-able level. The structural shift was in some respects faster than planned, but there was some return towards the previous position in 1969: the outcome, shown in Table 5.5, only corresponds very approximately to the intentions in the plan. Most remarkable of all was the success in agriculture although total investment in the 1966–70 period was only 3% more than in 1961–65. This had been recognised, on the basis of international comparisons, as the very

Table 5.5. *Investment in the main sectors of industry in 1968 and 1970 relative to 1965, measured in 1977 prices*

	1968	1970
All	101.6	124.0
Fuel	54.9	62.6
Energy	72.8	87.4
Steel	56.5	80.0
Chemicals	136.3	140.7
Building materials	213.5	240.6
Engineering	133.1	146.1
Glass and ceramics	183.2	113.1
Textiles	115.2	230.2
Food	128.4	163.2

Source: Calculated from *HSR*, pp. 179–80.

weakest part of the economy, but it still received far less attention than industry.

The year 1966 appears as a clear break in its fortunes and this can be related to a number of changes. The organisational structure was stabilised after collectivisation and a wave of mergers in the period up to 1962. The growth in fixed assets per head was especially rapid in the 1959–62 period, but the real benefits came with a slightly younger, more stable and better-educated labour force later in the decade as higher purchase prices allowed a rise in cooperative farmers' earnings – to 74% of the average of other employees in 1965 and 84% in 1970. There was to be a new system of management, using financial levers so as to allow for specialisation among farms, but it was never expected to bring rapid results.[123] Nevertheless, collectivisation had been firmly consolidated and, to judge from opinion polls, was regarded by the great majority as unequivocally beneficial in bringing higher living standards and making work easier.[124]

6   The reform falters

The principal economic issue during 1966 was the leadership's acceptance, in view of the failure of past economic policies, of the need to
accelerate the implementation of the reform.[1] The political case was
obvious in view of its promised benefits especially when set against
growing disillusionment among much of the population. Many delegates to the Thirteenth Congress in June referred to apathy of young
people: Novotný even accused many of them of acquiring 'a destruc-
tive relationship to the values of our society'.[2] The official youth
organisation was losing members rapidly while its student section's
leadership had been persecuted after calling for the right to be more
critical of the party leadership.[3] The feeling was continuing to grow
even within the central apparatus that something was seriously
wrong.

The pre-Congress discussion gave this a focus with 7436 of a total of
10 082 comments from party organisations being on economic questions. Some favoured a return to centralised administrative allocation
to overcome delivery problems, but overwhelmingly they criticised
the structure and the system of management. From 'almost every
workplace' came demands 'not only for more authority, but also
responsibility both from managers and from workers'.[4] Despite the
hopes aroused from talk of reform some delegates objected that, 'so
far nothing has happened'.[5]

The leadership seemed to be speaking ever more the language of
reform, but many clearly wanted to push them further. The key figure
was again Šik[6] who claims that Novotný allowed him in as only the
penultimate speaker at the Congress while Brezhnev sat ice-cold and
tight-lipped through his contribution.[7] He was characteristically sharp
in his criticisms of 'some comrades' who were still trapped in dogmatic thinking and exhibited unnecessary distrust and reservations
towards all changes. Others he accused of fighting for their personal

interests while some leading officials were allegedly blocking the work of specialist commissions by binding their representatives to the organisation's previously decided position. The essential message was that the reform could fail just as it had in 1958 thanks to those who wanted only to incorporate market relations into the old method of planning. He was publicly offering himself as the most credible figure opposing unnamed holders of power. He remembers receiving a fifteen-minute ovation.

His essential argument was that a market-oriented reform, offering substantial improvements in performance, was hampered primarily by political opposition from the top. Subsequent events suggest that he was oversimplifying the obstacles, as policy measures had to confront enterprises defending sectional interests and the reality of an economy still diagnosed as suffering from 'disequilibrium'. Flaws in the basic conception also became apparent around the issue of 'delevelling'. Although it appealed to much of the rising white-collar intelligentsia, Šik's conception of greater inequality was based on an unrealistically abstract vision of a market system and did not correspond either to what the economy needed or to what large sections of the employed population found acceptable.

Too much equality?

The theme, that somehow there was too much pay equality in Czechoslovakia, was brought to the centre of attention in the pre-Congress discussion. Many party organisations referred to the issue with the numbers supporting 'delevelling' approximately equal to those 'indicating distrust' and suggesting that those in high positions were already doing quite well enough.[8] As the natural tendency is to agree with the leadership and as managers often have a strong position in party organisations, this could certainly imply a powerful body of potential opposition.

Šik argued that without 'delevelling' there could be no substantial technological advance. The means to achieve this was to be market pressures which would then force enterprises to put order into their payment systems. Aware of the potential unpopularity of this, he called on the party to combat egalitarian attitudes. There was nothing exceptional in this: Novotný and several others also criticised 'levelling', but with far less public enthusiasm.

This argument of 'too much' equality took a number of different forms and seemed to have gained widespread approval in intellectual circles and within the party leadership. It was, in a sense, well established long before the 1960s with the acceptance even in the 1940s of Stalin's condemnation of 'petty bourgeois egalitarianism', the emphasis on piece-rates as an incentive device, attempts to raise the pay of foremen in 1955 and a major effort to raise differentials for managers in 1958. It was backed up with a priori reasoning of the possible negative effects of excessive equality, with evidence on particular pay differentials, with international comparisons and it was even incorporated into a more general critique of the prevailing system under Novotný.

Simple deduction indicated that, without inequality, there would be a lessening of workers' interest in achieving higher output and bitterness among people who felt they were undervalued. Qualified, demanding work would be less inviting so that the level of managerial competence and the authority of management would be lowered. Such was the argument of the leading authority on wage and payment systems[9] and it certainly seemed that this sort of negative feature could be found everywhere. Thus, for example, there was typically a 'gentleman's agreement' between workers and the foreman on how much could be produced, partly because the wage control system prevented higher payments: a new system of management allowing greater differentials could surely lead immediately to higher total output.[10]

The argument was strengthened by figures on lifetime earnings for various occupations as shown in Tables 6.1, 6.2 and 6.3. Generally speaking, qualifications were a financial advantage, but there appear to have been some dramatic exceptions even in individual workplaces where foremen were very frequently paid less than the average pay of workers.[11] There are grounds for quibbling with the figures presented, which do not appear to be consistent and assume, for example, that students receive no income and that a full working life is likely to be spent at a coal face. Nevertheless this kind of evidence made a tremendous impact in the later 1960s. It was perhaps particularly persuasive because the differential for qualifications in industry, the most accessible single indicator of levelling, had so clearly fallen at the start of the decade as shown in Table 6.4. The categories of 'engineering-technical' and 'administrative' workers were not clearly differentiated but the former includes the most qualified employees. In 1937 office workers had been earning 261.5% of the pay of manual workers.[12]

A major sociological study of stratification among men in Czecho-

Table 6.1. *Relative average monthly and lifetime earnings of employees with differing levels of education in 1963*

	Monthly pay	Lifetime earnings
Basic education (i.e. up to 15)	100	100
Full middle school (i.e. up to 18)	116.5	106.1
Higher education	153.2	119.1

Source: F. Charvát, *Sociální struktura ČSSR a její vývoj v 60. letech* (Prague, 1972), p. 78.

Table 6.2. *Average monthly and lifetime earnings (Kčs) in various occupations, calculated from 1963 figures*

	Average salary	Lifetime earnings
Coal-face worker (Ostrava-Karviná)	3360	1 612 000
Fitter	2450	1 176 000
Foreman in engineering workshop	1930	903 000
Chief engineer	2700	1 134 000
Scientific worker, highly qualified	3070	1 178 880

Source: Charvát, *Sociální*, p. 78.

Table 6.3. *Lifetime earnings (Kčs) in the engineering industry, calculated from October 1965 figures*

Lathe operator	949 860
Fitter	991 945
Erector	1 127 290
Lawyer	887 321
Engineer	988 958

Source: Průša, *Ekonomické*, p. 92.

Table 6.4. *Relative pay for manual workers, 'engineering-technical employees' and administrators in Czechoslovak industry*

	Manual workers	'Engineering-technical employees'	Administrators
1948	100	165.4	124.5
1950	100	159.1	116.8
1955	100	127.8	85.7
1960	100	132.7	87.2
1961	100	130.6	85.7
1962	100	127.3	84.0
1963	100	126.6	83.7
1964	100	130.3	84.3
1965	100	135.3	86.3
1966	100	140.5	88.6
1967	100	142.2	90.2
1968	100	141.0	89.3
1969	100	137.2	86.1
1970	100	132.7	83.9

Source: Figures up to 1968 are calculated from J. Šrůtka, *O rozvoji životní urovně pracujících za socialismu* (Prague 1962) p. 159; *SR*, 1965, p. 189; 1969, p. 238; and 1970, p. 235. Later figures are calculated from statistics published annually in *Práce a mzda*.

slovakia in 1967 seemed to confirm that there was something strange in the pattern of income distribution. The team under Pavel Machonin[13] examined five indicators of social differentiation. These were complexity of work, level of education, life-style including leisure activities, participation in power, and pay. There was differentiation within each of these and the patterns were, they felt, broadly consistent with each other, enabling them to divide society roughly into four strata.

There was, however, a great deal of evidence to suggest that income was not the dominant factor differentiating society. It was considerably less important than in comparable capitalist countries. Moreover, Machonin and his colleagues found many cases in which income systematically deviated from the other indicators of a person's standing in society. They even suggested that 12–23% of men had to be placed in two, or possibly three groups outside the main pattern of stratification. One group had all the characteristics of the lowest stratum (i.e. low education, unskilled work, etc.), but an income of 125–155% of the average. Another group had reasonably good education and yet incomes only about 80% of the average. There was also a small group of skilled manual workers earning over 155% of the average.

Machonin's explanation for these apparent anomalies was to suggest that the regime had favoured a section of the working class. It had, he said, made 'concessions to egalitarian feelings' in an effort to bolster its support. Thus political motives had led to excessive 'levelling'. He even referred to a 'bureaucratic–egalitarian' type of social relations which, he claimed without providing any further evidence, 'were demonstrably the main obstacle to the further maturing of a primary industrial culture'.[14]

This linked up with Šik who, on the basis of figures showing relative average earnings of broad categories of employee, could claim that 'levelling' was 'hampering scientific and technical development'.[15] He pointed to the 'existence of conservative or even regressive attitudes' not just at the highest levels but among 'part of the employees in enterprises'.[16] The enemies of reform could include workers 'who had become used to poor quality work'. Its supporters were to include, it seemed, those who could see through widely held prejudices and recognised just 'how strenuous and exceptionally complicated creative mental work is'.[17]

Despite their popularity with a significant section of the population, none of these analytical methods is satisfactory. International comparisons do show a very low level of earnings inequality in Czechoslovakia relative to other countries in both Eastern and Western Europe. Table 6.5 shows the narrow range within which earnings are concentrated. In fact, hardly anybody fell below the legal minimum of around 60% or above three times the median. Even within earned income, there were far more very high relative earners in Britain although, of course, in both cases top earnings might be supplemented by substantial perks.[18]

Compared at least with Britain, however, Czechoslovakia shows wide variations among male and female *manual* workers which overlap to a very great extent with non-manual earnings. The reason, however, is not to be found in political decisions to favour certain social groups. The point is rather the need to pay high wages to some manual workers to overcome an otherwise unbearable labour shortage in key sectors of the economy.

Heavy engineering, railways, metallurgy and especially coal-mining suffered from chronic labour shortages and rapid turnover. In the twenty years up to 1965 half a million men had worked on a temporary brigade system in the Ostrava-Karviná mines. That was

Table 6.5. *Distribution of full-time earnings in Czechoslovakia, excluding agricultural cooperatives*

	1961	1968	1977
P10/median	63	65	64
P25/median	78	78	78
P75/median	125	125	126
P90/median	156	154	155
P95/P5	307	308	310

Note: Figures are percentages with P10, P25, referring to the earnings of the tenth, twenty-fifth, etc. percentile.
Source: Calculated from *SR*, 1967, p. 117; 1976, p. 129; and 1980, p. 209.

the only way to get enough workers, but very few were prepared to stay there permanently. As a result, the inexperienced workforce could never make full use of new mining equipment and productivity could not rise in line with investment. Frequently throughout the 1950s and 1960s special measures were taken following discussions in the government and party Central Committee. A major sociological study in the mid-1960s left little doubt about why, despite high pay and excellent pension rights, so few men were prepared to spend their working lives in the crucially important mines of Ostrava-Karviná. The nature of the work, the ease of finding employment elsewhere and the poor living conditions in the Ostrava area were the main problems.[19] This was despite an average pay in mining around 150% of the level for industry as a whole.

Machonin's account completely ignored the functioning of the economic system. He implicitly assumed that there should be correspondence between his five indicators of stratification. This need not be true under the particular conditions of the Czechoslovak labour market. The point is that, rather than the Czechoslovak economy over-valuing simple work, Machonin and his colleagues were under-valuing unpleasant work.[20] Similarly Šik, having correctly argued that material reward is still the principal motive for working, missed the point that many other factors may enter into the precise choice of a job.[21]

In fact, the real difference from Britain is not that the market has less of an influence on pay in Czechoslovakia but rather the opposite. In a study of the British case, it was concluded that supply and demand

Table 6.6. *Average monthly earnings of workers and 'engineering-technical employees' in selected sectors of Czechoslovak industry in 1967*

	Manual workers	'Engineering-technical employees'	Ratio (× 100)
All	100	142	142
Coal-mining	143	206	144
Engineering	102	132	130
Chemicals	102	151	149
Consumer goods	83	136	163
Food	90	132	148
Construction	113	151	133
Railways	107	130	121

Note: The first two columns are percentages of the average for all workers.
Source: Calculated from *Práce a mzda*, XVII, p. 166 (1969).

were typically far less influential than long-established custom and widely held views of what was right.[22] As long as pay was high enough to attract a workforce adequate to the employer's needs, market forces need not have any impact at all and they were particularly unimportant in explaining differentials between skill grades within a workplace. There was in fact a 'zone of indeterminacy' over which the market had no effect. Exactly the same principle holds for Czechoslovakia, except that there are many more occupations where pay has reached the lower limit.

The supply and demand for categories of labour certainly do not explain the whole pattern of inequality in Czechoslovakia. Wide variations among manual and non-manual workers are strongly influenced by vagaries of the payment and incentive systems. Above all, the convention is still accepted that authority should find expression in higher pay. That was used in mining to justify a substantial differential for managers and engineers over manual workers, even though the former spent little time underground and were never in particular shortage.[23] In less favoured sectors, if there was pressure for workers' pay to rise, the differential had to be allowed to decrease, almost disappearing in the case of heavy engineering.[24] The consequent overlap between the pay of some manual workers, such as miners, and 'engineering-technical employees' (managers and qualified engineers) in other sectors can be seen in Table 6.6.

The basic difference from Britain is, of course, approximate full employment in the Czechoslovak case. That does not mean the maximum possible employment. There were still some women reporting in the 1960s that they would like to take a job if it were available although, at 45% of the total labour force in the mid-1960s, employment of women was very close to the maximum. There were also social barriers, such as opposition from the husband,[25] and regional differences with slack increasingly concentrated in rural parts of Slovakia. Full employment therefore has to be given a flexible meaning which can change as social attitudes, and even child-care facilities, alter the numbers seeking work.

Moreover, approximate full employment does not rule out substantial specific shortages. In fact it could appear that Czechoslovakia suffered a general labour shortage ever since the expulsion of the German minority. Estimates have been made suggesting, for example, half a million vacant workplaces in industry in the early 1970s. These, however, assume a target level of shift work which is high relative to Western Europe and, again because of attitudes within society, is probably unattainable.[26] In fact, the whole notion of a labour shortage is highly questionable. The appearance is generated by the behaviour of enterprises which, seeking security against the need for 'storming' towards the end of a plan period or higher plan targets generally, report shortages and take on more workers whenever they can. They also put off scrapping obsolete equipment thereby delaying the release of potentially surplus labour. A faster rate of replacement of equipment would lead to a higher rate of productivity growth and relax tensions on the labour market. The labour force barrier is therefore not the result of an absolute labour shortage but 'of a shortage at the given level of organisation'.[27]

Looking at the economy as a whole it appeared that the real shortage was for jobs requiring higher education, many of which were taken by people with inadequate qualifications. The link to pay relativities seemed plausible[28] and it was even claimed that people sometimes hid their qualifications in an effort to gain a better-paid job.[29] The fault, however, might well be in the inability of the education system to provide enough trained manpower as there is plenty of evidence of people seeking higher qualifications even without the expectation of massive financial reward.[30]

In fact, shortage was felt most severely in *manual* occupations. This could have been partly a consequence of a system that emphasised immediate output above the longer-term success which depends more on the most highly qualified. There were, however, many cases of specific, manual occupations throughout industry and construction where pay was simply inadequate to ensure stability. By way of contrast the actual workplaces for people with the higher qualifications were being filled, even if 50% of non-manual workers in 1965 were said to lack the necessary qualifications.[31]

In fact, the strongest grounds for complaint were excessive and unjustified inequality between sectors. The pattern here was no less unequal than before the war, and was remarkably stable after the early 1950s. 'Non-productive' sectors, such as health and education, were paid on average less than industry, although the employees' level of qualification was much higher. Non-priority sectors of industry, such as textiles or food, had earnings below 80% of the average for industry as a whole. There were clear cases of identical work receiving less in some sectors than others.

In the early 1950s, favouring key sectors was itself associated with a battle against the egalitarian 'slogan of equal stomachs' which implied that everyone's needs were the same so that they should be paid the same. The new differentials were justified, in the face of strong resentment expressed through some trade union organisations,[32] by classifying sectors in precise detail according to their 'social importance'. The criterion was partially dropped in the early 1970s, but very little changed in the broad pattern of inter-sectoral earnings differentials. The 'social importance' of a sector was really a formal justification for a level of pay that emerged from measures to stabilise a labour force at the level required by the central planners.[33] Thus coal-mining could claim great importance because its product was crucial to all other sectors in the economy and the work was so unpleasant as to make it very difficult to recruit a stable labour force.

At the other end of the scale the textile industry was of importance only to consumer demand. Moreover, unlike heavy industry generally, there were no social barriers to recruiting women. Although equal pay had been legally enforced since 1945, women still earned on average only just over two-thirds of the average for men. They tended to occupy lower positions and to predominate in those sectors where pay was lowest: thus in 1967 10% of employees in mining were women compared with 26% in construction, 68% in consumer goods and 79% in health. This last sector in particular had expanded very rapidly with significant shortages only in some nursing jobs. Surveys suggested that women were less likely than men to express dissatisfaction over pay and, contrary to a widely held prejudice, were frequently less likely to change their job.[34] The view was deeply rooted that jobs with authority and certain kinds of manual work were less appropriate for women. There was also a common assumption that women needed less pay as they were typically not the principal breadwinners.[35]

Thus the social position of women accentuated the shortage of labour in certain sectors – engineering enterprises found parental pressures dissuading girls from applying for apprenticeships[36] – and facilitated recruitment at low rates of pay in others. It tied in with the low level of technology in traditionally non-priority sectors and made it very difficult to retain the male skilled labour needed for greater mechanisation. Surveys suggested that this problem was felt throughout the economy but was more severe for manual than non-manual workers and was especially serious in the food and consumer goods industries.[37]

A picture was painted of parts of the food industry desperately needing a doubling of investment,[38] but that alone would solve little. The capital-intensive breweries and sugar refineries could barely maintain existing pre-war machinery as the older qualified workers retired and younger ones drifted into better-paid work elsewhere.[39] There was, then, a very strong case for changing a pattern that was derived from the operation of a market for labour within an otherwise planned economy and creating greater equality for manual workers between sectors – differences between other categories were anyway much smaller – and that was to be one of the factors overwhelming the attempt at 'delevelling'.

At first, however, progress seemed to be possible as a result of economic reform. Differentials between enterprise earnings were to rise at once with the new system of self-financing and that would be reflected in wages through the workers' share in profits. Top managers were given scope for higher bonuses – up from 30% to 55% of basic pay depending on enterprise performance – and lower managers were to receive a larger than average share in profits. There were enormous variations between enterprises in the criteria used for allocating available funds, which were set out in 'collective agreements' between management and the trade union committee without the mass of employees knowing much about it;[40] but the first results in 1967 showed a clear rise in differentials for the highly qualified. Enterprises even made out plans for reaching a target ratio of 'engineering-technical' employees' to manual workers' pay with differentials of up to 70%.

It was repeatedly emphasised that differentials among manual workers were just as important. In practice, however, the share in profits could only raise earnings in industry by about 2% in 1966 rising to 4% in 1968. The amount available for manual workers was fairly small and it was a very common policy to try to ensure that all got at least something so as to create interest in the enterprise's performance. As the intention was a very substantial increase in differentials between manual workers, another means had to be found and attention shifted back towards piece-rates and the elimination of any upper limit on earnings. This was successful in some enterprises but those most able to benefit were often the least skilled and the overall effect was to narrow the scope for increasing the differential for the highly qualified.

Moreover, the shortage of certain categories of manual worker continued to bite, probably influencing the softness of piece-rates and directly contradicting other aspects of the delevelling process. As an example, the management in ČKD was trying to get approval for significant pay rises for machine-tool operatives at exactly the same time as it was working out plans for raising the differential for engineers and managers.[41] As with other aspects of reform, the whole issue of delevelling was far more complicated than was originally assumed.

The price reform

The central theme in public discussions around the time of the Thirteenth Congress was the inadequacy of the first reform measures. Enterprises faced less obligatory indicators and were meant to link wages to their income rather than fulfilment of plan targets. In reality, however, the inadequacies of the price system compelled the retention of subsidies and differentiation of payments into the state budget. The changes already made therefore pointed logically towards the next step being reform of wholesale prices.

Previously most experts had seen even a time limit of 1969 as 'rather precipitate',[42] but rapid acceleration seemed to be possible with a new method of calculating prices using a computer. Previously they had been set in stages, starting with raw materials and working through the production chain. A full revision usually took up to 30 months by which time it was bound to be inaccurate. Moreover, there was plenty of scope for enterprises to spot which prices were rising, overstate their use of that input and thereby ease their own financial position.

The new method was said to overcome this danger by calculating all prices simultaneously for 27 000 product groups. A later stage was to bring adjustments to the total of one-and-a-half-million specific products after which market relations between enterprises could become a reality.[43] As no prices were known in advance enterprises should have no incentive to distort information about inputs.

The aim was an average price rise of 19% to enable enterprises to pay obligations to the state which had been increased by the charge on fixed assets. In practice the average was 29% and profitability was three times the intended level with very wide variations between sectors and enterprises.[44] The crucial point must have been that, aware of the far greater importance of prices for themselves, enterprises put more pressure than ever on the centre. A frequent criticism then and in later years was of 'inadequate preparedness', leaving scope for 'machinations' with the centre wrongly yielding to pressure from below.[45] Even taking more time need not have helped as it is always very difficult to counter enterprises' monopoly of information. Moreover, the appropriate prices for a later date would inevitably be different so that a slower process brings its own inaccuracies.

It is not even clear exactly what the price adjustments were to achieve. One view certainly was that conditions for enterprises should be tougher.[46] The authors of the reform were less ambitious suggesting that it could make no fundamental difference as it only altered the way in which enterprises were financed.[47] In these terms it was judged a success.[48] In fact Černík was very clear that real pressure could only come with flexible prices responding to supply and demand.[49] He even gave reassurances that 'we have done everything to prevent an undeserved effect on enterprises'.[50] Such an attitude could easily open the door for an upward bias on prices.

Nevertheless, this must be judged a major setback for the reform. The general 'strategy' was outlined most clearly by Turek. He had great faith in the powers of the market mechanism but saw no alternative to proceeding by compromises. This was partly a question of political realism – 'conservative forces' could only be persuaded to depart gradually from 'the old "proven" methods' – but there was also a policy of quite deliberate restraint. It was impossible to go at once for the full pressures of the domestic and world market because 'the medicines would most likely have killed the patient'.[51]

The decision to adjust all wholesale prices at the start of 1967 – made attractive as the next step by the promise of a speedy and reliable method of calculation – was fully in line with Turek's strategy and he optimistically saw it creating 'the nucleus of the new system'. It was still not 'complete victory', but the new system was now to start functioning with the remaining compromises appearing visibly as anomalies. The most serious of these was that prices were still set from the centre. It was, however, to be the last such operation 'in the directive model of management' and would logically be followed by increasing price flexibility.[52]

In fact, the system that emerged seemed to differ only in superficial appearance from what had existed before. There were still obvious anomalies, with even more cases of wholesale prices above retail.[53] There was no evidence of a real change in enterprises satisfying consumer demand: shortages still coexisted with spare capacity and excess stocks for some consumer goods and many enterprises saw no immediate hope of satisfying demand. Only in exceptional cases was there much sign of a genuine buyers' market and many enterprises actually complained of worsening relations with suppliers.[54] The hope had been for stable financial conditions enabling a longer perspective with investment undertaken after calculations of its profitability. Instead, surveys throughout 1967 show no greater restraint on the desire for investment. Fully half of all enterprises would use spare resources in this way and all were aware of inadequate supply in the investment field.[55] Investment was still said to be a much easier option than seeking out reserves.[56]

Most important of all, bargaining still continued between different levels in the hierarchy. This was no longer over precise plan targets – there was no such detailed plan for 1967 – but was rather over import limits, subsidies, credits and exemptions.[57] The only way to eliminate this was judged to be further price reform.[58] To some extent the administration of the subsidisation process was decentralised into associations which had the power to redistribute between profit- and loss-making enterprises. Thus a useful part of a highly centralised system could find an analogous role in a system based around financial instruments: it eased the task of the centre. Many enterprises were unhappy with this infringement of their financial independence. Turek accepted it with some reluctance, insisting that cross-subsidisation should gradually be eliminated. It is, however, difficult to see an alternative. Many enterprises inevitably were unprofitable, but they could usually blame higher authorities for refusing them investment thereby forcing them to produce goods vital to plan fulfilment throughout the economy on the basis of obsolete technology. Once associations took on that allocative function it is difficult to see, apart from central pressures, why they should give priority to their worst enterprises. Excluding closures, the subsidisation of loss-makers is very hard to eliminate.

Despite his previous optimism Turek was soon assessing this as no more than a 'transitional' model. The question, however, is whether there was a real alternative in 1967. The possibility of a forceful introduction of world prices appears even less realistic. It is meaning-less for non-traded goods and would create chaos unless associated with opening the country to imports. If, for example, the price of oil relative to coal were based on relativities outside, the result would have been a phenomenal excess demand for oil leading inevitably back to rationing and centralised allocation. Opening the country at once to free imports would bring dangers of massive disruption and destruction of whole sectors. At the very least it would have to be preceded by selective measures from the centre to encourage enter-prises that could hope to become competitive.[59]

This must increase doubts about the chosen reform strategy and strengthens the case, from the purely economic point of view, of accepting a slower transition still using the centre to direct structural change. A frequent exponent of this kind of position was Černík, but the dangers must have appeared immense to advocates of reform who were aware of political opponents trying to use arguments for caution as a cover for outright opposition and as a means to kill any chance of real change. It anyway seemed in early 1967 that progress could be resumed with another adjustment from the centre which, it was hoped, would create a buyers' market, at least for investment goods. It tied in with the belief that the greatest threat to the economy was 'disequilibrium', as had been stated clearly in authoritative party documents.

Equilibrium and shortage

There are two major problems in defining equilibrium in a socialist economy. The first is the theoretical one relating to how broadly the system is defined. A persistent state of market imbalance may be the normal economic condition to which 'that system is continually driven': in that case it must be regarded as 'equilibrium rather than disequilibrium'.[60] Keynes could refer to equilibrium in a capitalist economy operating below full employment so, similarly, persistent shortage could represent equilibrium in another economic system. That argument has been presented in great detail by Kornai.[61]

Some economists in the 1960s used the term 'inflation' to mean excess demand but frequently equilibrium was understood in terms of the relationship between supply and demand with the almost universal acceptance that the latter was excessive.

The second problem is whether, under centralised planning, there is any relevance to the notion of aggregate disequilibrium. In an open, free market economy there are close relationships between the markets for investment goods, consumer goods and labour and the foreign trade balance. Under central planning each of those spheres is regulated by quite distinct instruments so that imbalance in one need not spill over into another. Thus excess consumer demand need not affect the trade balance, unless the centre deliberately decides to counter it with more imports or a cut in exports. Conversely, a balance of payments problem could be solved without changing domestic current consumption if all the weight were put on cutting investment.

It is therefore necessary to take each sphere separately and to see how they interrelate. Tensions on the labour market could delay investment projects but the level of employment is itself determined by demand throughout the economy. The shortage of labour therefore cannot be seen as an active agent spreading disequilibrium throughout the economy.

There was concern about foreign trade, but information was still not published on the balance of payments. It seems that the deficit with socialist countries in 1968, shown in Table 6.7, enabled high domestic demand to be satisfied and was based on the repayment of past loans. The hard-currency position was superficially more healthy but the surplus there depended heavily on exports to developing countries from which payment was often delayed and irregular. Difficulties here could have forced restrictions on importing equipment or encouraged the use of domestic capacity to achieve higher machinery exports. Hard-currency problems were often named as such a contributor to domestic shortage and sometimes, taking a longer-term view, as the most fundamental problem of all. With greater export competitiveness, any domestic shortage could be overcome.

Far more concern was expressed about imbalance on the consumer goods market. Unspent financial resources, made up of cash and savings deposits, had fluctuated averaging 2.4% of money incomes in the period 1953 to 1963. Then there was a definite increase to an average of 3.4% for the next four years.[62] The fear was that this saving was at least partly involuntary and anyway could threaten the stability of markets at any time.

Table 6.7. *Czechoslovakia's trade balance with socialist and non-socialist countries in the late 1960s in million Kčs*

	Socialist	Advanced capitalist	Developing
1966	+36	−514	+543
1967	+878	+19	+429
1968	−635	−555	+673
1969	−578	−123	+883
1970	+826	−959	+833

Source: Calculated from *HSR*, pp. 320–21.

Some attempts at measuring market imbalance supported such fears. One study assumed a constant desired rate of saving and, obviously, the conclusion was of growing imbalance.[63] It is, however, more plausible to look for a definite break in savings habits associated with changing consumption patterns. Basic consumer goods, such as food and textiles, were reliably available in adequate quantities and were therefore no longer the subject of periodic panic buying. Instead, fluctuations could now appear in purchases of goods 'for long-term consumption', such as cars, for which a larger base of savings was needed.[64]

A number of economists, including Goldmann and his colleagues, persistently argued that there was no real problem here and, when allowance was made for deliberately saving for flats or cars, it appeared that aggregate supply of consumer goods exceeded aggregate demand up to 1966. There was a small reversal in 1967, but the overall message was that there was no great danger.[65] The same conclusion could be drawn from a comparison with much higher savings rates in Western Europe or even in pre-war Czechoslovakia. Total deposits were around only one-quarter of annual disposable incomes. Questionnaires similarly indicated that, while some people were seeking loans, there was a growing tendency towards conscious and deliberate saving, although it was often for a vague, unspecified future rather than something specific such as a car. If there were financial resources that could not be spent then it was a problem only for specific groups, such as older people.[66]

Despite this the view persisted of real danger on the consumer goods market. Part of the reason was the nervousness of central planners for whom behaviour was judged irrational if 'it does not respect the intentions of the plan'[67] and they had worked on the assumption of a saving rate of around 2%. A rising level of savings could also leave them nervous as economic development would depend on 'psychological factors' which were beyond their control.[68]

Moreover, the prejudices of planners seemed to fit with consumers' awareness of persistent shortages. The clearest cases were for imported consumer goods. There were also several examples of surpluses suggesting an inflexible system unable to match supply with demand at the detailed level. The consequences for behaviour are not so much forced savings as forced substitution and often excessive spending on potentially scarce goods when they become available. To the consumers, of course, the distinction between overall and specific shortage need not be important: they are in both cases annoyed that they cannot buy what they want.

Nevertheless, the greatest concern was definitely not with consumer goods but rather with investment. There were two separable questions; first, whether there was excess demand for investment and, then, whether high investment caused further disequilibrium throughout the economy. Although more figures are available than for earlier periods, the first question is very difficult to answer as neither supply nor demand are easy to define. There is no doubt that enterprises always push for more investment. Their 'almost insatiable' appetite has frequently been explained by the desire for security against higher plan targets, by the attractions of larger size bringing power and status and by the prestige associated with modern technology. At the level of the enterprise with its 'soft budget constraint', none of these needs be set against calculations of likely returns to the investment outlays.[69]

The centre, of course, battles to control this, but it frequently allows too many, poorly prepared projects to be started. This is regarded as a clear 'disequilibrium', but its precise measurement seems to be impossible. To use a comparison with plan targets, as is sometimes done, amounts to employing a subjective criterion as if it were an objective yardstick. Equilibrium can, of course, be taken as an average on the assumption that the system as a whole seems to be tending towards this point. It is anyway only possible to estimate relative levels of tension between supply and demand using a number of measures relating to investment demand none of which is fully satisfactory.[70] For the 1960s it seemed reasonable to make comparisons with the start of the decade which was generally agreed to have been a time of over-investment.

Table 6.8. *Measures of excess investment demand in the 1960s*

	Ratio of remaining costs to investment[a]	Ratio of investment to growth in fixed assets[b]
1961	1.50	1.32
1962	1.54	1.27
1963	1.62	1.19
1964	1.53	1.17
1965	1.59	1.50
1966	1.49	1.81
1967	1.44	1.42
1968	1.38	1.53
1969	1.49	1.58
1970	1.43	1.16

Notes: a. In current prices.
   b. Numerator in 1977 prices denominator in 1967 prices.
Source: Calculated from *HSR*, pp. 161, 169, 175 & 183.

Two possible measures, used in Table 6.8, can illustrate the problems. The relationship of investment to the remaining expenditure needed to complete projects could indicate how much of investment is being lost in work-in-progress and in excessive delays. A high figure therefore implies over-investment. The relationship of investment to growth in fixed assets similarly indicates whether the input is yielding results or being lost as a 'leakage'. Again, accepting the possible reservations expressed in Chapter 4, a higher figure suggests a worsening situation although we still have no idea what level corresponds to equilibrium.

The first measure provides confirmation for the slow recovery after 1962, but suggests a considerably easier situation later in the decade. The second measure points roughly to the opposite conclusion suggesting growing difficulties in the latter half of the decade. Part of the difference could be due to the use in the second measure of fixed prices, albeit from different base years, which eliminate the effect of the 1967 price adjustment. Nevertheless, it would seem impossible to reach a clear conclusion from this kind of evidence.

In fact, the argument at the time centred on the rising shares of accumulation and, to a lesser extent, investment in national income shown in Table 6.9 suggesting that these were so high as to be causing 'an overheated cyclical peak'.[71] The price reform probably raised the

Table 6.9. *Investment, accumulation and leakages relative to national income in the 1960s, measured in current prices*

	Accumulation as percentage of national income	Change in stocks and projects under construction as percentage of national income	Investment as percentage of final product
1960	17.6	6.0	23.5
1961	20.5	8.7	23.6
1962	18.4	8.8	22.2
1963	13.4	4.7	20.7
1964	10.3	− 1.5	21.8
1965	9.1	0.5	21.6
1966	13.2	5.6	21.5
1967	22.6	8.9	26.6
1968	23.2	9.9	26.2
1969	24.9	11.6	26.9
1970	26.9	10.3	28.0

Source: Calculated from *HSR*, pp. 90 & 169.

relative price of investment goods, but accumulation was also rising because of a growth in 'leakages' after 1965. Investment, however, was picked on as the principal source of 'inflationary tensions' throughout the economy[72] not least because it was the fastest growing element. Calculations also suggested that an increase in investment could raise total wages by almost twice as much.[73] The longer it took to raise final output the more likely this was to cause excess demand for consumer goods. The solution therefore had to be a cut in investment, although it need not amount to a 'pogrom'.[74]

The end of the economic reform?

This, then, was the complex background to the Central Committee meeting of May 1967. The principal report was delivered by Černík[75] who spoke with more understanding for the reform than was typical among political leaders. While others seemed to speak only in vague terms of the possibility of linking plan and market in general, he spelt out the relationship making it explicit that 'the market should serve for the objectivisation of value relationships'.[76] In part he took on board the reformers' ideas, but the policy he outlined could even be seen as the effective death of reform efforts.

The centre of concern was 'equilibrium'. He rejected fears of excess purchasing power and saw the greatest threat in excessively rapid growth since 1965. The planned level was to be around 5% but, estimated at over 10% for the period 1965–6, it was judged to be 'above the upper limit of the optimum': later figures actually show national income growing 9.1% in 1966 and averaging 6.9% for the 1966–70 period. The priority now was not growth but 'an anti-inflationary policy aiming to free the tension that has arisen'. He could, of course, have boasted about successful expansion, but he had absorbed the arguments from Goldmann and others, although they were not directly involved in policy formulation, and pointed to accumulation leaking into stocks and unfinished investment. Judged against the economy's apparent potential, there was 'no reason for exaggerated optimism'. Obviously, then, the long-term solution was reform.

First, however, there had to be a firm brake on new investment and even some under construction might have to be abandoned. The only means to achieve this had to be intervention from the centre because, despite a declared intention to solve the problem by 'linking the function of the plan and the market', 'economic instruments were not yet up to the task'. The aim was to cut investment in comparison with the Five Year Plan proposals and simultaneously institute a stronger structural shift towards chemicals, consumer goods and building materials. It seemed possible to cut investment more rapidly in coal and electricity, sectors that yielded slow returns, despite 'the undesirable social consequences for redundant workers', who were to be found work elsewhere. More difficult was the decision to resist 28 projects which would add another 25% to starts and were all judged beneficial to the economy. They could only be begun if something else were postponed and there were no acceptable candidates. They were therefore left to wait in line.

One means to reduce this pressure would have been financial instruments differentiated between enterprises. That, however, was judged as a return 'to subjectively set indicators' which would devalue and deform value relations. Ultimately something had to be done about enterprises' enormous financial resources particularly as they were matched by an inevitable shortfall in the state budget. In the end the state simply took what was regarded as excessive earnings. Černík's long-term solution was further price adjustments.

He was, however, convinced that a 'functioning, normalised market', the very basis for the operation of the reformed system, was still not realisable. There was still pressure for further increases in wholesale prices. He did not believe that a restrictive finance and credit policy would be enough to force enterprises into voluntary price reductions when they still had 'excessive incomes'. That could only happen after 'a radical restriction of demand' leading to 'a crisis situation with significant unused productive capacity, with workers discarded from the labour process and with a decline in the standard of living'. Such a policy was, under socialism, 'unacceptable'.

Having rejected that 'risky experiment', the only alternative was to retain central regulation. He dashed the hopes that the January 1967 adjustment would quickly be followed by freer price setting and also proposed central restrictions linking wage rises to productivity. The existing situation, he felt, was creating real dangers as highly unequal profitability led to unjustified wage rises, in turn creating pressure for wage increases elsewhere on grounds of comparability. The overall price level could, he thought, be held stable with some prices rising but with those in firms making big profits being driven down. Such a policy would obviously be very difficult as it contradicted the general state of market disequilibrium. He plausibly foresaw 'a situation of substantial conflict between the centre and enterprises' with the latter exhibiting no 'great enthusiasm'.

The crucial question was how this approach fitted with the reform. Černík acknowledged a number of points. The centre was keeping a grip on wholesale and retail prices. It retained plan directives for foreign trade and to some extent for investment. He reiterated, however, that the new system had never been understood as 'a retreat from planned management' and that there was always going to be a transitional stage using a combination of economic and directive instruments. He was very firm that the centre had a responsibility to use counter-inflationary policies to create the conditions for a 'new equilibrium'.

He went some way to differentiate himself from reform economists. He saw less need now for 'one-sided emphasis and talk about a future model of the economy which is anyway some way away in time'. That, he claimed, only created illusions about what was possible and continual calls for acceleration, without regard to the results of what had been achieved. In effect, this was a challenge from the leadership to the reformers to convert their general, abstract ideas into concrete policies.

There were already growing signs of lack of interest, and even opposition, from enterprise managements that had shortly before-hand been a major support for the reform.[77] Some were even saying that it had achieved nothing especially when set against the very pragmatic objective of finding a means to distinguish 'good' from 'bad' enterprises.[78] It was not difficult to join in the condemnation of theoreticians who endlessly repeated 'basic, general conclusions' and who won applause for 'generally correct, blanket propositions' without providing useful conclusions for those involved in practice.[79]

There had, however, been an attempt to provide a specific alternative, although its practicability is questionable. The proposal, in the approach to the Central Committee meeting, was to cut investment by enough to create a buyers' market and thereby overcome the inflationary pressures. The belief was that this would not hit living standards. One problem, however, was that, if priority to the most deserving sectors was to be maintained, then the scope for cuts was really restricted to the traditional heavy industries: some economists were reported to be advocating reductions of more than the total volume of investment in fuel, energy, metallurgy and engineering.[80] The leadership's view was that substantial cuts, hitting projects under construction, would threaten long-term prospects, leading at once to a run down in the construction industry and unused capacity in heavy engineering. In view of the long-term nature of trade agreements with socialist countries, this could not rapidly be shifted to exports. Restoring equilibrium therefore appeared as a task that would take time and that could not be achieved by the new system.

There was unhappiness at this conclusion. To judge from published comments, the crucial question was whether a milder deflation, which could be achieved through undifferentiated financial instruments, could achieve equilibrium without the serious dangers Černík had outlined. Šik accepted the policy, albeit calling for a more rapid structural shift – with investment tied to profitability – and showing less fear at stopping projects under construction. His theoretical work argued strongly that disequilibrium was an inherent feature of the centralised system and he wrote encouragingly of freer price movements after a restrictive credit policy had created a 'mild excess supply'.[81] How this could have worked with the arbitrarily variable levels of profitability remains unclear.

Turek too found it impossible to deny that there were many arguments for what had been done.[82] He still could not recommend free prices, but he saw real dangers in the centre retaining a permanent grip on them and thought harsher restrictions on credits and state grants could restore equilibrium.[83] He thought enterprises would be forced to seek out export markets, so that restoring equilibrium on the domestic market would improve the external balance too. Most controversially of all, he acknowledged that such a policy would lead to 'some social problems' such as 'a certain transitional unemployment'. Rejection of this he characterised as 'an ideological problem from the old conception of social certainty' which had for so long been presented 'as an achievement of socialism'. It would, then, need strong measures from the centre, plus 'active ideological preparation'. He did not foresee 'general unemployment', nor 'crisis phenomena' such as factory closures. Instead, there would be measures to help a rapid transition to other jobs. This was ridiculed as 'our own, little, socialist unemployment' which was not to be allowed.[84]

The fundamental problem, however, was that the transition to the 'economic model' was proving far more difficult than its advocates had realised. Turek and others wanted equilibrium restored by means of price, tax and credit policies. As he acknowledged, the price reform had created only a weak basis as it left a price system that was still essentially irrational. Based purely on cost-plus, prices did not even correspond to Marx's notion of 'socially useful labour', which depends on the most efficient production technique. Neither did they reflect world prices which should have been influencing the allocation of investment.[85] Rationality could therefore only be achieved by interventions from the centre, contradicting the criterion of profitability derived from existing prices.

Criticisms were therefore always cautious and hedged with reservations. There was some disagreement with the decision in July to limit wage increases by relating them to growth in an enterprise's productivity measured in terms of gross output. Not only was the old, discredited indicator creeping back, but this also appeared as a retreat from allowing 'the uneven distribution of income'. This, it was claimed, should have been accepted as 'a positive fact', while controls over wages could only hamper the creation of an innovative climate.[86] The danger here was that variations in profitability were too arbitrary to justify differences in earnings. One enterprise had even managed a profit rate of over 100% purely because of the price changes, while some had suffered during the process without any obvious justification in terms of their behaviour.[87]

These cases gained publicity and created a sense of injustice. Nevertheless, the effect on wages was not usually very substantial and was often evened out between enterprises by the associations. Whether the few cases of wages increasing by 20% were really a threat remains an open question. Some research apparently suggested that these bonuses often were justified, although others strongly contested that conclusion.[88] Novotný, however, was always unhappy about easy pay rises[89] and fears of disequilibrium gave his view very wide acceptability.

There were several conflicting assessments of the economic policy adopted after May 1967. To some it was a very sensitive and sober approach, recognising just how long the transition was to take.[90] Černík insisted that it was not a matter of reactions from one day to another, but rather 'a new strategy for the party's economic policy'. Others, however, were clearly getting frustrated with the slow pace of change. Having thought they were over the top of the hill, they saw old instruments reappearing. There undeniably was 'conservative' opposition, but even those in the leadership who were likely to be sympathetic could not be convinced to move more rapidly. Nevertheless, the stagnation of the economic reform was to be a powerful factor in the strengthening of opposition to the Novotný leadership.

7   1968

1968 began with the Central Committee removing Novotný and electing the competent but seemingly unexceptional 46-year-old Slovak party leader Alexander Dubček as First Secretary.[1] Much of the argument centred on the undesirability of the same man being party leader and head of state simultaneously. It was unclear at first whether the new leadership intended the major changes that swept through political life that year and made January 1968 far more than just a simple change in leadership. The previous years had, however, seen the gradual development of a very specific situation. The key element was not the blocking of reform by a conservative leadership. In fact, Novotný was characterised by chronic indecisiveness – possibly reflecting recognition of his own personal inadequacies and fears at the general direction of changes in the Soviet Union – alternating between acts of petty repression and implicit encouragement for ideas for reform.[2] These developed in the context of Czechoslovakia's uniquely strong heritage of socialist ideas – the Communist Party had been the largest in the world relative to the country's population at the time of its foundation and could claim massive backing in February 1948 – which had left even many high-ranking officials with a genuine commitment to their professed ideals. The change of leadership therefore opened the floodgates for a movement which, despite enormous and inevitable diversity, was essentially directed towards creating a democratised version of socialism.

Conflict with the Soviet Union, as made clear in publications at the time, centred around the related issues of the leading role of the party, interpreted as an unquestionable right to absolute power, and the possibility that Czechoslovakia might choose to pursue more independence in its international orientation. The economic reform was of secondary importance, although it was later to be linked in the Soviet perception with the reform movement as a whole such that the

Czechoslovak events coincided with an unannounced defeat for economic reform in the USSR.[3] In fact, 1968 did see major changes in the nature of Czechoslovakia's economic reform as it was enriched by political democratisation so that, at last, trade unions and other representative bodies were to play an active role.

Above all, the party's position was being redefined. The question of whether it should control everything or step back completely appeared irrelevant in the new situation with party organisations taking political initiatives in formulating ideas for democratisation. It was heading towards a different kind of leading role which was to be won not by repression, or by a constitutional guarantee of the ultimate right to overrule all other bodies, but by the strength and popularity of its own ideas. Such a perspective was embodied in the new leadership's first significant policy statement, the Action Programme produced in April which, despite its name, contained a general theoretical overview of the ideas for democratisation that had been maturing in intellectual circles in the mid-1960s. Power was no longer to be 'monopolised either by a single party or by a coalition of parties'. Instead it was to be 'open to all political organisations of the people'.[4]

Although he misread the external constraints, Dubček's personality matched the new internal situation perfectly. His basic philosophy was to persuade and trust people and to reach agreement whenever possible. His ideals seemed particularly credible in view of his perceived personal genuineness and lack of any hint of demagogy. At the theoretical level he saw the root of the inner-party conflict in evaluations of the social and economic situation after the completion of the 'foundations of socialism'. His view was that a new stage of 'non-antagonistic relations' led to the need to develop a new 'political system that would correspond to that new situation'.[5] It was to be a system that would win people for active participation overcoming the widespread apathy and growing passivity that he saw as the greatest weakness of the existing system. Many elements, such as the need for trade unions to play a more active role in defending workers' interests and influencing management, could be found in party documents of preceding years. Reasons for the absence of real progress had to be sought 'in the area of politics'.[6]

Despite a rather low-key presentation, he accepted it as a 'courageous' policy which would enable 'Czechoslovakia, with its democratic tradition, to contribute significantly to socialist ideas and to their attractiveness in the world'. It was also immensely popular at home. The simple philosophy of trusting people led at once to freer international contacts and a huge escalation in travel to capitalist countries: there were over 900 000 tourist trips in 1968 and 1969 compared with little over 100 000 in 1964. There was also a speedy end to press censorship which unleashed criticism against the old guard. Party organisations no longer passively reflected directives from above: instead they became the first major vehicle for putting immediate pressure on the leadership. Many quickly joined demands for Novotný's resignation as President – apart from other failings he had been able to block investigations of the show trials of the early 1950s which had been vital to his own promotion – and he went at the end of March. A new government was appointed on 8 April with Černík as Prime Minister.

There was no doubting the growing popularity of the new leadership which rose even higher when it publicly resisted Soviet attempts to stem the tide of internal change. An opinion poll in July already showed 51% expressing trust in the party and only 4% claiming outright distrust: only 23% reported trust before January 1968 which was barely above the proportion of party members.[7] A point frequently emphasised by party leaders was that they heard practically no demands for a return to capitalism: again, opinion polls confirmed this with figures around 90% for the further development of socialism. This rapid turnround from widespread apathy to support in general for a reformed model of socialism must be judged an extraordinary achievement. There was a widespread desire for the ideals of socialism and of the Communist movement to work and, at last, that latent hope seemed realisable with the new leadership.

There were doubts and scope for conflict once those very general principles were to be put into practice. For economic policy one of the key questions was the position of the working class, with the old guard trying to imply that reform was a betrayal of traditional supporters. They could hope for some backing with one opinion poll in May suggesting that 21% saw no benefit from the reform for workers and peasants.[8] There was a potential conflict with the strong body of opinion advocating 'delevelling' and other measures to reverse some of the perceived injustices against other strata in society committed in the name of the dictatorship of the proletariat.

More significant for the general direction of development were very strong pressures, especially from cultural journals, for taking political change further. Although treated with caution by the leadership, not least because selected sentences were being used by the Soviet leadership as evidence of impending 'counter-revolution', they were getting a good hearing within the party. There was no immediate likelihood of competing parties, particularly as the Communist Party was seen to be at the centre of initiatives for change, but, according to one poll, a clear majority of members agreed that contested elections between independent parties – rather than just democracy within their own party – was the only true guarantee of socialist democracy.[9] The point seemed self-evident outside the party, but it was also logical in a country where party activists' experiences suggested that they had more to fear from uncontrolled state power than from their own people. Zdeněk Mlynář, the rising ideologist who wrote the sections of the Action Programme concerned with the political system, privately foresaw ultimately freely contested elections.[10] The time for that had not yet come, but a survey of 40 000 delegates to district conferences in August showed 75% convinced that the party should no longer be directing state and economic organs: they were moving away from the conception of the party as a holder of all power. Not surprisingly, almost 90% expressed dissatisfaction with personnel changes[11] that still left many of the old guard in power.

The issue was to come to the fore at a special party congress organised for September for which delegates had already been elected. Some of those people who had still to be removed arranged with the Soviet leadership for a military invasion by five Warsaw Pact armies starting on 20 August. It was met with mass demonstrations of opposition but no military resistance. It did not mean an immediate end to the reform movement. Thanks to popular pressure isolating the intended new leadership, Dubček was released from Soviet captivity and allowed to remain in office subject to imposed conditions until April 1969. Even then his replacement was Husák, a man who had been imprisoned in the 1950s and only found a place in politics again in 1968.

The hope continued for some time that he would be able to follow Kádár, the man who led Hungary out of 1956 while preventing a return to the Stalinist past, and save some of the reforms. The difference may have been that in Hungary those in power were genuinely frightened and saw the need to mend their ways. In Czechoslovakia, where there was no hint of the authority of the state collapsing, there was no reason to doubt the possibility of restoring the old power structure.[12] Despite the initial appearance of almost unanimous opposition to the invasion, there was a very small group that supported it and a far larger number who were prepared to accept the new reality. The period after August therefore saw the gradual removal of supporters of reform.

Political barriers to economic reform

Advocates of economic reform had increasingly seen 'not the obsolete price system but the obsolete political system'[13] as the major obstacle to their efforts and therefore actively joined a coalition pushing for Novotný's removal. Ideas on the relationship between political and economic issues were fairly simple, but it seemed clear that the way should now be open for a faster pace of economic reform. It was natural to assume that 'freeing the economy from administrative directive methods of management' would run into trouble if those methods persisted elsewhere.[14] The reform had met barriers 'in the political sphere', but the necessary political conditions for further progress were 'now being created'.[15]

There were theoretical problems in linking democracy and the market. The obvious argument was that the market allowed for independence at lower levels and could take power away from an existing bureaucracy.[16] One of the frequent criticisms of the old leadership, however, was that it had lacked the courage to take the necessary unpopular decisions to raise labour morale and overcome structural weaknesses.[17] Linking 'bureaucratic-directive forms' and 'egalitarianism in pay' was a logically consistent way to show the political system holding back reform. Apart from weaknesses in the argument, it changes substantially the relationships of social groups to economic reform. Hardly anybody was harmed by an end to 'directive methods of management' in the media or in cultural policy. In the economic field there was the potential for much more scepticism, if not outright opposition.

Although the economic section of the Action Programme, written by Šik, reiterated the general principles of combining plan and market, economic reform received a low priority during 1968. Mlynář later saw that as a weakness: he complained of the dominance of 'a diverse mixture of predominantly general political problems'. At the time he had warned strongly against a rush of spontaneous workers' demands, but later argued that the leadership should have encouraged working-class pressure to bring attention back to economic issues.[18] The trouble was partly that working-class pressure could conflict with existing ideas on reform and partly that those ideas were still unclear and at times impracticable.

In the freer atmosphere there were a few attempts at outright criticism, with accusations that changes had already caused the economy enormous losses.[19] Generally, however, discussion was firmly dominated by the advocates of reform. The general objective was to overcome the 'inconsistencies and limitations' in past measures which left the market obstructed by subsidies and price anomalies,[20] but it was still unclear how to achieve this. Turek wanted freer trade to encourage competition, but he acknowledged the dangers in view of Czechoslovakia's low level of competitiveness. He wanted market relations to overcome long-term weaknesses, but acknowledged that the centre had to step in to overcome inflationary pressures which were themselves the result of these long-term weaknesses. His solution was for the centre to announce a 'binding programme of gradual transition towards free trade':[21] that would frighten enterprises into improving themselves and they could be given help and encouragement to do so. The government actually did talk of opening the economy and achieving convertibility within five to seven years.[22] The trouble with making such a target binding is that it would need to be very realistic before enterprises would believe it: a deadline pulled out of a hat frightens nobody because the centre could be expected to end up bargaining and compromising until nothing changed.

Considerably more was said in this period on foreign trade, with the obvious suggestion that it should be associated with enterprises' calculation of profitability rather than exchanges in physical terms.[23] This raised the sensitive question of the organisation of the CMEA and its persistent failure to satisfy Czechoslovakia's hope for genuine specialisation and integration of manufacturing industry.

Even more controversial were government hopes of a hard-currency loan.[24] In view of the belief that the new system would bring improvements, this seemed a possible way to accelerate structural change and modernisation while minimising domestic inflationary pressures. Šik talked first of asking the Soviet Union.[25] Its attitude towards structural aspects of Czechoslovakia's reform was never clear, but it might well have been sceptical and uneasy at a reorientation towards exporting consumer goods to all markets.[26] Šik was soon referring to $300–500m from the West with no political conditions to be allowed.[27] Comments from the USSR suggest a failure to appreciate the economic argument at the time. Although they too were soon seeking credits from capitalist countries, and better relations with Western Europe, this independent initiative was actually portrayed as part of a deliberate political reorientation towards West Germany.[28]

This, anyway, was an idea for the future which could not overcome the absence of a concrete programme for reform. While a number of economists, such as Turek, were formulating general principles in more detail and with more clarity, those in charge of the economy were taking a slightly different approach. Černík, whose view had for a long time been of the centre setting general structural changes while detailed improvements depended on the pressure of the market on enterprises, could point to the great success in the reallocation of investment.[29] He was for continuing gradually putting pressure on enterprises and lazy workers, albeit 'with more determination than before':[30] there was still to be no question of allowing unemployment.

The new government's programme in April put the emphasis on structure – referring to the effects of the embargo, of the cold war and of the 'dogmatic' conception of giving priority to heavy industry – and saw as the second major problem the 'tensions' in all economic relationships. It even asked for parliament's understanding as the problem was 'seemingly contradictory': a solution to one problem could hamper solving the other.[31] Significantly, there was no claim that reform provided an immediate solution.

Alongside this uncertainty over policy was organisational weakness in economic management. Šik became Deputy Prime Minister with responsibility for the reform, but his efforts increasingly went into political battles. An Economic Council was formed, but it was not to be a new central organ with its own apparatus standing outside the government. Instead, it was to be a committee of those government ministers most concerned with economic issues.[32] That left the previous powerful sectional interests untouched. Moreover, its remit was as an advisory body coordinating economic policy, preparing the basic economic decisions and working out measures for the current running of the economy.

This was at just the time when one point of unanimity among advocates of reform seemed to be the need for 'the existence of a programmatically strong centre'.[33] Instead, with the downgrading of the State Planning Commission, there was going to be weaker direction than ever before. The reasons for this, apart from the strength of ministerial interests, may have related to personalities: Šik was said to be distrusted by Černík and Dubček[34] but, by making him no more than an ordinary member of the Economic Council, his government post was effectively devalued. Another related factor may have been policy differences: the Council was chaired by former party official Štrougal, by then a Deputy Prime Minister, while its secretary was Komárek, an economist who consistently saw the main weaknesses in sectoral structure.[35] The result, however, was a body which could not solve the fundamental problem for economic policy. As Komárek put it, there was no 'real, concrete, economic strategy for Czechoslovakia which would realistically solve its problems and ensure the necessary consolidation'.[36]

By August confusion and disorientation were said to be rife throughout the economic apparatus. People did not know what the centre was doing and they did not know the relationship between organs. At the same time, economists seemed to have 'lost the strength' to exchange views and discuss. The danger was that even when the political situation became 'more or less normal', they would still have no solutions to the immediate problems.[37]

Growing scepticism was voiced throughout the summer of 1968 with references to the reimposition of wage and other regulations, which appeared as arbitrary panic measures, from mid-1967 onwards having ruined the reform. It seemed natural to many party and union organisations to point a finger at the same people in charge.[38] Possibly even more serious were growing public fears over the state of the economy. A number of factors probably contributed to this. One was a belief, although formal censorship had been abolished, that not all information was available and that could suggest that something was wrong: there were frequent acknowledgements of calls for the government to state openly what the real condition of the economy was.[39] A second factor must have been the receptiveness to critical comments, after being fed in the past with propaganda of success that was clearly exaggerated. Moreover, advocates of reform naturally found themselves criticising: otherwise they could hardly make a powerful case for changes that were going to hurt some people. A third factor could have been the awareness that the reform was not working and that the government could not produce a clear policy.

On his appointment as Prime Minister, Černík was confronted with criticisms both of past responsibility for the 'steel' conception, which he did not accept, and also of encouraging unjustified optimism by giving too positive an account of the economic situation.[40] A detailed reply was soon provided on some of the specific concerns.

One major issue was the state of international payments. The information available confirmed that the country was not heavily in debt. It was in fact a net creditor albeit suffering from short-term debts to advanced countries alongside long-term credits to developing and socialist countries. An even bigger area of concern was the possibility of a repeat of the 1953 currency reform. It was again made clear that such fears were unfounded.[41] The government produced a brief and objective statement – largely confirming what could have been gleaned from specialist journals – asserting that 'our economy is a long way from a state of crisis'.[42] It kept promising, but never delivered, a detailed analysis.

Šik, however, gave a series of television talks in June and July which was possibly the best popular presentation ever of the case for reform.[43] He referred back to the ideas of a Czechoslovak road as an opportunity smothered by centralisation and by the structural changes which he could now openly blame on the relationship with the Soviet Union. He showed by detailed comparisons of technology and living conditions that, contrary to the picture of success so often presented by a few selected indicators, Czechoslovakia had not done particularly well since 1948. His account could appear negative, as he referred to weaknesses rather than successes, but he was not pointing towards any particular disaster. He saw good prospects, with a perspective of achieving convertibility and hence an end to financial restrictions on foreign travel – the usual allowance for a tourist trip was £4 – and then of catching up with Western Europe. The process was not to be that painful either. Some prices would rise and others fall with the gradual standardisation of turnover tax rates. There would almost certainly be some 'pockets of short-term unemployment' while redundant workers were being trained:[44] although this seemed to go against the constitutional guarantee of the right to work, it is difficult to see any alternative if genuine flexibility was to be achieved.

Šik's broadcasts had an enormous impact. They amplified his previous characterisation of the situation as 'serious but by no means hopeless'[45] and were accompanied by warnings from the Economic Council of disequilibrium getting worse and hence of the need for tough policies in 1969.[46] The effect of all this was revealed in an opinion poll at the start of July showing 53% seeing the situation as either hopeless or very critical with no improvement for a long time. A massive majority of those with an opinion expected to lose out of the reform and fully 43% foresaw a substantial significant rise in living standards either never or after more than five years. Only 1% saw the prospect of such a rise within one year[47] which is considerably less even than the proportion of households becoming car owners for the first time during 1968.

It is true that very few were predicting, or behaving as if they predicted, outright disaster, and the overwhelming majority in other polls named foreign interference as a far bigger danger,[48] but this is a remarkably pessimistic view in a period characterised by rapidly rising living standards as new goods – especially cars – were becoming more widely available. The general atmosphere *was* one of optimism and to some extent opinion poll results may have reflected a new-found confidence, such that people felt able to make negative comments. Nevertheless, some public confusion, uncertainty and nervousness may have contributed to the ease with which the economic reform could be killed in the 1970s.

Another investment boom

Alongside its possible impact on public opinion, indecisiveness from the centre had a more direct impact on economic policy. Pressure for more investment was already very strong at the end of 1967 while the leadership even warned that there could be an emergency cut in new starts in the new year.[49] Instead, with only 10% of associations satisfied with their investment allocation, some were trying to get round restrictions by giving investment another name.[50] One major stimulus for this pressure must have been the easy financial position of enterprises after the price reform.[51]

A remarkable feature was that in some sectors preparation was under way at the start of the year to begin projects that were not being allowed.[52] The government sounded tough, reiterating its structural policy and talking of 'sharply limiting even justified demands'.[53] The reality already seemed different. The trouble may partly have been that the centre could not fully control lower levels. The volume of projects under construction was consistently above the intended level because projects were extended while under construction, enterprises were failing to stick to their contracts and too many projects were started.[54] Tensions, however, could not all be blamed on lower levels.

It seemed that the structure inherited from the past itself generated pressures for investment which would then reproduce that structure.[55] Thus on 13 March the government yielded and allowed two new metallurgy projects in Kladno. There were, however, very strong complaints, backed up with arguments that there could soon even be surplus steel capacity.[56] Shortly beforehand Černík had agreed to the redevelopment of the Nejedlý mine, also in Kladno, and he was again accused of naïvety in diverting resources towards something which could not possibly be the top priority.[57]

Political democratisation as such was not the cause of the problem. It rather created scope for public opposition to the results of wrangling behind closed doors. It also brought out into the open the pressure under which Černík had been. The director of the Kladno steel works explained that the government had been convinced of the case for investment when they came round the old steel works. This, he claimed, would actually make it profitable, while he was unconvinced by vague talk of alternative jobs after closure, which seemed the likely alternative.[58] The union organisation put the case even more forcefully: they were aware of public opinion moving against them but had to speak for 8000 steel-workers' jobs. The crux of their case was that continual delays and low investment in the past – while others had been benefiting – was the root cause of low productivity. Now, it seemed, they were to be disadvantaged in the new system too.[59]

Their determination could have been strengthened by the long-running battle for the nearby Nejedlý mine. The party organisation, having pushed the case throughout the mid-1960s, now saw its prime responsibility as defending the security of 7000 miners and also of maintaining their living standards. They were not tempted by suggestions of alternative employment in a pharmaceutical factory, which anyway would have paid less. They asked to be made an exception, with calculations showing likely future profitability, and a clear announcement was made in May that the redevelopment would continue.[60]

The possibility of closure was always a sensitive issue, and even led to short protest strikes in a few cases. Miners in particular felt insecure as the government was talking of using more oil and gas from the Soviet Union. Union organisations from North Bohemia, claiming that the policy of closing unprofitable mines was hitting them harder than others, indicated that they could resist closures even to the extent of strike action.[61] The management meanwhile presented the case for open-cast brown coal as the best basis for the immediate future of electricity generation.[62] They had some grounds for concern as projections for electricity demand for 1980 were being cut drastically: they were still considerably above the level that was to be achieved. In fact, the general case for brown coal was never questioned and there was no labour surplus in mining. Fears in the mines of Ostrava-Karviná were unjustified too, although the 1980 target for steel was cut from 24 million tonnes to 13 million tonnes. Some even suggested – wrongly as it turned out – that this was more than could possibly be sold on internal or external markets.[63]

The best guarantee against closure always seemed to be new investment. These fears and the resulting political pressures therefore helped push the allocation of investment back towards the existing sectoral structure: heavy industry accounted for only 15% of new starts in 1967 but was back up to 20% in 1968 and 30% in 1969.[64] Moreover, by yielding to these pressures the centre itself contributed to a 29% increase in the volume of projects started in 1968. The problem was not just the easy financial position of enterprises. In chemicals and heavy industry the government was allowing projects after which the bank had no choice but to grant credits even if it did not have the resources to cover them. Money was therefore reduced again to a purely formal role of confirming decisions taken on the basis of other criteria.[65]

There was some disagreement in the summer of 1968 as to how serious this situation was. A mid-year assessment referred to 'a state of deep disequilibrium'.[66] The good work of May 1967 seemed to have been undone and without equilibrium in investment the reform could never be effective. Some were beginning to suggest that the dangers might be overstated,[67] fearing possibly that this could be an excuse to strengthen the centre's powers. Others produced arguments similar to those used in 1967 to indicate again that investment was the major problem.[68] The familiar threats were heard again later in the year of the need to cut new starts in industry so that any increase in total investment could be devoted to housing.[69] Despite Novotný's promises at the start of the decade, the wait for a flat in Prague was around seven years and the ratio of housing units to households had actually fallen from 54% in 1961 to 50%.

An end to 'delevelling'?

Political pressure was even more obvious in another aspect of possible disequilibrium – the growing fears of a 'wages explosion'. Trade unions had for years played no independent role but shortly after Dubček's election as First Secretary basic organisations began holding workplace meetings. Sometimes the resolutions passed supported official positions, but the overall effect was to shift the priorities in incomes policy away from 'delevelling' towards long-standing sectoral differentials, towards pensions and towards helping the lowest paid.

The extent of suspicions about 'delevelling' began to emerge from a number of opinion surveys. One in mining, carried out purely as an exercise to reveal what problems there might be, produced striking results. A significant minority (almost 20%) effectively argued that there should be no differentials. More generally, there was a wide-spread feeling that differentials among manual workers were already too large. This view was less strongly held by the top grade, but about a third still favoured a significant reduction in inequality.[70]

Mining, of course, had for long been a favoured sector. The results, however, gave no more support to the 'delevelling' case in consumer goods, as revealed by a survey of attitudes in six selected enterprises. The method used was to ask what employees felt would be a just reward to positions above and below their own. There was little variation in their opinions which suggested that the existing situation was more or less acceptable. In fact, if anything, it seemed that non-manual workers would be more likely to accept a reduction than to demand an increase in their differential. Manual workers also tended to favour a reduction in foremen's relative earnings, although their pay was only just above the level of the highest manual workers. The obvious conclusion was that 'delevelling' would not be easy. 'People are used to equality and they see it as one of the benefits of a socialist society', it was pointed out.[71]

Very occasionally it seemed that dissatisfaction with pay rose slightly with earnings.[72] Generally, however, surveys showed about 40% dissatisfied with higher figures for the lower paid. Only among those with higher education could a small majority be found for the view that qualifications are not adequately rewarded.[73] Even then discontent was usually mild. In the Škoda engineering enterprise, for example, a clear majority of managers expressed general satisfaction with their pay. This surprised those conducting the survey as under 2% of managers were earning more than three times the average for all employees in the enterprise. They seemed, however, to put an enormous effort into their jobs, working up to twelve hours every day.[74]

Perhaps most surprising of all for the advocates of 'delevelling' was the discovery that the good and experienced workers were especially suspicious, seeing it as an attempt to benefit a narrow group of professionals.[75] In May 1968 the new trade union leadership began to express a similar view in public. Having only a year previously accepted 'delevelling' as a prerequisite for raising productivity – they even suggested changes in pricing policy to allow for a clearer differ-entiation in consumption patterns[76] – they now accepted as justified some criticisms of high rewards for managers and argued that 'delevelling' in practice was benefiting many bad workers.[77]

These, however, were secondary issues for the unions representing large sections of the economy. Their first priority was the unjustified differentiation between various sectors. This had sometimes been diverted into an argument about alleged excessive equality: doctors suffered a fall in money wages while prices rose from 1957 to 1965 and could see their qualifications undervalued, with pay only 53% above the average industrial wage. The real issue, however, was the under-valuing of the whole sector with serious labour shortages at lower levels of qualification.[78] In some industries demands were sometimes backed up with talk of strike action. The case was pressed by the new trade union chairman Poláček who, as the former Minister of the Engineering Industry, may have felt under pressure to prove that he was not just another stooge. The government's response was very careful: the demands 'could not be given a blanket rejection, but obviously not a blanket acceptance either'.[79] They needed a concrete ordering of priorities.

As Černík pointed out, they had to be very careful in responding to the greatest concentration of trade union demands at any time since 1945 without unleashing further inflationary pressures.[80] The leader-ship's desire, however, was 'to win the trust of the workers'.[81] They therefore agreed in July to the most pressing wage rises, which were judged to be railways, food and the consumer goods industries: the latter were intended soon to reach the industrial average.[82]

By making these demands the trade unions were implicitly chang-ing their role within society. They still saw themselves as a 'respon-sible' force. They fully accepted that there was no point in raising pay ahead of productivity, but they were no longer going to behave as 'transmission belts' merely repeating policies decided on by the party leadership. There was, they believed, scope for them to play a more active role as representatives of the working people.

The key to this was to be a joint agreement between the government and the trade unions. It was negotiated throughout the latter part of 1968 and signed on 11 November.[83] It did not represent any major shift in the stated aims of social policy, but there had been clear differences of emphasis during the discussion. It covered a wide range of issues affecting living standards, although it was accepted that not everything could be achieved at once. Some changes would be implemented in gradual stages.

There were proposals on housing policy, safety and hygiene at work, on raising the lowest pensions and family allowances and for increasing maternity leave to two years. There was also a lot of concern about wage and price policies. On the latter, the aim was to ensure that any inflationary tendencies associated with the economic reform did not harm the poorest in society. Thus the unions saw themselves playing a major role in protecting the least vocal sections of the population, such as pensioners, while within enterprises they were arguing for general cost-of-living increases to protect the lowest paid. To this end, they insisted on a continuation of controls on the prices of a large number of basic consumer goods. The unions had clearly moved from their 1967 position of supporting greater differentiation in consumption.

Proposals on wages included selective increases in transport, which faced special problems, alongside work over the next year to agree on a long-term conception of pay differentiation over the 1971–5 period. Immediate increases were also agreed for different sectors of the economy for 1969 which would continue to give more to consumer goods and make major headway in improving the positions of health and education. Table 7.1 shows what was achieved in industry. Workers' pay in previously non-favoured sectors did rise for a time, but not long enough to achieve parity with the rest of industry. The net effect was to reduce overall inequality and to strengthen fears of excess spending power, an issue pursued below.

Towards enterprise independence?

Trade unions also became involved in one of the most fundamental issues of the economic reform giving a sudden burst of life to the previously stunted debate on the status of the enterprise by tying it to democratisation. There had been much discussion at least from mid-1966,[84] but nothing significant was published until the end of 1967. The issue followed logically from ideas on economic reform as enterprises had to have 'separation from the state apparatus' if they were to be active agents within a market system.[85] Practice was already confirming this in the persistence of administratively created monopolies.

The danger of monopoly was publicly acknowledged. Some economists concluded that the degree of concentration was simply too much for a market to exert pressure on enterprises.[86] Others emphasised that perfect competition could never become a reality and accepted the case for considerable concentration and specialisation.[87] Galbraith's notion of countervailing power may even have encouraged confidence that a strong monopoly in internal trade, with a material interest in selling, could keep a check on monopolies in

Table 7.1. *Percentage increases in pay for manual workers and 'engineering-technical employees' in 1968, 1969 and 1970 over the preceding year*

	Manual workers			'Engineering-technical employees'		
	1968	1969	1970	1968	1969	1970
All industry	6.3	6.1	4.7	5.5	4.8	1.3
of which						
Mining	6.9	6.1	3.8	5.6	4.8	−2.0
Chemicals	5.8	5.7	5.4	4.3	3.0	0.5
Engineering	4.9	5.7	5.6	4.5	4.1	1.5
Textiles	8.6	7.1	3.9	6.5	7.1	2.3
Leather		8.4	4.8		7.8	0.1
Garments		7.3	3.6		6.4	1.4
Food	12.0	7.0	3.8	11.3	10.4	2.2
Construction	5.8	7.1	4.5	6.2	7.1	0.6
State farms	9.4	8.3	1.1	13.2	6.1	−2.5
State forestry	9.4	7.4	6.6	13.9	7.0	1.0
Railways	21.2	10.2	0.1	11.1	10.7	0.3
Road transport	7.6	12.5	1.9	4.4	10.0	−1.8

Sources: Práce a mzda, XVII p. 166; XVIII, p. 129; and XIX, p. 151.

production.[88] All of this, however, was a secondary issue. The problem did not seem to be market structure in the normal sense and neither was it shortage giving producers an automatic advantage: stocks of many goods were rising precisely because they could not be sold.

The issue was rather the persistence of the hierarchical administrative structure which had been built up to serve 'the logic of the directive plan'.[89] 'Hidden directives' were experienced by many enterprises – nine out of twelve surveyed in the clothing industry and 29 out of 70 in the food industry – with around half in these consumer goods sectors clearly favouring abolition or restriction of powers of the next level up the hierarchy. Despite formal changes in the system, the same people with the same habits were said to be blocking the logic of reform.[90] The freedom to choose customer or supplier had changed nothing: customers typically had to accept what they were offered even if other producers could easily have provided more appropriate goods. This was put down partly to inertia from buying organisations –

regional franchising in the food industry persisted because it did not seem worth the effort to hunt around for better suppliers – and partly to lack of initiative from producers to challenge each other. Their reluctance is understandable as they were frequently part of the same organisational structure with higher levels allocating production between enterprises and, obviously, also appointing their directors.[91]

Thus a genuine socialist market system requires a definition of who is to be the entrepreneur. It needs, it was increasingly felt, a complete transformation of power relationships between enterprises and central bodies 'to create two separate spheres . . . between which there is no relationship of subservience'.[92] This argument linked up with pressure from some enterprises to break free from their associations. The government accepted that integration had often been based purely on administrative convenience so that many associations had 'no economic foundation'.[93] There were some who clearly disagreed even with that criticism. They pressed for inactivity on the pretext of opposition to the 'atomisation' of the economy to achieve 'domestic competition at any price'.[94] Others were much more eager to see internal competition, but the government's preference was to proceed cautiously, to beware of profitable enterprises trying to break free for purely financial reasons and to put off any general reorganisation when there was so much else on the agenda.[95] Leading managers in associations were happy with the proposal for only very exceptional changes before January 1969.[96]

Many difficult questions were left unanswered particularly as to the form integration between enterprises was to take. It was intended to base this on voluntary agreements between independent units so that they could arrange their own cooperation and specialisation. The possibility of joint stock companies or the sale and purchase of shares were mentioned but not explored.[97] A group of young economists, who had been studying orthodox Western theory, became convinced during 1968 of the need for a genuine 'capital market',[98] but Šik and many others had not been interested. The problem ultimately was to find a mechanism to overcome the persistent fragmentation of industry. A full capital market could, at least in theory, facilitate the speedy elimination of backward technology while the inertia of vested interests within the existing system was undoubtedly a barrier to the most effective specialisation.

The most explosive issue at the time, however, was self-management, which fitted logically alongside any notion of giving enterprises independence from higher levels. The suggestion came from economists, one of whom published the suggestions for a co-existence of state enterprises, cooperatives and self-managed enterprises answerable to an elected council which appoints the director but is subject to various legal and financial constraints.[99] The new appeal of this was the obvious link to democratisation. The Action Programme referred vaguely to combining the traditions of the works councils of 1945–8 with modern management experience to create 'democratic bodies' in enterprises as the ultimate authority over the director but with otherwise 'limited' powers over enterprise administration.[100]

Up until then the principal strength of the reform movement had been among intellectuals. They now found plenty of workers clearly suspicious of who was exercising the 'leading role' and willing to dismiss economic reform as no more than a shallow trick that would leave the same people in charge.[101] There seemed a real danger of the movement failing to link up with the everyday concerns of workers many of whom were said to be unconvinced that 'socialist democracy' would mean any improvement for them.[102] There was, then, a very strong desire to show that democratisation meant something in workplaces too beyond just the scope for wage demands. Economic issues had influenced political change and now it seemed the debt could be repaid with the creation of conditions for deeper democracy in the economy. The precise form of participation was still uncertain but 'the principle is clear'.[103]

Discussion among specialists revealed a range of views revolving around the place of specialist managers and the authority of higher levels in the apparatus. Doubters could produce some very sensible objections to self-management, such as the argument that workers' representatives would always be at a disadvantage compared with better informed specialists with access to the necessary details: the result would be a false impression of being a joint owner.[104] This is close to Yugoslav experience. Others complained that it was an invention of 'the representatives of theory' while 'the people did not feel the problem so intensely'. It anyway seemed premature to push this new issue when the courage was still lacking to solve many other economic questions and when Yugoslav experience had not been particularly positive.[105]

Some were far more favourable. By the early summer, ideas for elected councils were beginning to emerge from enterprises, not necessarily 'from below'[106] in the sense of manual workers, but frequently reflecting dissatisfaction with top management. A major stimulus was the view that incompetents were holding high positions thanks to political considerations. Figures showed only 22% of directors to be graduates compared with 30% in Poland where the turmoil of 1956 helped towards better qualified management.[107] It is hardly surprising that there was always opposition from some managers, albeit tempered by another view that recognised the need to link employee administration with modern management methods.[108] One of the major issues was to remain 'cadre policy' and the desire to remove bad management was one of the causes, alongside wages and opposition to closure, of the small number of strikes and strike threats before 20 August.[109] Self-management was later condemned as an attempt to do away with 'the leading role of the party':[110] it certainly was recognised that party bodies clinging to the right of appointment helped maintain the existing hierarchies and were incompatible with democracy in the economy and with genuine enterprise independence.[111]

The first concrete proposals brought together the notion of an independent organ with the need for specialist managers. Thus from an employee in the rubber enterprise in Kralupy came a proposal for a 10–15 member council, elected by direct secret ballot and meeting twice a year to discuss basic issues of development, organisation and cadre policy. Its role was to be quite distinct from that of the party, of which 20% of employees were members, or of the trade union which was concerned with the division of available funds and with taking up specific complaints against the director. There was not even any need for an immediate change in the law as the director could formally be appointed by the higher organ 'on the recommendation' of the management council.[112]

The main practical alternative was for a council predominantly nominated by the centre; this was justified by the fear either that the quality of management would be threatened or that an enterprise council would defend sectional interests against those of the whole of society. Šik, having shown no interest in the issue before, was soon convinced that only 10–30% of the councils' members should be outside specialists and even they should be chosen by elected members. He also saw a case for the state, or a bank that had given a loan, to be represented.[113] He remembers a battle in the government, with the majority twice opposing the general introduction of enterprise councils.[114] At the end of June it adopted proposals which followed Šik's principles, but suggested a law only at the end of the year and advised a prior period of experimentation.[115]

This was a toning down of proposals from trade unions which were taking up the issue as they broke free from their previous passive role. It was also beginning to be overtaken by events as the first councils were established in June and produced their own statutes. The invasion then led to a very rapid escalation: one, probably exaggerated estimate suggests growth from 19 in September to 260 at the end of the year[116] while official figures show 300 in June 1969.[117] This may have been encouraged by the emergency Fourteenth Congress, held in Prague in later August in defiance of the occupation. It produced general proposals for political change, with a number of possible forms for contested elections,[118] and referred to making employees into 'genuine owners, dominating and directing the production of their own lives'.[119] It had a lot in common with Solidarity's later notion of a 'self-managing republic'. In Czechoslovakia the notion of phasing out the state's repressive power and replacing it with organs of self-administration was linked to a transition to communism while in Poland such Marxist terminology was to be consciously avoided.

Of all the ideas in economic or political life, the key strength of enterprise councils was that they could be created 'from below' as a demonstration of defiance. On 24 October the government tried to call a halt, but that provided a new impetus around fears that they would soon be abolished.[120] They never covered a majority of employees, but may have represented more than one million – around 15% of the active population – and could even claim to be 'the symbol of positive efforts made since January on the economic front'.[121]

Their position still seemed secure with the publication of a draft for the law on the socialist enterprise in January 1969. Previously, when regarded as just a part of the state system, enterprises had not needed such formalisation of their status. Now, the enterprise council was to act 'collectively as entrepreneur'.[122] It looked as if the only opposition was from existing councils feeling that some formulations did not go far enough. Then the Czech government, established within the new federal framework, won support at a large meeting of association and enterprise directors for a formulation emphasising the specialist nature of management. They effectively wanted to reduce the council to the role of a consultative organ in which employees' representatives would not have a majority.[123] The trade unions continued to fight against this, but discussion of the draft was suspended immediately after Dubček's removal and finally, in July 1970, a straightforward ban was imposed on enterprise councils.

The political polarisation after the invasion made it very difficult to look objectively at what appeared to be one of the more resilient elements of the reform movement. There are, however, serious questions that need to be answered. The first is whether they really did get in the way of specialist management. Advocates were able to point with great pleasure to the election of predominantly very well-qualified employees and often of a clear majority of party members. One argument for retaining a central authority seemed unfounded.[124]

A second question relates to the overall economic system. Some economists definitely saw self-management as the decisive step for enterprise independence.[125] Others were unconvinced having become familiar with abstract models of labour management which imply possibly perverse behaviour from a firm aiming to satisfy its employees' demands for the maximum income per head at the expense of employment and higher output, even in the face of high demand.[126] There were serious doubts about full self-administration for the employees and about whether the whole issue was not being overstated while the real need was still for 'a concrete programme of economic policy'.[127]

The point, however, remains that reform required a means to define enterprise independence which under capitalism is implicit in private ownership. If directors are not answerable to a higher authority then they must be answerable to somebody else. If that is only the employees, then there are obvious dangers: they could spend all the resources on wages and then all leave to work elsewhere. Šik later proposed that employees should become shareholders, gaining a share in profits depending on length of service.[128] There were other suggestions for legal and financial instruments to ensure the best use of society's assets, but the discussion had hardly begun. It remains perhaps the crucial unsolved problem in ideas for using the market within a socialist economy.

'Normalising' the economy

The status of the enterprise may not have been the most pressing economic issue, but it was an area in which progress could still be made even after August. When reform depended on initiatives from above, its chances were much weaker. Šik, in Yugoslavia at the time of the invasion, never returned. The Soviet leadership was anyway insisting on his removal.[129] The government had, understandably, lost its confidence as everybody's position was under threat. Černík was even believed to have advised intellectuals in general that he could no longer guarantee their future.

Despite diminishing chances of success, 'the overwhelming majority of economists were still convinced of the need to continue the reform. They were, unfortunately, still as unsure as ever on how to proceed. The emergency congress gave no lead, acknowledging difficulties and postponing the formulation of a 'long-term' programme.[130] Months later economists were still writing of how little had really changed and of the 'barriers' created by disequilibrium, by the wrong price structure and 'social barriers' such as opposition to 'delevelling'.[131] Generally the key problem was felt to be inflationary pressures and the solution was, in effect, a tougher version of May 1967. Somebody had to find the courage to take the strong measures that had previously been avoided.[132]

Discussion of price policy was still trapped in seemingly imponderable generalities. Equilibrium prices would lead to huge gains for some and justify an irrational structure from the viewpoint of integration into the world economy.[133] The same was true of existing prices, while world prices could not be introduced at once.[134] Retail prices, it was openly stated, would have to rise to eliminate the enormous subsidies on rent and food and to allow for 'delevelling' and an easier adjustment of sectoral differentials.[135] The prospect was 'not too pleasant' especially for a government which had, since 1953, propagated the notion that price reductions were the result of its 'far-sighted acts'.[136] The central message must have been that 'to revive the economy will not be a popular business'.[137]

This position was to become increasingly irrelevant as the government found a means to tackle disequilibrium that actually appeared to be popular. The problem, due already to high investment and rising incomes, was sharply accentuated in the 'special situation' after August 1968.[138] There was an immediate loss of output and disruption to the transport of finished goods which was made up fairly quickly:[139] people were even willing to work extra 'Dubček shifts'.

At the same time, the invasion stimulated a bout of panic buying. Monthly figures show August and September as times of withdrawal of savings deposits (normally there is a small increase in these months), with some held as cash alongside immediate spending on food. By September the panic had shifted towards textiles and industrial goods.[140] For some specific products, such as bed linen and sewing machines, even boosting output by up to 60% could not cover demand.[141] Generally, however, the gap was filled by credits from the socialist countries and by slaughtering more animals: neither measure could be repeated.[142] However, 1969 was another high spending year with people again often prepared to make do with lower quality goods that might otherwise have gone into stock-building. Unusually heavy savings withdrawals occurred in June and July which could have related to the expectation that this would be many people's last chance of a visit to Western Europe. The money had to be changed on the black market at a rate which was, quite exceptionally, above the comparable rate for foreign currency shops. Some found its way back in higher spending on public catering,[143] presumably from the enormous number of Western tourists.

Throughout the first nine months of 'normalisation' economic questions received very little attention in the centres of power. The stated policy was to continue with restricting new starts. There was, however, scope for 'a compromise between the objective need to lower the volume of projects under construction ... the pressure of sectoral and group interests and the demand for sectoral restructuring'.[144] Then the May 1969 Central Committee meeting, assessing investment starts which were some 37% above the guidelines, decreed blanket restrictions even on projects that had been approved and without regard to previous sectoral policies.

There was still a verbal commitment to using the market, but only after equilibrium had been restored. One hope was to begin a gradual transition after 1972 by which time propaganda might have prepared people for the hard things to come.[145] Attempting to use 'indirect' instruments at once, with all the economy's deformations and shortages, would lead to 'ever growing economic disequilibrium' and 'the total disorganisation of the economy'.[146]

The priority for the consumer goods market was much stricter wage controls. Demands for more pay were partly stimulated by 'extra-economic' factors, partly by a quest for security and partly, even in better paying sectors, by the desire to share in the general rise. Enterprises were using their greater independence to allow this.[147] It was now to end and the government, which had itself approved half the aggregate increase in the 1968 wage bill,[148] was to allow no more exceptions. The agreement with the trade unions had been for a 5% rise in nominal wages, but they were already running considerably above that level.

Linked to this was a decree to outlaw all retail price increases from 1 January 1970. The aim was very clearly political, to show all consumers the government's determination to 'reinstate' central manage-

Table 7.2. *Factors relating to consumer spending, 1967–1971*

	Total disposable incomes	Real incomes	Consumer spending	Saving	Retail prices
1967	107.5	105.9	106.7	131.6	102.0
1968	111.9	110.7	112.5	98.4	101.3
1969	111.4	107.5	112.4	85.1	104.0
1970	104.5	102.8	102.6	178.1	101.7
1971	105.5	105.9	105.0	115.7	99.7

Note: Previous year = 100
Source: Calculated from *HSR*, pp. 201 & 349–51.

ment of price policy: it was named as 'the chief front in the battle for economic consolidation'.[149] The point was even clearer after the strikes in Poland in December 1970. Supplying the population with meat was then described as 'not only an economic problem but an important political question'.[150]

Opinion polls suggest that the price freeze was overwhelmingly well received, despite strong suspicions that regulations were sometimes broken. There was a new expectation, expressed by 53% compared with 9% in December 1968, of price stability.[151] Optimism about the economy as a whole also grew with 20% in November 1969 expecting an improvement and 68% two years later.[152] Since people had expected things to get much worse, especially after the invasion, a government achieving its objectives helped restore the feeling that the material side of life was not that bad.

Table 7.2 shows the effect of wage and pension increases in 1968 and 1969 which raised spending above the rate of growth of productivity. The gap was accentuated by the drop in savings, down to 2.7% of disposable incomes in 1969, and was covered partly by a trade deficit in 1968 and then by retail price rises in the following year. Tables 7.3 and 7.4 show that, as consumption bore the brunt of the subsequent adjustment, there was no disruption to production. Even the poor result in agriculture in 1970 caused no serious problems as output was still up to the 1967 level. The apparent success in industry and construction is, however, partly due to the failure to control investment: its share in final product actually rose to 27.7% in 1970.

Table 7.3. *Components of final product in terms of expenditure, 1968–1971*

	Final product	Personal consumption	Social consumption	Change in stocks	Net exports	Investment
1968	100.0	51.4	16.6	3.5	0.3	26.9
1969	107.8	54.8	17.3	3.6	1.1	29.5
1970	112.9	55.4	18.0	4.8	1.7	31.2
1971	119.0	58.3	20.0	3.6	2.1	33.0

Note: All figures are percentages of final product in 1968, in 1967 prices. Losses are omitted.
Source: Calculated from HSR, pp. 84 & 91 and SR, 1975, p. 208.

Table 7.4. *Components of national income in terms of production, 1968–1971*

	National income	Agriculture	Industry	Construction	Others
1968	100.0	11.5	60.7	11.6	16.2
1969	107.3	12.0	64.7	11.6	19.0
1970	113.4	10.9	69.8	12.3	20.4
1971	119.6	11.3	73.8	13.5	21.0

Note: All figures are percentages of national income in 1968, in 1967 prices.
Source: Calculated from HSR, p. 88.

This success was only partially due to restrictive policies. Balance was comparatively easily restored because the previous disequilibrium was partly temporary in nature and partly exaggerated. High spending in 1968 and 1969 on consumer durables could not be repeated for a few years, while spending on foreign travel related to very specific circumstances. Moreover, it soon became clear that measures of the extent of shortages were highly unreliable: in 1969–70 there were estimated to be up to 300 000 people waiting for a car. By 1972, having been presented with the opportunity, it was clear that only one in five of these was seriously interested in buying. The others either did not have the money available or had simply put their names down because they had heard of the shortage.[153] As a result, even a decelerating increase in supply quickly eliminated the shortage.

Despite this success, the next stage was definitely not the revival of reform. A new concept was appearing in the determination to bury the politics of 1968. Society was being described by late 1969 as 'real existing' socialism, to be set against speculative 'models' of what socialism could be.[154] Although there was some revival of the jargon of the early 1950s, the essential message was very different. This was 'a reign of anti-utopia'.[155] The system was justified not on the grounds that it was leading to a better future but, on the most conservative grounds possible, that it 'existed'. It certainly had brought benefits and, as there was now going to be no possibility of an alternative, the message was that people might as well accept it.

There was little prospect of enthusiastic support for this approach, but it could win acquiescence especially by playing on doubts about the reform movement. One economic factor, apart from price rises, was structural policy with some voices consistently pressing the central importance of heavy industry and effectively hoping for it to be treated as a firm priority.[156] The 'Šikites' were accused by some of undervaluing this sector,[157] and the 'reputation' of engineering was said to have 'suffered significantly',[158] but the argument was not pressed: there was moreover continuing satisfaction that 1967 saw the beginnings of modernisation and reconstruction in the consumer goods industries.[159] 1968 saw the creation of unions of enterprise managements to lobby for the 'rehabilitation' of those sectors with the argument that only by 'the activisation of the whole sector' could past discrimination be overcome.[160] These formal bodies quickly disappeared, but relative wages and shares in total investment were eroded very slowly and there was no change in the plans to reduce investment in iron and steel.

Miners were sometimes claimed, unlike other workers, to have adopted a 'Marxist–Leninist' position of 'proletarian internationalism' which meant that they had been less active in opposing the invasion.[161] Their attitude could certainly have been influenced by lower investment and uncertainty about the industry's future. In practice there was no change in government policy. During the 1960s the aim had been the maximum of energy autarky which was very unusual for an advanced European country. There was now to be a rapid rise in oil imports from the USSR.[162] Miners may have been reassured as the implications were made clearer,[163] but there was no change in objective circumstances.

The principal weapon of normalisation was carefully controlled repression. Husák at first gave reassurances that there would be no purge, but the new leadership soon went beyond the step-by-step removal of top officials. Possibly a third of party members were expelled.[164] Those most active in 1968 were punished with dismissal from responsible jobs and discrimination against their children in education. Active opposition soon weakened largely because there seemed little chance of it achieving anything.

By the end of 1969 the Economics Institute had abandoned its 'revisionist' research programmes.[165] By the end of the next year it was starting a 'serious' analysis with a powerful critique of Šik's line. The failing in policy was said to have been in 'the lack of a clear conception' and in the 'one-sided conclusion on the necessity for changes in the mechanism of functioning of the economy'.[166] Šik was soon condemned as a 'rightist adventurer'.[167]

It was still claimed at the Fourteenth Congress, held in May 1971 – the emergency congress of 1968 was annulled on Soviet insistence – that the aim was to continue with a reform 'purged of its revisionist ballast'.[168] Unfortunately, although verbally still confirming the principles adopted in January 1965, it was felt necessary to condemn the price reform, and the 'political crisis': right-opportunist and anti-socialist opinions were accused of bringing the country to the brink of 'economic catastrophe'.[169] Without 1968, it was implausibly claimed, the economic situation would have been much better. Before long, even the use of the word 'reform' was outlawed and the whole experience of the 1960s disappeared from political discussion.

The new leadership placed great stress on a Five Year Plan, and their task was eased by work in the preceding years on a long-term perspective through to 1980. Goals were modest and realisable: this was a leadership that boasted of promising no more than stability, certainty and a 5% annual growth rate. Economists were still as aware as ever of the long-term problems and of the need to improve the system so as to facilitate 'intensive' growth. In practice, success was being judged against one-year plan targets.

Moreover, short-term emergency measures were increasingly being presented as a permanent solution and finding ratification in statutes. There was unquestioning approval for the renewal in 1971 of the full system of material balances.[170] The logic was clear as 'that which is solved by the market in a capitalist economy must be solved in a socialist economy by a centre for the whole society'.[171] Even in 1972 Husák was still talking of 'expanding the economic reform', but it was now to rely on 'using the results and experiences of the Soviet economic reform'. Moreover, the way to improve the system of management was to depend on 'renewal of central organisation and planning'. That meant more concentration and centralisation and, for lower levels, 'discipline'.[172]

A few elements of the reform consistently received verbal support from the new leadership, most notably much of the argument for 'delevelling' which was repeated in textbooks and party resolutions. In practice, measures of overall inequality show no changes and the differential for non-manual work has continued to decline. The immediate cause was the reconstruction of a strict system of wage control, seen as the only means to keep the lid on inflation, which was linked again to plan fulfilment. Overfulfilment was to be rewarded with a less than proportional increase in the wage bill and this primarily restricted non-manual workers' pay.[173] Manual workers could enjoy the benefits of piece-rates and other output-related bonuses while some, especially in mining, transport and heavy engineering, were granted several pay increases to help overcome chronic shortages. In a number of heavy engineering enterprises manual workers' average pay was either equal to or above the level for non-manual workers by the early 1980s.[174]

Despite instructions to enterprises in 1974 to formulate clear aims on pay differentiation,[175] the real barrier to 'delevelling' in the 1970s seems to have been 'weaknesses of a subjective character',[176] meaning the lack of interest of enterprise managements. Regulations allow considerable discretion over individual wages, but bonuses are typically paid at a uniform rate to those on the same grade or in the same unit. Nobody seems to have found precise means to measure individual performances and neither is there a clear conception of the 'optimal' differentiation of pay. In fact, there is no agreement in practice on the relative importance of earnings and payments systems as an incentive to work.[177] Managements prefer to use tradition and the pressures of labour shortages to evade what could become a very sensitive issue. Thus, although the general principle of deeper differentiation of pay is accepted, it remains in practice 'a mere proclamation'.[178]

Normalisation in the economy started from ad hoc measures to overcome specific problems. It has been argued that 'there was no return to the pre-1966 system',[179] and it is true that a number of financial indicators were retained. In practice, however, these were of little relevance and were easily swamped by the re-emergence of 'old-fashioned success indicators' around binding annual plans in 1971.[180] As these were soon given a firm ideological justification, full return to the essence of the old system was practically inevitable.[181] Nevertheless, that never stopped leading officials from criticising symptoms of the system's weaknesses: they could see central organs overburdened, lower levels failing to communicate and pursuing sectional interests and, most consistently of all, the failure to overcome problems with investment and innovation.

8 Intensification or stagnation?

Almost unparallelled success?

The 1970s were presented at the time as a period of success. Equilibrium had been restored quickly and maintained in more or less all markets, and growth rates in national income, in industrial and agricultural output and in living standards were respectably rapid. Moreover, they were very close to plan targets, at least for the first half of the decade, and only just behind the average for the CMEA as a whole. Later the tendency was to deviate downwards to an extent and with a consistency that cannot be explained by chance events such as bad harvests alone. Table 8.1 shows the stability of the early 1970s. The apparent break in 1976 does coincide with poor harvests but 1979 is usually regarded as marking the start of an altogether less happy period.

Statements from political leaders naturally included boasts of economic achievements which were used as evidence both of the correctness of their policies and, even more questionably, of their support from the population. Leading economists, such as Goldmann, viewed the early 1970s as 'among relatively the most successful periods in the development of the Czechoslovak economy'.[1] The stability of investment impressed him as making a major contribution to overall stability.

Having been excluded from a leading role in the economic reforms of the 1960s, and thanks also to a poor relationship with Šik, he could take over as director of the Economics Institute and maintain solid research in macroeconomics. In his view real dangers continued in foreign trade performance. All the signs were of a gradual drop in competitiveness from which the domestic economy was temporarily shielded. Within the CMEA it was no longer possible to continue as a monopoly supplier of investment goods. In fact, its machinery

Table 8.1. *Economic stability in the 1970s as indicated by annual growth rates*

	National income	Deviation from plan	Industry	Deviation from plan	Agriculture	Deviation from plan	Real incomes	Investment
1970	5.7	+0.5	8.7	+3.3	1.1	−1.6	2.8	5.8
1971	5.5	+0.3	6.9	+1.0	3.2	+0.2	5.9	5.7
1972	5.7	+0.7	6.0	+1.0	3.9	−0.8	6.3	8.9
1973	5.2	+0.1	6.7	+0.9	4.7	+0.4	6.2	9.0
1974	5.9	+0.7	6.3	+0.5	2.2	−1.6	4.2	9.1
1975	6.2	+0.6	6.9	+0.5	−1.1	−5.9	3.1	8.3
1976	3.6	−1.4	5.1	−0.4	−2.4	−6.9	3.9	4.4
1977	4.2	−1.0	6.3	+1.0	9.1	+0.9	3.0	5.7
1978	4.3	−0.7	4.9	−0.1	1.5	−1.9	2.1	4.1
1979	3.1	−1.2	3.7	−0.8	−0.04	−3.76	0.7	1.8
1980	3.0	+0.1	3.3	−0.2	6.0	−0.8	0.7	1.4

Source: P. Kynštetr, 'K analýze růstové dráhy čs. ekonomiky v 70. letech', *PE*, XXIX, p. 1282 (1981) and calculations from *HSR*, p. 349.

exports were growing considerably more slowly than trade in those products between European socialist countries generally. Soviet statistics show Czechoslovakia's share falling from 21% of Soviet machinery imports in 1965 to 16% in 1970 and 11% in 1975. Moreover, despite historically a higher level of development, trade in machinery with Bulgaria, Hungary, the GDR and Poland was, by 1978, in balance. In other words, the quality of Czechoslovak products had slipped so badly that its machinery 'was accepted only on the condition of a balancing export of machines from those states'.[2]

To some extent this was compensated by faster growth and a substantial surplus in consumer goods. Their importance is illustrated by a rise in the trade surplus with socialist countries from 25% in 1970 to 39% of that for machinery in 1980. On the face of it, this was a very sensible switch, but Goldmann's complaint was that it was occurring without adequate domestic preparation. The technological level and capacity for domestic production were improving. The shift in the sectoral structure of investment in the late 1960s was largely maintained, but the improvement was so slow that exports had to be at the expense of the range and quality of goods on the domestic market.[3]

Goldmann warned that Czechoslovakia's changed position within the CMEA was the bottleneck for its whole economic development. Without measures to adapt, which were not impossible in view of the flexibility of much of its productive capacity and the highly qualified labour force, the economy would become unstable and vulnerable. Such warnings were, however, easily played down amid satisfaction over domestic performance and complacency that instability and declining growth rates had been banished to the past.

Nevertheless, it was very soon clear that the target for an average annual growth rate of around 5% in the 1976–80 plan was over-optimistic. There was no sudden crash, but rather a gentle downward drift. The average annual growth rate in national income was 3.7% compared with 4.4% for European CMEA countries and that latter figure was pulled down by the exceptionally bad Polish performance. It could seem, yet again, that it was impossible for an advanced country to continue indefinitely with 'extensive' development.

There were still repeated official pronouncements on the necessity of a switch to 'intensive' growth, but favourable external conditions in the 1970s had made it possible to put that off. This, however, had not been a simple reversion to exactly the same kind of growth as in the 1950s. There was neither the scope for rationalisation in the first years of that decade nor the extreme emphasis on basic and heavy indus-

Table 8.2. *Shares of the main components in final product in the 1970s in percentages*

	1970–72	1973–78	1979–80
Personal consumption	48.0	48.3	47.4
Social consumption	15.8	17.4	17.6
Change in stocks	4.2	3.6	5.6
Net exports	2.1	− 1.0	0.4
Investment	28.3	30.5	27.9

Note: Losses are omitted.
Source: Calculated from *HSR*, pp. 84, 90, & 170.

tries of the Second Five Year Plan. Nevertheless, growth did depend on a high level of investment and substantial imports of raw materials. A major novelty was the availability and use of oil from the Soviet Union which was vital for the prosperity of the decade.

At first external conditions were universally favourable with a slight improvement in the terms of trade and a surplus in both world markets. In 1973, rising commodity prices and continuing declining competitiveness turned that into a substantial deficit which was more pronounced with the non-socialist countries where it was covered by running down reserves and then by substantial external borrowing. Table 8.2 shows that, during the period from 1973 to 1978, the trade deficit was used to allow for some growth in consumption but for a considerably greater increase in investment.

The trade gap would have been still greater but for the favourable CMEA pricing system which was formalised in 1975 to use a five-year moving average of world prices. The aim was said to be minimisation of fluctuations in commodity prices, but it helped raw material importers especially by delaying the impact of the rising price of oil. In fact, Vanous and Marrese estimated that the Soviet Union gave Czechoslovakia an effective subsidy of $6 billion in the 1973–8 period. They assumed that raw materials would otherwise have cost the world price, which seems reasonable, and also tried to estimate a subsidy in the price of Czechoslovak exports of manufactured goods. They may actually have been generous to the Czechoslovak side as the procedure required generalising from a comparison of prices of goods sold in both socialist and non-socialist markets: those could well have been only the most favourable.[4]

This Soviet generosity they attributed to a trade-off between economic costs and the political, strategic and military benefits of retaining Czechoslovakia's loyalty. This probably understates the economic benefits derived from greater security of supplies of a wide range of vital products, possibly including unpublicised military production. They also acknowledge that this Soviet beneficence could be a mixed blessing for Czechoslovakia as it has been associated with the unquantifiable costs of incorporation into the Soviet bloc and hence restricted contacts with much of the world economy. Nevertheless, Soviet goodwill, along with Western credits, made it possible to support a growth process relying on rising inputs of fuel and raw materials.

As Table 8.3 shows, the enormous expansion in these imports from socialist countries was largely covered by exports of machinery and consumer goods but, for the first time, Czechoslovakia was also being allowed to run a persistent deficit. The growing deficit with non-socialist countries reflected a worsening balance across several categories, especially machinery, but also food and 'other materials', which includes chemicals and non-mineral industrial raw materials. It presented no immediate problems when Western credit was easy after the 1973 oil price rise.

For a time, then, there was no need for internal changes to accommodate to the effects of external events. Enterprises themselves were, of course, shielded from higher import prices by the state monopoly of foreign trade and they actually gained slightly from the rise in export prices.[5] At the end of the decade government leaders were still boasting of the country's rapid growth and rising living standards. External deficits passed unnoticed amid claims that things were going well *despite* worsening external conditions.[6]

Events after 1979 are quite distinct as there was a clear shift in the source of immediate problems and hence in policy which moved towards overcoming the hard-currency deficit. The obvious reason was the toughening of credit conditions as a number of debtor countries – the most significant from Czechoslovakia's point of view being Poland – seemed unable to service their existing debts. Reversing the hard-currency deficit, with the only reservation being that 'the achieved standard of living' was to be maintained, had therefore become the key issue even before it was given prominence in the Seventh Five Year Plan for 1981–5. It was linked to the domestic economy as part of a diagnosis of general 'disequilibrium' which was said to be visible in, apart from the hard-currency balance, the areas of

Table 8.3. *Czechoslovak foreign trade balances in the 1970s in million Kčs*

	Socialist		Non-socialist	
	1970–72	1973–79	1970–72	1973–79
Total	+3433	−9267	+168	−16937
Machinery	+15707	+44676	+120	−8135
Fuel & mineral raw materials	−9216	−54891	+3589	+6731
Food	−6338	−15652	−2099	−8421
Consumer goods	+5896	+22470	+3205	+14010
Other materials	−2616	−5870	−4647	−21122

Source: Calculated from HSR, pp. 326–7.

energy, agriculture and investment. External relations were undoubtedly the crucial issue so it may be more accurate to see the problem as a coincidence of difficulties in trade with both non-socialist and socialist states. Difficulties in investment and agriculture were shown up by foreign trade.

The hard-currency squeeze

The solution to this 'disequilibrium' evolved partly through a considered reaction and partly through panic measures. The Five Year Plan for the 1981–5 period set the lowest growth target ever. National income was to rise by 14–16% and industrial production by 18–20%: the former had grown by 20% in the previous five years while the latter had grown by 18%. Agriculture was to grow by 10% which was again similar to the 1976–80 result, although that had been biased by a bad harvest at the start and a good one at the end of the period. The absolute priority was to be the restoration of 'equilibrium' even though the methods used must in some cases hamper solving the longer-term problems that led up to the difficulties. That aspect was, however, played down amid hopes that 'intensification' could enable lower consumption of energy and materials and greater competitiveness on international markets. The key to this was a 'package of measures', discussed below, which probably achieved nothing.

In fact, the plan was soon in trouble as attempts to overcome the trade deficit by export promotion met little success. The aim in 1980, for a 10% increase to non-socialist countries was nowhere near achieved and results were just as disappointing in the following years. Moreover, much of the growth that did occur was due to raw materials: the hope of really big increases in manufactured goods proved unrealistic. There were a few successes such as glassware in a number of Western European countries, but the really impressive increases were for wood and cellulose. In other words, the only effective export promotion involved a shift towards raw materials and more homogeneous products where quality was less variable. Inevitably, restoring the balance in hard currency also required reducing imports, which became quite a savage cut in 1981. Pressure was further increased when, after the declaration of martial law in Poland in December 1981, *all* further credits from the West were stopped.

The embargo only lasted for a few months, and after that Western bankers began to drift back into Prague with tempting offers. By then, however, the government had changed its policy from keeping the level of hard-currency debt stable to eliminating it altogether. This was encouraged possibly by a sudden realisation of the feasibility of withstanding the internal repercussions of a surplus with the capitalist world, but more obviously by cold war noises especially from the USA. The view was gaining ground there that the USSR and Eastern Europe might be more susceptible than ever before to an embargo policy concentrating on the most modern technologies. There were, of course, even attempts to block sales of grain in 1980–81 and trade relating to the Soviet gas pipeline in 1982. The USA was clearly thinking of broadening export controls beyond products of obvious military relevance. Such efforts were far less likely to succeed than in the days of US dominance through Marshall Aid, but they encouraged Eastern European fears that links with the West were inherently unreliable. Even apart from that danger, the experience, especially of Poland, seemed to prove that debts could be dangerously destabilising. Czechoslovakia therefore aimed to free itself completely from the perceived dangers of dependence on Western financial institutions.

There certainly was a logic to this approach, but it was not general throughout Eastern Europe. Hungary, East Germany and the USSR continued to take out new loans. It appears that Czechoslovakia did accept some in 1985, but they were probably essential within CMEA energy projects and its new debt for the whole 1981–5 period was only 1.3% of that for Eastern Europe and the Soviet Union as a whole.[7] It had been about the most cautious European CMEA country throughout the 1970s too after the condemnation of the proposal to seek Western loans in 1968. When Czechoslovakia did begin to build

Table 8.4. *Czechoslovakia's economic relations with non-socialist countries in the early 1980s*

	Exports (million Kčs)	Imports	Balance	Net indebtedness (billion $)
1979	19 409	21 985	−2576	—
1980	24 364	24 326	+38	—
1981	25 328	23 436	+1892	3.0
1982	24 961	22 010	+2951	3.0
1983	26 384	21 485	+4899	2.6
1984	27 411	22 127	+5284	2.1
1985	27 579	23 251	+4328	2.4

Source: HSR, pp. 326–7; SR, 1986, p. 443, and United Nations Economic Survey of Europe in 1986–1987 (New York, 1987), p. 309.

up a significant level of debt, towards the end of the decade, an unusually large amount was wisely spent on new machinery.[8] In view of this, the decision taken in 1982 is perhaps particularly surprising as it inevitably threatened a further loss of ground relative to more advanced economies.

As Table 8.4 shows, the deficit was quickly turned into a substantial surplus – even encouraging hopes of eliminating all debts by 1987 – but the key change was the substantial fall in imports. Czechoslovakia does not publish foreign trade figures in physical terms for different trading areas but, in relation to advanced capitalist countries, real exports seem to have fallen in 1981 and grew by only 10% over the 1981–5 period.[9] Net indebtedness fell slightly more rapidly than the average for the region, even when the exceptional case of Poland is excluded, but still left a debt service ratio of 20% in 1984, compared with 22% in 1981. The only European CMEA country with a lower figure was the USSR.

Breaking trade down into broad product groups shows that every category contributed towards the surplus with machinery and raw materials each responsible for 36% of the change. Despite the importance attached to agriculture, food contributed only 16% of the change. Imports had risen to cover for bad harvests in the late 1970s but proved very hard to reduce.

The effects of all this on the domestic economy were very varied. There was probably not much impact on the quantitative availability of consumer goods because export promotion was unsuccessful.

Table 8.5. Division of final product measured in expenditure terms, 1980–1985

	Final product	Personal consumption	Social consumption	Change in stocks	Net exports	Investment	Investment as share
1980	100	45.9	15.5	5.2	1.8	29.7	29.7
1981	100.8	46.7	16.3	2.3	4.7	28.4	28.1
1982	101.4	45.6	16.4	2.7	6.1	27.7	27.3
1983	104.1	46.5	17.0	2.6	7.7	27.9	26.8
1984	107.9	47.3	18.1	1.8	9.8	26.7	24.7
1985	111.3	48.2	18.8	2.1	10.0	28.1	25.3

Note: All figures are percentages of final product in 1980 measured in 1977 prices except the last column. Losses are omitted.
Source: Calculated from *SR*, 1986, pp. 132, 141 & 205.

Imports from capitalist countries were cut both absolutely and as a proportion of the total, from 7% in 1979 to 5% in 1983, but that made little difference to the total domestic market. There must have been a noticeable effect in a small range of luxury products not easily substituted. The wider issue of tensions on the consumer goods market is discussed below. The most serious effects were likely to be felt in investment. Existing projects were generally allowed to continue but new starts were slashed by 37% by 1981.

A brief halt for investment?

The determination to cut investment could be linked very directly to balance of trade difficulties via national income accounts. Table 8.5 shows how the cut in investment helped generate an export surplus while consumption was subjected to minimal pressure. At a more disaggregated level the link appears to be less direct. Better trade figures depended also on cutting raw material imports which enter into current production as much as investment. Lower investment could help by cutting machinery imports, by releasing industrial and even construction capacity for export and by reducing the need to use foreign construction workers. All of those factors were significant, but there was also a cost to the domestic economy. The failure to fulfil hopes for higher machinery exports probably contributed to the high level of stock-building in 1980: to that extent directing capacity away from domestic investment embodied a waste of resources. Moreover, both labour and fixed assets were squandered in under-utilisation in the construction industry as indicated by a 19% fall in the productivity of assets in the 1980–85 period and stagnation in the productivity of labour.

In fact, the problems in investment were usually presented in terms of the familiar arguments about excess demand and poor completion rates. As in some previous periods, the 1970s had seen plans which balanced at the start of the period but became overloaded as new projects were added and no existing ones were cut. In the early 1970s the culprits were petrochemicals, cars, nuclear power and steel pipes, added in under CMEA programmes. Investment was then held in check reasonably well, until the end of the decade saw renewed pressure especially from energy projects and the motor industry.[10] Table 8.6 shows the effects of this, and of the continuing micro-level problems described in previous chapters: contracts still seem often to have been negotiated at quite low levels without checking the avail-

Table 8.6. *Measures of excess demand in investment*

	Ratio of work remaining on unfinished projects to investment		Ratio of starts to completions
1961–65	1.56		1.02
1966–70	1.45		1.27
1971–75	1.45		1.28
1976–80	1.51		1.23
1981–85	1.42		0.90
	Ratio of work remaining on unfinished projects to investment	Starts (× 100m Kčs)	Completions (× 100m Kčs)
1978	1.48	959	655
1979	1.64	1090	749
1980	1.64	948	949
1981	1.51	683	841
1982	1.41	744	854
1983	1.36	870	1047
1984	1.43	1009	1055
1985	1.39	1085	1096

Note: All calculations are from annual figures in value terms at current prices.
Source: Calculated from *HSR*, pp. 175–83 and *SR*, 1986, p. 211.

ability of capacity, thereby defeating attempts at central control. The year 1979 looks like the worst ever for excess investment demand with starts running 46% ahead of completions: the comparable figure for 1961 was 26%.

The usual argument was that this had to be cut to allow for completion of priority projects.[11] There is evidence that this had already been attempted in the late 1970s but, owing to the low substitutability of investment capacity, the main effect was simply to slow the overall growth in investment, and hence in national income.[12] Experience in the early 1980s was very similar. Cuts extended into 18% of projects already under construction, 93% of which were in the 'non-productive' sector, and the losses are clear in lower output, unused capacity and slower completion of schools, hospitals and other communal facilities. There was, however, no evidence at all of any compensating benefits. The paradoxical effect was 'a certain form of legalisation of pre-existing delays in construction'. Elsewhere the available evidence 'confirmed the continuation of unsatisfactory fulfilment of individual deadlines and of deadlines for putting capacity into operation and for completing priority projects'.[13] A longer time period might have brought results but, apart from the uncertainty as to how far inadequate capacity rather than the incentive structure was the limiting factor on completion times,[14] it is difficult to believe that the energy sector had been permanently under-represented in investment. In fact 1982 saw energy – meaning just fuel and electricity – taking 31% of all industrial investment, which was the highest proportion since 1959. If all related projects are included, then the figure is one-quarter of investment for the economy as a whole.[15]

There were soon significant successes in completing energy projects, and throughout industry as a whole the ratio of the increase in fixed assets to the level of investment improved. All of these encouraging indicators, along with the apparent decline in excess demand for investment, need not prove that work in progress was being completed more quickly. They could simply be a result of the investment wave of the late 1970s working its way through.

In fact, there could even be scope for concern at the revival of investment starts which were approaching the 1979 level by 1985. Already in 1982 they were growing faster than investment while the trend line for the volume of uncompleted projects was accelerating above the line for completions immediately after the cutback of 1981.

The point was confirmed with the help of an econometric model, using data for the period 1967–83, which related investment starts to the likely pressure from enterprises and the likely will of the centre to resist that pressure. The former was represented by the volume of starts in the previous period and the latter by the change in the volume of projects under construction, which is known to be watched carefully by central planners. The rate of change in the level of investment was also included as it could indicate capacity and hence again the centre's will to resist.[16]

The results for the 1967–83 period were reasonably good, but among the years with a high level of starts relative to the model's predictions were, not surprisingly, 1968 but also, and far more strikingly, 1983 and 1984. Thus if there was over-investment before 1981, the implication was that it had reappeared with a vengeance by the middle of the decade.

This conclusion needs to be treated with some caution as the model does not claim to predict accurately the economy's *capacity* for investment: it is concerned rather with the determinants of its volume. The cut in 1981, leaving some sectors probably unable even to maintain existing capacity,[17] created plenty of slack rather than exact, overall equilibrium. This must further strengthen the suspicion that the cut in investment, meaning strong resistance to demands from lower levels, was only possible when it contributed to overcoming a serious balance of payments problem.

A new start for agriculture?

Agriculture's problems were far more obviously and explicitly tied to the hard-currency deficit. Its contribution was not enormous, but it was clearly undesirable and appeared unnecessary. Czechoslovakia had planned to move towards self-sufficiency in agriculture to limit the disturbances due to unreliable imports and unstable world market prices. Moreover calculations clearly demonstrated the benefits of domestic production rather than importing from the capitalist world. It might have been even better to import some products from socialist countries, but one of the many faults of the CMEA was that it had never really developed specialisation in agriculture as so few of its members could guarantee substantial exports. The objective therefore had to be the maximum possible degree of self-sufficiency. By the end of the 1970s that level varied from 60% for fruit to 80% for cereals while there was actually a surplus of meat for export. The overall figure was around 92% for the 1976–80 period.

Behind that apparent success lay a deeper problem. From the time of the First Five Year Plan there was a consistent intention to redirect agriculture more towards animal products. By the end of the 1950s it had even become necessary to import animal feed. The following decades saw a further rise in meat consumption, especially in the early 1970s, which put Czechoslovakia at a very high level on this measure relative to other indicators of living standards.

It was now in animal products that 'the achievements of large-scale socialist production' were the most pronounced.[18] The chosen price structure encouraged large cooperatives to concentrate on factory farming of pigs and poultry – one factory even contained half a million chickens – which gave quick results for comparatively little investment. Cattle, which are easier to feed but need a three-year cycle, were under-developed with the selling price of both beef and milk below the cost of production. The chosen method for rapidly saturating the demand for meat therefore led towards an import-intensive

Table 8.7. *Agriculture's performance in the early 1980s relative to previous periods*

	Output	Productivity of fixed assets	Productivity of labour	Grain per hectare
1966–70	118.1	84.3	128.3	120.4
1971–75	113.3	82.8	127.5	130.6
1976–80	107.9	70.2	119.5	108.5
1981–85	109.7	71.9	112.9	112.2

Note: Each figure is an average for the five-year period relative to the previous five-year period.
Source: Calculated from HSR, pp. 146, 166, 213 & 218, and SR, 1986, pp. 184, 232, 265 & 285.

form of agriculture. The domestic deficit in animal feed was covered at first by imports paid for in hard currency, but that became increasingly expensive with rising world prices in the 1976–80 period.[19]

The Five Year Plan for the early 1980s aimed to eliminate this problem by giving priority to an expansion of grain output, which had clearly decelerated in the preceding years. Only on that basis could meat production increase again. This consideration overshadowed the original targets after a bad harvest in 1981 and a failure to reach the target in the following year. The reaction then was for a sharp rise in the price of meat – over 50% for roasting pork – leading to an immediate fall in consumption. By 1983 grain imports had been cut to little over a third of the 1979 level. The next few years saw good harvests: crop production grew faster than planned and, in fact, faster than in any previous post-war period allowing a speedy restoration of the previous meat consumption level. This cannot be attributed to genuine 'intensification' in agriculture, but there were some positive developments that could be built on in the future. Table 8.7 shows performance relative to previous periods.

Earlier productivity improvements can largely be explained by the full mechanisation of harvesting – 96% for grain by 1973 and for sugar in 1982 – and the greater use of fertilisers. The former offered little scope for further progress while the latter was also heading towards its limit in the mid-1970s: in many parts of the country excessive use of fertilisers was even damaging water supplies.

The period 1970–75 also saw a cut in the number of cooperatives by 64% as the authorities encouraged a wave of mergers. The justification was the alleged economies of scale in modern animal husbandry. Probably more important reasons were the administrative ease for higher bodies setting plan targets and the desire to eliminate backward and poorly managed farms. The organisational uncertainty may even have contributed to a decline in growth rates in the later 1970s by which time the unstated policy seemed to have shifted to encouraging mergers only for good economic reasons rather than on grounds of administrative expediency.

Farming in the 1980s could benefit both from organisational stability and from four other improvements. The first was the rise in relative earnings: cooperative farmers' pay passed the average for the rest of the economy in 1980. Even that left some serious labour problems. There had, of course, been a shortage for many years, but it takes on a different significance when, especially around Prague and in some frontier regions, one person leaving an unpleasant job may put an expensive industrial piggery out of action.

The second improvement was in relative as well as absolute purchase prices. Suddenly beef and milk were back in favour: purchase prices rose by 45% and 25% respectively between 1979 and 1982 compared with 13% for pork. The result took planners completely by surprise. The new financial incentive disproved previous assumptions about output per cow: milk deliveries grew by 22% between 1979 and 1985. Cooperatives had previously been subjected to fixed quotas for the number of cows in an effort to maintain milk production despite financial disincentives. This result was achieved from slightly fewer cows and even exceeded the capacity of the processing industry.

The third improvement was the encouragement of non-agricultural activities. From the very beginning some cooperatives had been involved in providing local services, such as transport or cleaning snow from roads. After a relaxation of controls in 1967 some moved into transport, construction, catering and manufacturing to such an extent that these activities could account for 90% of gross output, but there was strong disapproval during 'normalisation'. They were accused of poaching workers from the key projects in state enterprises: they were 'a reflection of the incredible spread of indiscipline'.[20] By the 1980s, however, the idea was in favour again as cooperatives were putting substantial profits back into agriculture with very impressive results.

The best known example both in the 1960s and now, is the very large Slušovice cooperative in Moravia, formed by often difficult mergers ending in 1976, with nearly 5000 employees and a maximum grain output per hectare of 6.71 tonnes in 1984. This was 22% up on the 1980 level and compared with an average for the republic of 4.80. Milk production per cow showed an understandable 24% growth from 1980 to 1985. The cooperative's other activities include manufacturing agricultural machinery, for which it has been building an additional factory 250 km away in Poprad to service demand in Slovakia.[21] It also produces microcomputers – 2000 in 1986 – aims for the peak position in Czechoslovak microelectronics with the production of components for an eager Western firm, and sells software under its own trademark. It enters motor rallies, runs horse-races, hotels and a travel agency, and sells ice cream in Prague; it also researches alternative sources of energy. Its agricultural achievements have won international recognition with visits and praise from the Soviet Union including a glowing vote of confidence from Gorbachov's economic adviser Abel Aganbegyan.[22] Gross agricultural production was, however, only 19% of total output in 1980 and 5% in 1986.[23] This is an exceptional case but several other, small cooperatives are not far behind. Overall, more than 20% of agricultural cooperative members are engaged in non-agricultural activities. The enterprise of these cooperatives – many of which are now expanding into the service sector by opening restaurants in Prague and other cities – could be a substantial boost to part of the economy.

The fourth improvement, in contrast, is less certain in its effects. This is the attempt to improve the planning system. Until 1982 it continued to be based on detailed directives from purchasing authorities which, in the interests of administrative convenience, ignored the possibility of specialisation according to local conditions. 1982 saw a replacement of detailed administrative controls by only two binding indicators covering sales of grain and meat: the precise mix within those categories and other products such as milk and eggs were to be left to the price mechanism. In practice, however, even stricter controls have been exercised on inputs because of the situation throughout the economy, with agriculture suffering particularly severe restrictions on fuel, and this would seem to cancel out the apparent freedom over production.

This is one of the crucial weaknesses of Czechoslovak agriculture which explains much of its disappointing performance. Despite rapid growth in output in the 1966–74 period, international comparisons suggest a gap with Western Europe: milk and meat production per employee lag by maybe one-third.[24] This is consistent with figures on the overall structure of employment showing agriculture's share still 14% in 1982, which is much higher than the Western European level.[25] This cannot all be explained by backwardness inherited from before the war. In fact, the gap seems to have widened in the 1970s when the decline in agricultural employment slowed down in socialist relative to advanced capitalist economies. Clearly this cannot still be due to the chaos during collectivisation. Today the largest cooperative farms tend to have the best results in agriculture.

To some extent inefficiency has been encouraged by a price system that distorts incentives, possibly contributing to wasteful use of bulk animal feed and industrial fertiliser: consumption of both of these is considerably above the levels implied by international comparisons.[26] The key issue, however, is the place of agriculture within the economic system as a whole. In the 1950s that meant its role in providing resources for industry. The issue today is its exceptional susceptibility to periodic shortages and irregular deliveries. Unlike industry, work often cannot be delayed or made up with extra shifts weeks or months later. If fertiliser, heating oil or fuel for transport fails to arrive when needed that can seriously damage a whole year's work.

It is also harmed by the lack of international integration. There are shortages of machinery, as domestic production goes partly for export and integration within the CMEA has been only partially successful, and of certain types of animal foodstuffs such as soya and fish meal. The solution has been to experiment with domestic production – without success – and again, to use far more grain per animal than is usual in Western Europe. This suits the government with its objective of maximum self-sufficiency and the policy in the early 1980s must be judged successful as greater autarky meant that agriculture was no longer a 'destabilising' element in the economy.

Growth was, however, achieved without any 'fundamental turn-round'[27] in the relationship between inputs and outputs. Investment, having fallen to its lowest level in 1980, went over the planned level in 1985. Employment stabilised and began increasing in 1984, although that is probably accounted for by non-agricultural activities. Meat consumption recovered rapidly after 1982, but this was not due to a switch towards more 'intensive' growth. That would require greater internal, and especially international specialisation which does not appear imminent.

Table 8.8. *Oil deliveries to Czechoslovakia from the USSR in the early 1980s*

	1980	1981	1982	1983	1984	1985
Quantity	100	96	89	89	87	88
Value	100	141	183	216	242	261

Note: The quantity figures show deliveries via the Friendship pipeline.
Source: Calculated from *SR*, 1984, p. 466 and *SR*, 1986, pp. 434 & 447.

Oil from the Soviet Union

Problems with agriculture were almost trivial in comparison with the impact of the Soviet restriction on oil supplies in 1982. The stimulus from the Soviet side was the need to repay its own hard-currency debt and the decision to give some convertible loans to Poland. The world price of oil was simply too tempting and, just as the CMEA price was itself rising, it forgot previous commitments and cut its deliveries, as shown in Table 8.8. Of course, more could have been bought with hard currency, but that was hardly feasible. The immediate impact was therefore a sharp tightening of the energy constraint.

It was already regarded as a limiting factor, because of delays over the nuclear power programme and in opening new open-cast mines. In the long-term it could present an absolute barrier so that there was already an awareness of the desirability of cutting energy consumption per unit of output. Targets were set to achieve this – for example a 0.5% reduction in fuel and energy consumption for 1981 – but they were made to seem pitifully inadequate after 1982.

This did contribute to a worsening of the trade deficit with socialist countries, which had almost disappeared in 1981 but, as Table 8.9 shows, the gap was held in check by a rapid increase in exports. This unplanned success was actually made possible partly by the failure to reach plan targets for exports of machinery and consumer goods into non-socialist markets. It also partly reflected rapidly rising demand for Czechoslovak investment goods especially from the USSR which continued with a programme of expansion facilitated by the higher price of oil. In fact, contrary to repeated claims of Soviet concern at the quality of imported goods, it appeared from the Czechoslovak side that the power of the 'petro-rouble' made this again their softest

Table 8.9. *Changes in trade balances with socialist countries in the early 1980s in million Kčs*

	1976–80	1981–85	Difference
Balance	−13517	−15963	−2446
of which			
Machinery	+41910	+104653	+62743
Mineral raw materials	−54885	−143939	−89054
Food	−11250	−12778	−1528
Consumer goods	+20265	+37726	+17461
Other	−9557	−1625	+7932

Source: Calculated from *HSR*, pp. 320–21 and *SR*, 1986, p. 456.

export market. By 1985 Czechoslovakia was again supplying over 15% of Soviet machinery imports and Table 8.10 shows the early 1980s as a striking reaffirmation of the trade structure developing in the early 1950s. 1985 saw the highest share of socialist countries in exports of any year apart from 1953 while the shares of the Soviet Union and of machinery were both much higher.

There was also some expansion from some of the other CMEA countries – a 54% rise in machinery exports, measured in current prices, to Poland and the GDR compared with 82% to the USSR over the 1980–85 period[28] – as hard-currency problems forced them to turn back to Czechoslovakia. For once, then, economic difficulties within the Soviet bloc did not hit Czechoslovakia especially hard: instead its bias towards heavy machinery proved to be advantageous. There was no sign of the disruption throughout industry experienced after 1953 or 1962 and, in fact, output of investment goods appears as a stabilising factor on the economy's overall performance.

Nevertheless, there was some restriction on the domestic consumer goods market both in terms of quantity and variety. Imported cars, mostly Soviet-made Ladas, fell from 36% to 13% of a declining domestic market and even became an attractive proposition for black marketeering. The crucial internal adjustment, however, was an even more noticeable cut in the consumption of oil products, achieved by direct restrictions and by continuing the trend since 1979 of raising the price. Comparing 1982 with 1981, heating oil consumption fell by 19%, diesel oil by 11% and petrol by 5%. Internal flights were reduced to carry barely one-fifth of the previous number of passen-

Table 8.10. *Structure of Czechoslovak exports in the early 1980s relative to earlier periods (average share in total exports)*

	1951–55	1956–60	1961–65	1966–70	1971–75	1976–80	1981–85	1985
Socialist countries	71.0	68.9	73.5	70.5	70.3	72.6	74.5	77.0
Soviet Union	32.9	32.2	37.4	33.5	32.0	34.8	41.4	43.7
Machinery	37.6	42.7	47.1	49.8	48.7	51.0	55.7	57.0

Source: Calculated from *HSR*, pp. 316 & 325–6 and *SR*, 1986, pp. 456–7.

gers and many company cars disappeared from the roads. These, then, were short-term measures which minimised the impact on the living standards of the mass of the population but had no direct link to a long-term 'intensification' of the economy.

For a time the energy problem was further complicated by difficulties in electricity generation: output actually fell in the North Bohemian coalfield in 1980. The efforts to complete investment projects then began to bear fruit and output in 1984 was 9% above the 1980 level. With new nuclear power capacity as well, electricity output could rise by 11% during the Seventh Five Year Plan. This, along with the recent appearance of Soviet natural gas, made possible the substitution of other forms of energy for oil. The higher price of oil to enterprises made coal a cheaper source of energy,[29] although less efficient for industrial heating.

There was therefore no break in the continuing rise in electricity consumption per unit of output. By way of contrast, energy use in Britain was rising in road transport alongside a fall in electricity demand. Part of that decline was due to domestic users switching to gas and part to the disappearance of energy-intensive industries. There was also a better use of electricity in industry. Steel output, for example, fell by 27% from 1979 to 1985 while its energy consumption fell by 39%:[30] thus around two-thirds of energy saving was due to lower output and the other third to better technology. Steel output in Czechoslovakia grew by 10% during the Seventh Five Year Plan, but the electricity consumed in the iron and steel industry also increased by 6%.[31]

As was admitted by the State Planning Commission's Chairman Svatopluk Potáč, the aim of cutting the very high metal consumption by an annual average rate of 4.5–5% depended on serious preparations in construction and technology and in finding substitutes. The same can be said for energy consumption but there was not much sign of the necessary work being done.[32] He was, however, able to give a cautiously optimistic account at the start of 1984. 'Balance' had been set before 'growth' and that objective had been achieved. As Table 8.11 shows, the economy was growing again and it was eventually to satisfy a number of the objectives of the Seventh Five Year Plan.

Considering the difficult circumstances, this could be judged a success especially as there seemed to be a recovery after 1982. It was, however, a success bought at a price. Moreover, the apparent recovery from the depths of 1982 depended partly on good luck – an easy winter putting little strain on energy followed at last by plan overful-

Table 8.11. *Basic economic indicators during the Seventh Five Year Plan*

	1981	1982	1983	1984	1985	1985/1980	1981–85/1976–80
Social product	99.5	100.6	102.7	101.7	102.2	106.8	110.9
National income	99.3	99.2	101.2	102.6	102.5	104.8	109.0
Industry:							
gross	100.0	100.4	102.3	102.0	101.6	106.3	109.1
net	99.3	98.5	100.8	104.0	102.3	104.8	108.0
Agriculture:							
gross	97.9	106.1	105.5	103.9	103.3	117.7	117.7
net	85.5	111.1	98.6	107.6	98.2	99.0	97.6

Note: Previous period = 100; figures in 1977 prices.
Source: Calculated from *SR*, 1986, p. 136.

filment in coal and nuclear power in the next year – and partly on positively harmful developments. Thus the plan for steel was for a 1% reduction, as it was an energy-intensive sector, but a 2.8% increase in output was achieved. Similarly construction did well: the hope had been to hold investment spending in check but it overran plan targets as projects proved very difficult to complete.

Evidently, measuring success by a gross output indicator is potentially misleading when the aim is to cut output in some sectors. The point was very clear for 1985 when the volume of gross output was 0.9% above the plan while the value-added indicator was 0.2% below target.[33] 'Success' therefore depended on higher use of inputs. Investment was again judged to be excessive and unduly concentrated towards expanding rather than modernising. Electricity output was above the planned level, but so too was consumption.

There were differing interpretations of these phenomena as became clear at a panel discussion in the State Bank in 1983.[34] There were several such attempts to bring economists from different institutions together in the early 1980s and the debates were published in a journal allowed a print run of little over 100. Both were stopped after 1984. On this occasion the theme was whether 1983 marked a turning point from stagnation to growth. Much of the argument in favour was that the economy had done well to weather a difficult period. Broadly speaking, the set objectives had been achieved and it seemed churlish to be too pessimistic about the future. Čáp, the Deputy Chairman of the Federal Statistical Office, who writes regular summaries of the economy's performance, could give a cautious 'yes'. He based this on figures showing revival from the lowest level and the appearance that the economy was becoming less energy-intensive. He had to acknowledge that this might not represent a lasting recovery owing to doubts as to how far it was really based on the application of scientific and technical progress.

More definite pessimism came from Josef Fogl of the Prime Minister's office who saw balance restored by cutting imports without any sign of a change in the structure of production: the ageing stock of machinery could hardly make that possible. There was, to him, no hint of a change in micro-level behaviour away from input maximisation. Recovery was based rather on energy-intensive sectors relying on imports. He concluded that 1982 was 'rather a turning point towards predominantly the traditional technical-balance growth relations'. This was a disappointing view for those who had hoped that changes to the system of management would lead to radical changes in enterprise behaviour.

Another reform that changed nothing

The objective had been to introduce the 'package of measures' gradually after 1980. It was derived partly from ideas in the USSR and had a great deal in common with Rozsypal's reform of the late 1950s. Although there were elements new to Czechoslovakia, they could not give it any greater chance of success. Rather, its failure is even clearer, as it can be followed in more detail thereby avoiding the possible misconception that it would have given good results but for changed external circumstances.[35]

The changes can be summarised as a new importance for the medium-term plan, a revival after nearly thirty years of counter plans and a new set of success indicators. The key was the greater role for the Five Year Plan with the hope that more serious medium-term planning would overcome the short-term time horizon at the micro level. Unfortunately, that was to place immense demands on the plan: it had to be reasonably stable and reliable down to the micro level so that enterprises themselves could use it as a basis for their own one-year plans. No annual guidelines were to be provided from the centre.

This could probably never have worked. External conditions were bound to change for a small, relatively open economy. Even without this difficulty, so accurate a plan was bound to take time to work out and was, in the event, not ready for the start of the period. Instead, enterprises had only the familiar annual guidelines up until 1983 and even after that they complained of frequent changes in directives. Moreover, even if that weakness could have been overcome, the details of the Five Year Plan would have lacked credibility. Realistically, it would have to be based on information from enterprises and would degenerate into planning from the achieved level, only this time to cover a five-year instead of a one-year period. It is simply not possible for the centre to make serious predictions of changes in enterprises' inputs and outputs which could depend on totally unpredictable technological changes. Neither could enterprises themselves make serious predictions. It is well known that they waste little energy on formulating long-term perspectives when all the operational incentives relate to the one-year period. One survey actually showed a quarter of enterprises and associations using effectively no method at all to work out forecasts while the great majority just extrapolated past trends.[36] They evidently lack serious experience in the area vital for the new planning system.

Nevertheless, a stable and reliable Five Year Plan was the logical precondition for the next element in the 'package'. This was a revival of 'counter plans'. In effect, the aim was to encourage enterprises to reveal their reserves by making it more advantageous for them to accept and reach a tough target than to overfulfil a soft plan. This should not lead to an excessive pressure on inputs, as limits were already clearly specified. In practice, however, input supplies were not stable. Moreover, it was an obvious weakness that enterprises did not need to establish links with each other during this plan formulation period: they could certainly be aiming to produce goods nobody wanted. Obviously, accepting a harder target could have implications for the next plan period as the centre would have been given a good view of that enterprise's potential. The whole idea therefore assumes that the haggling over targets has somehow ended: that might be nearly true at the start of a planning period, but fears about revealing full potential would grow again towards the end of the five years.

In practice, as one-year guidelines continued to be set, enterprises remained understandably cautious, leaving counter plans 'a supplementary and marginal affair'.[37] For 1984 it was reported that 52% were participating,[38] but by then the whole idea had become an 'embarrassment' as enterprises had learnt how to manipulate it.[39] One method was to reject a reasonable plan target and then make a great exhibition of accepting it later as a counter plan. Thus the targets finally accepted for 1985 were ultimately no more demanding than the original proposals. Another possibility – made easier by the continuing instability of central directives which must often have ignored enterprises' specific circumstances – was to accept a tough target, but then claim later that it was no longer realisable due to unpredicted changes in circumstances or breakdowns. The enterprise could then keep the additional bonuses. Sometimes they were effectively forced into this practice as the original guidelines could threaten them with a lower wage fund than that previously achieved. It seems, then, that counter plans were fairly easily incorporated into the plan formulation game and were so widely regarded as an irrelevance to improving actual performance that even enterprises not accepting tougher targets were often not penalised.

In practical terms, then, counter plans made no difference because they did not alter the fundamental relationship involved in plan formulation. The same was true of new success indicators which were intended to shift attention towards 'quality' rather than just 'quantity' of output. A huge number remained, but a new significance was now

Table 8.12. *Annual percentage change in financial indicators and material inputs in economic units in the early 1980s*

	1981	1982	1983	1984	1985
Industry					
Output	8.0	6.9	2.4	9.1	3.6
Value added	—	2.3	5.9	3.6	4.8
Materials	8.4	8.9	1.0	11.4	3.2
Materials per unit of output	+0.3	+1.7	−1.3	+2.1	−0.3
All state & cooperative organisations					
Output	4.1	6.2	2.8	8.8	3.3
Value added	—	3.1	1.7	5.2	4.0
Materials	5.6	7.8	1.6	10.6	3.2
Materials per unit of output	+1.4	+1.6	−1.2	+1.7	−0.1

Note: — Missing data.
Source: SR, 1982, p. 173; *SR*, 1983, p. 161; *SR*, 1984, p. 152; *SR*, 1985, p. 161, and *SR*, 1986, p. 155.

given to a measure of value-added which determined the total wage bill. Managers' bonuses were linked to indicators of profitability and export performance. As an enterprise director argued, the profitability indicator 'has no functional value' while 'counter-measures have already been created to deform it'.[40]

In fact, Table 8.12 suggests that the real success in cutting inputs came in 1983 and should be attributed to one-off measures. Even though 1985 later showed a glimmer of hope (which was however firmly extinguished in the following year), costs continued to rise to such an extent that the 1981–5 period actually compares rather unfavourably with earlier periods when the incentive was ostensibly for maximum output irrespective of the cost. The average change in material costs per unit of output was significantly higher than during the 1970s. Part of this can be explained by higher energy prices at the start of the decade, but energy consumption in physical units against gross output in fixed prices, in Table 8.13, is again unfavourable for the early 1980s. International comparisons are also uncomfortable as the 1980–85 period saw, for example, a 10% drop in energy use per unit of GDP in the United Kingdom:[41] it was almost the best post-war period in that respect.

None of this should be surprising. The precise success indicator

Table 8.13. *Changes in energy use per unit of social product in the early 1980s relative to earlier periods (annual average growth rates)*

1950–55	1955–60	1960–65	1965–70	1970–75	1975–80	1980–85
2.0	2.3	−0.6	−3.6	−2.7	−1 5	−0.9

1981	1982	1983	1984	1985
−1.2	−1.9	−1.5	0.9	−0.2

Source: Calculated from *HSR*, pp. 84–5, 87 & 268 and *SR*, 1986, pp. 23, 126 & 355.

chosen is of less importance than the method used to select its magnitude. Inevitably, it has to be set in relation to the achieved level and enterprises can then haggle to be allowed a slow growth in value-added, a small rise in exports or even, if pressure is put on to improve quality, to gain acceptance for a large number of faulty products. Moreover, the indicators chosen are actually inconsistent with the logic of plan formulation. The centre inevitably has to balance in quantity terms. Frequent plan changes respond to and in turn create shortages of specific materials.

Thus there is a panic if a mine fails to deliver a quantity of coal, but it is less disastrous for its customers and hence in its immediate impact on the economy as a whole if it fails to reach a value-added target. The latter could not be the basic ingredient of planning especially once the unrealisable hope of a stable Five Year Plan had collapsed. Instead, enterprises continued to behave as if the real issue was the quantity of outputs and of available inputs. Value-added targets were just a criterion for allocating wage funds with no further operational significance.

The package of measures was greeted with a great deal of quiet scepticism. Official statements carried contradictory messages that it represented no fundamental change – certainly nothing like the ideas for 'reform' in the late 1960s – while it was also 'not just a change of indicators, but a change in the whole approach to planning management'.[42] It did at least indicate a new willingness to accept that serious failings in the existing system of management could lie behind weaknesses in economic performance. Generally, however, economists were cautious, not least because the public discussion of the 1960s and even of Hungary's experience were taboo areas. There were continuing criticisms from within the management apparatus where lack of faith in the ability of central planners was as strong as ever. As in

Table 8.14. *Indicators of consumption in the early 1980s compared with earlier periods*

	Personal consumption	Meat per head	Car purchases	Housing completed (area)
1956–60	137	128	—	153
1961–65	122	110	126	133
1966–70	127	130	253	150
1971–75	127	115	173	148
1976–80	117	108	111	111
1981–85	104	101	74	83

Note: Figures are percentages of the previous period.
— denotes that the number purchased was extremely low.
Source: Calculated from *HSR*, pp. 91, 370, 338 & 185 and *SR*, 1986, pp. 23, 39, 496 & 216.

earlier periods, that pressure alone pointed in no constructive direction.

Maintaining living standards

This was certainly not a period of visible mass discontent, but living standards did not escape unscathed. This was the five-year period with the lowest growth in consumption. There was a decline in 1982 of which the most dramatic indicators were purchases of meat and cars. To some extent they were substituted by other foods and a growth in some other consumer durables. This was accompanied by an adjustment problem as, for a short time, demand outstripped supply for eggs (and some other substitutes) and public transport. In the case of cars the effect was muffled as, being goods for 'long-term consumption', lower sales were still compatible with rising ownership. Tables 8.14 and 8.15 show the changes in selected indicators of consumption.

This suggests a reservation over claims to have maintained living standards. It is certainly hard to take seriously official boasts of 'improved quality' of consumption. Nevertheless, Czechoslovakia did well in comparison with other countries. There was no substantial unemployment, as in Western Europe at the time, and there was certainly no dramatic, or 'qualitative' decline in living standards as happened in Poland.

Another factor that could discourage discontent was the govern-

Table 8.15. *Indicators of consumption during the Seventh Five Year Plan*

	Personal consumption	Meat per head	Car purchases	Housing completed
1978	100	100	100	100
1979	99	101	90	97
1980	99	103	69	102
1981	101	104	63	79
1982	99	96	54	86
1983	101	101	58	81
1984	103	102	67	79
1985	104	103	71	88

Note: Figures are percentages of the 1978 level.
Source: As Table 8.14

ment's ability to maintain equilibrium on much of the consumer goods market. As in 1953 and after 1969, the crucial issue need not be the growth in purchases of consumer goods but the absence of widespread shortages. Attempts to measure this, or even just estimate its extent, lead into a difficult and controversial area. It is reasonable to assume that the centre can maintain, via wage control policies, a rough overall balance between spending power and the availability of consumer goods. That, however, can coexist with considerable areas of specific shortage as there is neither the freedom to import scarce goods nor any significant price flexibility. Under these circumstances there could well be forced saving as well as forced substitution.

Several indicators of shortage are known to be unreliable, especially the length of 'queues', for reasons explained in Chapter 7. One interesting method has been developed from surveys through internal trade organisations. Estimates have been collected systematically since 1967 for a selected range of products which are then classified on a five-point scale to indicate degree of consumer satisfaction with supply. Further questions concern the change over the previous year and the results are then used to calculate an overall index for broad categories. There are obvious disadvantages, especially as aggregation can allow for the cancellation of shortages against surpluses, but the results should indicate the general trend. Moreover, detailed figures could be used which registered a shortage if demand could not be satisfied for one particular product within one of the 240 classification groups. Results in the 1970s showed less of a problem for food but considerable and fluctuating shortages for industrial consumer goods. The explanation seemed to be that consumer selectivity was growing faster than the economy's ability to adapt.[43]

An alternative approach is to use econometric studies of consumer behaviour. If consumption does not correspond to likely determinants of what consumers would like to spend, then that suggests that supply could be determining consumption. The most popular method has been to apply a Houthakker-Taylor model, which relates consumption to past spending and current incomes and seems to give good results in capitalist economies. It does seem to fit for tobacco products which are in plentiful supply but not for bicycles which are a typical case of a good subject to frequent shortages.[44] It appears, on the basis of data for 1960–75, that there is a similar stable relationship in European socialist countries between incomes and saving with the latter growing in relation to the former. The only marked deviation from the trend was in Czechoslovakia in the late 1960s.[45]

There are more sophisticated disequilibrium methods which purport to find aggregate supply and demand from existing data without assuming them to be equal. The best known such study, which again found a stable relationship explaining consumer spending, suggested excess supply in nine of the years between 1955 and 1975.[46] The authors were cautious in their conclusions and some of the specific results suggest that such modesty is justified. The greatest excess demand appeared to be in 1971 and 1972 which are generally regarded as years of widespread excess supply.

A deeper insight on consumer behaviour came from a study of short-run fluctuations in spending. Growth rates in the 1970s varied from 1.7% in 1970 to 7.5% in 1974 to 3.2% in 1975 and 5.7% in 1978: consumption had become a less stable element in national income than investment. The cause was not sudden availability: high spending seemed to go with greater shortage and lower stocks. It seemed to be an 'autonomous' reaction of the population. There could even be a consumption cycle with a length of around 3–4 years. That might be related to the lifetime of some consumer durables, making an analogy with Goldmann's explanation for the investment cycle, but small bouts of panic buying also seemed to stem from rumours of shortages or of imminent price rises. It was as if savings were building up without any obvious purpose and could then be released when a 'consumer vanguard' was frightened into over-spending. It would then take a few years for the conditions to be created for the next buying spree.[47]

The power of these subjective factors is widely accepted,[48] although other contributors could be the number of new households, the appearance of new products and even the availability of some particularly expensive goods.[49] Record car sales and a new model at a higher price could almost account for the abnormal growth in spending in 1978 relative to the previous few years. 1974 was also a good year with car exports down by almost a third and domestic sales up enough to cover half of the above average growth in total spending. Studies for specific products might therefore lead to a different conclusion relating spending more closely to availability.

One attempt used a Houthakker-Taylor model to estimate desired spending on furniture. It was assumed to depend on past incomes, growth in incomes, the stock of furniture already held by the population and changes in the relative price.[50] The data were used to calculate a separate supply function which included gross domestic output, imports and past consumption. The two were then compared and this suggested the expected excess demand in 1968 and 1969 followed by excess supply in the next two years. 1974, however, was another very good year for customers as domestic production rose by 8% and imports increased by 39%. On this measure at least, there would be no justification for panic buying. By way of contrast, 1978 saw clear excess demand which could relate to expectations of a price rise at the same time as reductions in imports. There is, then, the possibility that some saving may be forced in the sense that it is waiting for the availability of specific goods. A fall in savings deposits could therefore indicate either a shortage, leading to panic buying; or a surplus, mobilising pent-up purchasing power.

The figures from internal trade surveys have inspired attempts to find evidence of forced saving from econometric models of consumer behaviour. One study produced remarkably good results in terms of the relevant statistical tests. It started from the assumption that a significant proportion of all saving above 2.2% of disposable incomes, the lowest figure in any year which was assumed to be a minimum level, was forced while fluctuations in food purchases included forced substitution away from unavailable manufactured goods. These figures were then incorporated into a Houthakker-Taylor consumption function with the implication that forced saving would fit as an element of desired consumption.

One reason for doubting this method is that, on the basis of figures for 1965 to 1985, it showed the highest satisfaction of consumer demand for manufactured goods in the years of highest spending. It had failed to separate low saving due to availability from low saving due to panic buying. Thus for 1979 demand was almost 98% satisfied while the lowest figure was 91% for 1973. Internal trade surveys indicate that shortage tended to be higher in big-spending years.

The issue is important for an assessment of the early 1980s. The conclusion from figures for the 1981–85 period was that 40% of the growth in savings deposits was forced saving while about a third of that amount was spent on food as forced substitution. This was set alongside an even less plausible measure of excess demand for investment. The method was to assume a relationship with the level of gross national income and past investment and with past trends in those variables. It is inevitable, when investment has been cut, that total demand calculated by such a method will be greater than the realised level of investment. This may be a fair estimate of what enterprises, or even higher bodies, would like to invest but it does not relate in any way to excess demand in the sense of projects started beyond the capacity of the economy. Nevertheless, the conclusion was that 'the problems of external economic equilibrium have been solved to a significant extent at the expense of internal equilibrium'.[51]

Internal trade surveys suggest a more complex picture with a sudden worsening in food shortages in 1981, but then a dramatic improvement to create an overall position of excess supply by 1983. There were still shortages for fruit, some categories of which had to be imported, but an understandable surplus of milk and milk products. The key to this improvement was the good performance in agriculture plus an 8.6% increase in nominal food prices in 1982 after an average inflation rate of zero for 1971–6 and 1.4% for 1976–80.[52]

Shortages of manufactured goods seemed to be decreasing too, although price rises were below the 2.3% average of the late 1970s. This is a surprising result in view of export promotion and restrictions on imports. In fact the aggregate measure concealed a number of sharply increasing shortages including televisions and refrigerators and freezers.[53] The econometric evidence for furniture also showed the highest ever indication of excess demand in the early 1980s.[54] This might put a different angle on the high rate of saving. Running at 3.7% of disposable incomes it was above the level expected by planners and seemed to be a stabilising element. Despite the slow growth in disposable incomes, saving accounts for 41% of that growth in the 1981–5 period compared with 17% in 1966–70 and just under 30% throughout the 1970s.[55] It seemed that, despite price rises on a scale that would have been unthinkable in any other period since 1953, 'the trust of citizens in the economic situation' was growing.[56]

This, however, was growth from a very low level. In early 1982 an opinion poll showed only 5% thinking the state of the economy and living standards had improved from the previous year; in contrast, 67% correctly saw a worsening. Comparable figures for autumn 1978 were 27% and 11%. By the autumn of 1983, 10% thought things were getting better[57] although official figures suggest far more grounds for optimism. This could suggest deep dissatisfaction compatible with a form of reluctant saving due to the poor quality of consumer goods. The slow pace of innovation in domestic industry was clearly visible from a comparison with goods in foreign currency shops. There had been little lag in introducing black and white televisions in the early 1950s, but colour televisions appeared on general sale only in 1982. Video-recorders were promised for the future as part of a joint manu-facturing deal with Philips and the first compact disc factory in the CMEA was due to be built in Czechoslovakia. Another bout of panic buying could clear the stocks of unwanted furniture and electrical equipment, but knowledge of what is available in some neighbouring countries may be helping to make consumers too choosy for that. This might be interpreted as a form of confidence that the desired goods would eventually be available, but is hardly a welcome phenomenon.

Problems on the domestic market could have two further effects. One, which is beginning to attract attention and seems plausible in view of the shortages most strongly felt in Czechoslovakia, is the possible impact on work incentives. Attention has been drawn to the coincidence of low growth in labour productivity, relative to other CMEA countries, and low growth in personal consumption.[58] It is, however, difficult to prove direct causation.

The other possibility is that discontent could be expressed publicly. The example at the start of the decade was obvious, but there was hardly a thought of copying Poland's mass protest. Workers in Czechoslovakia have anyway staged no major strikes since 1953 with the exception of symbolic protests in August 1968. Poland's crisis with almost universal shortages was on a totally different level from Czechoslovakia's problems which concern mostly the range and quality of manufactured consumer goods. Moreover, the Polish events were widely felt to have exacerbated difficulties first by the restriction of coal supplies in 1981 and then by causing greater hard-currency restrictions. Thus Czechoslovakia seemed to be paying for the bungles of the Polish leadership and then for what many were willing to believe were further economic costs imposed by the strikes and protests of 1980 and 1981.

Overall, the leadership did have some grounds for satisfaction. The country had achieved a hard-currency surplus. It had maintained a reasonably rapid growth rate: for industry the use of the gross output indicator suggested that it was faster than all significant Western European countries. It had one of the lowest inflation rates in Europe at 10% for the whole 1980–85 period. The evidence was of an improved market situation for food and a number of basic manufactured consumer goods. The country had also avoided any signs of mass unemployment. Leading officials were boasting of their success in 'the gradual implementation of intensive directions of development'[59] as evidence that the economy could achieve substantial positive results. In fact, the successes of the early 1980s – in running an export surplus without too much harm to living standards – were achieved by putting off measures that could contribute to the modernisation of the economy. Buoyed up by the habit of complacency, they attached no urgency to major changes that might be needed to reverse the gradual, long-term relative decline of the Czechoslovak economy.

9   Relative decline

The slowdown in the late 1970s and stagnation at the start of the next decade were not unique to Czechoslovakia. All the European socialist countries experienced a worsening in performance and it is reasonable to assume some degree of common explanation. One obvious and plausible suggestion is the gradual exhaustion of raw material sources leading to 'the enormous growth of extraction and other costs' in distant and almost inaccessible parts of the Soviet Union.[1] This could never be a complete explanation on its own as it begs the question of why the same raw materials could not be bought on the world market. It needs to be combined with a recognition of declining competitiveness particularly in the face of newly industrialising countries.

Tentative studies, moreover, suggest that higher costs explain little of the decline in Soviet growth rates,[2] and the major problems for other CMEA countries related, until the early 1980s, to rising prices from the agreed use of the five-year moving average. An almost absolute barrier in raw materials is, however, plausible, at least for Czechoslovakia. Econometric studies have shown an extraordinarily close and stable relationship between gross industrial output and raw material imports.[3] It is even possible to construct a reasonably good model of the Czechoslovak economy as a whole starting from the assumption of a fixed relationship between output and imports.[4] The link also holds at the more disaggregated level. The ratio of crude iron production to imported iron ore over the 1960–78 period changed from 0.65 to 0.64 with only small deviations outside that range.

The inability to improve this relationship could have been particularly serious as other CMEA countries were industrialising and becoming dependent to some degree on imported fuel and raw materials. Each wanted trade relations with a deficit in these commodities.[5] Declining competitiveness in manufactured goods could have left Czechoslovakia losing ground in relation to the chief supplier, the USSR. The inability to earn adequate hard currency to buy replacements on the world market inevitably held Czechoslovakia's growth in check. There was a similar slowdown elsewhere in Eastern Europe, but Czechoslovakia's performance was slightly worse than the average despite a smaller level of hard-currency debt: it may have been due more to its position within the CMEA and less directly to hard-currency problems.

Ultimately the blame must lie not with external changes but with the internal operation of the economy which failed to raise international competitiveness or adapt to the need to survive without continually expanding material inputs. The simplest view of internal weaknesses is the familiar argument that centralised planning becomes 'increasingly unable to cope with the problems of a modern industrial society'. As it becomes more advanced and complex so it could be 'reasonable to see' its weaknesses 'becoming more acute through time'.[6] This is very similar to the Goldmann-Kouba argument of the 1960s. It can be made more specific by the use of precise measures of performance. The conclusion seems to be that Czechoslovakia, more clearly than any other CMEA country, suffered from a gradual relative decline from the early 1950s onwards. The root causes are located in lack of innovative activity and international integration. Generally speaking, whenever flexibility and change was needed, the system seemed unable to cope satisfactorily.

Factor productivity and production functions

The key to exposing what had been happening is to go beyond figures on growth in output alone and relate them to the use of inputs. The simplest way is to find the quantities of each separate input needed for a unit increase in output. The figures in Table 9.1 provide a basis for this and would show, obviously enough, a low growth in output per unit increase in fixed assets, with particularly bad periods in the early 1960s and late 1970s. The trend for labour appears to be similar in that productivity performed badly in that first period. The trend in the consumption of energy seems to have improved after 1965 while the trend for other raw materials seems extraordinarily consistent.

This is useful information but, without a weighting of the various inputs, it gives no clear overall measure of the economy's performance. The notion of total factor productivity aims to overcome that

Table 9.1. *Growth in output and factors of production for the productive sphere of the Czechoslovak economy 1960–1980*

	Output	Fixed assets	Labour	Energy	Materials
1960	100	100	100	100	100
1965	120.0	126.9	102.3	121.6	126.9
1970	166.9	157.8	108.8	129.8	177.8
1975	220.9	208.7	111.0	145.5	236.8
1980	265.4	281.0	113.5	159.7	284.4

Source: J. Klacek & A. Nešporová, 'Modelování variantních trajektorů ekonomického růstu', *PE*, XXX, p. 935 (1982).

weakness. Its origins are in neo-classical economic theory, but the basic principle is still applicable without assuming that payment to factors of production depends on their marginal products. In essence the theory is that a growth in output depends on a growth in inputs. Assuming constant returns to scale, then if all inputs really are included, the growth in inputs will fully explain the growth in output. In practice, not all inputs can be quantified. Studies typically use a limited number, such as capital and labour, and the resulting unexplained growth is termed total factor productivity. The more inputs that are included, such as making allowances for the better quality of labour, the more of growth is explained. There is, however, always a 'residual' which is often ascribed to technical progress as the most obvious source that cannot otherwise be quantified.

Various different attempts have been made to adapt the concept of total factor productivity to Czechoslovak conditions. Recent studies have embodied some innovations which relate to concern at specific barriers to growth.[7] Instead of just labour and fixed assets, it is possible to use three and ultimately five inputs – labour, fixed assets and raw materials later divided into energy, metals and other materials – so that growth can be subdivided into the simple quantitative increase in each input plus the improvement in its utilisation. A logical consequence is the use of a *gross* output measure for national income.

Growth in total factor productivity appears as the weighted arithmetic average of the individual improvements in the utilisation of the five inputs. Weights were based on those inputs' shares in total costs of production. There is little alternative to this although it is clear that internal prices for inputs, additional charges per employee and the

Table 9.2. *Average annual growth rates in national income and total factor productivity in CMEA countries, 1961–1984*

		1961–70	1971–75	1976–80	1981–84
Czechoslovakia	nat. inc.	4.4	5.7	3.6	1.5
	TFP	1.1	1.5	0.6	0.0
Hungary	nat. inc.	5.4	6.2	2.8	2.1
	TFP	1.4	1.6	0.4	0.3
GDR	nat. inc.	4.4	5.4	4.1	4.3
	TFP	1.1	1.3	0.7	1.0
European CMEA	nat. inc.	—	6.4	4.1	3.1

Note: — Not available in source.
Source: Janáček, *Hlavní*, pp. 82–3.

arbitrarily set depreciation rate need not relate to true costs to society. Nevertheless, the authors of these studies are confident that their broad conclusions are not sensitive to plausible variations in these magnitudes.

The picture that emerges is of sharp year-to-year fluctuations, but there is some evidence of secular decline at least from 1966 onwards and the impression is unmistakable that the slowdown in overall growth rates was due to worse use of inputs rather than just an absolute restriction on the latter. Tables 9.2 and 9.3 show the results since 1961 in terms of comparisons within the CMEA and of the breakdown into individual factor productivities indicating the improvement in the utilisation of that input. The picture that emerges is bad: only Poland did worse in the early 1980s, and the decline is especially marked in the productivity of fixed assets. In view of the improved utilisation of energy, this would be consistent with an energy barrier leading to the underutilisation of other inputs. That need not rule out a simultaneous long-term decline and there are claims of a declining quality of fixed assets in some sectors.[8]

If this slowdown was caused by a particular barrier, then it needs to be explained why the shortage of one input could not be overcome by substituting another. The best way to analyse this is to find elasticities of substitution from a production function. The simplest forms actually assume a fixed degree of substitutability so that the most meaningful results need an extremely general one such as the tran-

Table 9.3. *Individual factor productivities in Czechoslovakia 1961–1980*

	Total productivity	Productivity of labour	Productivity of fixed assets	Productivity of all materials		
				total	non-energy	energy
1961–65	0.2	3.3	−1.2	−1.3	−1.1	−0.3
1966–70	2.0	5.6	2.2	0.1	−0.2	5.4
1971–75	1.5	5.3	0.0	0.1	−0.1	3.4
1976–80	0.6	3.2	−2.3	0.2	0.0	1.8

Source: M. Toms & M. Hajék, 'Proces intenzifikace a prognózování růstu souhrnné hospodárnosti čs. ekonomiky', *PE*, XXX, p. 929 (1982); J. Klacek & A. Nešporová, 'Modelování', p. 941.

scendental logarithmic function. Its complex mathematical form also avoids assumptions of constant returns to scale and of the separability of the contributions of different inputs.[9]

This was applied to the Czechoslovak economy over the 1960–80 period using as inputs fixed assets (measured at their original cost in fixed prices and corrected to allow for variations in the degree of utilisation), labour (uncorrected for improvements in quality), energy and other materials. Annual figures, of which a sample are given in Table 9.1, were used to estimate the production function. The conclusions, however, have to be regarded in the words of the authors, as 'tentative'.[10] It was impossible to obtain satisfactory results from the familiar ordinary least squares method as the effects of increases in different inputs cannot be separated. Good results were only possible with the use of ridge regression which, according to some authorities, should not be trusted.[11]

It was, however, the only method that could produce usable results. Partial elasticities of substitution[12] between the four factors of production were calculated for each year up to 1980 and the results suggested that, from 1975 onwards, no substitution at all was possible between *any* of the inputs. Previously, there had been substitution between fixed assets and energy (up to 1964), between assets and materials (up to 1975) and between energy and materials (up to 1961).[13] The implication of this is that any input could now be a barrier restricting growth. For some reason, flexibility that had once existed had declined and then vanished.

The same production function could be used as an alternative measure of the growth in output unexplained by quantitative growth

in inputs. More than any other method, it suggested that Czechoslovakia was the worst of the European CMEA countries over the
whole 1960–80 period, although the Soviet Union was even more
dependent on increasing inputs by the late 1970s.[14] The obvious
explanation, for Czechoslovakia at least, was some form of inflexibility combined with restrictions on raw materials leading to under-
utilisation of other inputs and hence declining total factor productivity. Energy was especially likely to be the operative barrier as
output per unit of energy continued to grow as it did throughout the
CMEA. Czechoslovakia's particularly bad performance could then be
due, at least in part, to its high energy dependence and specific
difficulties in changing the structure of its economy towards less
energy-intensive activities.

One very serious reservation to this relates to the measurability of
fixed assets. Capital equipment, made up often of unique products of
monopoly producers, is particularly susceptible to price inflation disguised behind bogus improvements.[15] The price index also seems
unable to take account of the rapidly rising prices of imported
machinery, of higher development costs, of additional repair bills
following the forced substitution of raw materials, of the need to build
under less favourable conditions and several other factors. The difference that this makes is suggested by a study of machinery in the
engineering industry over the period 1970–81. By looking at what the
machines could actually do rather than the prices paid for them, the
total growth was scaled down from 121% to 32%.[16] If this distortion
were general, and there is evidence of massive cost increases from
other industries which appear much greater than recorded inflation,[17]
then much of the decline in the productivity of assets, and hence in
total factor productivity, would disappear, with the remainder caused
by lower utilisation due to the restriction of other inputs.

There is believed to be no important difference up to the mid-1970s,
but disguised inflation on investment goods is estimated at slightly
over 2% per annum from 1978 to 1985, made up of 1.5–1.75% on
construction work and 3.0–3.3% on machinery.[18] The implications are
wider even than the conclusions of these particular studies. Doubt is
cast on aggregate national income figures and on the share of investment in national income both of which may have been exaggerated.

In fact, the same study using labour and fixed assets figures corrected for quality, still found no *ex post* substitutability between those two
inputs. Substitution between energy and fixed assets or raw materials
remained relatively easy, but it was still possible to attribute the

deceleration of growth in the 1970s primarily to restrictions on energy and raw materials.

A corrected figure for fixed assets would therefore probably make little difference to the corollary of the original study with the four-factor production function. This was a prediction of future performance based on reasonable guesses at the rate of growth of inputs and at changes in their partial productivities. Assuming, as seemed likely, a minimal increase in energy inputs, a slow growth in the labour force and a low productivity per unit increase in fixed assets – due not least to the commitments to projects such as nuclear power with long gestation periods – there seemed no chance whatsoever of fulfilling the political leadership's dream of a return to growth rates of around 5%. More likely were figures around 2% in the early 1980s and between 1 and 3.4% in the later 1980s. Higher growth rates could only be achieved by a dramatic improvement in the utilisation of inputs.

What is intensification?

A further attraction in these sorts of studies is that they seem to provide the basis for a more rigorous definition of extensive and intensive growth. Marx himself referred to two possible methods for expanding the reproduction of capital. One, extensive, depends on more inputs while the other, intensive, depends on their more effective utilisation.[19] This easily links up with the approach derived from neo-classical theory to give two poles of purely extensive and purely intensive growth. In reality growth is usually somewhere between these extremes but, so it is suggested, can be described as extensive if more than half can be attributed to a greater quantity of inputs and intensive if more than half is due to better utilisation of inputs. Intensification need not mean achieving purely intensive growth: it can be defined as raising the share of intensive factors in the rate of growth of output.

There have been serious reservations over the attempt to find precise measures and theories of intensification that may 'push the qualitative characteristics into the background'[20] and mask the desirable changes in the nature of growth in the Czechoslovak economy. The origins of the concept are in agriculture and relate to the better use of one input, namely land. When applied more generally with multiple inputs, problems arise of aggregation and of what to include. This would not matter except that different methods can produce very different results. Moreover, excessive formalisation and theorisation

leads to strange conclusions. Thus the degree of intensification has
been subdivided into no less than seven zones with the hypothesis
that, as an economy develops, it will move through a series of stages
with a certain balance between intensive and extensive factors.[21] This
is not borne out by changes over time, which suggest a consistent shift
back towards extensive sources of growth after 1975, nor by comparisons between socialist economies which suggest no strong link
between level of development and share of intensive sources.[22]

Despite this cautionary note, something can be learnt from applying the concept: a comparison with Austria, Japan and the USA
produced some instructive surprises.[23] There was more similarity
than expected to Czechoslovakia and particularly the USA seemed
unable to achieve 'intensive' growth in the period studied. This result,
derived from a four-factor production function and a measure of gross
output, was quite different from the result from a two-factor function
which suggested 'intensive' growth from the mid-1950s.[24] Tables 9.4
and 9.5 are derived from some of the figures used for the study. The
partial productivity of fixed assets in the USA performed very badly
after 1969 while the use of energy and other raw materials suggest
little for Czechoslovakia to be ashamed of. The share of 'intensive'
factors – derived from the difference between growth in output and a
weighted sum of growth in inputs – in a lower rate of growth was
probably not much higher at around 21% for the 1965–77 period.[25]

Japan's growth process, however, appeared to have undergone a
transformation around 1973. Expansion was still possible despite a
reduction in energy inputs and it is hard to imagine any conceivable
set of weights that would not attribute the great bulk of growth to
better utilisation of inputs. Japan seemed to have moved from 'the
predominantly extensive' to the 'predominantly intensive' phase of its
growth. 'Intensive' factors, calculated as for the USA, accounted for
only 17% of growth for the 1965–78 period but 57% for the 1973–78
period.[26] It was, however, a transition that required a continued
expansion of material inputs and that was based on a massive
accumulation of capital. These points have important implications for
Czechoslovakia if it is to follow a similar path of 'intensification'.

This still only provides part of the practical meaning for intensification. All the methods considered so far imply that growth can be
equated with saving on inputs or increasing the quantity of outputs.
There is no indication of how far that depends on the introduction of
new products rather than just finding better methods to produce
existing ones. Both should be seen as intensification as a better

Table 9.4. *Output and inputs of US manufacturing industry, 1958–1977*

	Output	Fixed assets	Labour	Energy	Materials
1958	100	100	100	100	100
1977	204	161	128	202	199

Source: Calculated from Klacek, 'Relace', p. 57.

Table 9.5. *Output and inputs of Japanese manufacturing industry, 1965–1978*

	Output	Fixed assets	Labour	Energy	Materials
1965	100	100	100	100	100
1973	271	375	112	240	249
1973	100	100	100	100	100
1978	115	116	88	98	109

Source: Calculated from Klacek, 'Relace', p. 58.

product should command a higher price. That relationship need not be precise within the Czechoslovak institutional framework and it is anyway valuable to use the quality of output as a further indicator of the economy's performance.

Prices of new products actually depend on an essentially subjective assessment of how far they represent an improvement over old ones. That either means estimating just how radical a change an innovation represents, which hardly gives a simple quantitative indicator, or attempting a comparison of 'newness' in relation to existing products of that enterprise, within Czechoslovakia, within the CMEA or throughout the world.[27] Such measures are notoriously unreliable, although it must have some significance that only around 2% of Czechoslovak products are judged as reaching world quality. Unfortunately, the measure seems to be influenced by hopes of which sectors should do well and by pressure from enterprises, periodically countered by insistence on stricter criteria. Trends are therefore meaningless: the share of world quality products in the clothing industry increased from 6.4% in 1976 to 9.3% in 1980 while neither figure was reflected in export performance. Some figures appear quite bizarre, such as the 0.0% for the well-established glass, ceramics and porcelain sector in 1978.[28] Ultimately the only way to test product quality is by export success and that can give very different results.

The slump in competitiveness

No single measure satisfactorily summarises foreign competitiveness over the whole post-1948 period. One useful indicator, at least for the period up to the 1970s, is based on the difference between domestic prices, corrected for taxes and profits so as to come nearer to an indication of internal costs, and export prices. An index of comparative efficiency derived from this shows a slow but, with the exception of a couple of years, absolutely continuous decline from 1953 to the mid-1970s.[29] The measure is still used as an indicator of the profitability of exports, but the necessary data for its calculation are not published, possibly because they could be quoted as evidence of dumping. Calculations anyway become far more difficult in a period of rapid inflation and fluctuating exchange rates, but no other measure exists which relates export performance to domestic costs.

The only other indicator available over a very long period is the terms of trade. Unfortunately, published figures have only very recently differentiated between the various world markets. They are calculated from a selection of goods covering 70% of the value of imports and exports which may not be fully representative; and there are obviously dangers in comparisons over long time periods when the structure of trade and relative prices can vary substantially. Over short periods they could reflect factors beyond the country's control. A persistent worsening, however, for a country exporting predominantly manufactured goods, suggests a failure to adapt to changes in the world economy or a failure to maintain international competitiveness.

Czechoslovakia's experience can usefully be divided into five periods.[30] The late 1940s were an exceptionally favourable time with high export prices. They fell rapidly, probably particularly in relation to non-socialist economies, with the economy's integration into the Soviet bloc while raw material import prices remained high through the Korean war. Then followed a long, fairly stable period with little substantial change until the end of the 1960s. A brief, favourable interlude around 1970–71, associated with the high export prices into non-socialist countries, was followed by a sharp and continuing decline in relation to both trading blocs.

This is the period in which the figures are the least reliable owing to the scale of fluctuations in price levels, but the worsening cannot be attributed to rising raw material prices. Over the period 1971–80 the index of raw material prices, excluding oil, rose only marginally faster than the price of manufactured goods. The higher price of oil on the world market was, for much of that period, almost irrelevant to Czechoslovakia which should therefore have been performing *better* than advanced capitalist countries. Instead, it experienced a growing trade deficit with the developed economies of Western Europe which were exporting engineering goods in exchange, to a great extent, for raw materials. West Germany's exports, for example, were 50% machinery and 10% food and raw materials while 40% of its imports from Czechoslovakia were made up of raw materials.

Along with a number of other advanced capitalist countries, it was able to react to the changing world situation and limit the decline in its terms of trade, as shown in UN statistics, to only 4% over the 1973–9 period, compared with 12% for Czechoslovakia. The commodity structure of exports and imports of those two countries are fairly similar overall and it does seem reasonable to conclude that Czechoslovakia's difficulties 'relate rather to difficulties with selling our machinery with its unsatisfactory technical level'.[31] The decline in terms of trade was more immediate with the socialist than with the non-socialist countries,[32] the latter still less than 10% down on 1973 at the end of the decade. By 1984, however, the index relative to 1975 was 73.7 with the socialist countries and 73.4 with the non-socialist world.[33]

Stronger evidence in this direction comes from a study of Eastern European manufacturing exports to a number of capitalist countries.[34] The general picture since the late 1960s, as shown in Table 9.6, is of a slow but steady decline of Czechoslovakia's share in imports into the 22 selected countries, although some product groups showed signs of stabilisation in 1981–2. For Eastern Europe as a whole, there was far more success in the mid-1970s as Poland and Hungary in particular seemed to be doing well. Moreover, there clearly was scope for advance as shown by the performance of newly industrialised countries and Southern Europe (Turkey, Greece, Spain and Portugal) which has a very similar export structure to Eastern Europe as a whole.

The next step was to use the method of constant market shares to separate out the effects of the territorial structure of exports, the demand for particular groups of commodities and a residual that

Table 9.6. *Percentage share in imports from various countries of manufactured goods into developed market economies*

	1965	1970	1975	1977	1981
Eastern Europe	1.56	1.48	1.71	1.71	1.46
Czechoslovakia	0.48	0.45	0.41	0.37	0.33
Newly industrialised countries	2.74	2.99	4.41	5.44	6.95
Southern Europe	0.84	1.10	1.85	1.90	2.10

Source: 'Exports', p. 459.

includes a variety of factors assumed to relate to competitiveness. For the selection of products chosen, it again appeared that Czechoslovakia had done uniformly badly across the whole period and across almost the whole product range. Declining export performance explained more than half the fall in export share in the late 1960s and in the 1978–81 period. During the rest of the 1970s it even overwhelmed a favourable shift in demand for products. The only sign of hope was a recovery in the performance indicator in the early 1980s due to good results for chemicals.

The same approach was used for 18 selected groups of engineering industry products at the level of the three-figure SITC classification.[35] Overall, for the period 1965–80, Czechoslovakia's share in engineering exports into non-socialist countries fell by around 48% and the performance indicator proved important throughout the 1970s, especially for exports to the advanced capitalist countries, both at the level of the commodity groups and of the sector as a whole. As in the UN study, it appeared that up to 1977 Czechoslovakia's share would have fallen more rapidly but for a *favourable* shift in demand structure. For 1978–81, declining competitiveness explained around three-quarters of a 41% drop in market share for the whole engineering industry. The only consistent exceptions were the groups including domestic electrical appliances, agricultural machinery and aircraft.

It was not difficult to eliminate a number of possible explanations for this negative trend. Czechoslovak export prices rose more slowly than the average for advanced capitalist countries and even for Hungary's exports, so that factor should have given a competitive advantage. There was no shortage of productive capacity: in fact some products aimed at capitalist markets could not be sold. There may have been some impact from protectionist trade policies; but the principal explanation must be the worsening relative quality of Czechoslovak goods.

Still stronger evidence is provided by the kilogram prices of exports. This is the subject of considerable interest inside Czechoslovakia with a general assumption that a high price per kilogram of product reflects a high input of 'qualified labour'. Official statements even refer to this measure as a desirable target for economic policy. Foreign trade statistics, however, make it impossible to calculate a figure for any product so that Czechoslovak economists have had to rely on EEC trade statistics which helpfully break down imports by country of origin.

The measure has been suggested in Britain as an indicator of the technological level of machinery, and it does correspond in some cases at least to the foreign trade performance of individual products.[36] It seems far more attractive as a measure of comparative product quality of an Eastern European country able to produce and export even highly uncompetitive products. A low figure, for example for cars, suggests the need to sell more to achieve the same financial return.

There are, however, three reservations. The first is that an apparently good performance might be achieved at an enormous cost in investment or development expenses; in other words, it is purely an indication of the quality of the end product and not of the profitability of producing or exporting it. The second reservation is that it is largely a meaningless measure for raw materials and becomes most significant only for the most differentiated products. The third and most important reservation is an ambiguity over exactly what is being measured. A low price-to-weight ratio for a broad product group could reflect either lower quality or a bias towards inherently heavier products: even the latter could be judged a possible indication of technological backwardness, but that need not always be true. To solve this ambiguity by using highly disaggregated figures limits the scope for comparisons over time and actually eliminates one of the benefits of the whole method. Thus, for example, the apparent recent decline in performance of Czechoslovak machine tool exports is largely due to the failure to win a foothold in the market for the most advanced products which did not exist as a detailed classification a few years ago. In this case it is very reasonable to assume that a range of products biased towards a low price per kilogram does reflect technological backwardness.

Accepting these reservations, the measure can be used to indicate, again, the low and declining relative level of Czechoslovak products. A study in the 1960s[37] compared the price per kilogram of Czechoslovak exports into the EEC with the price of exports from EEC countries themselves which was assumed to represent a high level of international competitiveness. It is well known that a fairly small difference in quality can lead to very substantial differences in price and that was confirmed for what was intended to be a representative sample of engineering industry products. For some, such as sewing machines, electric motors and mining equipment, the Czechoslovak selling price was 20–40% of the level achieved by other exporters. Tractors and cars reached 40–60% while only in textile machinery, at 153% in 1964, was Czechoslovakia able to charge a price above the average level.

The situation was remarkably similar even for products of the steel industry and still worse for some consumer goods. Shoes, for example, had a selling price in 1964 little over 25% of the level from advanced capitalist countries. Generally speaking, however, the further advanced along the production process, so the worse Czechoslovakia's competitive position. The best results were achieved with cut timber. As has been indicated, these are the least meaningful figures: competitiveness in raw materials and similar relatively homogeneous products can only really be assessed in terms of costs of production as the quality of final product should not vary much.

These figures show changes over the relatively brief period from 1959 to 1964 and in most cases there was a worsening. An extension and expansion of this method, using product groups that maintain a significant position in EEC imports over a twenty-year period, leaves little doubt about the trends. In general, very few product groups perform really well and a number have fallen from around the 60% level to the 30–40% level below which it is maybe no longer worth exporting. Table 9.7 needs to be interpreted with the obvious reservation that the EEC expanded its membership in the early 1970s and the calculations take no account of that.

It is impossible not to comment on the sheer extent of the implied gap between Czechoslovak and world products. The measure used is likely to exaggerate differences. A small variation in quality or failure to respond to the latest changes in fashion for some consumer goods could make a product almost unsaleable and hence force its price down a very long way. There are two issues here apart from the technological level of Czechoslovak products. The first is the apparent indifference of Eastern European exporters to the potential of their

Table 9.7. *Price per kilogram of selected Czechoslovak exports to the EEC as a percentage of the price per kilogram of intra-EEC trade*

	1963	1966	1972	1975	1978	1981	1983
Glass bottles	37	37	38	38	36	42	38
Glassware	149	145	176	188	194	166	199
Steel bars & rods	77	88	79	77	85	85	54
Tractors	63	63	52	51	42	43	37
Machine tools	67	42	44	41	41	33	30
Cars	52	68	55	46	41	32	31
Lorries	90	83	71	65	53	55	56
Mens' & boys' outer garments	67	52	65	68	66	64	62
Footwear (upper leather)	25	—	33	37	38	39	36

Source: Calculated from relevant years of Eurostat, *Analytical Tables of Foreign Trade*.

products: Western importers often believe that a small investment and small improvement could make an immense difference. Instead, administrative convenience encourages enormous production runs of standardised products with minimum variability. That is adequate for the domestic market, but makes it difficult to export machinery and especially fashion goods. Foreign trade organisations seem happy with a practice of 'disaster pricing' whereby goods are sold, often as part of barter deals with Western firms, at absurdly low prices.[38]

The second issue is the pricing policy itself. Despite claims to be researching Western market conditions, it seems that many export prices are little more than an adaptation from domestic wholesale prices which is the simplest way to ensure adequate profitability of foreign trade.[39] The low price per kilogram figures are therefore only partially a reflection of weaknesses in the Czechoslovak economy as a whole. They also reflect the specific lack of interest in an orientation towards exporting into the most competitive capitalist markets.

To some extent they may also reflect deliberate discrimination, as is believed by foreign trade organisations. An attempt to allow for this by comparing prices per kilogram of Yugoslavia's imports certainly yields an improvement for some products: Czechoslovak lorries, for example, rose to 93% of the average for all imports in 1984. The general picture, however, remains unchanged. Moreover, a comparison with other CMEA countries is highly uncomplimentary. By 1983 the price per kilogram of engineering products sold into the EEC was lower than that of any CMEA country apart from the Soviet

Union and even that was at the same level.[40] The comparison is slightly deceptive as Czechoslovakia holds a more substantial market share than the other small CMEA countries in important sections of engineering such as the motor industry, but the trend is obviously significant.

It is remarkable how closely trade performance matches with measures of internal performance. One link is the dependence of internal growth on export performance. Worsening conditions for earning foreign currency meant that imports suffered from increasingly severe restriction while ever more domestic resources had to be directed into exports at the expense of domestic investment and modernisation. A second possible link is that both could be indicators of the level of innovative activity within the economy. A high level could be expected to produce competitive products, savings of inputs and flexibility in face of worsening external conditions. The available evidence points to a rather disappointing performance.

Investment and integration

Strictly speaking, a thorough analysis should distinguish innovations in processes from those in products, but that seems to make little difference to the conclusion. More significant is a classification by the extent of disruption caused by an innovation which suggests that Czechoslovakia performs relatively worse the wider the effects. Evidence in the previous section points both to backwardness, relative to the most advanced countries in the world, and to a widening gap. This is supported also by the impressionistic method of a questionnaire to 342 'experts' in technological development. There was agreement that the pace of change was speeding up but 88% thought the rate was slower in Czechoslovakia than in capitalist countries: only 2% thought it was faster. Moreover, the lag was becoming most noticeable in the fastest growing areas.[41]

There is a common assumption in Czechoslovakia that performance at the invention stage is good, but that it is let down by barriers to further development and implementation. Figures show Czechoslovakia occupying first place in the world for patents per head in the 1980s.[42] This, however, is a highly unreliable statistic as an individual patent gives little indication of the real value of the invention. Using the percentage share of non-resident US patents, Czechoslovakia accounts for 0.23% compared with 0.37% for Hungary, almost 10% for the United Kingdom and over 30% for Japan.[43]

The size of the research base is also open to exaggeration. Crude comparisons, using a published figure of 181 000 research workers and 3.8% of national income, suggest a position ahead of any capitalist country. Using strictly comparable figures for full-time equivalents of scientists and engineers in engineering and scientific research, Czechoslovakia's figure falls to 39 700, which is well behind Japan and the USA. It still looks respectable, but resources devoted per qualified research worker are only around one-third to one-half of the level of the advanced capitalist countries. This fits with very frequent complaints that research is stifled by inadequate resources.[44]

It also appears that central attempts to direct these resources are frequently distorted by the entrenched interests in the economy. A small number of big projects have been selected which are intended to cut through the boundaries between ministries, but they usually end up fragmented or tied to particular interest groups. Thus the project for energy was sensibly conceived to cover production, consumption and conservation. In practice, it slipped into proposals for the energy industry alone. It is much harder to organise conservation, which links with no specific interest group and depends rather on innovations that may cut across sectoral boundaries and on knowledge, confidence and the incentive at low levels.[45]

The fragmentation of research effort is a logical consequence of the fragmentation of economic organisation. This is often attributed to the necessity to produce an enormous range of goods as a consequence of Czechoslovakia's semi-autarkic structure. Figures are quoted suggesting that 70% of the world range of engineering products are manufactured, thus dispersing research and limiting scope for mass production.[46] The result is no less than 30 000 tasks for applied research – roughly one for every specialist research worker – which inevitably forces concentration towards very minor innovations.[47]

There is an important reservation to this argument as the 70% figure relates to quite broad classification groups. Narrower ranges would show, for example, that very few specific car models are manufactured in Czechoslovakia. It might even be argued that the economy is highly specialised, with visible consequences in the narrow range of consumer goods. There are serious difficulties in achieving international integration, as discussed below, but possibly as serious a problem is the low level of *internal* specialisation. Thus for the manufacture of robots several enterprises make their own final product and their own components, each trying to use its own research base and traditions. There are still four lorry manufacturers, with motors and drive mechanisms based on very different principles: there could be clear gains from the concentration of research and production facilities onto one concept.

The problem was clearly recognised by the late 1950s when a great deal of publicity was given to narrowing the range of products by standardisation. Success was soon claimed for tractors, with 80% of components in common for the different sizes of motor, and the hope was to apply the same principle in lorries and buses.[48]

Traditions and regional interests not only hampered this, but even threatened further fragmentation. Thus in 1968 a proposal came from an Ostrava mine for a car factory which, they argued – perhaps naïvely – would provide employment for women and miners with damaged health. The idea won a lot of local support, but there was even stronger pressure from Slovakia for a new factory to produce 100–150 thousand small cars under licence from a Western firm. The justification was the desire to eliminate quickly the 180 000 waiting list for new cars, although that was later to appear as a great exaggeration of demand. Had the proposal gone ahead it would have created overcapacity and fragmented production. The government's preference was therefore to satisfy Slovak demands, which they interpreted as 20 000 employment places, by building a specialised branch factory as a component of the whole Czechoslovak industry.[49] In effect, new capacity has been used in this way, but a Czech belief persists that greater Slovak lobbying power in the 1970s has created unnecessary capacity for prestige reasons only.

International integration was recognised as valuable from the time of the CMEA's foundation. It is not crucial for all sectors: in the heavy chemicals industry, stages in the production process depend so closely on each other that the case is overwhelming for a single giant complex. In engineering, however, final products often depend on a vast number of separate production processes giving enormous scope for specialisation between developed countries. The conditions were believed to exist for this by the late 1950s. Specialisation agreements, mainly with the GDR, then aimed to specify which country would concentrate on which kind of lorries and buses with the hope of using as many common components and concepts as possible. Czechoslovakia seemed to be gaining as it dropped the production of various kinds of agricultural equipment, machine tools and other engineering products.[50] It was, however, often a tough battle to persuade partners to drop an existing product.

Subsequent evidence suggests deepening integration of engineering through the 1970s, but its benefits are uncertain. A major limitation was a relative emphasis on end-product specialisation. Capitalist countries were increasingly trading semi-finished products while Czechoslovakia and the CMEA generally were missing this area.[51] There is a similar situation for consumer goods, in which mutual trade is partly organised by barter between big department stores. It is possible that, taking account of the country's level of development and despite a widely held contrary belief, the level of imports relative to national income is within the range that would be expected for a capitalist economy of similar size.[52] Integration, however, could be taking a form that misses some of the biggest potential benefits especially in the engineering industry.

A great deal has been written on the persistent barriers to deeper integration of the CMEA economies. The most important seems to be that it is, in practice, always subordinated to immediate aims within the essentially bilateral trading system. Thus countries aim to balance their trade whenever possible and give priority to imports that cover particular shortages. An enormous number of agreements drawn up independently of these considerations seem to have had no significant impact.[53]

This primarily 'defensive' integration fits with the internal systems of centralised planning which are geared towards protecting economies from external disruption. Improved international planning could never overcome this without destroying the independence of sovereign states. Khrushchov, apparently with Czechoslovak support, tried to achieve that in 1962 but fell foul especially of Romanian opposition.[54] A genuine alternative would require a whole number of changes. Despite a universally declared interest in integration, negotiations have proven extremely difficult. Even common standards cannot be agreed.[55] Ultimately, trade and integration would need to be linked to the use of prices and money and to calculations of its profitability. Internal and trade prices would have to be unified instead of the latter alone relying on world prices with no relationship to internal economic mechanisms. Exchange rates within the CMEA would have to be harmonised ultimately allowing currency convertibility and that would also require harmonisation of price systems which, in practical terms, would mean relating them all to world prices. There would also need to be a harmonisation of systems for, as long as enterprises aim to fulfil plan targets set on the basis of the achieved level, the incentive for integration from lower levels will centre on specific shortages only.[56]

Cooperation agreements in practice are frequently encouraged and receive financial assistance without reference to financial returns, but institutional peculiarities often make them unprofitable for enterprises. Moreover, delivery is less reliable than from domestic producers: despite agreements allowing for the establishment of direct links between enterprises, daily contacts are usually ruled out by the need to work through foreign trade organisations. Above all, no CMEA country has a great interest in being a supplier of components for another's prestige project. They are not obliged by market pressures to admit their own backwardness relative to each other. It actually seems easier to achieve joint production with Western firms which are seeking lower labour costs and a volume of guaranteed sales enabling a larger scale of production. A current example is Philips with a joint production agreement and a new factory in Bratislava for video-recorders which should strengthen its position in relation to Japanese competition.

Even when production specialisation and integration between CMEA countries has been successful its benefits in terms of raising competitiveness are often questionable. The obvious case is military production where Czechoslovakia is probably undertaking branch operations totally dependent on Soviet technology. It can anyway bring no benefits for civilian technology as it remains shrouded in secrecy. There has also been widespread criticism of end-product specialisation in chemical machinery which appears as a continuation of the strategy of the early 1950s and actually limits scope for developing the most advanced technology. Czechoslovakia gained experience during the difficult construction of the petrochemicals industry in Slovakia, and the same kind of technologically simple equipment has been exported to the Soviet Union for the expanding fertiliser industry. The domestic industry then had even less interest in the most modern kind of equipment: by the early 1980s only 8% of production was for domestic investment while some orders were actually being refused.[57] As a result the chemical industry suffers from two forms of specialisation. Oil-based heavy products are exported to non-socialist countries while specialised products are exported to socialist countries.[58] Raising the level of the latter to the world level is judged highly desirable, but must be difficult when the average age of equipment is rising.[59]

Innovation and the system of management

The barriers to internal and international integration discussed in the previous section clearly relate to the system of management. There is a widely held view that the main barrier to technological progress generally can be seen from a simple comparison between economic systems. Under capitalism the pressures from consumer demand and from competition create a natural drive for innovation. The firm under centralised planning is free from these pressures. A major study in Soviet industry saw this as 'the most potent single factor impeding innovation'. It seemed that, 'in the absence of initiatives from below, the centre becomes the main guarantor of technical progress' with political leaders becoming 'the major force for change in the system'.[60] Evidence from Czechoslovakia suggests that this understates the barriers associated with the internal workings of the system and gives unjustified credence to pronouncements from the centre.

There certainly is a disincentive at the level of the enterprise and many observers are convinced of the existence of a pool of unused inventions often held in reserve for when higher levels put on the pressure. To some extent this follows directly from success indicators rewarding average performance and punishing failure, but it is difficult to distinguish incentives from the consequence of further aspects of the system. A questionnaire to 342 selected specialists found that many barriers were named simultaneously, suggesting that they need not be separable. The highest scores for 'strong' barriers to speeding up technological progress went to the low interest in innovation in enterprises (89%) and inadequate support from the system of plan indicators (85%). The scores were almost as high for the unavailability of some materials and for the inability to make use of foreign technology[61] which would appear to be absolute barriers. Moreover, bad experiences in those areas might well contribute to the disincentive.

Other surveys, including a study of 100 enterprises in 1980 and 1981, put even more emphasis on the impossibility of buying the most progressive technology or the best materials. Two-thirds saw investment limits and hard-currency restrictions as 'the decisive influence on the low tempo'.[62] Another survey of 208 directors, who certainly might underestimate the significance of their own allegedly unenterprising attitudes, put still more emphasis on barriers 'outside' the enterprise. Even among 1700 specialists, including research workers, only 39% saw the main obstacles 'inside'.[63]

There is considerable evidence that at least some enterprises are actively seeking to innovate but, because of lack of interest from higher levels, they are pushed back into minor innovations which do not transcend the enterprise's boundaries. A study of 1000 innovations over a ten-year period showed the predominance of this latter type. Only 26% could be classed in the desirable category of 'automation and complex mechanisation': international comparisons suggested that the proportion should be over one-third.[64] This is also encouraged by a system of success indicators giving financial rewards for products of a 'high technological level' – the criterion can often be satisfied by trivial adjustments – but the barriers to genuine innovations are wider than this alone. They reflect also a low level of interest from the centre such that, in the context of the existing incentive structure, organisational difficulties dog practically every stage of the innovation process once it requires investment or substantial disruption to existing links with other enterprises. Difficulties become enormous when, as is likely for a small country specialising in engineering, international contacts are required.

Part of the problem seems to be that the aspiration level from the centre is low: the nucleus of the innovation strategy of the early 1980s, which was to be supplemented by a stream of smaller innovations, aimed for a level that would accentuate the lag.[65] It appeared to be putting rather old ideas into practice rather late. The same attitude affected lower levels where, for example, it was judged quite adequate to develop new electrical appliances up to the level of foreign products. Given the inevitable delays, they are obsolete when launched.[66]

More important, however, is the relationship of innovation to investment. The latter is on average very slow relative to capitalist economies, but that would not be too serious if innovations enjoyed priority status. In practice, investment is more likely to go to cover a particular shortage than to a long-term technological objective, which is itself only vaguely quantifiable.[67] There has long been a stated aim of planning technological progress, but it is contradicted by the separation from investment. They are planned over different periods, with the innovation cycle, meaning the period between major innovations, in much of the manufacturing industry lasting around twelve years, and often by different bodies. This is very clear even in the chemical industry where technological progress is probably more dependent on investment than in any other sector. Despite frequent proclamations to the contrary, planning of innovations remained for many years a supplementary activity rather than being the starting point for investment decisions.

Some major innovations, all of which depended on licence purchases, were treated as priorities. Smaller innovations encountered the familiar delays. By the late 1970s the whole innovation cycle was being planned, but it was still separate from the planning of investment. They were even the responsibility of different levels and there is evidence that two distinct departments in the ministry had no knowledge of what each other was doing. Incorporation into the plan under such circumstances is meaningless as operational plans are subject to frequent adjustment. There was even at least one major enterprise which satisfied its investment needs by informal links without signing a formal contract.[68]

Apart from the need for investment, the system discourages innovation whenever it depends on a large number of contacts outside the enterprise. This is the typical case in the engineering industry. The decision was taken in 1955 to launch a new, lightweight small car and three prototypes were ready within a year. The project finally came to fruition in 1964[69] and was reflected in an improved kilogram price. The rear-engine concept was then widely used in Western Europe as a means to economise on materials, but had lost favour by the next decade. Mass production of a Czechoslovak front-wheel-drive small car was not due to commence until June 1988.

Part of the difficulty is the absence of international cooperation as other Eastern European countries are said to have rejected overtures. There is, however, also a lack of interest from domestic producers who have become unaccustomed to the need for change. It is not too difficult for those already exporting, such as glass manufacturers. Others are governed by the familiar enterprise-level disincentives which are not counterbalanced in their case by the rewards in higher prestige that could be expected to spur on the manufacturer of the final product.

There are marked differences here from innovation in capitalist countries, alongside a few similarities. A common feature is the frequent need for a long battle, starting from a small, informal group governed primarily by a creative urge. Innovation is often a 'political' process with precise calculations extremely difficult and figures often fiddled to make the project look attractive.[70] There is, however, an agreed criterion in profitability, even if its estimation is a highly uncertain process. This should apply less for the diffusion of new ideas which, to judge from a number of studies, is fastest for the most profitable and takes place most readily in firms with large financial resources.[71]

In the Czechoslovak case calculation is even less reliable both for completely new ideas and for the adoption of existing innovations. A survey of 100 enterprises showed 56 different indicators being used in various combinations with only five using the same criterion. Even when rate of profit was said to be used, it turned out to be measured sometimes against costs, sometimes turnover or sometimes fixed assets.[72] Thus, as much of the benefit to an enterprise is derived from the prestige and status of modern technology rather than any precisely quantifiable gain, so there need be no unified means of calculating its justifiability. The decision will therefore depend even more on political processes and it will be even harder to give priority to the most promising.

A further crucial difference is the scale and persistence of organisational obstacles after a decision has been taken. This applies, obviously, where investment is required, but can even be true of the development of a new product. Thus, after a new idea has emerged, often in response to customer demand, and its exponents have overcome conservatism within the enterprise, they still need to wait for inclusion in the plan. This has been formulated to balance, so that there should be little spare capacity. Sometimes research institutes even undertake limited production outside the plan and sometimes innovations are nurtured in defiance of the strict regulations, but more typically the battle continues with the next level up the hierarchy.

The association provides resources for research and development, but it is usually so stretched that it allocates to all its enterprises as if they will spend steadily. There is little scope here for unpredictable additional expenses. At best, the battle for resources from the time of inclusion in the plan could be expected to waste a year relative to competitors. There are then further delays if a prototype is to be produced, although this need not be a major problem for capitalist firms as long as they are large enough to have the financial resources.

As the aim is to compete on the world market, the materials must be of the highest quality. Unfortunately, domestic suppliers are often interested only in bulk deliveries and foreign trade organisations also find tiny quantities contribute little to fulfilling their plan targets. These difficulties may have intensified with the import restrictions of the early 1980s and mean that, according to a complaint from the research institute for transport equipment, a four-month task could be dragged out over four years. The prototype is already obsolete, but if testing shows up the need for changes, as can happen anywhere, then the same delays are repeated.[73]

Despite these obstacles, some sectors of Czechoslovak industry have maintained a high level of competitiveness. The most successful have been traditional industries that were allowed to re-emerge in the late 1950s. A method has been constructed for assessing enterprises' foreign trade performance in both trading blocs by a combination of indicators of exports, relative to production and to production costs, that supplements the standard difference between the domestic and the export price. The extremely small number of consistently good performers were typically enterprises with long traditions. They were not large and were located in smaller towns with low rates of labour turnover. They were not very dependent on research and neither did they need extensive links with other domestic producers. They had not been specially rewarded with resources in the past.[74]

This must be a clear indictment of the heavy engineering industry and probably of much of the Slovak economy. Success stories probably include some of the textile enterprises created in the early 1950s, the 200-year-old artificial jewellery industry which was almost left for dead in 1952 and only revived later in the decade and, above all, the even older glass industry which had been allowed to fall way behind the world level until the 1960s.[75] The highest percentage of production exported for hard currency is found in the crystal industry. It relies on the highest quality domestic raw materials and innovation, which involves introducing a new range every six months, depends largely on the creativity and skills of individual workers.[76]

This is atypical. Most enterprises are very reluctant to look for exports at the possible expense of a safe domestic market. Even workers in the crystal industry felt themselves penalised by the hard route they had been given to reach plan indicators.[77] Generally enterprises have little faith in information from foreign trade organisations[78] and, without well-established contacts, probably stand little chance of producing what foreign customers want. There have, however, been some success stories from the engineering industry which has always been the major source of hard-currency earnings from manufactured goods.

The greatest achievement was winning world domination in a range of kinds of textile machinery from the mid-1960s well into the next decade. The position was eventually lost after the sale of licences to Japan and other countries. The original inventions came from within a specialised industry – it only made 10% of the world range[79] – and somehow they won resources for investment even during the difficult period of the early 1960s. The outside impression was that it was done very quickly, showing the enormous potential for a powerful state to concentrate on the development of a new product and on preparations for its mass production. Moreover, it seemed to be a model in the close contacts with customers and the continuing collaboration between production and research workers with the latter still involved after the commercial launch so that difficulties could be ironed out quickly.[80]

The search for solutions

These examples are becoming increasingly atypical, partly as the years of isolation from the world market take their toll and partly as the level of technology slips further behind. A new twist has been added by an extreme weakness in modern electronics. Machine tools were once exported in substantial quantities into Western Europe, despite neglect of their potential in domestic investment and complaints of an amateurish sales and marketing effort. They now compete, albeit without great success, only when supplemented with West German control systems.[81]

There is, of course, enormous concern within Czechoslovakia at the decline in competitiveness and new solutions are continually being tried. One element could be the expansion of purchases of foreign licences, but it is certainly no panacea on its own. An immediate consequence could even be the intensification of difficulties as it can create the need for even more international contacts. Their use remains very limited with figures for the 1980s suggesting only 4% of total production dependent on licences compared with 10–15% in comparable capitalist countries. Annual purchases are around 60, only seven of which were in electronics in 1984, amounting to 1% of spending on research and development. The comparable figure for West Germany is 43%.[82]

This extreme aspect of autarky has persisted long after the 1950s, despite open encouragement of purchases since 1964.[83] Enterprises have remained very slow and cautious and have not even been exhausting the available hard currency. Difficulties are least in consumer goods, but problems mount with the need for investment and with dependence on component suppliers as is typical in heavy chemicals and engineering.[84] The experience has been that a licence for one product may be little use if inputs are inadequate to reach the desired level of quality and potential component suppliers lack either the motivation or the capability. Associated costs therefore tend to quadruple the hard-currency bill. As a result, enterprises see licences largely as a means to fill particular gaps when their own technology can go no further.[85] They are not integrated into the domestic research effort, which remains internationally isolated, and there is certainly nothing comparable to the large number of Japanese organisations permanently on the look-out for foreign technological developments.[86]

Solutions have instead concentrated on incentives at the micro level and organisational forms. Under capitalism there can be enormous financial rewards from getting in quickly with new products and these help offset the obvious risks. A system of automatic cost-plus pricing offers no comparable financial gain and may even mean losses in view of inevitable disruption to production programmes. Alternatives have been sought, such as a 20% supplement for a set period for 'technologically progressive' products or prices based on international comparisons, but they suffer from the familiar weaknesses of attempts at simulating the market. Comparisons are hampered by ambiguities over the exchange rate and are anyway extremely difficult: there is always scope for haggling and winning excessive rewards for 'fictitious' innovations. One counter-productive consequence of allowing higher prices for 'improved' products is that customers may prefer the old ones creating a new disincentive to innovation.

Another popular solution is to fiddle with the organisational structure, an approach given support by research on an enormous number of product innovations in the mid-1970s in a selection of associations.[87] They were categorised by their novelty, depending on whether they represented new variants of an existing product, the start of a new generation or an altogether new kind of product. It appeared that enterprises were able to cope on their own with variants of existing products which typically required minimal investment and little research and development spending. The association, however, sometimes had to step in when difficulties arose, and solutions often required going even beyond its boundaries.

The association also tended to take the initiative in higher order product innovations but here there was a clear impression of organisational disjunction. The implications typically went beyond the association's boundaries. The solution was to shift those boundaries so that they coincided more with the 'action radius' of the innovation.

This could never hope to be precise and reorganisations certainly did not eliminate organisational problems. The evidence over the years was of disappointing results from 'complex' innovations. The ramifications were consistently underestimated as innovations appeared poorly prepared, sometimes making unexpected demands on others and sometimes producing unwanted goods.[88] It is, however, difficult to blame this on the association management in view of the uncertainties imposed by the wider planning system.

10 The politics of 'restructuring'

This disappointing economic performance provided the background for the new interest in reform developing even before Gorbachov's appointment as the Soviet party's General Secretary in March 1985. The impact on much of the population as he developed and strengthened his ideas for 'restructuring' was one of enormous interest. He seemed to be using much of the language of 1968 and that could only arouse hopes in a way that was unique in Eastern Europe. While other countries had enjoyed histories of their own – Poland with its crises, East Germany with its international recognition, Hungary with its reforms – Czechoslovakia had been left waiting for Brezhnev to go.

It was acknowledged in 1986 that Gorbachov's policies were arousing unprecedented public enthusiasm, as demonstrated by letters protesting at suspected censorship by the Czechoslovak media of some of his major statements[1] and by the rapid sales of Soviet newspapers. This pressure from below could not be opposed openly, but there were plenty of signs of nervousness. Books by both Goldmann and, more surprisingly, Komárek whose ideas have received ample publicity and are referred to below, were printed but halted at the distribution stage in 1985, presumably on instructions from a very high level in the party.

There were clear indications of lack of interest in following the new Soviet policies[2] until Gorbachov had proven his likely permanence and especially until after he asserted his authority at a crucial Central Committee meeting in January 1987. Shortly afterwards Husák – by then 74 years old and judged ready for retirement – indicated his inability to ignore such immense pressure from below and announced his full acceptance of the whole policy of 'restructuring'. There was no sign at all of it signalling changes in policies towards culture and the media or towards the political system itself. It looked as if a deal had been done whereby the Czechoslovak leadership would give verbal support, thereby weakening a potential anti-Gorbachov front, and in return they would still receive Soviet approval.[3] Real change could be highly dangerous for Gorbachov as it would almost inevitably raise the embarrassing issue of 1968.

The only area where reform seemed to mean anything was the economy, and even there official statements were shrouded in cautious ambiguity. The most forthright was Štrougal, who had taken over from Černík as Prime Minister in January 1970. He was strong on criticisms of the 'package of measures'. They remained, he warned at the party's Seventeenth Congress in March 1986, 'only partial, lacking in comprehensiveness and the necessary depth'. Moreover, 'a number of measures had been applied inconsistently and with many compromises'.[4] He went further at a January 1987 Central Committee meeting, when Gorbachov seemed secure, pointing to past 'dogmatic interpretations' on theoretical questions such as commodity relations and the law of value. He referred to 'the objective function of value instruments' which were to be used actively 'within the framework of the plan'. Above all, he praised the programme adopted at the Thirteenth Congress as 'corresponding to the level of understanding and the needs of the time'. He had to add that it had been 'misused' and fundamentally changed into 'a conception of unrestricted market relations, pulverisation of social property and abandoning the principle of planning'. Nevertheless, he seemed to be indicating that the proposals that really were made in the 1960s could be brought forward again and he even acknowledged the value of 'altogether open discussions and polemics'.[5]

This contrasted with other contributions unequivocally condemning 1968. The summing-up speech from Jakeš, the man who led the purge in the early 1970s, vaguely presented the basic problem as the persistence of 'old thinking'. There were, he acknowledged, 'shortcomings' in the system, 'but its possibilities have not been exhausted'. Old methods, such as mobilising employees' initiative around public appeals from above, seemed to him valuable in cutting energy consumption and setting the economy onto a path of 'intensive' growth. Following his appointment as party General Secretary in December 1987, he repeatedly used the previously forbidden term 'democratisation', but made it very clear that there was no intention of repeating the ideas of 1968 and he made no mention of anything positive that could be learnt from the Thirteenth Congress. Although talking of the need for 'broad restructuring', the specific issues he noted related to failings from 'state and economic organs' and to indiscipline such as lower levels falsifying results. He only acknowledged 'some retarding factors in the existing system of management and planning'.[6]

Official documents seemed to be treading between these positions. The Eighth Five Year Plan, as adopted at the Seventeenth Congress in 1986 contained, as is usual, a little addendum on the need for changes in the system. A commission discussed the details throughout the year. This time they were following closely thinking in the Soviet Union and were aware that such terms as 'market' could soon be in vogue again. Discussions centred around the familiar themes of relating incentives to actual achievements, establishing horizontal links between enterprises, using profit as the dominant criterion, achieving self-financing for enterprises, creating greater inequalities and incorporating the influence of world prices. A draft was approved in February 1987[7] with the hope that the new system would influence the Eighth Plan and be fully in place for all preparations for the Ninth Plan starting in 1991.

As finally approved by the Central Committee in December 1987, and supplemented by a government document shortly afterwards,[8] 'the most revolutionary change in the management of economic processes since February 1948'[9] appeared as a weaker version of the ideas from the mid-1960s in terms of specific proposals, of their theoretical justification and of the recognition of the need to discuss and develop them further. The greatest limitation is in the isolation of economic from political change, which is taken up later. In economic terms, the centre is to be allowed to retain its primacy, abandoning no policy instruments and explicitly retaining the right to intervene at least as vigorously as, for example, in 1967 and 1969, in such a way as to contradict any independence given to lower levels. Moreover, it is still to set norms, tasks and limits with the hope that their scope could gradually be reduced as shortages of energy, raw materials and hard currency are overcome. This depends both on maintaining macroeconomic stability and on other aspects of the reform encouraging a rapid and substantial improvement in performance, neither of which seems likely. If all went well then, as in the 1960s, a growing share of wages would be derived from profit-related bonuses. The centre, however, is explicitly permitted to freeze wages and block enterprise funds should it feel the need to do so.

There are hopes for substantial change with an 'active' role for 'value instruments', but a functioning market is not seen as a necessary starting point for planning. The first step, as in 1967, is to be a price reform on a cost-plus basis to be implemented in January 1989.

This time it is not to be linked to such exaggerated hopes and it is also made clear that the state will retain control over prices. There is, however, also a very strong emphasis on the desirability of achieving an open economy with competition between domestically produced and imported goods, a gradual transition to a united, flexible exchange rate and ultimate currency convertibility. This, as is recognised, depends on the attitudes of other CMEA countries. The Czechoslovak position is, as always, for greater integration, but the means now advocated to achieve it point towards far more substantial internal changes and, in fact, possibly constitute the strongest case for market-oriented elements in the reform.

There is immense lack of interest by the public, and even suspicion towards these proposals, with a widespread belief that they represent a dishonest charade, appearing to copy Gorbachov while actually changing nothing. The reality is probably slightly more encouraging. Uncertain of how to counter the hopeful expectations that the period opened by 'normalisation' is about to end, but still afraid to allow free discussion among specialists which would have wider political repercussions, the decision seems to have been taken to mimic Soviet economic reforms. Some elements are slightly different, but the clearest example of this approach was the draft for a law on the socialist enterprise, published in July 1987.

Favourable references to the attempt to introduce a similar law in 1969 are still unthinkable. It is therefore not surprising that there was no sign of internal pressure, and even its authors were sceptical of the value of starting with this particular measure when other elements of the reform, which would be decisive in determining its significance, had yet to be discussed.[10] The stimulus is quite obviously a similar Soviet law.[11] The justification is said to be to strengthen enterprise independence and to create the conditions for stimulating involvement and initiative towards 'intensification' of growth. It could indeed be part of a new system, but there are enough ambiguities to enable central organs to retain the same powers as before. Some sentences are very close to the Soviet version, but others are weaker. There is, for example, little left of a firm statement that 'socialist competition' is for satisfying the demands of customers and should force enterprises to improve themselves. The need to attack 'monopoly positions' has been lost in translation and 'self-management' takes a weaker form. In the Soviet case a council is to be elected by a plenary meeting of the workforce which also has the ultimate power to elect and control the director. In Czechoslovakia, one-third of council members are to be chosen 'on the recommendation of the director' and the powers of the state to overrule the plenary meeting are clearly specified.

Thousands of meetings were held in workplaces to discuss the proposal and the leadership claimed 'full support'.[12] Even in the Soviet Union, however, self-management is encountering major resistance: within the existing Czechoslovak political structure it might make absolutely no headway. There has been no sign of pressure for it, which would surely have been stamped on as an attempt to revive one of the most dangerous ideas from 1968, and it has not figured at all in the thinking of the economists most prominent in proposing reform measures. Moreover, the 'leading role of the party' is strongly emphasised in the law, more so than in the Soviet version, and that can mean the power to overrule other constitutional guarantees. There are already laws allowing anyone to stand in parliamentary elections but they have no practical meaning: the chances for an election process under party 'leadership' and with no other specified nomination procedures need be no better. By April 1988 the first few factories had elected councils by secret ballot, albeit from a single list recommended by the party organisation, but it is too early to judge their significance.

Although the discussion itself was still limited, at least an atmosphere was being created in which problems could begin to come out into the open. Thus, for example, the need was recognised for a greater impact of world on domestic prices.[13] There was a quick reminder of the view from the past that world prices could bring chaos into a closed economy: their use depended on the degree of its openness.[14] On the law of the enterprise itself there were a lot of specific criticisms on individual points and ambiguities, but behind the scenes the central theme was the depressingly familiar battle to ensure that nothing changed. It seemed that everyone was for 'restructuring', but only so long as 'it does not affect the position and work of individuals much'.[15] The key battle was around the position of associations, which were to suffer from the greater independence given to enterprises. The loophole was that those associations with a genuine economic justification could themselves become enterprises and continue as before. As they typically do organise cooperation and specialisation among their enterprises, there was plenty of scope for argument.

The crucial weakness of these reform proposals stems ultimately from the general political situation. Opposition from those defending positions of power is still very strong while potential proponents of deeper reform remain uncertain and sceptical. Nobody is openly opposing 'restructuring', but the work of specialist commissions has already shown the ability of powerful institutions to defend their own powers and interests thereby weakening any coherent idea of comprehensive reform. In contrast to the mid-1960s, enterprise directors appear as part of that opposition. They may not like all aspects of the existing system, with arbitrary directives and plan changes often several times a month, but they seem to have learnt to live with it. Above all, they seem happier to go through the centre for deliveries – they have now learnt to manipulate that system so as to minimise uncertainties to themselves – rather than facing the hazards of dependence on direct links. They also have reason to be unhappy about measures that could put greater pressure on them, and particularly pressure from the world market.

Pressure therefore comes from the centre, where the weaknesses of overall performance are visible, and from specialist economists especially in research institutes. It may well be that the Prime Minister's office has wanted the latter to push harder with more coherent ideas, but that is very difficult. The constraints are partly political including the continuing blanket condemnation of the ideas of 1968 and the restricted nature of discussion among economists. Even the debates in the State Bank in the early 1980s, which did bring together economists from different institutions, were not open to the public and had to respect existing taboos. Political change could quickly stimulate debate, without any need for it to retrace the gradual learning process of the early 1960s, but the collective voice of professional economists could still sound confused and chaotic.

It need not lead to a single conception of reform as there are probably more doubts and disagreements than ever before. There is far more awareness of developments in economic theory around the world and of developments in other socialist economies. Both provide scope for a greater plurality of approaches. Even Hayek's ideas, amounting to a total rejection of socialism, command some support. That could conceivably link up with a naïve trust in all things capitalist by a significant section of the population which has learnt to distrust the official media to such an extent as to believe the reverse of what they are told. This, however, contributes little for practical policies as it typically implies a rejection both of the current system and of reformed versions of socialism. An uncontrolled market system implying also a fully open economy would, in practice, have such obviously catastrophic economic and social consequences as to stand only a minimal chance of winning significant support.

Another possibility could be a simple return to 1968, and that certainly is appealing to many political opponents of the current leadership. A few of the leading economists from that period are still active, especially Kouba and Turek, and still support broadly the kind of economic system that they advocated then. There is, however, no denying that the transition encountered serious difficulties, and the price reform of 1967 is widely seen among economists with long enough memories as a crucial turning point. Unanswered questions from that period only add to political constraints to make it impossible to present a strong united position for repeating the past.

This caution is further strengthened by the very ambiguous experience of the Hungarian reform launched in 1968 which bore strong similarities to the Czechoslovak proposals of that period. Its twists and turns have been followed closely both through personal contacts and through publications from Hungary in English. Public discussion is limited. Articles in Czechoslovak journals typically pick on individual aspects of the Hungarian planning system implying, if anything, that there is no substantial difference in the conceptions underlying the management of the two economies. Many officials are privately hostile to what they see as a weakening of central planning, while firm advocacy of the Hungarian system is prevented, that being the most likely reason for the fate of Goldmann's last book due for publication after his death in 1984. He, and a few others, believed that Hungary's system of management has contributed to a more flexible domestic economy and a better foreign trade performance,[16] but there is considerable scepticism about this and any difference is certainly not dramatic. In fact, a Czechoslovak study showing very similar shortcomings in the two countries' adaptation mechanisms in the face of worsening conditions in the world economy was received with considerable interest by Hungarian economists critical of the inadequate and partial nature of their own reform.[17]

The Hungarian experience is often argued as showing the limitations of that kind of reform. It may have significance in the scope allowed for private and cooperative enterprises, although that view is not officially sanctioned in Czechoslovakia, but less has changed for the major industrial enterprises which respond to 'informal commands' and haggle over prices and credits instead of plan targets.[18] The implication could be that reform needs to be taken much further with measures to strengthen enterprise independence: that either stirs memories of doubts over the applicability of self-management in state-owned enterprises or points towards some privatisation of ownership.

In practice, then, a combination of past repression and difficult experiences has hampered progress towards a plausible concept of reform. Alternatives are not clearly differentiated, but it seems that economists can be divided into three distinct camps even on the question of how to initiate change. Some point to the need for structural change, others to the need to overcome macroeconomic disequilibrium and still others to the system of management in the sense of the incentives and behaviour of decision makers.[19] There are substantial links between these areas, as is argued below, but politically the most headway is probably being made by the first.

The key figure is Komárek who could be creating a possible centre for a future 'restructuring'. He has recently regained prominence following an unproductive period after 1970 and became director of a unit, elevated to the status of a full research institute in 1987, charged formally with preparing forecasts for the economy and society. The work goes far beyond bland predictions and involves the study and international comparison of trends that determine economic performance. It must be significant – showing support from someone in a very powerful position – that the institute can use a number of people who were purged after 1969 and refused employment in other research institutes.

Komárek's central argument, as in the 1960s, is that there needs to be a major shift in the sectoral structure of the economy. He is amazingly prolific with articles and books, sometimes developing, but more often restating a case that is now stronger than ever. It is based partly on international comparisons suggesting the ossification of a structure appropriate for a less advanced country. Thus, for example, industry in 1984 still accounted for 46% of employment, services for only 40% and agriculture for 14%. For West Germany, which has had a similar economic structure, the comparable figures are 41%, 53% and 6%.[20] Within industry itself Komárek has concentrated on the Czechoslovak bias towards basic industries and controversy has been most acute around the case of steel.

Part of the argument is derived again from international comparisons. Steel production per unit of national income is way above the level for the chosen comparators in Western Europe. Moreover, demand, production and employment in advanced countries has fallen rapidly in the 1980s. Taking into account the high Czechoslovak consumption of other materials, a tempting prospect is presented of raising output by two-thirds if the efficiency levels of Western Europe could be attained. Despite the impression he has sometimes given, Komárek has accepted that these 'reserves' will not be easy to mobilise.[21] There is no miracle cure, but there must be a strong case for cutting investment in steel and putting resources into modernising sectors of industry that can bring quicker returns and into services which, if the potential for tourism were developed, could even become major hard-currency earners.

The steel industry is politically quite strong enough to defend itself, with its deputy minister suggesting that 'some people are getting niggled by steel'.[22] In his view, the raw materials are available, in the iron ore from the Soviet Union and in domestic reserves of coking coal. The experience and traditions are there. Moreover, there is scope for enormous gains from specialisation – the Czechoslovak industry still covers practically all domestic needs and provides a large amount for export making a total of 4360 product types[23] – and modernisation. Continuous casting, used for 8% of production in 1985 compared with 86% in Japan in 1983, could save on both iron ore and energy.[24] Komárek has no quarrel with this last point, but cannot see how the resources could be found to modernise the *whole* industry. He sees no alternative to plant closures even suggesting a target of halving the share in gross output. Attempts in this direction have already encountered obstacles because, in the deputy minister's words, 'lots of human problems are linked with that'.

The urgency of overcoming such obstacles is further emphasised by a very high level of energy consumption per head: Czechoslovakia occupies fourth place in the world, behind the USA, Canada and the GDR. Comparisons of consumption per unit of national income, which must be taken as approximate only, show a level around twice that of Austria and several other Western European countries.[25] A detailed comparison with West Germany showed that there was not much difference in the efficiency of the energy industries in their use of raw materials, although Czechoslovak dependence on brown coal certainly does impose additional costs in the form of environmental damage. There was little difference either in energy per unit of output in individual industries. The gap was largely due to the higher production per head of iron, steel, cement, lime, fertilisers and other basic materials with very high energy demands.[26] These structural factors have forced the high level of investment in energy, limiting the development of other sectors.

At current rates of extraction, brown coal reserves will be exhausted in around thirty years. The emphasis has therefore had to go on nuclear power, but that still accounted for only 9% of electricity in 1984. Despite a belief until quite recently that it was a cheaper form of generation, investment costs have been 50–70% above the agreed level and are significantly higher than in other advanced countries – at all stages of construction – including the USSR.[27] The blame has commonly been put on the Škoda heavy engineering combine with its monopoly position in supplying equipment. Its management blames overambitious targets, poor documentation from the Soviet Union and the need for links with hundreds of suppliers which in turn have to grapple with making new products.[28] There certainly seems to be no easy solution and total generating costs may rise by another quarter following the introduction of additional safety measures in response to the disaster at the Chernobyl power station in 1986.

Expensive investment – maybe 5–10% of the total – is also needed to prevent and counter environmental damage. Czechoslovakia occupies third place in Europe – behind the GDR and Belgium – for sulphur dioxide emissions per unit of land area with conditions so bad in some parts of the country that schools have been officially closed on certain days and people advised to stay indoors. The principal culprit is the energy sector and there is a commitment to reduce sulphur dioxide emissions quickly. This, however, requires expensive imported technology and, in view of the delays and costs of nuclear power, part of the solution should be a cut in the economy's energy-intensity.

A possible reservation to Komárek's argument is that structure cannot be separated from the system of international integration and, above all, from the relationship with the Soviet Union. There is likely to be some change as the CMEA price of oil is now falling rapidly, with Czechoslovakia beginning to show the first signs of a trade surplus. The USSR could finally begin to become a more discerning customer. As is now being said publicly, changes could be dramatic if Gorbachov's economic objectives are achieved and the Soviet economy modernised.[29] It is, however, far from certain that Soviet interests will favour a Czechoslovak structural policy geared towards integration into a wider world economy, which would be the only way to achieve the highest technological levels, anymore than they did in 1968.

A further objection is that, by emphasising structure rather than the system, Komárek makes the solution seem much easier than it really is.[30] Recent articles suggest that he is putting more emphasis on strengthening market elements[31] and the case for combining these two kinds of change is probably stronger today than ever before. The new meaning given by Gorbachov to the term 'restructuring', implying much more than a shift in sectoral structure of the economy, is even more relevant to Czechoslovakia. Thus, in the practical terms of the argument around Komárek's proposals, a reduction in steel production depends on a reduction in its consumption which necessarily depends on the system of management and the level of international integration. It is not even clear that reducing steel can be the starting point. Modernisation in other sectors depends on new machinery – Czechoslovakia already boasts the oldest stock in the CMEA and keeps its machinery in use for twice as long as the average for advanced capitalist countries[32] – which depends on steel: the current plan is to redirect investment massively towards machinery rather than construction work.

Moreover, steel can be exported at a reasonable price and for immediate hard-currency payment. Komárek and many others are convinced that, in view of the higher world prices of energy and iron ore, it can no longer be profitable,[33] but the situation may be even worse for many sectors of engineering.[34] It is, of course, the historical failure of other exports that has made the sale of steel necessary. The solution has to start by finding other exports that can gradually prove themselves. At the moment there is no sign of these being in the most modern and glamorous sectors. Microelectronics, for example, is stunted by a history of inadequate investment and inadequate hard currency. Czechoslovakia has struggled heroically with its own technology to little avail and produces personal computers at a cost that makes it unthinkable to sell them abroad, while Hungary and the GDR are now ready to export, at least into the Soviet Union.[35] For modern industries international integration is a necessity, but for that to get beyond the stage of proclamations there will need to be substantial changes in the system of management.

Fears of 'disequilibrium' leading to arguments for restraint could be a further obstacle to a process that will definitely require substantial investment and public spending. The strongest case derives from the hypothesis that 'disequilibrium', caused by macroeconomic policies, is itself a major cause of inefficiency leading, for example, to an investment policy which, in practice, directs resources to overcoming specific shortages. Even a new system with a new incentive structure would soon be grounded if this disequilibrium persisted.[36] The evidence in Chapter 8 did not support the view of general internal disequilibrium and it must be hoped that signs of shortage can be reduced through other changes creating greater efficiency. The implication otherwise is of the need to apply a sharply restrictive policy, which will take some years to bring benefits, at a time when living standards have stagnated and when the economy really has been 'living beyond its means'.

'Restructuring' must be seen as a more uncertain, more controversial and more difficult process than anything contemplated in the 1960s. That, however, was not reflected in the Eighth Five Year Plan prepared in the atmosphere of confusion and disagreement about the state and the potential of the economy from 1983 onwards. Simple extrapolation of past trends on the basis of likely input availability showed just how difficult it would be to accelerate growth rates and the first responses from enterprises suggested an annual average figure of 2.4%. The State Planning Commission raised this to 3.2% but the political leadership insisted on 3.5%, presumably suspecting that even the central planners were looking for an easy life. Jakeš, as quoted earlier, has rather implied that they could be blamed for not achieving it, but this target really was extremely ambitious. For the first time, 'intensification' was to enable output to grow on the basis of stagnant inputs. The key was to be structural change – with steel growing hardly at all over the five years while the new favoured sectors of electronics and pharmaceuticals were to grow by 60–65% and 40% respectively – and official statements also suggested exaggerated hopes of improvement from changes to the system of management which had still not been worked out.[37]

The plan was soon in trouble as, although output was rising at first, there was no progress either in the input savings or in the structural changes. The economy's long-term weakness was also pushed to the fore in 1987 by growing awareness of a hard-currency crisis. As a result ultimately of declining competitiveness, exports to developing countries during 1986 had become more dependent on long-term loans. Enterprises were perfectly happy with this, claiming the credit for achieving export targets, but the decline in immediate payments was particularly serious as a number of countries – including Libya, Syria, Iran and Iraq – were unable to service even their existing debts. Some others were being forced to offer goods rather than the desired hard currency. The economy's position was strong enough for this not to force major adjustments over the course of one year, but continuation of difficulties into 1987, when exports to non-socialist countries fell by 4.4% alongside a 5.3% growth in imports, was noted with increasing concern.[38] There is still no desire to abandon the aim of eliminating the hard-currency debt hopefully within the current plan period, but unless that changes the solution will soon require substantial cuts in living standards.

Economic reform therefore seems more essential than ever. For it to be successful, however, 'restructuring' cannot be seen as a purely economic issue. There will need to be changes in the education system. It is no longer adequate to boast of a highly skilled labour force when those skills are obsolete. There must be legal and financial provision for the contemplated scale of employment relocation. Above all, economic reform cannot succeed if it is isolated from a wider reform movement.

Inadequacies in the system of management have been recognised since the very first experiences in 1949 and yet, despite plenty of statements of good intentions and a whole string of adjustments, its basic features have remained remarkably resilient. This is partly attributable to the ideological belief in centralised planning, but the link to the political system runs deeper.

In practice, as previous chapters have argued, the system has steadily deviated from the abstract model of a 'command' economy towards one in which orders are set after bargaining with lower levels. Although it is impossible to organise outright opposition to the authorities, experience confirms that it is possible for any existing enterprise or sector to use every legal organisation – including party, local government, trade union and several other bodies – as a means of pressing its sectional interests. The system creates no objective criteria for assessing demands for investment or other resources, so that these decisions have to depend on political pressure. The consequences for the economic system must be a lack of flexibility. Only in the unique atmosphere of the early 1950s, when whole sectors were effectively deprived of a political voice, was rapid structural change possible.

Centralised planning, within the existing political system, therefore now appears as a system offering immediate protection to threatened interests. It is also the best means to help managers overcome immediate problems, such as a specific shortage, and it appears to offer a general atmosphere of stability and certainty to the population as a whole. Thanks to the plethora of limits and regulations, it ensures broad balance in macroeconomic aggregates. The obvious successes are full employment and relative price stability. The cost is borne in the gradual decline in international competitiveness as domestic stability is achieved by shielding the economy from outside influences rather than by fostering rapid adaptation.

The implication is that there is no specific social group with an immediate material interest in pushing for economic reform. A common view from higher levels in the power structure, encouraged by the continuous pressure from below to defend sectional interests, is that the mass of the population are simply unaware of how serious the situation could be becoming and hence of how much will need to change in their cosy life-styles. There is, however, not much sign of widespread faith in today's political leaders and attempts at hectoring fall on deaf ears.

There is certainly an objective basis for strong opposition especially to a proposed wholesale price reform allowing an average rate of profit of 4.5% which must mean losses in a lot of enterprises. That, together with the reduction in basic industries, would hit some regions particularly hard with a likely base for strong resistance in Slovakia. Equalisation of living standards has been regarded as one of the more impressive achievements of centralised planning. Consumer spending per head in Slovakia was, by 1983, 93% of the Czech level, compared with a figure of 68% in 1953. The key to this has been industrialisation pulling up Slovak national income per head from 65% of the Czechoslovak average in 1948 to 72% in 1953, rising to 81% by 1983. Unfortunately, the basis for this had to be the priority sectors of the time, creating a bias towards steel, heavy engineering and petrochemicals, and an emphasis on branch factories of predominantly Czech enterprises. There is currently no obvious source of pressure to counter this likely lack of interest particularly when past experience can be quoted as evidence that major reform attempts never seem to bring the promised benefits.

The way to overcome this probably depends on two preconditions. The first is a leadership with widespread trust, and that must depend on political democratisation, such that it could begin to win conviction and overcome doubts about the practical aspects of economic reform. The second is a careful approach to economic reform itself. Turek's sound advice from the 1960s, of the need for a gradual process to win over doubters by showing that measures work, is just as true today. In this context, a number of the measures being proposed could provide a very sensible beginning if they were part of a determined and coordinated programme. There will, for example, be a rapid start in internal trade and in public catering, with cooperatives and even individuals free to lease restaurants. This is an area where market elements can prove themselves without encountering major political opposition and without waiting for a wholesale price reform. Further steps include pressures on enterprises to earn their own hard-currency requirements. There are real difficulties with this as those enterprises justified in using hard currency are not necessarily those that can most easily earn it: there should continue to be considerable central allocation. There could, however, even be scope for using the assessments of enterprises' foreign trade performance, discussed in Chapter 9, to allocate resources. It would be a move towards a gradual process of rewarding export performance with the ultimate aim of convertibility and an open economy.

There should probably be a different emphasis from 1967 when so much faith was put on the speedy creation of a complete internal mechanism. The objective should still be to apply Turek's principle of selecting those measures which will logically point towards further extensions of market principles. As Marx argued, 'The exchange of commodities . . . first begins on the boundaries of such communities, at their point of contact with other similar communities.' Only later does the logic of that exchange lead to the penetration of the market into 'internal intercourse'.[39] Starting outside the key sectors of heavy industry and stimulating them first through foreign trade could well be politically the most feasible way to enable an economic reform to gather momentum.

The overall conclusion must be that economic reform is a necessity. The immediate benefits will be small – it will take years for international integration to develop and bear fruit – so that a wider reform movement would be treading a very dangerous course if it tied itself to promises of faster growth in living standards. Nevertheless, the prospects of success are better than ever before in the light of changes in the Soviet Union. Faith in the old system of management is weaker than ever throughout the European socialist countries. The term 'existing socialism', with all its conservative connotations, has disappeared from the official vocabulary. Ultimately, however, success in Czechoslovakia depends on following, and going beyond, the Soviet lead and linking economic to political reform. Only that can unleash a thinking community of economists, create the basis for public trust in the leadership and, above all, enrich the whole process by bringing together expertise and a mass movement for democratisation. That could still, as seemed possible in 1968, create the basis for a regeneration of socialism.

Notes

Introduction

1 These comparisons are from E. A. Radice, 'General characteristics of the region between the wars', and E. Lethbridge, 'National income and product', in M. C. Kaser (ed.) *The Economic History of Eastern Europe 1919–1975* (5 vols., Oxford, 1985–) pp. 31 & 534, and V. Dlouhý, 'Hrubý domácí produkt a economická úroveň Československa II.', *PE*, XXXV, pp. 585–91 (1987).

1 The end of the Czechoslovak road

1 All of this is discussed in M. Myant, *Socialism and Democracy in Czechoslovakia, 1945–1948* (Cambridge, 1981).

2 L. Frejka, *SSSR dnes* (Prague, 1946) p. 45.

3 K. Rozsypal, *Úvod do teorie národohospodářského plánování* (Prague, 1981) pp. 420–31; J. Goldmann & J. Flek, 'O dvouletce a první pětiletce', *Příspěvky k dějinám KSČ*, V, 3; K. Kaplan, *Znárodnění a socialismus* (Prague, 1968) chapter 2.

4 Rozsypal, *Úvod*, p. 427; V. Kobzár, 'Plánování investic', *PH*, I, 5, p. 114 (May 1948).

5 J. Halbhuber, *Hospodářská politika nového Československa* (Prague, 1946).

6 Frejka, *SSSR*, p. 45.

7 O. Berger (ed.) *Československá průmyslová delegace ve SSSR* (Prague, 1946).

8 M. Dobb, *Soviet Economic Development since 1917* (London, 1948) p. 17.

9 F. A. Hayek, *The Road to Serfdom* (London, 1944).

10 For a general discussion see K. Kaplan, 'Úvahy o první pětiletce', *Příspěvky k dějinám KSČ*, VII, 5 (1967).

11 From Prime Minister Zápotocký's speech to parliament, 7 October 1948, in *Základy první československé pětiletky* (Prague, 1948) p. 21.

12 K. Gottwald, *Long-term Planning in Czechoslovakia* (Prague, 1947) p. 14.

13 Zápotocký, in *Základy*, p. 21.

14 Kaplan, 'Úvahy', p. 709.

15 Gottwald, *Long-term*, p. 9.

16 Ibid., p. 10.

17 K. Kaplan, *Utváření generální linie výstavby socialismu v Československu* (Prague, 1966) p. 211.

18 Ibid., e.g. pp. 246–53.

19 *Statistický zpravodaj*, IX, 2, p. 427 (December 1948).

20 In the words of Central Committee member Josef Frank, quoted in V. Brabec, 'Vztah KSČ a veřejnosti k politickým procesům na počátku padesátých let', *Revue dějin socialismu*, 1969, 3, p. 376.

21 R. Olšovsky & V. Průcha (eds.) *Stručný hospodářský vývoj Československa do roku 1955* (Prague, 1969) pp. 472–3.

22 Kaplan, *Utváření*, pp. 212–14.

23 For evidence see K. Kaplan, 'Zamyšlení nad politickými procesy', in 3 parts, *NM*, XXII, p. 783 (1968).

24 V. Široký, speaking at the Slovak party's Central Committee on 27 September 1948, *Komunistická strana Slovenska Dokumenty z konferencií a plén 1944–1948* (Bratislava, 1971) p. 709. For a general account of these events see Kaplan, 'Zamyšlení'.

25 K. Kaplan, *Dans les archives du Comité Centrale* (Paris, 1978) pp. 164–6.

26 D. Machová, *ČSSR v socialistické mezinárodní dělbě práce* (Prague, 1962) p. 106.

27 Kaplan, 'Zamyšlení', part II, and *Utváření*, esp. pp. 196–200.

28 M. Kaser, *Comecon: Integration Problems of the Planned Economies* (London, 1967) p. 22.

29 Ibid., pp. 28–9. See also J. M. van Brabant, *Socialist Economic Integration: Aspects of Contemporary Economic Problems in Eastern Europe* (Cambridge, 1980) pp. 47–53.

30 For an account see G. Adler-Karlsson, *Western Economic Warfare 1947–1967* (Stockholm, 1967).

31 G. Myrdal, in Adler-Karlsson, *Western*, p. xii.

32 J. V. Stalin, *Economic Problems of Socialism in the USSR* (Moscow, 1952) p. 35.

33 *RP*, 24 February 1950, p. 1.

34 K. Kaplan, *The Overcoming of the Regime Crisis after Stalin's Death in Czechoslovakia, Poland and Hungary* (Cologne, 1986) pp. 6–7.

35 K. Gottwald, in *Zasedání Ústředního výboru Komunistické strany Československa 21.–24. února 1951* (Prague, 1951) p. 35.

36 J. Dolanský, in *Zasedání*, p. 96.

37 L. Frejka, 'Urychlená přestavba našeho průmyslu', *PH*, III, 2–3, p. 93 (February–March 1950).

38 Calculated from *Historická statistická ročenka*, henceforth *HSR* (Prague, 1985) p. 273.

39 Calculated from figures of workers employed and gross output for each sector of industry in *HSR*, pp. 249–50 & 253–4. The more helpful figures for value added are not given.

40 E. Kučera, 'Rozvoj a úkoly chemického průmyslu v ČSR', *Chemický průmysl*, II, p. 97 (April 1952); Dr. Němeček, *Chemický průmysl*, I, 26, p. 322 (December 1951).

41 J. Kresta, *PH*, IV, p. 773 (December 1951).

42 G. Kliment, *RP*, 18 March 1950, p. 3.

43 'Přehlídka tvůrčích výsledků práce textiláků a oděvářů', *Textil*, XV, pp. 121–3 (April 1960). Calculations from *HSR*, pp. 161–5.

44 J. Ševčovič, 'Pohled na potravinářský průmysl v 20. roce osvobození', *Průmysl potravin*, XVI, p. 165 (1965), 'Rozvoj masného průmyslu do 25. výročí osvobození ČSSR', *Průmysl potravin*, XXI, p. 129 (1970); J. Kohout, 'Vývoj masného průmyslu v letech 1945 až 1960 a jeho úkoly ve třetí pětiletce', *Průmysl potravin*, XI, p. 61 (1960).

45 An account of rationalisation in many sectors of industry is given in Olšovský & Průcha, *Stručný*, part V, chapter 3.

46 R. Olšovský et al., *Přehled hospodářského vývoje Československa v letech 1918–1945* (Prague, 1961) p. 521.

47 'Úspěchy čsl. automobilového průmyslu v r. 1948–1958', *Automobil*, II, pp. 33–4 (February 1958); K. Výška, '15 let výroby nákladních automobilů v ČSR', *Automobil*, IV, pp. 97–101 (April 1960).

48 J. Pivrnec & J. Schulmann, 'Situace ve světové výrobě a odbytu jednostopých motorových vozidel', *Automobil*, I, 3, pp. 74–5 (March 1957); J. Rybka, in *Celostátní konference Komunistické strany Československa* (Prague, 1956) p. 144; J. Pivrnec, 'Třicet let technického vývoje československých motocyklů Jawa', *Automobil*, III, pp. 325–6 (1959); V. Janza, 'Československý průmysl jednostopých motorových vozidel v údobí 1945–1960', *Automobil*, IV, pp. 69–73 (March 1960).

49 E.g. L. Karásek, in *XII. sjezd Komunistické strany Československa* (Prague, 1962) p. 456.

50 *Statistická ročenka Republiky československé 1958*, henceforth *SR*, 1958 (Prague, 1958) p. 116.

51 A. Zápotocký, in *Zasedání*, p. 223. The account here relies heavily on Kaplan, 'Zamyšlení' and Brabec, 'Vztah'.

52 *Zasedání*, pp. 49–52.

53 Quoted in Brabec, 'Vztah', p. 379.

54 Quoted in Brabec, 'Vztah', p. 380.

55 Cf. Kaplan, *Dans les archives*, pp. 166–9.

56 Kaplan, 'Zamyšlení', p. 932.

57 Brabec, 'Vztah', p. 367.

58 Kaplan, 'Zamyšlení', p. 1062.

2 Towards the Soviet system of management

1 Quoted in Rozsypal, *Úvod*, p. 28.

2 Quoted in E. H. Carr, *The Bolshevik Revolution*, 3 vols. (London, 1952) vol. II, pp. 115–16.

3 F. Kolár, *Zestátnění průmyslu a peněžnictví* (Prague, 1945) pp. 30–33; Frejka, *SSSR*, p. 36.

4 B. Lehár, *Dějiny Baťova koncernu* (Prague, 1960) pp. 99–101; Kaplan, *Utváření*, p. 231.

5 Kaplan, *Utváření*, p. 209.

6 V. Sedlák et al., *Národohospodářské plánování v ČSSR* (Prague, 1963) p. 5.

7 Rozsypal, *Úvod*, p. 24.
8 J. Dolanský, 'Prohloubením plánovací metodiky k zajištění zvýšených úkolů 5LP', *PH*, IV, 2, p. 68 (February 1951).
9 J. Goldmann, 'Některé problémy plánovací techniky a metodiky', *PH*, III, 4–5, pp. 219–20 (April–May 1950).
10 From Slánský's speeches in November 1948 and early 1949 reproduced in R. Slánský, *Za vítězství socialismu: stati a projevy 1925–1951*, 2 vols. (Prague, 1951) vol. II.
11 Z. Valouch, *RP*, 10 February 1949, p. 2, and 3 June 1949, p. 3.
12 Cf. C. Littler, *The Development of the Labour Process in Capitalist Societies* (London, 1982) esp. pp. 117–45.
13 *RP*, 10 February 1949, p. 3; F. Zdobina, *RP*, 4 June 1952, p. 2.
14 Slánský criticised the extent of such practices at the party congress in May 1949, but seems not to have worried later on, *Za vítězství*, vol. II, p. 318.
15 In Škoda-Plzeň, *RP*, 10 February 1949, p. 3.
16 E.g. in the Mila enterprise in Opava, Z. Šulc, *RP*, 28 January 1949, p. 3.
17 *RP*, 18 January 1949, p. 3.
18 E.g. M. Slunečko, 'Nová metodika plánování v chemických závodech', *Chemický průmysl*, II, p. 193 (July 1952).
19 A. Růžička, *RP*, 1 December 1952, p. 2.
20 E.g. E. Kaifoš, 'Věrnost, oddanost a láska', *Tvorba*, XVIII, p. 191 (1949).
21 Slánský, *Za vítězství*, vol. II, pp. 277–8.
22 J. Provazník & F. Vlasák, *Socialistické soutěžení v ČSR* (Prague, 1960) p. 173.
23 *RP*, 23 October 1949, p. 1; F. Krajčír, *RP*, 21 March 1950, p. 4.
24 Figures calculated from *RP*, 29 May 1949, and subsequent congress reports.
25 *RP*, 10 February 1949, p. 3.
26 E. Erban, *RP*, 22 March 1950, p. 3.
27 'K historii a dalšímu výhledu koncentrace v potravinářském průmyslu', *Průmysl potravin*, XV, p. 113 (1964) and the report of the February conference on the food industry, *Průmysl potravin*, VI, 4–5 (1955).
28 *RP*, 18 January 1949, p. 3.
29 M. Hronský, *Odměna za práci v ČSSR* (Prague, 1960) p. 157.
30 Provazník & Vlasák, *Socialistické*, pp. 9–10.
31 Provazník & Vlasák, *Socialistické*, p. 94.
32 F. Krajčír, *RP*, 21 March 1950, p. 4.
33 Z. Šulc, *RP*, 14 June 1949, p. 5.
34 G. Hnilička, *RP*, 13 February 1953, p. 2.
35 V. Kaigl, 'Socialistické soutěžení a náš tisk', *Tvorba*, XVIII, p. 611 (1949).
36 Gottwald, quoted in Provazník & Vlasák, *Socialistické*, p. 109.
37 J. Frank, *RP*, 3 March 1950, p. 3.
38 Ibid.
39 Slánský, at the party congress in May 1949, *Za vítězství*, vol. II, p. 294.
40 J. Frank, *RP*, 3 March 1950, p. 4; E. Erban, *RP*, 22 March 1950, p. 3.
41 Provazník & Vlasák, *Socialistické*, p. 145.
42 J. Čepelák & V. Čech, *ÚRO*, 3 July 1947, p. 7.
43 M. Derco & M. Kotlaba, *Mzda v ČSSR* (Prague, 1977) pp. 184–94.

44 *SR*, 1957, p. 180.

45 *RP*, 1 March 1950, p. 3.

46 *RP*, 21 March 1950, p. 4.

47 B. Strużek, *Rolnictwo europskych krajów socjalisticznych* (Warsaw, 1963) p. 133.

48 V. V. Marjinová & G. P. Murašková, *Rozorané medze* (Bratislava, 1971) pp. 41–2.

49 J. Spáčil, 'Některé výsledky kolektivizace na střední a severní Moravě v letech 1952–1953', *Příspěvky k dějinám KSČ*, VII, 6, p. 882 (1967).

50 S. Najmr, *Zemědělský pokrok*, XV, p. 32 (January 1948); J. Brda, 'Mechanisace v plánovitém zvyšování produktivity živočíšné výroby', *Zemědělský pokrok*, XVII, p. 80 (May 1950); A. Aubrecht, 'Úpravy kravínů pro JZD a ČSSS', *Zemědělský pokrok*, XVII, p. 99 (June 1950).

51 L. Frejka, 'Urychlená přestavba našeho průmyslu', *NM*, IV, p. 307 (1950).

52 M. Špindler, 'JZD v čele pokroku', *Zemědělský pokrok*, XVII, p. 191 (November 1950).

53 Kaplan, *Utváření*, p. 252.

54 Marjinová & Murašková, *Rozorané*, p. 55.

55 This is implied by the only accurate figures on ownership from 1930 in V. Krkoška, 'Niektoré aspekty materiálno-technických predpokladov socializácie československého poľnohospodárstva', in *Kapitoly z dejín socialistického poľnohospárstva v Československu* (Bratislava, 1982) p. 103.

56 Marjinová & Murašková, *Rozorané*, p. 107; J. Kmoníček, J. Doležal & J. Pekárek, 'Skúsenosti zo začiatkov kolektivizácie poľnohospodárstva vo východných Čechách', in *Kapitoly*, pp. 258–9.

57 G. Nečas, *Zemědělské noviny*, 26 March 1949, quoted in Marjinová & Murašková, *Rozorané*, p. 70.

58 Kmoníček et al., 'Skúsenosti', p. 248; Ž. Kratochvílová, 'Prvé kroky pri socialistickom združstevňovaní československého poľnohospodárstva', in *Ku vzniku a začiatkom JRD v ČSSR* (Bratislava, 1985) pp. 26–7.

59 Marjinová & Murašková, *Rozorané*, p. 73.

60 *RP*, 28 May 1949, p. 4.

61 J. Pešek, *Přerod jihočeské vesnice* (České Budějovice, 1985) p. 40.

62 Slánský, *Za vítězství*, vol. II, p. 307.

63 Krkoška, 'Niektoré', pp. 98–121.

64 Marjinová & Murašková, *Rozorané*, p. 41.

65 Olšovský & Průcha, *Stručný*, p. 466.

66 A. Vanko, 'Výkup poľnohospodárskych výrobkov v období kolektivizácie v Československu', in *Ku vzniku*, pp. 84–109.

67 M. Štefanský, 'Vplyv industrializácie na tempo kolektivizácie poľnohospodárstva v podmienkach Hornej Nitry', in *Kapitoly*, p. 237; Kmoníček et al., 'Skúsenosti', p. 248.

68 O. Zdycha, 'Úloha kovoroľníkov v prvých rokoch združstevňovania na strednom Slovensku (1949–1953)', in *Kapitoly*, p. 210.

69 R. Slánský, *RP*, 2 March 1950, p. 3.

70 Ibid.

71 J. Pelikán, 'Cesta vesnice k socialismu', *NM*, IV, pp. 135–6 (1950); J. Krblich & J. Pelikán, 'Ekonomický význam společného obdělávání půdy v JZD', *NM*, IV, pp. 642–7 (1950).

72 J. Uher, at the Central Committee meeting, December 1953, *PH*, VII, p. 17 (1954).

73 K. Jech, 'Sociální pohyb a postavení čs. zemědělského obyvatelstva v letech 1948–1955', *Revue dějin socialismu*, 1968, special issue, p. 1126.

74 Marjinová & Murašková, *Rozorané*, p. 134.

75 V. Uhlíř, in *Celostátní konference Komunistické strany Československa Praha 1952* (Prague, 1953) p. 127.

76 From a local government meeting in Olomouc, June 1952, quoted in Spáčil, 'Některé', p. 884.

77 *RP*, 10 December 1952, p. 1.

78 *RP*, 8 June 1952, p. 4.

79 D. Vojtal, in *Celostátní 1956*, p. 85.

80 Spáčil, 'Některé', p. 897.

81 L. Marek, *RP*, 7 January 1953.

82 M. Trapl, F. Kraváček & M. Pospíchal, 'Realizácia roľníckej politiky KSČ pri združstevňovaní poľnohospodárskej malovýroby v horských a podhorských oblastiach Českomoravskej vrchoviny (1949–1955)', in *Ku vzniku*, p. 298.

83 Spáčil, 'Některé', p. 896.

84 Z. Hejzlar, *Reformkommunismus* (Cologne and Frankfurt, 1976) p. 93.

85 K. Kaplan, *Political Persecution in Czechoslovakia 1948–1972* (Cologne, 1983) p. 15.

86 K. Jech, 'Sociální', p. 1132.

87 Slánský, *Za vítězství*, vol. II, p. 328.

88 Brabec, 'Vztah', p. 374.

89 J. Vohnout, *RP*, 6 June 1952, p. 2.

90 *RP*, 18 June 1952, p. 1.

91 Marjinová & Murašková, *Rozorané*, p. 196.

92 M. Ďuriač, 'Skúsenosti z práce straníckych organizácií v Banskobystrickom kraji pri socialistickej prestavbe dediny vo rokoch 1949–1955', in *Ku vzniku*, p. 223.

93 *Celostátní 1956*, p. 74.

94 E.g. J. Nepomucký (Minister of Agriculture), *PH*, V, 7, p. 522 (1952).

95 Central Committee resolution of 26 May 1952, *PH*, V, 6, p. 499 (1952); *RP*, 9 April 1953, p. 1.

96 L. Frejka, *RP*, 24 November 1952, p. 4 and 27 November 1952, p. 6.

97 Kaplan, *Utváření*, p. 218; E. Loebl, *My Mind on Trial* (London, 1976) p. 4.

98 Brabant, *Socialist*, p. 45.

99 *RP*, 27 November 1952, p. 6.

100 E.g. *RP*, 31 December 1952, p. 1.

101 J. Maurer, *Strojírenství*, III, p. 2 (1953).

102 E.g. O. Šimůnek, 'Do 4. roku Gottwaldovy pětiletky', *Chemický průmysl*, II, 1, pp. 2–3 (January 1952).

103 Z. Půček, 'Za zlepšení metodiky plánování rozvoje národního hospodářství v ČSR', *PH*, V, 4, pp. 242–9 (April 1952).
104 Z. Půček, 'O pojetí a methodách socialistické plánování', *NM*, IV, p. 617 (1950).
105 Brabec, 'Vztah', p. 368.
106 *RP*, 30 November 1952, p. 1.
107 *Celostátní 1952*, p. 21.
108 Kaplan, 'Zamyšlení', p. 1064.
109 F. Šobr, in *Celostátní 1952*, p. 196.
110 F. Pecha, in *Celostátní 1952*, p. 155.
111 Z. Bluďovský, in *Celostátní 1952*, p. 143.
112 *Celostátní 1952*, p. 149.
113 A. Růžička, *RP*, 1 December 1952, p. 2.
114 K. Sarauer, in *Celostátní 1952*, pp. 169–70.
115 Ing. Martinů, *Strojírenství*, III, p. 465 (June 1953).
116 V. Brabec, 'Životní úroveň a některé stránky diferenciace čs. společnosti v padesátých letech', *Revue dějin socialismu*, 1968, special issue.
117 *SR*, 1975, p. 90.
118 Brabec, 'Vztah', p. 382; Kaplan, 'Zamyšlení', p. 939.
119 Z. Mlynář, *Nightfrost in Prague* (London, 1980) pp. 37–8.
120 Kaplan, *Political*, p. 24.
121 *RP*, 31 May 1953.
122 *RP*, 1 June 1953, p. 1.
123 Kaplan, *Political*, p. 15.

3 A New Course without a new strategy

1 R. Baring, *Uprising in East Germany: June 17, 1953* (Cornell University, Ithaca, 1972) pp. 17 & 20.
2 *RP*, 13 June 1953, p. 3.
3 Kaplan, *The Overcoming*, p. 14.
4 T. Jodko, 'Handel zagraniczny a wzrost gospodarczy NRD', in J. Soldaczuk (ed.) *Handel zagraniczny a wzrost krajów RWPG* (Warsaw, 1969) p. 181.
5 From *Statisches Jahrbuch der Deutschen Demokratischen Republik* (Berlin, 1955).
6 S. Jankowski, 'Warnuki bytu ludności', in J. Kaliński & Z. Landau, *Gospodarka Polski Ludowej 1944–1955* (3rd edn, Warsaw, 1986) p. 456.
7 A. Jezierski & B. Petz, *Historia gospodarcza Polski Ludowej 1944–1975* (Warsaw, 1980) p. 217.
8 J. M. Montias, *Economic Development in Communist Rumania* (Cambridge, Massachusetts, 1967) pp. 46–7; Kaser, *Comecon*, p. 55.
9 Calculated from *HSR*, pp. 253 & 307.
10 R. Vintrová, *Národohospodářská bilance: nástroj analýzy reprodukčního procesu v ČSSR* (Prague, 1979) pp. 86–9.
11 *For a Lasting Peace For a People's Democracy* 20 November 1953, quoted in Kaplan, *The Overcoming*, p. 101.
12 R. Barák, in *X. sjezd Komunistické strany Československa* (Prague, 1954) p. 827.

13 K. Rozsypal, 'Dvacet let vývoje plánování a řízení československého národního hospodářství', in *Vývoj a cíle národohospodářské politiky ČSSR* (Prague, 1968) pp. 41–2.

14 Ibid., p. 7.

15 J. Púčik, 'O štátnom pláne rozvoja národného hospodárstva ČSR na rok 1954', *PH*, VII, 2, p. 108 (1954).

16 V. Kolár and M. Schmotzer, in *X. sjezd*, pp. 821–3.

17 J. Marko, in *X. sjezd*, p. 788, and L. M. Kaganovich, in *XX. sjezd KSSS* (Prague, 1956) p. 258.

18 J. Dolanský at the Central Committee meeting of October 1954, in *Od X. do XI. sjezdu KSČ: Usnesení a dokumenty ÚV KSČ* (Prague, 1958) p. 10.

19 V. Široký, in *X. sjezd*, p. 719.

20 A. Novotný, in *X. sjezd*, p. 671.

21 V. Široký, in *X. sjezd*, p. 739 and the final resolution, p. 896.

22 G. Embree, *The Soviet Union between the 19th and 20th Party Congresses 1952–1956* (Nijhoff, 1959); J. Dolanský at the Central Committee meeting of 6–7 October 1954, in *Od X.*, p. 25.

23 O. Káňa, 'Septembrové plénum ÚV KSČ roku 1953 a realizácia jeho záverov', in *Ku vzniku*, p. 425.

24 J. Žatkuliak, 'Činnosť národných výborov na úseku poľnohospodárstva na Slovensku v prvých rokoch výstavby socializmu', in *Ku vzniku*, pp. 207–8.

25 M. Kormaník, in *X. sjezd*, p. 775.

26 Káňa, 'Septembrové', pp. 440–41.

27 M. Ďuriač, 'Skúsenosti', p. 239.

28 *RP*, 2 August 1953.

29 Káňa, 'Septembrové', p. 423.

30 Pešek, *Přerod*, p. 124.

31 Marjinová & Murašková, *Rozorané*, p. 170.

32 A. Novotný, in *X. sjezd*, p. 682.

33 Marjinová & Murašková, *Rozorané*, esp. pp. 180–84 & pp. 210–11.

34 For a full discussion see Kaplan, *The Overcoming*.

35 Embree, *The Soviet Union*, p. 317; *RP*, 31 March 1956.

36 V. Kopecký, in *Celostátní 1956*, p. 160.

37 *Celostátní 1956*, pp. 25–6.

38 *RP*, 30 April 1956, p. 1.

39 *RP*, 6 May 1968, p. 2.

40 V. Kopecký, and P. Colotka, in *Celostátní 1956*, p. 164 and p. 81.

41 Kaplan, *The Overcoming*, p. 40.

42 J. Bureš, in *Celostátní 1956*, p. 181.

43 Cf. Z. Mlynář, *Nightfrost*, p. 41.

44 *RP*, 7 March 1956, p. 1.

45 N. Khrushchov, in *XX. sjezd KSSS* (Prague, 1956) p. 58.

46 *XX. sjezd*, p. 508.

47 N. Bulganin, in *XX. sjezd*, p. 349.

48 M. Michenka, in *Celostátní 1956*, p. 169.

49 *Od X.*, p. 411.

50 From the Central Committee meeting of 1 September 1955, *Od X.*, p. 462.

51 V. Široký, in *Celostátní 1956*, pp. 222–3.

52 *RP*, 4 April 1956, p. 1 and 7 April 1956, p. 3.

53 Kaser, *Comecon*, p. 78; J. Košnár, *RVHP výsledky a problémy* (Bratislava, 1964) pp. 51–5.

54 *RVHP a ČSSR. Štvrťstoročie spolupráce a perspektívy so zameraním na zahraničný obchod* (Bratislava, 1974) p. 141.

55 *Celostátní 1956*, p. 223.

56 *Celostátní 1956*, p. 62.

57 O. Šimůnek, in *Celostátní 1956*, p. 197.

58 *Problémy nové soustavy plánování a financování československého průmyslu* (Prague, 1957) p. 3.

59 Ibid., p. 24.

60 *Celostátní 1956*, p. 62.

61 J. Pajestka & K. Secomski, *Doskonalenie planowania i funkcjonowania gospodarki w Polsce Ludowej* (Warsaw, 1968) pp. 18–22.

62 A. Novotný, in *XI. sjezd Komunistické strany Československa 18.6.58* (Prague, 1958) p. 17.

63 J. Bránik, 'O ekonomické úloze socialistických financí', in *Úloha financí v současné ekonomice Československa* (Prague, 1959) p. 17.

64 *Problémy*, p. 20.

65 Ibid., p. 22.

66 Ibid., p. 70.

67 Ibid., p. 40.

68 Ibid., p. 49.

69 Ibid., p. 55.

70 Ibid., p. 129. See also Z. Blažej, 'Základní fondy v hospodaření podniku', in *Úloha*, pp. 82–109.

71 *Problémy*, p. 130.

72 Rozsypal, *Úvod*, pp. 465–6.

73 *PH*, XI, 4, p. 242 (1958).

74 *XI. sjezd*, pp. 76–7 & 116.

75 Rozsypal, *Úvod*, p. 470.

76 *Celostátní 1956*, p. 46.

77 J. Bukal, 'Za vyšší technologii ve strojírenství', *Strojírenství*, IV, p. 402 (June 1954).

78 J. Budík, 'Možnost přechodu kusové a malosériové strojírenské výroby na vyšší organizační typ', *Strojírenství*, IX, pp. 615–18 (August 1959).

79 J. Kareš, 'Úkoly specializace strojírenské výroby', *PH*, XV, 7, pp. 23–4 (1962).

80 J. Kozák, 'Rekonstrukce a modernizace základních fondů', *PH*, XIV, 3, pp. 213–14 (1961).

81 J. Houska, 'Úkoly techniků v nové organisaci textilního průmyslu', *Textil*, XII, p. 161 (May 1958); J. Drtina, 'Textilní průmysl do roku 1959', *Textil*, XIV, pp. 81–2 (March 1959).

82 *Celostátní konference KSČ 5.7–7.7.1960* (Prague, 1960) p. 37.

83 *XI. sjezd*, p. 40.

84 Kaplan, *Political*, p. 26.
85 *Usnesení a dokumenty ÚV KSČ: Od listopadu 1962 do konce roku 1963* (Prague, 1964) p. 145.

4 From confidence to crisis

1 *United Nations Economic Survey of Europe in 1958* (Geneva, 1959) p. 33.
2 *Financial Times*, 5 November 1956.
3 *United Nations Economic Bulletin for Europe*, XII, 3, p. 30 (November 1960).
4 A. Novotný, in *Celostátní 1960*, p. 18.
5 *RP*, 23 November 1961, p. 3.
6 L. Kurowski, 'Handel zagraniczny a wzrost gospodarczy Węgier', in Soldaczuk, *Handel*, p. 225.
7 Jodko, 'Handel', p. 203.
8 *United Nations Economic Bulletin for Europe*, XIV, 2, p. 17 (November 1962).
9 O. Šimůnek, in *Celostátní 1960*, p. 43.
10 *Celostátní 1956*, p. 113.
11 Ibid., p. 205.
12 Strużek, *Rolnictwo*, p. 195.
13 *Usnesení a dokumenty ÚV KSC: Od XI. sjezdu do celostátní konference 1960* (Prague, 1960) p. 43.
14 *HSR*, pp. 153–4.
15 Strużek, *Rolnictwo*, p. 149.
16 V. Široký, in *Celostátní 1956*, p. 52.
17 Košnár, *RVHP*, pp. 124–5.
18 A. Czepurko, 'Handel zagraniczny a wzrost gospodarczy Československacji', in Soldaczuk, *Handel*, p. 128. See also Z. Vergner & M. Souček, *Teoretické otázky ekonomického růstu ČSSR* (Prague, 1967) pp. 80–100.
19 See Table 9.7.
20 V. Wacker et al., *Ekonomika zahraničního obchodu ČSSR* (Prague, 1968) p. 205.
21 A. Novotný, in *Usnesení a dokumenty ÚV KSČ: Od celostátní konference KSČ 1960 do XII. sjezdu KSČ*, 2 vols. (Prague, 1962) vol. 2, p. 228.
22 Wacker, *Ekonomika*, p. 205.
23 Ibid., p. 199.
24 *United Nations Economic Bulletin for Europe*, X, 1, p. 33 (May 1958).
25 A. Novotný, in *Usnesení: Od celostátní*, vol. 2, p. 230.
26 J. Ďuriš, *RP*, 23 November 1961, p. 4.
27 O. Šimůnek, *RP*, 1 December 1961, p. 2.
28 J. Ďuriš, *RP*, 23 February 1962, p. 3 and the letter from the Central Committee 27 February 1962, in *Usnesení: Od celostátní*, vol. 2, pp. 182–3.
29 Rozsypal, 'Dvacet', p. 79.
30 *Statistické zprávy*, 1963, p. 353.
31 Wacker, *Ekonomika*, pp. 161–2.
32 Košnár, *RVHP*, p. 123; Wacker, *Ekonomika*, p. 162.
33 Central Committee resolution of 11 July 1961, in *Usnesení: Od celostátní*, vol. 2, p. 590.

34 K. Rozsypal, 'Príspevok k analýze predchádzajúceho úsilia o zdokonaľovanie sústavy riadenia', in J. Iša (ed.) *Revizionizmus v československej ekonomickej teórii* (Bratislava, 1976) p. 531.

35 P. Rett, 'Za splnění akčního programu', *Sklář a keramik*, XIII, p. 198 (August 1963).

36 A. Novotný at the Central Committee meeting of 12 April 1962, in *Usnesení: Od celostátní*, vol. 2, p. 245.

37 *Usnesení: Od celostátní*, vol. 2, pp. 224–54; *XII. sjezd*, esp. pp. 29–43.

38 A. Indra, 'O úkolech dalšího rozvoje naší socialistické společnosti', *PE*, X, 9, p. 749 (1962).

39 E.g. A. Novotný, in *Celostátní 1956*, pp. 11–12 and Central Committee resolution of 28 July 1959, in *Usnesení: Od XI.*' p. 419; or O. Šimůnek, in *Celostátní 1960*, pp. 45–6.

40 Indra, 'O úkolech', p. 758.

41 'K úkolům státního plánu rozvoje národního hospodářství na roku 1962', *PH*, XV, 3, p. 11 (1962).

42 Rozsypal, 'Príspevok', p. 529.

43 E.g. K. Kodeš, *XII. sjezd*, p. 575.

44 Rozsypal, 'Dvacet', p. 82.

45 Goldmann et al., *Úvod do makroekonomické analýzy* (Prague, 1978) p. 250. Slightly different figures are given in J. Bedrunka, 'Rozestavěnost v investiční výstavbě', *PH*, XIV, 2, p. 125 (1961).

46 Z. Mačica, 'Tempo růstu a model řízení', *PH*, XVIII, 2, p. 37 (1965).

47 Bedrunka, 'Rozestavěnost', p. 126; Z. Kundrátek, 'Nedostatky v investiční výstavbě národních výborů', *PH*, XIV, 9, p. 794 (1961).

48 P. J. Wiles, *Communist International Economics* (Oxford, 1968) p. 113.

49 Calculated from *HSR*, pp. 169 & 183 and Bedrunka, 'Rozestavěnost', p. 126.

50 V. Kupka, *Investice a ekonomický růst v ČSSR* (Prague, 1983) p. 90.

51 Bedrunka, 'Rozestavěnost', p. 126. O Černík, *RP*, 30 October 1958, p. 3 quotes a figure of 20 000 for the start of 1958.

52 V. Komárek, 'K výsledkům celostátní porady o investiční výstavbě', *PH*, XII, 1, pp. 6–7 (1959).

53 V. Komárek, *Technika a ekonomika investic* (Prague, 1982) pp. 54–5.

54 Cf. a more cautious view in Goldmann, *Úvod*, p. 124.

55 Sedlák, *Národohospodářské*, pp. 381–2; M. Krupička, *RP*, 8 October 1960, p. 2.

56 Goldmann, *Úvod*, p. 123. See also Central Committee resolution of 22 July 1958, in *Usnesení: Od XI.*, pp. 99–101, and A. Dubček, *RP*, 28 September 1962, p. 2.

57 M. Krupička, *RP*, 8 October 1960, p. 2.

58 E.g. K. Šraier, *Celostátní 1960*, p. 116.

59 E.g. O. Beran, *RP*, 16 April 1961, p. 3; E. Gajdošek & O. Mesároš, 'Investiční výstavba metalurgie', *PH*, XV, 7, p. 19 (1962) and B. Macháčova-Dostálová, 'Úkoly investiční výstavby ve třetí pětiletce', *Textil*, XV, pp. 361–2 (October 1960).

60 E.g. O. Černík, *RP*, 30 October 1958, p. 3.

61 Rozsypal, *Úvod*, p. 471; Z. Šrein, *Plánovité řízení a efektivnost investiční výstavby* (Prague, 1984) p. 57.
62 K. Johanovský, 'Rozestavěnost v investiční výstavbě', *PH*, XXI, 4, p. 47 (1968).
63 V. Komárek, 'Efektivnost investic a tempo rozvoje', *NM*, XVI, p. 5 (1962).
64 A. Bichler, *RP*, 25 January 1963, p. 4; M. Vaculík, in *XII. sjezd*, p. 199.
65 Central Committee resolution of 28 January 1958, *Od X.*, p. 736.
66 J. Goldmann, 'Tempo růstu a opakující se výkyvy v ekonomice některých socialistických zemí', *PH*, XVII, 9 (1964); J. Goldmann & K. Kouba, *Economic Growth in Czechoslovakia* (New York, 1969); Goldmann, *Úvod*, pp. 240–61.
67 Goldmann & Kouba, *Economic*, pp. 43–4.
68 E.g. *United Nations Economic Survey of Europe in 1953* (Geneva, 1954) p. 63.
69 Goldmann, *Úvod*, p. 243.
70 A. Karpiński, *Polityka uprzemysłowienia Polski w latach 1958–1968* (Warsaw, 1969) chapter 3.
71 Kupka, *Investice*, p. 89.
72 Vintrová, *Národohospodářská*, pp. 118–23.
73 Kupka, *Investice*, pp. 89–91.
74 T. Bauer, 'Investment cycles in planned economies', *Acta Oeconomica*, XXI (1978).
75 T. Bauer, *Tervgazdaság, beruházás, ciklusok* (Budapest, 1981) chapter 4.

5 Towards economic reform

1 K. Kouba, 'Tempo rozvoje a struktura čs. hospodářství', *NM*, XVI, p. 1410 (1962).
2 V. Komárek, 'Dlouhodobý rozvoj národního hospodářství', *PH*, XV, 11, pp. 13–14 (1962).
3 D. Blažej, *RP*, 26 April 1968, p. 5.
4 R. Selucký, *Czechoslovakia: The Plan that Failed* (London, 1970) p. 47.
5 O. Šik, *The Third Way* (London, 1976) p. 9.
6 O. Šik, *Ekonomika, zájmy, politika* (Prague, 1962).
7 O. Šik, *The Communist Power System* (New York, 1981) p. 80.
8 Šik, *Ekonomika*, p. 381.
9 O. Šik, 'Překonat pozůstatky dogmatismu v politické ekonomii', *NM*, XVI, pp. 1025–1042 (1963); 'Socialistické zbožně peněžní vztahy a nová soustava plánovitého řízení', *PE*, XIII, p. 291 (1965).
10 *RP*, 22 December 1963, p. 4; Šik, 'Překonat', p. 1037.
11 O. Turek, *O plánu, trhu a hospodářské politice* (Prague, 1967) p. 12.
12 K. Kouba, *RP*, 9 October 1962, p. 2.
13 A. Birman, 'In which direction? What Soviet economists are debating about', in E. Liberman et al., *Theory of Profit in Socialist Economy* (New Delhi, 1966) p. 57. See also D. Dyker, *The Soviet Economy* (London, 1976) p. 58.
14 D. Schejbal & J. Vintera, 'K státnímu plánu na roku 1964', *PH*, XVI, 11, p. 1 (1963).

15 K. Johanovský, 'Zabezpečit hlavní úkoly investiční výstavby v roce 1963', *PH*, XVI, 4, p. 3 (1963); J. Ďuriš, *RP*, 25 January 1963, p. 3.

16 *RP*, 10 February 1965, p. 1.

17 K. Rozsypal, 'Co je a co není reálné', *HN*, 1964, 9 & 10, p. 3.

18 *RP*, 24 September 1968, p. 3.

19 O. Šik, 'Problémy nové soustavy plánovitého řízení', *NM*, XVII, p. 1165 (1964).

20 W. Brus, *The Market in a Socialist Economy* (London, 1972) p. 192.

21 Turek, *O plánu*, pp. 13–14 & 180.

22 Ibid., p. 23.

23 Č. Kožušník, 'Zbožní výroba a plánovitost', in K. Kouba et al., *Úvahy o socialistické ekonomice* (Prague, 1968) p. 94.

24 Ibid., pp. 115–16.

25 Brus, *The Market*, p. 27.

26 Kožušník, 'Zbožní', p. 119.

27 Ibid., p. 132.

28 K. Kouba, 'Plán a trh', in Kouba et al., *Úvahy*.

29 L. Mises, 'Economic calculation in the socialist commonwealth', in F. A. Hayek (ed.) *Collectivist Economic Planning* (London, 1935).

30 Hayek, *Collectivist*, pp. 203–4.

31 Ibid., p. 205.

32 Ibid., p. 237.

33 Kouba, 'Plán a trh', p. 205.

34 *Planning and Market Relations: International Economic Association Conference 1970* (Prague, 1970) p. 75.

35 Kouba, 'Plán a trh', p. 220.

36 O. Šik, *Plan and Market under Socialism* (Prague, 1967) pp. 106 & 131–2.

37 K. Kouba, 'Plán a ekonomický růst', *PE*, XII, pp. 293 & 295 (1965).

38 M. Kohoutek, 'K problematice plánu a trhu', *PH*, XX, 9, p. 17 (1967).

39 Kouba, 'Plán a trh', p. 224.

40 K. Kouba, M. Sokol & O. Turek, 'Nová soustava řízení a růst československého hospodářství', *PH*, XIX, 1, p. 17 (1966).

41 Kouba, 'Plán a trh', p. 226; Turek, *O plánu*, p. 294.

42 M. Rosický, *Společnost hospodářských možností* (Prague, 1969) p. 37.

43 E.g. Č. Kožušník & Z. Kodet, 'Monopolní výroba a soutěživost', *NM*, XX, 23, p. 19 (1966).

44 Cf. Mlynář, *Nightfrost*, p. 70.

45 *XIII. sjezd Komunistické strany Československa* (Prague, 1967) p. 39.

46 Ibid., p. 58.

47 J. Hendrych, *XIII. sjezd*, p. 294.

48 E.g. *RP*, 21 December 1966, p. 1.

49 *RP*, 24 March 1963, p. 4.

50 *RP*, 18 March 1964, p. 2.

51 O. Švestka, *RP*, 9 February 1965, p. 4.

52 *RP*, 29 October 1965, p. 2.

53 *RP*, 21 December 1966, p. 1.

54 *RP*, 30 January 1965, p. 1.

55 Rosický, *Společnost*, pp. 34–6.
56 Turek, *O plánu*, p. 13.
57 *RP*, 30 January 1965, p. 1.
58 *RP*, 17 February 1965, p. 2.
59 Central Committee resolution of 3 October 1958, in *Usnesení: Od XI.*, p. 126.
60 A. Novotný, speaking at the Central Committee meeting of 2–3 November 1960, in *Usnesení: Od celostátní*, vol. 1, p. 170.
61 *RP*, 30 January 1965, p. 4.
62 J. Hendrych, *RP*, 3 February 1965, p. 3.
63 M. Vaculík, in *XIII. sjezd*, p. 96.
64 F. Kašpar, *RP*, 7 February 1967, p. 3; V. Němec, *RP*, 7 March 1967, p. 3.
65 *RP*, 5 September 1967, p. 3.
66 F. Bárta, *RP*, 24 February 1965, p. 2.
67 O. Kýn, 'Czechoslovakia', in H-H. Höhmann, M. Kaser & K. Thalheim (eds.) *The New Economic Systems of Eastern Europe* (Los Angeles, 1975) p. 124.
68 Turek, *O plánu*, p. 178.
69 E.g. J. Dolanský, *RP*, 4 February 1965 and Z. Šulc, *RP*, 18 January 1965, p. 2.
70 *RP*, 9 February 1965, p. 3.
71 *RP*, 28 February 1965, p. 2.
72 Cf. Šik, *Plan*, pp. 138–42.
73 M. Rosický, 'Diskuse k analýze nové soustavy řízení ekonomiky', *PE*, XIX, p. 957 (1971).
74 Rosický, *Společnost*, pp. 80 & 82.
75 Ľ. Romančík, *Ekonomické problémy tvorby kombinátov v priemysle* (Bratislava, 1969) p. 131.
76 Rosický, *Společnost*, p. 96.
77 Cf. M. Rosický, *Organizace výrobní základny a plánovité řízení ekonomiky* (Prague, 1983) p. 101.
78 M. Horálek, M. Sokol, C. Kožušník & O. Turek, 'The economic of management – an outline of the conception of its further development', *New Trends in Czechoslovak Economics*, 4, pp. 29 & 28 (1968).
79 Kouba et al., 'Nová', p. 20.
80 A. Kapek, *RP*, 7 May 1967, p. 3.
81 J. Steinhauser, 'Malé strojírenské závody', *HN*, 1966, 2, p. 6; Kouba et al., 'Nová', p. 13.
82 Rosický, *Organizace*, p. 45.
83 J. Tabáček, *XIII. sjezd*, p. 376.
84 E.g. Z. Šulc, *RP*, 22 February 1965, p. 2.
85 B. Krejcar, J. Procházka & J. Tesař, 'Nová soustava řízení a ekonomické experimenty', *PH*, XIX, 1, p. 33 (1966); *RP*, 4 November 1965, p. 1.
86 B. Bugala, 'Skúsenosti s experimentom v nárdnom podniku Cementáreň, Liet. Lúčka', *Finance a úvěr*, XVI, p. 95 (1966); L. Hula, 'Nad výsledky experimentujících podniků v Jihomoravském kraji', *Finance a úvěr*, XVI, pp. 348–9 (1966).

87 F. Jaška, 'S poznatky z experimentů k dalšímu uplatňování nové sous-
    tavy řízení', *Textil*, XXI, p. 41 (1966).
88 J. Habr & J. Vepřek, 'Rozbor nové soustavy řízení z hlediska systé-
    mového přístupu', *PE*, XIX, p. 721 (1971).
89 Kýn, 'Czechoslovakia', p. 137.
90 *XIII. sjezd*, p. 36.
91 Kouba et al., 'Nová', p. 16.
92 Kýn, 'Czechoslovakia', p. 139.
93 Šik, *Plan*, p. 83. See also O. Šik, 'Příspěvek k analýze našeho hospo-
    dářského vývoje', *PE*, XIV, pp. 1–32 (1966).
94 *XIII. sjezd*, p. 683.
95 Ibid., p. 684.
96 Rozsypal, 'Príspevok', pp. 531–2.
97 B. Šimon et al., 'Cesty k ekonomické rovnováze', *NM*, XXI, 25, p. 11
    (1967).
98 *XIII. sjezd*, p. 751.
99 Kýn, 'Czechoslovakia', p. 123.
100 K. Soška, 'Dvě koncepce rozvoje československé ekonomiky', *HN*, 1966,
    16, p. 6; *RP*, 9 March 1966, p. 3.
101 Apart from the works subsequently referred to, the argument is devel-
    oped in J. Goldmann & A. Suk, *RP*, 18 January 1966, p. 3, and J.
    Goldmann, L. Jüngling & K. Janáček, 'Jaká je "druhá" koncepce rozvoje
    čs. ekonomiky', *HN*, 1966, 17, pp. 4–5.
102 K. Kouba, 'Vztahy mezi plánovitým řízením, dynamikou a strukturou
    výroby', *PH*, XVII, 12, p. 11 (1964).
103 Goldmann & Kouba, *Economic*, p. 66.
104 Ibid., p. 115.
105 Ibid., pp. 71 & 77–8.
106 Ibid., p. 112.
107 B. Levčík & V. Nachtigal, 'Disproporce ve struktuře národního důchodu
    a jejich řešení', *HN*, 1966, 12, p. 5; L. Jüngling, *RP*, 22 March 1966, p. 3.
108 Goldmann & Kouba, *Economic*, p. 114.
109 J. Goldmann, 'Postupná konsolidace a růst národního hospodářství',
    Ekonomický časopis, XIV, p. 288 (1966).
110 Goldmann & Kouba, *Economic*, p. 136.
111 Ibid., p. 135.
112 Goldmann, 'Postupná', p. 286.
113 Cf. V. Komárek, *Inovace a intenzifikace v hospodářství* (Prague, 1986) p. 189.
114 Goldmann & Kouba, *Economic*, p. 90
115 Cf. Kouba et al., 'Nová', pp. 12–13.
116 K. Rozsypal, *Československé národní hospodářství po 2. světové válce* (Prague,
    1974) p. 27.
117 Šik, *Plan*, pp. 86–8, 153–4 & 345–50, and 'Problémy', pp. 1166–7.
118 Rozsypal, 'Co je', *HN*, 1964, 9, p. 3.
119 A. Novotný, *XIII. sjezd*, p. 33.
120 D. Kolder, 'Pětiletka a nová soustava', *HN*, 1966, 41, p. 1.
121 *XIII. sjezd*, p. 688.

122 V. Rendl, 'Information on the main features of the proposed economic development in Czechoslovakia, 1966–1970', *Czechoslovak Economic Papers*, IX, p. 21 (1967).

123 J. Havelka, 'Nové řízení zemědělství', *HN*, 1966, 45, pp. 1 & 6.

124 J. Piekalkiewicz, *Public Opinion Polling in Czechoslovakia 1968–69* (New York, 1972) pp. 310–12.

6 The reform falters

1 A. Novotný, in *XIII. sjezd*, p. 36.

2 Ibid., p. 56.

3 H. Klímová & J. Kavan, 'Jak to bylo s těmi vysokoškoláky', *Literární listy*, 1968, 2, pp. 6–7. The general political background is covered more than adequately elsewhere especially in H. G. Skilling, *Czechoslovakia's Interrupted Revolution* (Princeton, 1976) and G. Golan, *The Czechoslovak Reform Movement* (Cambridge, 1971).

4 *XIII. sjezd*, p. 748.

5 J. Smetivý, in *XIII. sjezd*, p. 187.

6 *XIII. sjezd*, pp. 535–43 and his pre-congress contribution, *RP*, 18 & 23 February 1966.

7 *Guardian*, 14 April 1972. See also Hezlar, *Reformkommunismus*, p. 121.

8 *XIII. sjezd*, p. 752.

9 J. Průša, *Ekonomické řízení a mzdové soustavy* (Prague, 1969) pp. 84–5.

10 O. Kýn, *RP*, 4 May 1966, p. 3.

11 T. Hauptvogel, 'Diferenciace mezd v ČSR v roce 1970', *Práce a mzda*, XIX, p. 217 (1971); I. Baštýř, 'Současný stav výdělkových vztahů mezi dělníky a technicko-hospodářskými pracovníky v průmyslu a stavebnictví', *Práce a mzda*, XXII, p. 516 (1974).

12 J. Maňák, 'Problematika odměňování české inteligence v letech 1945–1948', *Sociologický časopis*, III, p. 531 (1967).

13 P. Machonin, *Československá společnost* (Prague, 1969).

14 Ibid., pp. 168 & 166.

15 Šik, *Plan*, pp. 77–8.

16 *RP*, 18 February 1966, p. 3.

17 *XIII. sjezd*, p. 539.

18 For more detail see M. Myant, 'Income inequalities in Czechoslovakia', *Coexistence*, XX, pp. 189–215 (1983), and M. Myant, 'Delevelling: the attempt to increase pay differentials in Czechoslovakia in the late 1960s', *Coexistence*, XIX, pp. 51–75 (1982).

19 K. Wysocki, in V. Lamser & D. Slejška, 'Pohyb pracovních sil jako sociologický problém', *Sociologický časopis*, III, pp. 91–2 (1967).

20 Cf. F. Charvát, J. Linhart & J. Večerník, 'Vývoj sociálně třídní struktury Československa v třiceti letech budování socialismu', *Sociologický časopis*, XI, p. 467 (1975).

21 Šik, *Plan*, pp. 175–6 & 198–9.

22 G. Routh, *Occupation and Pay in Great Britain 1906–1979* (London, 1980).

23 P. Brychca, 'Mzda a společenský význam práce', *Práce a mzda*, XVII, p. 493 (1969); J. Řezníček et al., *Hospodářská politika KSČ* (Prague, 1977) p. 513.

24 A. Mikuláš & D. Vojanec, 'Výsledky statistického šetření o mzdách delníků a THP za říjen 1976 v hlavních výrobních odvětvích', *Práce a mzda*, XXVI, p. 413 (1978).

25 J. Klacek & M. Toms, *Pracovní síla a modelování reprodukčního procesu* (Prague, 1976) p. 78.

26 Klacek & Toms, *Pracovní*, pp. 46–7 & 56–7; Z. Karpíšek, 'Směnost a časové využití strojů v čs. průmyslu', *PH*, XXVI, 3, pp. 17–18 (1973).

27 Klacek & Toms, *Pracovní*, p. 110.

28 L. Kalinová, *Máme nedostatek pracovních sil?* (Prague, 1979) pp. 130, 135 & 153.

29 J. Chromý, *RP*, 13 February 1968, p. 3.

30 J. Matusík & J. Kolbaba, 'Sociálně psychologický výzkum k některým otázkám odměňování v NHKG', *Práce a mzda*, XV, p. 199 (1967).

31 J. Fejgl, 'Diferenciace mezd v průmyslových podnicích Východočeského kraje', *Práce a mzda*, XVIII, p. 395 (1970).

32 F. Zupka and A. Zápotocký at the Central Council of Trade Unions meeting of 6–7 March 1951, in *Zhospodárněním výroby splnit zvýšené úkoly Gottwaldovy pětiletky* (Prague, 1951) pp. 21 & 65.

33 Cf. M. Koš, *Diferenciace mezd a produktivita práce* (Prague, 1964) pp. 75–81.

34 E.g. K. Bartek, 'Pracovná motivácia a spokojnosť v odmeňovaní', *Práce a mzda*, XVIII, pp. 388–92 (1970).

35 A. Heitlinger, *Women and State Socialism* (London, 1979) chapter 14.

36 J. Vesel, 'Príprava mládeže na povolanie v Slovenskej socialistickej republike', *Práce a mzda*, XXVIII, p. 257 (1980).

37 J. Urmínsky, 'Kvalifikácia z pohľadu riaditeľov v priemysle', *Práce a mzda*, XX, pp. 604–5 (1972).

38 J. Ševčovič, 'Zpracovatelské kapacity potravinářského průmyslu', *Průmysl potravin*, XV, p. 432 (1964); O. Závodný, 'Některé problémy obnovy základních fondů v potravinářském průmyslu', *Průmysl potravin*, XVII, pp. 483–8 (1966).

39 S. Rufert, 'Vliv nové techniky na profesní a kvalifikační strukturu a početní stavy pracovníků', *Práce a mzda*, XIV, p. 457 (1966); P. Tesák, 'Problémy potravinárskeho priemyslu na Slovensku', *Práce a mzda*, XVIII, pp. 62–4 (1970); F. Krakeš, 'Problémy diferenciace odměňování v pivovářsko-sladářském průmyslu', *Práce a mzda*, XVI, pp. 491–5 (1968).

40 Průša, *Ekonomické*, p. 222.

41 V. Hora, 'Jak se v ČKD Praha připravujeme na uskutečňování denivelizačního procesu', *Práce a mzda*, XIV, p. 400 (1966).

42 M. Sokol, 'Changes in economic management in Czechoslovakia', *Czechoslovak Economic Papers*, VIII, p. 10 (1967).

43 B. Sekerka & J. Typolt, 'The method used in the overall reform of wholesale prices in Czechoslovakia', *Czechoslovak Economic Papers*, X, pp. 48–52 (1968).

44 J. Typolt, 'Realizace ekonomické reformy a cenová politika', *PH*, XXI, 2, p. 51 (1968), and J. Tesař & B. Krejcar, 'K důchodové politice v nové soustavě řízení', *PH*, XXI, 4, p. 32 (1968).

45 L. Štrougal, *RP*, 28 September 1967, p. 2.
46 Horálek et al., 'The economic', p. 6.
47 J. Typolt, 'Hospodářská politika a ceny', *NM*, XXIII, p. 397 (1969).
48 E.g. V. Janza, *RP*, 22 November 1967, p. 1.
49 O. Černík, 'O ekonomických problémech', *HN*, 1966, 14, p. 6.
50 *RP*, 3 August 1966, p. 2.
51 O. Turek, 'Jak dál v nové soustavě řízení?', *HN*, 1966, 51–2, p. 1.
52 O. Turek, 'Ceny – klíčový problém nové soustavy řízení', *HN*, 1966, 3, p. 6; Turek, *O plánu*, pp. 227–8 & 230.
53 O. Černík, *RP*, 5 May 1967, p. 4.
54 Z. Šulc, *RP*, 9 March 1967, p. 2, and 15 September 1967, p. 2; Z. Nekola, 'Ředitelé podniků potravinářského průmyslu o hospodářské situaci', *Průmysl potravin*, XIX, pp. 182–3 (1968); Z. Nekola, 'Podnikoví ředitelé se vyjadřují k hospodářským problémům', *Textil*, XXIII, pp. 82–3 (1968).
55 Z. Nekola, 'Co si myslí podnikoví ředitelé', *HN*, 1968, 1, p. 9.
56 *RP*, 30 January 1968, p. 3.
57 J. Vintera, 'K předpokladům hospodářského vývoje v roce 1967', *PH*, XX, 7, p. 6 (1967).
58 Typolt, 'Hospodářská', p. 399.
59 Turek, *O plánu*, pp. 269–71.
60 V. Klaus, 'Úvod do zkoumání inflace v československé ekonomice', *PE*, XVIII, p. 257 (1970).
61 J. Kornai, *The Economics of Shortage* (Amsterdam and Oxford, 1980).
62 *HSR*, pp. 350–1.
63 L. Rychetník, 'Vývoj inflačního tlaku 1955–66', *PH*, XXI, 9, pp. 49–57 (1968).
64 R. Vintrová et al., *Reprodukční proces v ČSSR v 80. letech* (Prague, 1984) pp. 180–81.
65 J. Klacek & V. Klaus, 'Inflační nerovnováha na trhu spotřebních předmětů', *PE*, XVI, p. 996 (1968).
66 M. Horák, 'Nerealizovaná kupní síla ve Východočeském kraji', *Finance a úvěr*, XV, pp. 720–26 (1965); V. Zahálka, 'Je nerealizovaná kupní síla problém?', *Finance a úvěr*, XVI, p. 141 (1966).
67 K. Janáček, V. Klaus & V. Kupka, 'Úvod do zkoumání inflace v československé ekonomice', *PE*, XVIII, p. 303 (1970).
68 M. Sokol, 'Ekonomická reforma jako problém', *PH*, XXII, 1, p. 17 (1969).
69 Cf. V. Kupka, 'Investiční rozhodování a míra parametričnosti prostředí', *Finance a úver*, XXXII, pp. 264–5 (1982).
70 Cf. V. Kupka, *Investice*, pp. 49–56.
71 K. Houška & K. Špaček, 'Poučení z roku 1967', *HN*, 1968, 11, p. 5.
72 A. Bálek & K. Janáček, 'Investujeme hodně, nebo málo?', *HN*, 1967, 15, p. 5.
73 Janáček, 'Úvod', p. 297.
74 Bálek & Janáček, 'Investujeme', p. 5.
75 *RP*, 5 May 1967, pp. 3–4.
76 *XIII. sjezd*, p. 553.

77 Horálek et al., 'The economic', p. 5.
78 A. Kapek, *RP*, 29 September 1967, p. 3.
79 A. Kapek, *RP*, 7 May 1967, p. 4.
80 Vintera, 'K předpokladům', p. 7.
81 O. Šik, 'Cesty k překonání nerovnováhy v našem hospodářství', *NM*, XXI, 8, p. 25 (1967); and in Z. Bednařík, 'Z jednání československých ekonomů', *PE*, XV, p. 478 (1967).
82 O. Turek, 'O plánu, trhu a hospodářské politice', *HN*, 1967, 43, p. 9.
83 Turek, 'Jak' (1966), p. 1.
84 B. Šimon et al., 'Obsah a cíle', *NM*, XXI, 21, p. 17 (1967).
85 Turek, *O plánu*, pp. 249–50.
86 Horálek et al., 'The economic', p. 47; O. Turek, 'Jak dál v nové soustavě řízení', *HN*, 1968, 4, p. 5.
87 E. Moravec, 'Mzdová diferenciace a využití podílů na hospodářských výsledcích', *Práce a mzda*, XV, pp. 241–3 (1967).
88 C. Lorenc, 'Jaké budou podíly', *HN*, 1967, 11, pp. 4–5; M. Pospíšil, 'Co ukázala prověrka kolektivních smluv', *HN*, 1967, 40, p. 1.
89 *RP*, 29 October 1965, p. 2, and 4 November 1965, p. 3.
90 Kohoutek, 'K problematice', pp. 22–4.

7 1968

1 For accounts see Skilling, *Czechoslovakia's*, and G. Golan, *Reform Rule in Czechoslovakia* (Cambridge, 1973).
2 Cf. J. Batt, *Economic Reform and Political Change in Eastern Europe: A Comparison of the Czechoslovak and Hungarian Experiences* (London, 1988) pp. 174–80.
3 M. Ellman, *Planning Problems in the USSR* (Cambridge, 1973) p. 134.
4 *Akční program Komunistické strany Československa* (*RP*, 10 April 1968, supplement) p. 11.
5 *RP*, 2 April 1968, p. 1.
6 *RP*, 5 March 1968, p. 2.
7 *RP*, 13 July 1968, p. 1.
8 Piekalkiewicz, *Public*, p. 95.
9 *RP*, 27 June 1968, p. 5.
10 Mlynář, *Nightfrost*, pp. 82–6.
11 *RP*, 15 August 1968, p. 1.
12 For a different view see W. Brus, P. Kende & Z. Mlynář, 'Normalisation' *Processes in Soviet-Dominated Central Europe* (Vienna, 1982).
13 Kýn, 'Czechoslovakia', p. 110.
14 Č. Kožušník, 'Rozhodující krok dalšího rozvoje ekonomické reformy', *NM*, XXII, p. 589 (1968).
15 *RP*, 1 March 1968, p. 1; F. Vlasák, *RP*, 29 March 1968, p. 5.
16 Cf. *Akční*, p. 17.
17 E.g. A. Červinka, *RP*, 25 September 1968, p. 3; J. Kosta & J. Sláma, 'Ekonomická reforma a československé hospodářství', in *Systémové změny* (Cologne, 1972) p. 118.

18 Z. Mlynář, *Československý pokus o reformu 1968* (Cologne–Rome, 1975) p. 182; *RP*, 20 April 1968, p. 3.
19 J. Šuba, 'Za pravdu v ekonomice', *HN*, 1968, 17, p. 8.
20 *Akční*, p. 17.
21 Turek, 'Jak dál' (1968), p. 4.
22 *RP*, 26 April 1968, p. 1.
23 Horálek et al., 'The economic', p. 39.
24 *RP*, 25 April 1968, p. 4.
25 *RP*, 30 April 1968, p. 2.
26 Cf. J. Smrkovský, *The Story of the Czechoslovak Invasion of 1968 as Told by an Insider* (Australian Left Review pamphlet, 1976) p. 12.
27 *RP*, 16 May 1968, p. 5.
28 *On Events in Czechoslovakia* (Moscow, 1968) p. 113.
29 O. Černík, 'O ekonomických', p. 6; 'Přestavba čs. hospodářství a jeho výhledy', *HN*, 1968, 1, p. 1.
30 *RP*, 15 March 1968, p. 3.
31 *RP*, 25 April 1968, p. 3.
32 A. Indra, *RP*, 30 March 1968, p. 1.
33 E.g. K. Kouba, *RP*, 21 May 1968, p. 1.
34 Mlynář, *Nightfrost*, p. 105.
35 E.g. *RP*, 3 July 1968, p. 3.
36 Ibid.
37 V. Šilhán, *RP*, 21 August 1968, p. 1.
38 E.g. *RP*, 11 June 1968, p. 3.
39 E.g. O. Černík, *RP*, 9 April 1968, p. 2.
40 *RP*, 29 March 1968, p. 3.
41 Z. Vergner, *RP*, 28 March 1968, p. 5; O. Šik, *RP*, 30 April 1968, p. 2.
42 *RP*, 26 April 1968, p. 1.
43 O. Šik, *Czechoslovakia: The Bureaucratic Economy* (New York, 1972).
44 Ibid., p. 123.
45 *RP*, 16 May 1968, p. 5.
46 F.Vlasák, *RP*, 21 June 1968, p. 7.
47 *RP*, 20 August 1968, p. 2.
48 Piekalkiewicz, *Public*, pp. 51–3.
49 L. Štrougal, 'O současných ekonomických problémech', *Život strany*, 1967, 23, p. 14.
50 Z. Mačiča et al., 'Tendence vývoje ekonomiky v roce 1968', *HN*, 1968, 38, p. 7.
51 Cf. the half-year's assessment in *RP*, 25 July 1968, p. 3.
52 M. Reh, *RP*, 7 March 1968, p. 3.
53 *RP*, 25 April 1968, p. 4.
54 'Jak jsme na tom?', *HN*, 1968, 26, p. 8.
55 M. Reh, *RP*, 7 March 1968, p. 3.
56 M. Reh, *RP*, 20 March 1968, p. 1; J. Pleva, *RP*, 3 August 1968, p. 3; M. Reh, 'Charakteristické rysy současného investování', *Finance a úvěr*, XIX, p. 607 (1969).
57 *RP*, 21 March 1968, p. 5.

58 J. Reitmayer, *RP*, 22 March 1968, p. 1.
59 *RP*, 1 April 1968, p. 1.
60 *RP*, 28 March 1968, p. 6, and 19 May 1968, p. 1.
61 *RP*, 28 March 1968, p. 6.
62 *RP*, 9 April 1968, p. 6.
63 E.g. L. Jüngling, 'Tržní nerovnováha a struktura ekonomiky', *HN*, 1968, 32, p. 4.
64 Reh, 'Charakteristické', p. 608.
65 J. Adamec & M. Reh, 'Formy usměrňování investičního vývoje', *Finance a úvěr*, XIX (1969); Reh, 'Charakteristické'.
66 'Zpráva o vývoji národního hospodářství v 1. pololetí 1968', *HN*, 1968, 30, p. 11.
67 O. Šik, *RP*, 22 May 1968, p. 3; Horálek et al., 'The economic', p. 17.
68 E.g. A. Bálek & K. Janáček, 'Efektivnost investic a koncepce hospodářské politiky', *HN*, 1968, 37, p. 3; K. Janáček & V. Kupka, 'Konjunkturální situace a chování ekonomických subjektů', *HN*, 1968, 48, p. 3.
69 F. Vlasák, 'Tendence národního hospodářství', *HN*, 1968, 43, p. 1.
70 V. Šmolcnop, 'Sociologický a psychologický výzkum odměňování v hornictví', *Práce a mzda*, XVI, pp. 544–8 (1968).
71 F. Borecký, 'K průzkumu názorů pracovníků spotřebního průmyslu na výdělkové relace', *Práce a mzda*, XIV, pp. 450–55 (1966).
72 E.g. in an Ostrava steel works, Matusík & Kolbaba, 'Sociálně', pp. 195–200 (1967).
73 J. Nový, 'Některé poznatky z výzkumu veřejného mínění zaměřeného na problematiku hmotné zainteresovanosti', *Práce a mzda*, XXVII, pp. 667–8 (1979); K. Bartek, 'Pracovná', p. 388.
74 J. Kohout & J. Kolár, 'Výzkum pozice a role československých manažerů', *Sociologický časopis*, V, pp. 610–11 (1969).
75 M. Mracno. 'Denivelizaci k vyšším výkonům v pražském Koh-i-nooru', *Práce a mzda*, XV, pp. 76–8 (1967).
76 'VI. všeodborový sjezd a odměňování pracujících', *Práce a mzda*, XV, pp. 54–8 (1967).
77 K. Poláček, 'K novému pojetí mzdové politiky', *Práce a mzda*, XVI, pp. 193–5 (1968).
78 Derco & Kotlaba, *Mzda*, p. 152; Myant, 'Income', pp. 207–8.
79 O. Černík, *RP*, 4 May 1968, p. 1.
80 *RP*, 21 June 1968, pp. 1–2.
81 A. Dubček, *RP*, 19 June 1968, p. 3.
82 *RP*, 5 July 1968, p. 1.
83 Full text in 'O programu životní úrovně a sociálně politických opatření na rok 1969', *Práce a mzda*, XVI, pp. 476–82 (1968).
84 J. Řezníček & J. Toman, 'Demokratizace hospodářství a postavení podniku', *HN*, 1968, 16, supplement, p. 1.
85 Horálek et al., 'The economic', p. 13.
86 Kožušník, 'Rozhodující', p. 591.
87 B. Šimon et al., 'Nástroje řízení', *NM*, XXI, 26, p. 10 (1967); Turek, *O plánu*, p. 168.

88 Šimon, 'Nástroje', p. 11.
89 Kouba, 'Nová', p. 15.
90 Nekola, 'Podnikoví', p. 83; Nekola, 'Ředitelé', p. 183; O. Černík, *RP*, 15 March 1968, p. 3.
91 O. Kraus, 'Ještě k postavení podniku v naší ekonomice', *PH*, XXI, 2, pp. 15–24 (1968).
92 Horálek et al., 'The economic', p. 13.
93 *RP*, 27 April 1968, p. 1.
94 E.g. V. Vít, J. Sova & M. Kulka, *RP*, 12 May 1968, p. 3.
95 J. Toman, *RP*, 30 March 1968, p. 3; O. Šik, *RP*, 26 May 1968, p. 1.
96 *RP*, 4 May 1968, p. 1.
97 Horálek et al., 'The economic', p. 70; J. Ptáček, 'Decentralizovaný model socialistického hospodářství a úloha financí v národním hospodářství', *PE*, XIV, p. 919 (1966).
98 L. Mlčoch, 'Symposium o podniku', *PE*, XVII, p. 278 (1969).
99 R. Kocanda, 'Postavení podniku v socialistické ekonomice', *PH*, XX, 10, p. 18 (1967).
100 *Akční*, p. 18.
101 L. Vaculík, 'A co delníci', *Literární listy*, 1968, 6, p. 5.
102 V. Vörös, in 'Hledání společné řeči', *Literární listy*, 1968, 14, p. 3. See also K. Bartošek, *Reportér*, 8 May 1968, quoted in A. Oxley, A. Pravda & A. Ritchie (eds.) *Czechoslovakia: The Party and the People* (London, 1973) p. 194.
103 K. Matouš & J. Vlček, 'Kam směřujeme', *HN*, 1968, 12, p. 1.
104 V. Vít, J. Sova & M. Kulka, *RP*, 12 May 1968, p. 3.
105 V. Šilhán, in 'O demokracii v oblasti výroby', *NM*, XXII, pp. 950–51 & 957–8 (1968).
106 Hrdinová (Škoda–Plzeň), in 'O demokracii', p. 953.
107 L. Adamec, 'Nově jen s novými lidmi', *HN*, 1967, 31, p. 1.
108 Hrdinová, in 'O demokracii', p. 953.
109 V. V. Kusín, *Political Grouping in the Czechoslovak Reform Movement* (London, 1972) pp. 14–17.
110 V. Gerloch, 'Ideovo-politické hľadiská účasti pracujúcich na riadení výroby', in Iša, *Revizionizmus*, p. 291.
111 Cf. Horálek et al., 'The economic', p. 28.
112 E. Dvořák, *RP*, 14 May 1968, p. 6.
113 *RP*, 22 May 1968, p. 3.
114 Šik, *The Communist*, p. 121.
115 V. Fišera (ed.) *Workers' Councils in Czechoslovakia 1968–9: Documents and Essays* (London, 1978) p. 23.
116 Ibid., p. 12.
117 R. Vitak, 'Workers' control: the Czechoslovak experience', *Socialist Register*, 1971, p. 258.
118 *XIV. mimořádný sjezd KSČ (protokol a dokumenty)* (Vienna, 1970) p. 228.
119 Ibid., p. 205.
120 Fišera, *Workers'*, p. 62.
121 Quoted in ibid., p. 51.

122 Ibid., p. 78.
123 Ibid., pp. 113–8; A. Červinka, 'V čem jsou spory?', HN, 1969, 10, p. 3.
124 Vitak, 'Workers'', pp. 260–1; A. Komárek & V. Filip, 'Demokracii ve výrobe', NM, XXII, p. 146 (1969).
125 M. Sokol, 'Ekonomická', p. 21.
126 B. Ward, 'The firm in Illyria: market syndicalism', American Economic Review, XLVIII (1958); Kýn, 'Czechoslovakia', p. 114; V. Kupka, 'Podniková samospráva a ekonomická racionalita', NM, XXIII, p. 75 (1969).
127 K. Kouba, 'Rady pracujících a ekonomická reforma', NM, XXIII, p. 331 (1969).
128 O. Šik, 'Demokratické a socialistické tržní hospodářství', in Systémové, pp. 258–60.
129 Mlynář, Nightfrost, p. 215.
130 XIV. mimořádný, p. 234.
131 Sokol, 'Ekonomická', pp. 12–13.
132 V. Šíba, 'Ekonomická reforma a důchodová politika', PH, XXII, 2 (1969); M. Sokol, 'Existují vychodiska z těžkostí v hospodářství?' NM, XXIII, p. 750 (1969); and 'Cesty k ozdravení naší ekonomiky', NM, XXIII, p. 847 (1969).
133 K. Kouba, in 'Cesty', p. 854.
134 J. Typolt, 'Hospodářská', pp. 400–1.
135 M. Koudelka, in 'Cesty', p. 849.
136 Typolt, 'Hospodářska', p. 397.
137 Kouba, in 'Cesty', p. 857.
138 'K současným hospodářským opatřením', HN, 1969, 20, p. 1.
139 S. Potáč, RP, 12 September 1968, p. 3.
140 Statistické přehledy, 1968, 1, pp. 4–5 & 18, and 1969, 2, pp. 44–5 & 63.
141 Vintrová, Národohospodářská, p. 222.
142 'K současným', p. 1, and RP, 14 May 1969, pp. 1 & 3.
143 Statistické přehledy, 1970, 2, pp. 36–7 & 53.
144 D. Dvořák, 'Národní hospodářství v roce 1969', PH, XXII, 1, p. 7.
145 V. Šíba, RP, 29 April 1969, p. 5.
146 E. Moravec, 'Jaké poučení plyne z vývoje mezd v roce 1969', Práce a mzda, XVII, p. 512 (1969).
147 E. Moravec, 'Byl rok 1968 rokem mzdové exploze?' Práce a mzda, XVII, pp. 117–20 (1969).
148 A. Bálek, 'Inflační tlaky v československé ekonomice v období zavádění ekonomické reformy', PE, XIX, p. 543 (1971).
149 V. Knobloch, 'K zákazu zvyšování cen', PH, XXIII, 3, p. 1.
150 M. Parkan & K. Hotový, 'Problémy kolem masa', PH, XXVI, 7, p. 48. (1973).
151 S. Hejduk, 'Průzkumy veřejného mínění a cenová politika', PH, XXIV, 2, pp. 59–61 (1971).
152 Goldmann, Úvod, pp. 89–90.
153 Vintrová, Národohospodářská, pp. 221–2.
154 V. Gerloch, 'Do boje s pravicovým oportunismem', NM, XXIII, p. 1155 (1969).

155 L. Sochor, *Contribution to an Analysis of the Conservative Features of the Ideology of 'Real Socialism'* (Cologne, 1984) p. 5.

156 A. Kapek, *RP*, 25 January 1966, p. 3; R. Rychecký (ČKD director), in 'Hledáme odpověd' na aktuální problémy', *PH*, XXVI, 4, p. 18 (1973).

157 V. Klail, *XIV. sjezd Komunistické strany Československa* (Prague, 1971) p. 476.

158 J. Dittert, 'Ekonomika strojírenství a průmyslový výzkum', *Strojírenství*, XVIII, p. 817 (1968).

159 F. Semerák, 'Úkoly čs. textilního průmyslu v páté pětiletce', *PH*, XXV, 4, p. 45 (1972).

160 V. Sousedík, 'Budoucí postavení podniků v textilním odvětví', *Textil*, XXIII, p. 241 (1968), and the report of the creation of the Czech union for the textile and garment industries, *Textil*, XXIV, p. 1 (1969).

161 V. Purkrábek, in *XIV. sjezd*, pp. 233–4.

162 Z. Veselý, 'Čs. výroba a spotřeba energie v mezinárodním srovnání', *PH*, XXV, 9, p. 87 (1972).

163 L. Chrust, in *XIV. sjezd*, p. 246.

164 Brus, *Normalisation*, p. 18.

165 J. Vejvoda, 'Příspěvek k analýze naší ekonomické teorie v šedesátých letech', *PH*, XIX, p. 297 (1971).

166 Central Committee resolution, January 1970, *PE*, XIX, p. 685 (1971).

167 G. Husák, in *XIV. sjezd*, p. 30.

168 L. Štrougal, in *XIV. sjezd*, p. 153.

169 *XIV. sjezd*, pp. 571 & 591.

170 V. Hůla, 'Další kroky ke konsolidaci čs. ekonomiky', *PH*, XXIV, 1, p. 5 (1971).

171 V. Špěváček, 'Bilanční metoda v národohospodářském plánování', *PH*, XXIV, 7, p. 32 (1971).

172 G. Husák, in 'K další realizaci závěrů XIV. sjezdu v ekonomické oblasti', *HN*, 1972, 8, supplement, pp. 8–9.

173 T. Hauptvogel, 'K některým průřezům diferenciace mezd', *Práce a mzda*, XXIII, p. 39 (1975). For details on the present wage control system, see J. Adam, *Wage Control and Inflation in Soviet Bloc Countries* (London, 1979) chapter 10.

174 H. Rosická, *Mzdové diferenciační procesy v chozrasčotní sféře* (Prague, 1984), p. 50.

175 Derco & Kotlaba, *Mzda*, pp. 310–11.

176 Rosická, *Mzdové*, p. 72.

177 Ibid., p. 73; F. Čuba (chairman of Slušovice agricultural cooperative), *Vědotechnický rozvoj*, III, 1, p. 6 (1987).

178 Rosická, *Mzdové*, p. 71.

179 L. Rychetník, 'The industrial enterprise in Czechoslovakia', in I. Jeffries (ed.) *The Industrial Enterprise in Eastern Europe* (Eastbourne and New York) p. 115. See also J. Kosta, 'Aims and methods of economic policy in Czechoslovakia 1970–1978', in A. Nove, H-H. Höhmann & G. Seidenstecher (eds.) *The East European Economies in the 1970s* (London, 1982), pp. 165 & 175.

180 Kýn, 'Czechoslovakia', p. 132.
181 L. Csaba, *Economic Mechanism in the GDR and in Czechoslovakia* (Budapest, 1983) pp. 70–71 & 73. See also Kýn, 'Czechoslovakia', p. 105.

8 Intensification or stagnation?

1 J. Goldmann, 'Československá ekonomika v sedmdesátých letech', *PE*, XXIII, p. 3 (1975).
2 Vintrová, *Reprodukční*, pp. 160–1.
3 Goldmann, 'Československá', p. 11.
4 M. Marrese & J. Vanous, *Soviet Subsidization of Trade with Eastern Europe: A Soviet Perspective* (Berkeley, 1983) esp. pp. 108–9.
5 V. Dlouhý & K. Dyba, *Ekonometrický model československé obchodní bilance* (Prague, 1985) p. 19. For analyses of the process of adaptation, see K. Dyba & V. Kupka, 'Přizpůsobení československé ekonomiky vnějším nárazům (Makroekonomická analýza za léta 1973–1981)', *PE*, XXXII (1984); K. Dyba & R. Vintrová, 'Československá ekonomika v osmdesátých letech', *Finance a úvěr*, XXXV, pp. 444–56 (1985).
6 V. Hůla, 'Hlavní úkoly rozvoje čs. ekonomiky v roce 1980', *PH*, XXXIII, 1, p. 1 (1980).
7 Calculated from figures in *United Nations Economic Survey of Europe in 1985–6* (New York, 1986) p. 254.
8 *United Nations Economic Bulletin for Europe*, XXXVIII, p. 81 (1986). For a justification of the Czechoslovak policy, see F. Vencovský, 'Devizová rovnováha je nezbytnou podmínkou rozvoje', *HN*, 1987, 50, pp. 1 & 4.
9 *United Nations Economic Survey of Europe in 1985–6*, p. 243.
10 See the discussion of investment in *HN*, 1986, 45, pp. 8–9.
11 For a substantial analysis, see M. Strejček, 'Účinněji řídit rozestavěnost', *PH*, XXXV, 10 (1982).
12 Vintrová, *Reprodukční*, pp. 118–21.
13 J. Mitro, 'Úsilí SBČS o snižování rozsahu nedokončené investiční výstavby', *Finance a úvěr*, XXXVII, p. 652 (1987); A. Blaas, 'Spomalenie stavieb, investičná politika a menový plán', *Finance a úvěr*, XXXIV, p. 82 (1984).
14 Cf. V. Čap & K. Rybnikář, 'K Vývoji národního hospodářství v 1. pololetí 1982', *PH*, XXXV, 9, p. 12 (1982).
15 K. Janáček et al., *Hlavní tendence reprodukčního procesu československé ekonomiky a základní rysy strategie hospodářského rozvoje CSSR* (Prague, 1986) p. 196.
16 V. Klaus, 'Rozestavěnost investiční výstavby, model i empirická analýza', *Finance a úvěr*, XXXV, pp. 152–62 (1985); V. Klaus, 'Modelování investiční sféry centrálně plánované ekonomiky: diskuse problémů a demonstrace jednoho možného přístupu', *Ekonomicko-matematický obzor*, XXII, pp. 378–90 (1986).
17 Vintrová, *Reprodukční*, p. 122.
18 V. Häufler, *Ekonomická geografie Československa* (Prague, 1984) p. 313.
19 V. Čáp et al., *Fakty o sociálno-ekonomickom rozvoji Československa po roku 1945* (Bratislava, 1986) pp. 84–93.

20 R. Suchánek, 'Proč limity zaměstnanosti?', *PH*, XXIV, 2, p. 40 (1971).
21 *Naše cesta*, 19 September 1986, pp. 1 & 3.
22 *Naše cesta*, 30 October 1986.
23 *Vědeckotechnický rozvoj*, III, p. 1 (1987).
24 Z. Lukas, 'Die tschechoslowakische Landwirtschaft', *Osteuropa-Wirtschaft*, XXXI, p. 43 (1986).
25 Janáček, *Hlavní*, p. 233.
26 Ibid., p. 247.
27 V. Třeška, 'Úkoly plánu rozvoje zemědělství a výživy v ČSR v roce 1986', *PH*, XXXIX, 4, p. 1 (1986).
28 *SR*, 1984, pp. 502–4; *SR*, 1986, pp. 483–5.
29 Janáček, *Hlavní*, pp. 207–8.
30 *Annual Abstract of Statistics, 1988 Edition* (London) pp. 145 & 155.
31 Calculated from *SR*, 1986, pp. 67 & 357.
32 S. Potáč, 'Plán urychlení intenzifikace ekonomiky', *PH*, XXXV, 1, p. 4 (1982).
33 V. Ježdík, 'Vývoj národního hospodářství v roce 1985', *PH*, XXXIX, 3, p. 14 (1986).
34 *Ekonomické modelování*, 1984, 2, pp. 80–97.
35 Criticisms here rely heavily on I. Okáli & J. Vojtko (eds.) *Hospodársky mechanizmus v etape formovania intenzívneho typu rozšírenej reprodukcie* (Bratislava, 1983) pp. 77–85, contributions in *Zdokonaľovanie plánovitého riadenia národného hospodárstva* (Bratislava, 1983), L. Mlčoch, *Analýza procesu plánování v podnikové sféře* (Prague, 1983) and L. Mlčoch, 'Vstřicné plánování v hierarchickém plánovacím systému', *Ekonomické modelování*, 1984, 2, pp. 38–43.
36 Komárek, *Technika*, p. 188.
37 Okáli & Vojtko, *Hospodársky*, p. 79.
38 V. Filip, 'Vedle pozitiv i negativ', *HN*, 1985, 35, p. 9.
39 J. Váňová, 'Co povědí a co ne', *HN*, 1985, 36, p. 9.
40 P. Koch, in *Zdokonaľovanie*, pp. 91–2.
41 *Digest of UK Energy Statistics 1985* (London, 1985) p. 30.
42 J. Řezníček et al., *Základy hospodářské politiky KSČ* (Prague, 1984) p. 59.
43 Goldmann, *Úvod*, pp. 93–5; V. Klaus, 'Nepravidelnost spotřebních výdajů domácností v sedmdesátých letech', *PE*, XXVII, p. 458 (1979).
44 J. Mládek, 'Shortage – the barrier of modelling consumption in centrally planned economy', *Ekonomicko-matematický obzor*, XXIII, pp. 156–70 (1987).
45 V. Klaus & V. Rudlovčák, 'Komparace vývoje oběživa a vkladů obyvatelstva v některých socialistických zemích: formální analýza', *PE*, XXVI, pp. 707–22 (1978).
46 R. Portes & D. Winter, 'Disequilibrium estimates for consumption goods markets in centrally planned economies', *Review of Economic Studies*, XLVII, pp. 137–59 (1980).
47 Klaus, 'Nepravidelnost', pp. 455–68.
48 E.g. M. Bouchal, 'Příjmy a úspory obyvatelstva', *PH*, XXXII, 3, p. 48 (1979).
49 M. Kohoutek, 'K vývoji hotovostního oběhu a peněžních rezerv obyvatelstva v ČSSR v letech 1961–1985', *Finance a úvěr*, XXXVII, p. 165 (1987).

50 I. Šujan & B. Viktorínová, 'Rovnováha na spotrebiteľskom trhu a jej ovplyvňovanie hodnotovými nástrojmi', *Finance a úvěr*, XXXVI, supplement 4, pp. 260–72 (1986) and XXXVII, supplement 1, pp. 63–70 (1987).
51 I. Šujan, 'Analýza príčin spomalenia rozvoja čs. ekonomiky v r. 1980–1985', *PE*, XXXV, p. 301 (1987).
52 Vintrová, *Reprodukční*, p. 190; Mládek, 'Shortage', pp. 167–8; Janáček, *Hlavní*, pp. 152–3.
53 Janáček, *Hlavní*, p. 152.
54 Šujan, 'Rovnováha', p. 66.
55 Calculated from *HSR*, pp. 350–51 and *Statistický přehled*, 1987, 7, p. 209.
56 Janáček, *Hlavní*, p. 127.
57 Vintrová, *Reprodukční*, p. 190.
58 Šujan, 'Analýza', p. 300.
59 V. Janza, 'Do prvého roka ôsmej päťročnice', *HN*, 1985, 49, p. 1.

9 Relative decline

1 Janáček, *Hlavní*, p. 11.
2 P. Desai, *The Soviet Economy: Problems and Prospects* (Oxford, 1987) pp. 32–3; A. Bergson, 'Technological progress', in A. Bergson & H. Levine (eds.) *The Soviet Economy: Towards the Year 2000* (London, 1983) pp. 42–4.
3 Goldmann, *Úvod*, pp. 159–60.
4 V. Dlouhý, 'On the problem of macroeconomic modelling in centrally planned economies', paper presented to Models and Forecasts conference, Bratislava, 1985.
5 V. Lančaričová, 'Dlhodobý vplyv medzinárodnej socialistickej integrácie na rozvoj čs hutníctva železa', in *Problémy intenzifikácie ekonomického rozvoja a SEI* (Bratislava, 1983) p. 82.
6 A. Nove, 'Soviet economic performance: a comment on Wiles and Ellman', in J. Drewnowski, *Crisis in the Eastern European Economy: The Spread of the Polish Disease* (London, 1982) p. 169.
7 M. Toms & M. Hájek, 'Proces intenzifikace a prognózování růstu souhrnné hospodárnosti čs. ekonomiky', *PE*, XXX, esp. pp. 924–6 (1982).
8 M. Mach & M. Toms, *Teorie socialistické rozšířené reprodukce* (Prague, 1986) p. 138.
9 J. Klacek & A. Nešporová, *Produkční funkce a modelování ekonomického růstu v ČSSR* (Prague, 1983) chapter 2: L. Christensen, D. Jorgenson & L. Lau, 'Conjugate duality and the transcendental logarithmic production function', *Econometrica*, IV (1971).
10 Klacek & Nešporová, *Produkční*, p. 165.
11 G. C. Judge, W. E. Griffiths, R. C. Hill & T. C. Lee, *The Theory and Practice of Econometrics* (New York, 1980) pp. 471–5.
12 Following the method described in R. G. D. Allen, *Mathematical Analysis for Economists* (London, 1938) pp. 503–9.
13 Klacek & Nešporová, *Produkční*, p. 164.
14 J. Klacek & A. Nešporová, *Ekonomický růst a jeho intenzifikace – mezinárodní srovnání* (Prague, 1985) pp. 63 & 65.

15 Cf. Vintrová, *Národohospodářská*, p. 103.

16 A. Nešporová, 'Kvantifikace ekonomického potenciálu základních fondů a pracovních sil a odhad jejich vzájemného vztahu pro strojírenství ČSSR', *PE*, XXXII, pp. 813–28 (1984).

17 Komárek, *Technika*, pp. 201–3.

18 K. Johanovský, quoted in A. Nešporová, 'Analýza vývoje produktivity práce ve výrobní sféře ČSSR', paper presented at Macroanalyses 1987 conference, Bratislava, 1987, p. 7.

19 Mach & Toms, *Teorie*, pp. 145–6.

20 Komárek, *Inovace*, p. 96.

21 A. I. Anchishkin, *Prognozirovaniye rosta sotsialisticheskoy ekonomiki* (Moscow, 1973) pp. 72–3.

22 Klacek & Nešporová, *Ekonomický*, p. 65

23 Klacek & Nešporová, *Ekonomický*; J. Klacek, 'Relace mezi výrobními faktory v procesu intenzifikace', *PE*, XXXIII, p. 43–59 (1985).

24 M. Hájek, 'K některým otázkám činitelů ekonomického růstu USA', *PE*, XIV (1966).

25 Klacek & Nešporová, *Ekonomický*, p. 79.

26 Ibid., p. 79.

27 Mach & Toms, *Teorie*, pp. 214–18.

28 Ibid., pp. 91–2; S. Kalousek, 'Neprodává třída', *HN*, 1985, 49, p. 6.

29 Goldmann, *Úvod*, p. 276.

30 See K. Dyba, *Československé vnější ekonomické vztahy* (Prague, 1980) chapter 1, and K. Dyba & K. Kudlák, 'Agregátní cenové indexy v čs. zahraničním obchodě a čs. reálné směnné relace 1948–1978', *Statistika*, 1979, 8–9, pp. 370–9.

31 Komárek, *Inovace*, p. 116.

32 V. Dlouhý & K. Dyba, 'K problému modelování pohybu reálných směnných relací v centrálně plánované ekonomice', *Informační systémy*, XIII, p. 58 (1984).

33 Janáček, *Hlavní*, p. 24.

34 'Exports of manufactures from Eastern Europe and the Soviet Union to developed market economies, 1965–1981', *United Nations Economic Bulletin for Europe*, XXXV, pp. 441–534 (1983).

35 K. Dyba, 'K exportní výkonnosti čs. strojírenství v sedmdesátých letech', *Finance a úvěr*, XXXV, pp. 104–15 (1985).

36 R. Rothwell, 'The relationship between technical change and economic performance in mechanical engineering: some evidence', in M. Baker (ed.) *Industrial Innovation: Technology, Policy, Diffusion* (London, 1979) pp. 37–40.

37 J. Klacek & J. Pleva, 'Efektivnost zahraničně obchodních operací na trhu EHS', *PE*, XV, pp. 613–32 (1967).

38 S. Paliwoda, *International Marketing* (London, 1986) p. 269; M. Matějka, J. Matouš & J. Vrba, 'Exportní schopnost: negativní role velkoobchodních cen', *HN* 1985, 28, p. 8.

39 Matějka et al., 'Exportní', pp. 8–9.

40 Janáček, *Hlavní*, p. 98.

41 O. Landa & J. Loudín, 'Neúprosná výzva ke světovosti', *HN*, 1986, 17.
42 Janáček, *Hlavní*, p. 95.
43 P. Hanson & K. Pavitt, *The Comparative Economics of Research and Development and Innovation* (New York, 1987) p. 56.
44 K. Müller, 'Co určuje efektivnost výzkumu?', *HN*, 1985, 13, p. 9.
45 Cf. E. Hirst, W. Fulkerson, R. Carlsmith & T. Wilbanks 'Improving energy efficiency', *Energy Policy*, X, pp. 134–7 (1982).
46 Košnár, *RVHP*, p. 201; Komárek, *Inovace*, pp. 51 & 133.
47 V. Komárek et al., *Prognóza základních tendencí reprodukčního procesu čs. ekonomiky do roku 2000 (etapa 1981)* (Prague, 1982) pp. 134–6.
48 'Znovu o traktorech', *Automobil*, V, p. 221 (1961); K. Poláček, 'Úkoly automobilového průmyslu ve třetí pětiletce', *Automobil* V, p. 2 (1961).
49 *RP*, 14 August 1968, p. 2; V. Křenek & B. Měšťák, 'Nová automobilka v ČSSR?', *Automobil*, XII, pp. 22–3 (1969); K. Novotný, 'Úvahy o rozvoji čs. automobilového průmyslu', *Automobil*, XIII, p. 5 (1969).
50 K. Poláček, 'Úspěchy strojírenství v mezinárodní socialistické dělbě práce', *Strojírenství*, XIII, pp. 561–2 (1963); M. Vojtěch, 'Spolupráce mezi strojírenskými průmysly zemí tábora míru', *Automobil*, VI, p. 161 (1962); 'Mezinárodní dělba práce v automobilovém průmyslu', *Automobil*, VII, pp. 293–4 (1963).
51 M. Kolanda & O. Touš, 'Kompletační výrobky v mezinárodní dělbě práce ve strojírenství', *PH*, XX, 6, pp. 33–41 (1967); S. Novák, 'Od potenciálních ke skutečným efektům', *HN*, 1986, 25, p. 3.
52 Brabant, *Socialist*, p. 263; Goldmann, *Úvod*, pp. 283–8; B. Dybová & K. Dyba, 'The level of foreign trade in socialist and capitalist economies compared', *Ekonomicko-matematický obzor*, XXIII, pp. 25–37 (1987).
53 K. Pécsi, *Economic Questions of Production Integration within CMEA* (Budapest, 1978) p. 21.
54 Kaser, *Comecon*, pp. 106–9.
55 M. Káňa & Z. Škoda, 'Elektronika pro občana: ČSSR', *HN*, 1985, 32, p. 9.
56 For criticisms of current integration attempts see Novák, 'Od potenciálních', p. 3, P. Špaček & V. Válek, 'Systémové předpoklady', *HN*, 1986, 48, p. 3, P. Špaček & P. Parízek, 'Cíl – kurs a směnitelnost', *HN*, 1988, 1, pp. 8–9, P. Špaček & V. Válek, 'Sbližování místo autarkie', *HN*, 1988, 7, p. 3, and P. Chvojka & F. Fojtík, 'Příkaz intenzifikace: změna integračního soukolí', *HN*, 1986, 43, pp. 8–9.
57 S. Gistinger, 'Problematika vazeb technického a investičního rozvoje v chemickém průmyslu' (Kandidátská dizertační práce, VŠChT, Prague, 1984) pp. 46–9.
58 Komárek, *Prognóza*, p. 135.
59 J. Holeček & J. Kubečka, 'Chemie: od defenzívních k ofenzívním oborům!', *HN*, 1986, 21; A. Mlčoch, 'Kdo dobře zhodnotí, dobře prodá', *HN*, 1987, 12, p. 8.
60 R. Amann & J. Cooper (eds.) *Industrial Innovation in the Soviet Union* (New Haven, 1982) pp. 11–12, 22 & 26.
61 O. Landa, 'Řízení jako hlavní sociální faktor urychlování vědeckotechnického rozvoje', *Organizace a řízení*, XVI, pp. 12–13 (1987).

62 S. Mareš, 'Zvláštnosti inovačních procesů a jejich nároky na řízení', *Organizace a řízení*, XV, pp. 47–8 (1985).

63 J. Míšović, 'Růžovější brýle ředitelů', *HN*, 1986, 23, p. 5.

64 Mareš, 'Zvláštnosti', p. 47.

65 Komárek, *Prognóza*, pp. 184–8.

66 J. Bydžovský & I. Soukup, 'Spotřebiče nevedou k hospodárnosti', *HN*, 1986, 50, p. 6.

67 V. Kupka, *Analýza vývojových trendů investiční výstavby v ČSSR jakožto prostředků vědeckotechnického rozvoje československého národního hospodářství* (Prague, 1982) p. 21.

68 Gistinger, 'Problematika', esp. p. 86.

69 'Karosérie vozu Škoda 1000MB', *Automobil*, IX, p. 7 (1965).

70 C. Freeman, *The Economics of Industrial Innovation*, 2nd edn (London, 1982) p. 25 & chapter 8.

71 S. Davies, *The Diffusion of Process Innovations* (Cambridge, 1979) esp. chapters 2 & 9.

72 Mareš, 'Zvláštnosti', p. 45.

73 F. Madrý, 'Proč zaostávat kdyz nemusíme', *HN*, 1986, 11, p. 3.

74 M. Kolanda, 'K problémům exportních výkonů podnikové sféry čs. zpracovatelského průmyslu', *PE*, XXXII, pp. 1301–6 (1984).

75 J. Kopal, 'Bižuterie pro celý svět', *Sklář a keramik*, XI, p. 209 (1961); O. Klapetek, 'Dvacet pět let rozvoje průmyslu skla a jemné keramiky v ČSSR', *Sklář a keramik*, XX, p. 253 (1970).

76 F. Arnošt, 'Naše sklo zůstává pojmem', *HN*, 1985, 14, pp. 8–9.

77 F. Arnošt, 'Ohlédnutí po roce', *HN*, 1988, 6, p. 6.

78 K. Heřman, D. Kliková & J. Vydrová, 'Průzkum o průzkumu trhu', *HN*, 1985, 41, p. 8.

79 F. Adámek, A. Hrdlička & J. Handzel, 'Osvobození otevřelo nové možnosti a výhledy k rozvoji textilního průmyslu', *Textil*, XX, p. 211 (1965).

80 *RP*, 24 September 1965, p. 1; R. Rothwell, 'Innovation in textile machinery: the Czechoslovak experience', *Textile Institute and Industry*, 1977, pp. 421–2.

81 P. Štrougal, *RP*, 4 May 1966; M. Brožík, *RP*, 30 July 1965, p. 2; A. Gregor, 'K diskusi o průzkumu trhu', *Podniková organizace*, X, p. 249 (1956). See also I. Kršiak, 'Konkurenti jako pobídka', *HN*, 1987, 51–2, p. 15.

82 S. Sýkora, 'Nad licencemi zataženo', *HN*, 1985, 23, p. 8.

83 M. Hnízdo, 'Čs. licencní politika', *PH*, XIX, 8–9, pp. 122–30 (1966).

84 A. Volná, 'Licence v praxi', *HN*, 1985, 18, p. 5.

85 J. Brandýs, 'Licenční politika ve všeobecném strojírenství', *PH*, XXX, 12, p. 21 (1977); Sýkora, 'Nad licencemi', p. 8.

86 L. H. Lynn, *How Japan Innovates: A Comparison with the US in the Case of Oxygen Steelmaking* (Boulder, Colorado, 1982), p. 189.

87 F. Valenta et al., *Inovační proces v socialistickém průmyslu* (Prague, 1977) esp. 159–63; F. Valenta, 'Organizační struktury v intenzívním rozvoji', *HN*, 1985, 16, p. 3.

88 M. Rabiška, 'Plánování, programování a řešení komplexních inovací', *Podniková organizace*, XXXIX, pp. 370–74 (1985).

10 The politics of 'restructuring'

1 Acknowledged by J. Houfová, *RP*, 8 November 1987, p. 3.
2 K. Dawisha, *Eastern Europe, Gorbachev and Reform: The Great Challenge* (Cambridge, 1988) pp. 167–9.
3 Z. Mlynář, *7 Days*, 16 May 1987, p. 4.
4 *RP*, 26 March 1986, p. 4.
5 *Lidová demokracie*, 29 January 1987, pp. 3–4.
6 *RP*, 19 December 1987, p. 3, & 18 December 1987, p. 2.
7 'Konkretizace Zásad přestavby hospodářského mechanismu ČSSR', *HN*, 1987, 13, supplement.
8 *RP*, 22 December 1987, p. 3, and 'Směrnice k zabezpečení komplexní přestavby hospodářského mechanismu', *HN*, 1988, 8, supplement.
9 'Směrnice', p. 3.
10 V. Šlajer, 'Úvahy k zamyšlení', *HN*, 1987, 40, p. 6.
11 *HN*, 1987, 29, & 1987, 30, supplements.
12 *RP*, 5 December 1987, p. 1.
13 F. Vencovský, 'Sbližování cen', *HN*, 1987, 32, p. 3.
14 J. Fogl, 'O co jde při sbližování cen?', *HN*, 1987, 48, p. 3.
15 'Předmet sporu: VHJ = podnik?', *HN*, 1987, 41, p. 8.
16 E.g. J. Goldmann & K. Kouba, 'Terms of trade adjustment processes, and the economic mechanism', *Acta Oeconomica*, XXXII, pp. 137–60 (1984).
17 K. Dyba, 'Adjustment to international disturbances: Czechoslovakia and Hungary', *Acta Oeconomica*, XXXIV, pp. 317–37 (1985).
18 Cf. T. Bauer, 'The Hungarian alternative to Soviet-type planning', *Journal of Comparative Economics*, VII, pp. 304–16 (1983).
19 M. Hrnčíř, 'Princip demokratického centralismu a hospodářský mechanismus pro intenzívní typ rozvoje', *PE*, XXXV, p. 6 (1987).
20 V. Komárek, 'Ekonomika žádá revoluční změny', *HN*, 1987, 11, p. 9.
21 Komárek, *Inovace*, pp. 32–4.
22 Z. Suchý, in a debate with Komárek, in 'Ocelové otazníky struktury', *HN*, 1987, 10, pp. 8–9. See also Z. Suchý, 'Změnami struktury ke snížení kvant', *HN*, 1986, 13, p. 3.
23 Z. Suchý, 'Cesta, kterou jsme zvolili', *HN*, 1986, 51–2, p. 11.
24 J. Miksa, 'Hutnictví železa: Jakou cestou?' *HN*, 1985, 24, p. 9.
25 Janáček, *Prognóza*, p. 87.
26 M. Farský & P. Pešek, 'Palivové a energetické zdroje', *HN*, 1985, 39, p. 3; Janáček, *Hlavní*, pp. 209–11.
27 Janáček, *Hlavní*, p. 219.
28 I. Tupý, 'Disproporce podle plánu?', *HN*, 1987, 26, pp. 8–9.
29 K. Dyba, J. Kreuter & A. Suk, 'Na prahu nové etapy', *HN*, 1988, 3, pp. 8–9.
30 Cf. K. Janáček, 'Kontinuita ekonomických procesů', *HN*, 1986, 37, p. 3; K. Janáček, 'Zamyšlení nad hlavními výsledky ekonomické prognózy', *PE*, XXXV, p. 469 (1987).
31 V. Komárek, 'Budoucnost již začala', *HN*, 1987, 51–2, p. 1.
32 Janáček, *Prognóza*, p. 47.
33 E.g. Vintrová, *Reprodukční*, p. 84.

34 Cf. J. Svatoš, in 'Hutě ve světle souvislostí', *HN*, 1986, 2, p. 9.
35 A. Marhula, 'Víme, co musíme', *HN*, 1987, 19, p. 9.
36 V. Klaus, 'Nedostatečná efektivnost investic, rovnováha a nerovnováha', *Investiční výstavba*, XXII, pp. 197–200 (1984); 'Příspěvek k hledání nedostatečné efektivnosti čs. ekonomiky', *Finance a úvěr*, XXXVI, pp. 688–95 (1986); 'Ekonomický růst, nerovnováha a nerovnovážné impulsy', *Finance a úvěr*, XXXVII, pp. 479–91 (1987); I. Kočárník, 'Některé problémy obnovy zbožně-peněžní rovnováhy v čs. ekonomice', *Finance a úvěr*, XXXVII, pp. 793–8 (1987).
37 V. Věrtelář, 'Osmá pětiletka', *HN*, 1986, 3, pp. 1 & 4; 'Hlavní směry hospodářského sociálního rozvoje ČSSR na leta 1986–1990 a výhledy do roku 2000', *HN*, 1986, 15, supplement.
38 'Vývoj národního hospodářství a plnění planu v roce 1987', *HN*, 1988, 7, supplement, p. 7; K. Hájek, 'Výsledky roku 1986 v devizové oblasti a hlavní úkoly pro rok 1987', *Finance a úvěr*, XXXVII, pp. 433–41 (1987).
39 K. Marx, *Capital*, 3 vols., (London and Moscow, 1970–72) vol. I, p. 87.

Bibliography

Adam, J. *Wage Control and Inflation in Soviet Bloc Countries*, London, 1979

Adamec, J. & Reh, M. 'Formy usměrňování investičního vývoje', *Finance a úvěr*, XIX, 1969

Adamec, L. 'Nově jen s novými lidmi', *HN*, 1967, 31

Adámek, F., Hrdlička, A. & Handzel, J. 'Osvobození otevřelo nové možnosti a výhledy k rozvoji textilního průmyslu', *Textil*, XX, 1965

Adler-Karlsson, G. *Western Economic Warfare 1947–1967*, Stockholm, 1967

Akční program Komunistické strany Československa, RP, 10 April 1968, supplement

Allen, R. G. D. *Mathematical Analysis for Economists*, London, 1938

Amann, R. & Cooper, J. (eds.) *Industrial Innovation in the Soviet Union*, New Haven, 1982

Anchishkin, A. I. *Prognozirovaniye rosta sotsialisticheskoy ekonomiki*, Moscow, 1973

Annual Abstract of Statistics, 1988 Edition, London

Arnošt, F. 'Naše sklo zůstává pojmem', *HN*, 1985, 14

'Ohlédnutí po roce', *HN*, 1988, 6

Aubrecht, A. 'Úpravy kravínů pro JZD a ČSSS', *Zemědělský pokrok*, XVII, 1950

Bálek, A. 'Inflační tlaky v československé ekonomice v období zavádění ekonomické reformy', *PE*, XIX, 1971

Bálek, A. & Janáček, K. 'Efektivnost investic a koncepce hospodářské politiky', *HN*, 1968, 37.

'Investujeme hodně, nebo málo?' *HN*, 1967, 24

Baring, R. *Uprising in East Germany: June 17, 1953*, Cornell University, Ithaca, 1972

Bartek, K. 'Pracovná motivácia a spokojnosť v odmeňovaní', *Práce a mzda*, XVIII, 1970

Baštýř, I. 'Současný stav výdělkových vztahů mezi dělníky a technicko-hospodářskými pracovníky v průmyslu a stavebnictví', *Práce a mzda*, XXII, 1974

Batt, J. *Economic Reform and Political Change in Eastern Europe: A Comparison of the Czechoslovak and Hungarian Experiences*, London, 1988

Bauer, T. 'The Hungarian alternative to Soviet-type planning', *Journal of Comparative Economics*, VII, 1983

'Investment cycles in planned economies', *Acta Oeconomica*, XXI, 1978

Tervgazdaság, beruházás, ciklusok, Budapest, 1981

Bednařík, Z. 'Z jednání československých ekonomů', *PE*, XV, 1967

Bedrunka, J. 'Rozestavěnost v investiční výstavbě', *PH*, XIV, 2, 1961

Berger, O (ed.) *Československá průmyslová delegace ve SSSR*, Prague, 1946

Bergson, A. 'Technological progress', in A. Bergson & H. Levine (eds.) *The Soviet Economy: Towards the Year 2000*, London, 1983

Birman, A. 'In which direction? What Soviet economists are debating about', in E. Liberman et al. *Theory of Profit in Socialist Economy*, New Delhi, 1966

Blaas, A. 'Spomalenie stavieb, investičná politika a menový plán', *Finance a úvěr*, XXXIV, 1984

Blažej, Z. 'Základní fondy v hospodaření podniku', in *Úloha*

Borecký, F. 'K průzkumu názorů pracovníků spotřebního průmyslu na výdělkové relace', *Práce a mzda*, XIV, 1966

Bouchal, M. 'Příjmy a úspory obyvatelstva', *PH*, XXXII, 3, 1979

Brabant, J. M. van, *Socialist Economic Integration: Aspects of Contemporary Economic Problems in Eastern Europe*, Cambridge, 1980

Brabec, V. 'Vztah KSČ a veřejnosti k politickým procesům na počátku padesátých letech', *Revue dějin socialismu*, 1969, 3

'Životní úroveň a některé stránky diferenciace čs. společnosti v padesátých letech', *Revue dějin socialismu*, 1968, special issue

Brandýs, J. 'Licenční politika ve všeobecném strojírenství', *PH*, XXX, 12, 1977

Bránik, J. 'O ekonomické úloze socialistických financí', in *Úloha*

Brda, J. 'Mechanisace v plánovitém zvyšování produktivity živočišné výroby', *Zemědělský pokrok*, XVII, 1950

Brus, W. *The Market in a Socialist Economy*, London, 1972

Brus, W., Kende, P. & Mlynar, Z. 'Normalisation' Processes in Soviet-Dominated Central Europe, Vienna, 1982

Brychca, P. 'Mzda a společenský význam práce', *Práce a mzda*, XVII, 1969

Budík, J. 'Možnost přechodu kusové a malosériové strojírenské výroby na vyšší organizační typ', *Strojírenství*, IX, 1959

Bugala, B. 'Skúsenosti s experimentom v národnom podniku Cementáreň, Liet. Lúčka', *Finance a úvěr*, XVI, 1966

Bukal, J. 'Za vyšší technologii ve strojírenství', *Strojírenství*, IV, 1954

Bydžovský, J. & Soukup, I. 'Spotřebiče nevedou k hospodárnosti', *HN*, 1986, 50

Čáp, V. et al. *Fakty o sociálno-ekonomickom rozvoji Československa po roku 1945*, Bratislava, 1986

Čáp, V. & Rybnikář, K. 'K vývoji národního hospodářství v 1. pololetí 1982', *PH*, XXXV, 9, 1982

Carr, E. H. *The Bolshevik Revolution*, 3 vols., London, 1952

Celostátní konference Komunistické strany Československa Praha 1952, Prague, 1953

Celostátní konference Komunistické strany Československa, Prague, 1956

Celostátní konference KSČ 5.7–7.7.1960, Prague, 1960

Černík, O. 'O ekonomických problémech', *HN*, 1966, 14

'Přestavba čs. hospodářství a jeho výhledy', *HN*, 1968, 1

Červinka, A. 'V čem jsou spory?' *HN*, 1969, 10

'Cesty k ozdravení naší ekonomiky', *NM*, XXIII, 1969

Charvát, F. *Sociální struktura ČSSR a její vývoj v 60. letech*, Prague, 1972

Charvát, F., Linhart, J. & Večerník, J. 'Vývoj sociálně třídní struktury Československa v třiceti letech budování socialismu', *Sociologický časopis*, XI, 1975

Christensen, L., Jorgenson, D. & Lau, L. 'Conjugate duality and the transcendental logarithmic production function', *Econometrica*, IV, 1971

Chvojka, P. & Fojtík, F. 'Příkaz intenzifikace: změna integračního soukolí', *HN*, 1986, 43

Csaba, L. *Economic Mechanism in the GDR and in Czechoslovakia*, Budapest, 1983

Czepurko, A. 'Handel zagraniczny a wzrost gospodarczy Czechosłowacji', in Soldaczuk, *Handel*

Davies, S. *The Diffusion of Process Innovations*, Cambridge, 1979

Dawisha, K. *Eastern Europe, Gorbachev and Reform: The Great Challenge*, Cambridge, 1988

Derco, M. & Kotlaba, M. *Mzda v ČSSR*, Prague, 1977

Desai, P. *The Soviet Economy: Problems and Prospects*, Oxford, 1987

Digest of UK Energy Statistics 1985, London, 1985

Dittert, J. 'Ekonomika strojírenství a průmyslový výzkum', *Strojírenství*, XVIII, 1968

Dlouhý, V. 'Hrubý domácí produkt a ekonomická úroveň Československa II.' *PE*, XXXV, 1987

'On the problem of macroeconomic modelling in centrally planned economies', paper presented to Models and Forecasts conference, Bratislava, 1985

Dlouhý V. & Dyba, K. *Ekonometrický model československé obchodní bilance*, Prague, 1985

'K problému modelování pohybu reálných směnných relací v centrálně plánované ekonomice', *Informační systémy*, XIII, 1984

Dobb, M. *Soviet Economic Development since 1917*, London, 1948

Dolanský, J. 'Prohloubením plánovací metodiky k zajištění zvýšených úkolů 5LP', *PH*, IV, 2, 1951

Drtina, J. 'Textilní průmysl do roku 1959', *Textil*, XIV, 1959

Ďuriač, M. 'Skúsenosti z práce stranických organizácií v Bánskobystrickom kraji pri socialistickej prestavbe dediny v rokoch 1949–1955', in *Ku vzniku*

Dvořák, D. 'Národní hospodářství v roce 1969', *PH*, XXII, 1, 1969

Dyba, K. 'Adjustment to international disturbances: Czechoslovakia and Hungary', *Acta Oeconomica*, XXXIV, 1985

Dyba, K. *Československé vnější ekonomické vztahy*, Prague, 1980

'K exportní výkonnosti čs. strojírenství v sedmdesátých letech', *Finance a úvěr*, XXXV, 1985

Dyba, K., Kreuter, J. & Suk, A. 'Na prahu nové etapy', *HN*, 1988, 3

Dyba, K. & Kudlák, K. 'Agregátní cenové indexy v čs. zahraničním obchodě a čs. reálné směnné relace 1948–1978', *Statistika*, 1979, 8–9

Dyba, K. & Kupka, V. 'Přizpůsobení československé ekonomiky vnějším nárazům (Makroekonomická analýza za léta 1973–1983)', *PE*, XXXII, 1984

Dyba, K. & Vintrová, R. 'Československá ekonomika v osmdesátých letech', *Finance a úvěr*, XXXV, 1985

Dybová, B. & Dyba, K. 'The level of foreign trade in socialist and capitalist economies compared', *Ekonomicko-matematický obzor*, XXIII, 1987

Dyker, D. *The Soviet Economy*, London, 1976

Ellman, M. *Planning Problems in the USSR*, Cambridge, 1973

Embree, G. *The Soviet Union between the 19th and 20th Party Congresses 1952–1956*, Nijhoff, 1959

'Exports of manufactures from Eastern Europe and the Soviet Union to developed market economies, 1965–1981', *United Nations Economic Bulletin for Europe*, XXXV, 1983

Farský, M. & Pešek, P. 'Palivové a energetické zdroje', *HN*, 1985, 39

Fejgl, J. 'Diferenciace mezd v průmyslových podnicích Východočeského kraje', *Práce a mzda*, XVIII, 1970

Filip, V. 'Vedle pozitiv i negativ', *HN*, 1985, 35

Fišera, V. (ed.) *Workers' Councils in Czechoslovakia 1968–9. Documents and Essays*, London, 1978

Fogl, J. 'O co jde při sbližování cen?' *HN*, 1987, 48

Freeman, C. *The Economics of Industrial Innovation*, 2nd edn, London, 1982

Frejka, L. *SSSR dnes*, Prague, 1946

'Urychlená přestavba našeho průmyslu', *NM*, IV, 1950

'Urychlená přestavba našeho průmyslu', *PH*, III, 2–3, 1950

Gajdošek, E. & Mesároš, O. 'Investiční výstavby metalurgie', *PH*, XV, 7, 1962

Gerloch, V. 'Do boje s pravicovým oportunismem', *NM*, XXIII, 1969

'Ideovo-politické hľadiská účasti pracujúcich na riadení výroby', in Iša, *Revizionizmus*

Gistinger, S. 'Problematika vazeb technického a investičního rozvoje v chemickém průmyslu', Kandidátská dizertační práce, VŠChT, Prague, 1984

Golan, G. *The Czechoslovak Reform Movement*, Cambridge, 1971

Reform Rule in Czechoslovakia, Cambridge, 1973

Goldmann, J. 'Československá ekonomika v sedmdesátých letech', *PE*, XXIII, 1975

'Některé problémy plánovací techniky a metodiky', *PH*, III, 4–5, 1950

'Postupná konsolidace a růst národního hospodářství', *Ekonomický časopis*, XIV, 1966

'Tempo růstu a opakující se výkyvy v ekonomice některých socialistických zemí', *PH*, XVII, 9, 1964

Goldmann, J. et al. *Úvod do makroekonomické analýzy*, Prague, 1978.

Goldmann, J. & Flek, J. 'O dvouletce a první pětiletce', *Příspěvky k dějinám KSČ*, V, 3, 1965

Goldmann, J., Jüngling, L. & Janácek, K. 'Jaká je "druhá" koncepce rozvoje čs. ekonomiky', *HN*, 1966, 17

Goldmann, J. & Kouba, K. *Economic Growth in Czechoslovakia*, New York, 1969

'Terms of Trade adjustment processes, and the economic mechanism', *Acta Oeconomica*, XXXII, 1984

Gottwald, K. *Long-term Planning in Czechoslovakia*, Prague, 1947

Gregor, A. 'K diskusi o průzkumu trhu', *Podniková organizace*, X, 1956

HSR, see Historická statistická ročenka
Habr, J. & Vepřek, J. 'Rozbor nové soustavy řízení z hlediska systémového přístupu', PE, XIX, 1971
Hájek, K. 'Výsledky roku 1986 v devizové oblasti a hlavní úkoly pro rok 1987', Finance a úvěr, XXXVII, 1987
Hájek, M. 'K některým otázkám činitelů ekonomického růstu USA', PE, XIV, 1966
Halbhuber, J. Hospodářská politika nového Československa, Prague, 1946
Hanson, P. & Pavitt, K. The Comparative Economics of Research and Development and Innovation, New York, 1987
Häufler, V. Ekonomická geografie Československa, Prague, 1984
Hauptvogel, T. 'Diferenciace mezd v ČSR v roce 1970', Práce a mzda, XIX, 1971
'K některým průřezům diferenciace mezd', Práce a mzda, XXIII, 1975
Havelka, J. 'Nové řízení zemědělství', HN, 1966, 45
Hayek, F. A. (ed.) Collectivist Economic Planning, London, 1935
The Road to Serfdom, London, 1944
Heitlinger, A. Women and State Socialism, London, 1979
Hejduk, S. 'Průzkumy veřejného mínění a cenová politika', PH, XXIV, 2, 1971
Hejzlar, Z. Reformkommunismus, Cologne and Frankfurt, 1976
Heřman, K., Kliková, D. & Vydrová J. 'Průzkum o průzkumu trhu', HN, 1985, 41
Hirst, E., Fulkerson, W., Carlsmith, R. & Wilbanks, T. 'Improving energy efficiency', Energy Policy, X, 1982
Historická statistická ročenka, Prague, 1985
'Hlavní směry hospodářského a sociálního rozvoje ČSSR na léta 1986–1990 a výhledy do roku 2000', HN, 1986, 15, supplement
'Hledáme odpověď na aktuální problémy', PH, XXVI, 4, 1973
'Hledání společné řeči', Literární listy, 1968, 14
Hnízdo, M. 'Čs. licenční politika', PH, XIX, 8–9, 1966
Holeček, J. & Kubečka, J. 'Chemie: od defenzívních k ofenzívním oborům!' HN, 1986, 21
Hora, V. 'Jak se v ČKD Praha připravujeme na uskutečňování denivelizačního procesu', Práce a mzda, XIV, 1966
Horák, M. 'Nerealizovaná kupní síla ve Východočeském kraji', Finance a úvěr, XV, 1965
Horálek, M., Sokol, M., Kožušník, Č. & Turek, O. 'The economic of management – an outline of the conception of its further development', New Trends in Czechoslovak Economics, 4, 1968
Houška, J. 'Úkoly techniků v nové organisacii textilního průmyslu', Textil, XII, 1958
Houška, K. & Špaček, K. 'Poučení z roku 1967', HN, 1968, 11
Hrnčíř, M. 'Princip demokratického centralismu a hospodářský mechanismus pro intenzívní typ rozvoje', PE, XXXV, 1987
Hronský, M. Odměna za práci v ČSSR, Prague, 1960
Hula, L. 'Nad výsledky experimentujících podniků v Jihomoravském kraji', Finance a úvěr, XVI, 1966
Hůla, V. 'Další kroky ke konsolidaci čs. ekonomiky', PH, XXIV, 1, 1971

'Hlavní úkoly rozvoje čs. ekonomiky v roce 1980', *PH*, XXXIII, 1, 1980
'Hutě ve světle souvislostí', *HN*, 1986, 2
Indra, A. 'O úkolech dalšího rozvoje naší socialistické společnosti', *PE*, X, 1962
Iša, J. (ed.) *Revizionizmus v československej ekonomickej teórii*, Bratislava, 1976
'Jak jsme na tom', *HN*, 1968, 26
Janáček, K. 'Kontinuita ekonomických procesů', *HN*, 1986, 37
'Zamyšlení nad hlavními výsledky ekonomické prognózy', *PE*, XXXV, 1987
Janáček, K. et al. *Hlavní tendence reprodukčního procesu československé ekonomiky a základní rysy strategie hospodářského rozvoje ČSSR*, Ekonomický ústav ČSAV, Prague, 1986
Prognóza změn v reprodukčním procesu čs. ekonomiky do roku 2000, Ekonomický ústav ČSAV, Prague, 1984
Janáček, K., Klaus, V. & Kupka, V. 'Úvod do zkoumání inflace v československé ekonomice', *PE*, XVIII, 1970
Janáček, K. & Kupka, V. 'Konjunkturální situace a chování ekonomických subjektů', *HN*, 1968, 48
Jankowski, S. 'Warunki bytu ludności', in Kaliński & Landau, *Gospodarka*
Janza, V. 'Československý průmysl jednostopých motorových vozidel v údobí 1945–1960', *Automobil*, IV, 1960
'Do prvého roka ôsmej päťročnice', *HN*, 1985, 49
Jaška, F. 'S poznatky z experimentů k dalšímu uplatňování nové soustavy řízení', *Textil*, XXI, 1966
Jech, K. 'Sociální pohyb a postavení čs. zemědělského obyvatelstva v letech 1948–1955', *Revue dějin socialismu*, 1968, special issue
Ježdík, V, 'Vývoj národního hospodářství v roce 1985', *PH*, XXXIX, 3, 1986
Jezierski, A. & Petz, B. *Historia gospodarcza Polski Ludowej 1944–1975*, Warsaw, 1980
Jodko, T. 'Handel zagraniczny a wzrost gospodarczy NRD', in Soldaczuk, *Handel*
Johanovský, K. 'Rozestavěnost v investiční výstavbě' *PH*, XXI, 4, 1968
'Zabezpečit hlavní úkoly investiční výstavby v roce 1963', *PH*, XVI, 4, 1963
Judge, G. C., Griffiths, W. E., Hill, R. C. & Lee, T. C. *The Theory and Practice of Econometrics*, New York, 1980
Jüngling, L. 'Tržní nerovnováha a struktura ekonomiky', *HN*, 1968, 32
'K další realizaci závěrů XIV. sjezdu v ekonomické oblasti', *HN*, 1972, 8, supplement
'K historii a dalšímu výhledu koncentrace v potravinářském průmyslu', *Průmysl potravin*, XV, 1964
'K současným hospodářským opatřením', *HN*, 1969, 20
'K úkolům státního plánu rozvoje národního hospodářství na roku 1962', *PH*, XV, 3, 1962
Kaifoš, E. 'Věrnost, oddanost a láska', *Tvorba*, XVIII, 1949
Kaigl, V. 'Socialistické soutěžení a náš tisk', *Tvorba*, XVIII, 1949
Kalinová, L. *Máme nedostatek pracovních sil?* Prague, 1979

Kaliński, J. & Landau, Z. *Gospodarka Polski Ludowej 1944–1955*, 3rd edn, Warsaw, 1986

Kalousek, S. 'Neprodává třída', *HN*, 1985, 49

Káňa, M. & Škoda, Z. 'Elektronika pro občana: ČSSR', *HN*, 1985, 32

Káňa, O. 'Septembrové plénum ÚV KSČ roku 1953 a realizácia jeho záverov', in *Ku vzniku Kapitoly z dejín socialistického poľnohospodárstva v Československu*, Bratislava, 1982

Kaplan, K. *Dans les archives du Comité Centrale*, Paris, 1978
The Overcoming of the Regime Crisis after Stalin's Death in Czechoslovakia, Poland and Hungary, Cologne, 1986
Political Persecution in Czechoslovakia 1948–1972, Cologne, 1983
Utváření generální linie výstavby socialismu v Československu, Prague, 1966
'Úvahy o první pětiletce', *Příspěvky k dějinám KSČ*, VII, 5, 1967
'Zamyšlení nad politickými procesy', in 3 parts, *NM*, XXII, 1968
Znárodnění a socialismus, Prague, 1968

Kareš, J. 'Úkoly specializace strojírenské výroby', *PH*, XV, 7, 1962
'Karosérie vozu Škoda 1000MB', *Automobil*, IX, 1965

Karpiński, A. *Polityka uprzemysłowienia Polski w latach 1958–1968*, Warsaw, 1969

Karpíšek, Z. 'Směnnost a časové využití strojů v čs. průmyslu', *PH*, XXVI, 3, 1973

Kaser, M. *Comecon: Integration Problems of the Planned Economies*, London, 1967
(ed.) *The Economic History of Eastern Europe 1919–1975*, 5 vols., Oxford, 1985 –

Klacek, J. 'Relace mezi vyrobními faktory v procesu intenzifikace', *PE*, XXXIII, 1985

Klacek, J. & Klaus, V. 'Inflační nerovnováha na trhu spotřebních předmětů', *PE*, XVI, 1968

Klacek, J. & Nešporová, A. *Ekonomický růst a jeho intenzifikace – mezinárodní srovnání*, Ekonomický ústav ČSAV, Prague, 1985
'Modelování variantních trajektorů ekonomického růstu', *PE*, XXX, 1982
Produkční funkce a modelování ekonomického růstu v ČSSR, Prague, 1983

Klacek, J. & Pleva, J. 'Efektivnost zahraničně obchodních operací na trhu EHS', *PE*, XV, 1967

Klacek, J. & Toms, M. *Pracovní síla a modelování reprodukčního procesu*, Prague, 1976

Klapetek, O. 'Dvacet pet let rozvoje průmyslu skla a jemné keramiky v ČSSR', *Sklář a keramik*, XX, 1970

Klaus, V. 'Ekonomický růst, nerovnováha a nerovnovážné impulsy', *Finance a úvěr*, XXVII, 1987
'Modelování investiční sféry centralně plánované ekonomiky: diskuse problémů a demonstrace jednoho možného přístupu', *Ekonomicko-matematický obzor*, XXII, 1986
'Nedostatečná efektivnost investic, rovnováha a nerovnováha', *Investiční výstavba*, XXII, 1984
'Nepravidelnost spotřebních výdajů domacností v sedmdesátých letech', *PE*, XXVII, 1979

'Příspěvek k hledání nedostatečné efektivnosti čs. ekonomiky', *Finance a úvěr*, XXXVI, 1986

'Rozestavěnost investiční výstavby, model i empirická analýza', *Finance a úvěr*, XXXV, 1985

'Úvod do zkoumání inflace v československé ekonomice', *PE*, XVIII, 1970

Klaus, V. & Rudlovčák, V. 'Komparace vývoje oběživa a vkladů obyvatelstva v některých socialistických zemích: formální analýza', *PE*, XXVI, 1978

Klímová, H. & Kavan, J. 'Jak to bylo s těmi vysokoškoláky', *Literární listy*, 1968, 2

Kmoníček, J., Doležal, J. & Pekárek, J. 'Skúsenosti zo začiatkov kolektivizácie poľnohospodárstva vo východných Čechách', in *Kapitoly*

Knobloch, V. 'K zákazu zyvšování cen', *PH*, XXIII, 3, 1970

Kobzár, V. 'Plánování investic', *PH*, I, 5, 1948

Kocanda, R. 'Postavení podniku v socialistické ekonomice', *PH*, XX, 10, 1967

Kočárník, I. 'Některé problémy obnovy zbožně-peněžní rovnováhy v čs. ekonomice', *Finance a úvěr*, XXXVII, 1987

Kohout, J. 'Vývoj masného průmyslu v letech 1945 až 1960 a jeho úkoly ve třetí pětiletce', *Průmysl potravin*, XI, 1960

Kohout, J. & Kolár, J. 'Výzkum pozice a role československých manažérů', *Sociologický časopis*, V, 1969

Kohoutek, M. 'K problematice plánu a trhu', *PH*, XX, 9, 1967

'K výoji hotovostního oběhu a peněžních rezerv obyvatelstva ČSSR v letech 1961–1985', *Finance a úvěr*, XXXVII, 1987

Kolanda, M. 'K problémům exportních výkonů podnikové sféry čs. zpracovatelského průmyslu', *PE*, XXXII, 1984

Kolanda, M. & Touš, O. 'Kompletační výrobky v mezinárodní dělbě práce ve strojírenství', *PH*, XX, 6, 1967

Kolár, F. *Zestátnění průmyslu a peněžnictví*, Prague, 1945

Kolder, D. 'Pětiletka a nová soustava', *HN*, 1966, 41

Komárek, A. & Filip, V. 'Demokracii ve výrobě', *NM*, XXIII, 1969

Komárek, V. 'Budoucnost již začala', *HN*, 1987, 51–2

'Dlouhodobý rozvoj národního hospodářství', *PH*, XV, 11, 1962

'Efektivnost investic a tempo rozvoje', *NM*, XVI, 1962

'Ekonomika žádá revoluční změny', *HN*, 1987, 11

Inovace a intenzifikace v hospodářství, Prague, 1986

'K výsledkům celostátní porady o investiční výstavbě', *PH*, XII, 1, 1959

Technika a ekonomika investic, Prague, 1982

Komárek, V. et al. *Prognóza základních tendencí reprodukčního procesu čs. ekonomiky do roku 2000 (etapa 1981)*, Ekonomický ústav ČSAV, Prague, 1982

Komunistická strana Slovenska. Dokumenty z konferencií a plén 1944–1948, Bratislava, 1971

'Konkretizace Zásad přestavby hospodářského mechanismu', *HN*, 1987, 13, supplement

Kopal, J. 'Bižuterie pro celý svět', *Sklář a keramik*, XI, 1961

Kornai, J. *The Economics of Shortage*, Amsterdam and Oxford, 1980

Koš, M. *Diferenciace mezd a produktivita práce*, Prague, 1964

Košnár, J. *RVHP výsledky a problémy*, Bratislava, 1964

Kosta, J. 'Aims and methods of economic policy in Czechoslovakia 1970–1978', in A. Nove, H-H. Höhmann & G. Seidenstecher (eds.) *The East European Economies in the 1970s*, London, 1982

Kosta, J. & Sláma, J. 'Ekonomická reforma a československé hospodářství', in *Systémové změny*, Cologne, 1972

Kouba, K. 'Plán a ekonomický růst', *PH*, XII, 1965
'Plán a trh', in Kouba et al., *Úvahy*
'Rady pracujících a ekonomická reforma', *NM*, XXIII, 1969
'Tempo rozvoje a struktura čs. hospodářství', *NM*, XVI, 1962
'Vztahy mezi plánovitým řízením, dynamikou a strukturou výroby', *PH*, XVII, 12, 1964

Kouba, K. et al. *Úvahy o socialistické ekonomice*, Prague, 1968

Kouba, K., Sokol, M. & Turek, O. 'Nová soustava řízení a růst československého hospodářství', *PH*, XIX, 1, 1966

Kozák, J. 'Rekonstrukce a modernizace základních fondů', *PH*, XIV, 3, 1961

Kožušník, Č. 'Rozhodující krok dalšího rozvoje ekonomické reformy', *NM*, XXII, 1968
'Zbožní výroba a plánovitost', in Kouba et al., *Úvahy*

Kožušník, Č. & Kodet, Z. 'Monopolní výroba a soutěživost', *NM*, XX, 23, 1966

Krakeš, F. 'Problémy diferenciace odměňování v pivovářsko-sladářském průmyslu', *Práce a mzda*, XVI, 1968

Kratochvílová, Ž. 'Prvé kroky pri socialistickom združstevňovaní československého poľnohospodárstva', in *Ku vzniku*

Kraus, O. 'Ještě k postavení podniku v naší ekonomice', *PH*, XXI, 2, 1968

Krblich, J. & Pelikán, J. 'Ekonomický význam společného obdělávání půdy v JZD', *NM*, IV, 1950

Krejcar, B., Procházka, J. & Tesař, J. 'Nová soustava řízení a ekonomické experimenty', *PH*, XIX, 1, 1966

Křenek, V. & Měšťák, B. 'Nová automobilka v ČSSR?', *Automobil*, XII, 1969

Krkoška, V. 'Niektoré aspekty materiálno-technických predpokladov socializácie československého poľnohospodárstva', in *Kapitoly*

Kršiak, I. 'Konkurenti jako pobídka', *HN*, 1987, 51–2
Ku vzniku a začiatkom JRD v ČSSR, Bratislava, 1985

Kučera, E. 'Rozvoj a úkoly chemického průmyslu v ČSR', *Chemický průmysl*, II, 1952

Kundrátek, Z. 'Nedostatky v investiční výstavbě národních výborů', *PH*, XIV, 9, 1961

Kupka, V. *Analýza vývojových trendů investiční výstavby v ČSSR jakožto prostředku vědeckotechnického rozvoje československého národního hospodářství*, Ústav pro ekonomiku a řízení vědeckotechnického rozvoje, Prague, 1982
Investice a ekonomický růst v ČSSR, Prague, 1983
'Investiční rozhodování a míra parametričnosti prostředí', *Finance a úvěr*, XXXII, 1982
'Podniková samospráva a ekonomická racionalita', *NM*, XXIII, 1969

Kurowski, L. 'Handel zagraniczny a wzrost gospodarczy Węgier', in Soldaczuk, *Handel*

Kusín, V. V. *Political Grouping in the Czechoslovak Reform Movement*, London, 1972

Kýn, O. 'Czechoslovakia', in H-H. Höhmann, M. Kaser & K. Thalheim (eds.) *The New Economic Systems of Eastern Europe*, Los Angeles, 1975

Kynštetr, P. 'K analýze růstové dráhy čs. ekonomiky v 70. letech', *PE*, XXIX, 1981

Lamser, V. & Slejška, D. 'Pohyb pracovních sil jako sociologický problém', *Sociologický časopis*, III, 1967

Lančaričová, V. 'Dlhodobý vplyv medzinárodnej socialistickej integrácie na rozvoj čs. hutníctva železa', in *Problémy intenzifikácie ekonomického rozvoje a SEI*, Ekonomický ústav, SAV, Bratislava, 1983

Landa, O. 'Rizení jako hlavní sociální faktor urychlování vědeckotechnického rozvoje', *Organizace a řízení*, XVI, 1987

Landa, O. & Loudín, J. 'Neúprosná výzva ke světovosti', *HN*, 1986, 17

Lehár, B. *Dějiny Baťova koncernu*, Prague, 1960

Lethbridge, E. 'National income and product', in Kaser *The Economic*

Levčík, B. & Nachtigal, V. 'Disproporce ve struktuře národního důchodu a jejich řešení', *HN*, 1966, 12

Littler, C. *The Development of the Labour Process in Capitalist Societies*, London, 1982

Loebl, E. *My Mind on Trial*, London, 1976

Lorenc, C. 'Jaké budou podíly', *HN*, 1967, 11

Lukas, Z. 'Die tschechoslowakische Landwirtschaft', *Osteuropa-Wirtschaft*, XXXI, 1986

Lynn, L. H. *How Japan Innovates: A Comparison with the US in the Case of Oxygen Steelmaking*, Boulder, Colorado, 1982

Mach, M. & Toms, M. *Teorie socialistické rozšířené reprodukce*, Prague, 1986

Macháčova-Dostálová, B. 'Úkoly investiční výstavby ve třetí pětiletce', *Textil*, XV, 1960

Machonin, P. *Československá společnost*, Prague, 1969

Machová D. *ČSSR v socialistické mezinárodní dělbě práce*, Prague, 1962

Mačica, Z. 'Tempo růstu a model řízení', *PH*, XVIII, 2, 1965

Mačica, Z. et al. 'Tendence vývoje ekonomiky v roce 1968', *HN*, 1968, 38

Madřy, F. 'Proč zaostávat když nemusíme', *HN*, 1986, 11

Maňák, J. 'Problematika odměňování české inteligence v letech 1945–1948', *Sociologický časopis*, III, 1967

Mareš, S. 'Zvláštnosti inovačních procesů a jejich nároky na řízení', *Organizace a řízení*, XV, 1985

Marhula, A. 'Víme, co musíme', *HN*, 1987, 19

Marjinová, V. V. & Murašková, G. P. *Rozorané medze*, Bratislava, 1971

Marrese, M. & Vanous, J. *Soviet Subsidization of Trade with Eastern Europe: A Soviet Perspective*, Berkeley, 1983

Marx, K. *Capital*, 3 vols., London and Moscow, 1970–1972

Matějka, M., Matouš, J. & Vrba, J. 'Exportní schopnost: negativní role velkoobchodních cen', *HN*, 1985, 28

Matouš, K. & Vlček, J. 'Kam směřujeme', *HN*, 1968, 12

Matusík, J. & Kolbaba, J. 'Sociálně psychologický výzkum k některým otázkám odměňování v NHKG', *Práce a mzda*, XV, 1967

'Mezinárodní dělba práce v automobilovém průmyslu', *Automobil*, VII, 1963
Miksa, J. 'Hutnictví železa: Jakou cestou?', *HN*, 1985, 24
Mikuláš, A. & Vojanec, D. 'Výsledky statistického šetření o mzdách dělníků a THP za říjen 1976 v hlavních výrobních odvětvích', *Práce a mzda*, XXVI, 1978
XIV. mimořádný sjezd KSČ (protokol a dokumenty), Vienna, 1970
Mises, L. 'Economic calculation in the socialist commonwealth', in Hayek, *Collectivist*
Míšovič, J. 'Růžovějsí brýle ředitelů', *HN*, 1986, 23
Mitro, J. 'Úsilí SBČS o snižování rozsahu nedokončené investiční výstavby', *Finance a úvěr*, XXXVII, 1987
Mládek, J. 'Shortage – the barrier of modelling consumption in centrally planned economy', *Ekonomicko-matematicky obzor*, XXIII, 1987
Mlčoch, A. 'Kdo dobře zhodnotí, dobře prodá', *HN*, 1987, 12
Mlčoch, L. *Analýza procesu plánování v podnikové sféře*, Ústav pro ekonomiku a řízení vědeckotechnického rozvoje, Prague, 1983
'Symposium o podniku', *PE*, XVII, 1969
'Vstřícné plánování v hierarchickém plánovacím systému', *Ekonomické modelování*, 1984, 2
Mlynář, Z. *Československý pokus o reformu 1968*, Cologne and Rome, 1975
Nightfrost in Prague, London, 1980
Montias, J. M. *Economic Development in Communist Rumania*, Cambridge, Massachusetts, 1967
Moravec, E. 'Byl rok 1968 rokem mzdové exploze?' *Práce a mzda*, XVII, 1969
'Jaké poučení plyne z vývoje mezd v roce 1969', *Práce a mzda*, XVII, 1969
'Mzdová diferenciace a využití podílů na hospodářských výsledcích', *Práce a mzda*, XV, 1967
Mracno, M. 'Denivelizací k vyšším výkonům v pražském Koh-i-nooru', *Práce a mzda*, XV, 1967
Müller, K. 'Co určuje efektivnost výzkumu', *HN*, 1985, 13
Myant, M. 'Develelling: the attempt to increase pay differentials in Czechoslovakia in the late 1960s', *Coexistence*, XIX, 1982
'Income inequalities in Czechoslovakia', *Coexistence*, XX, 1983
Socialism and Democracy in Czechoslovakia, 1945–1948, Cambridge, 1981
Nekola, Z. 'Co si myslí podnikoví ředitelé', *HN*, 1968, 1
'Podnikoví ředitelé se vyjadřují k hospodářským problémům', *Textil*, XXIII, 1968
'Reditelé podniků potravinářského průmyslu o hospodářské situaci', *Průmysl potravin*, XIX, 1968
Nešporová, A. 'Analýza vývoje produktivity práce ve výrobní sféře ČSSR', paper presented at Macroanalyses 1987 conference, Bratislava, 1987
'Kvantifikace ekonomického potenciálu základních fondů a pracovních sil a odhad jejich vzájemného vztahu pro strojírenství ČSSR', *PE*, XXXII, 1984
Novák, S. 'Od potenciálních ke skutečným efektům!' *HN*, 1986, 25
Nove, A. 'Soviet economic performance: a comment on Wiles and Ellman', in J. Drewnowski (ed.) *Crisis in the Eastern European Economy: The Spread of the Polish Disease*, London, 1982

Novotný, K. 'Úvahy o rozvoji čs. automobilového průmyslu', *Automobil*, XIII, 1969

Nový, J. 'Některé poznatky z výzkumu veřejného mínění zaměřeného na problematiku hmotné zainteresovanosti', *Práce a mzda*, XXVII, 1979

'O demokracii v oblasti výroby', *NM*, XXI, 1968

'O programu životní úrovně a sociálně politických opatření na roku 1969', *Práce a mzda*, XVI, 1968

'Ocelové otazníky struktury', *HN*, 1987, 10

Od X. do XI. sjezdu KSČ: usnesení a dokumenty ÚV KSČ, Prague, 1958

Okáli, I. & Vojtko, J. (eds.) *Hospodársky mechanizmus v etape formovania intenzívneho typu rozšírenej reprodukcie*, Bratislava, 1983

Olšovský, R. et al. *Přehled hospodářského vývoje Československa v letech 1918–1945*, Prague, 1961

Olšovský, R. & Průcha, V. (eds.) *Stručný hospodářský vývoj Československa do roku 1955*, Prague, 1969

On Events in Czechoslovakia, Moscow, 1968

Oxley, A., Pravda, A. & Ritchie, A. (eds.) *Czechoslovakia: The Party and the People*, London, 1973

Pajestka, J. & Secomski, K. *Doskonalenie planowania i funkcjonowania gospodarki w Polsce Ludowej*, Warsaw, 1968

Paliwoda, S. *International Marketing*, London, 1986

Parkan, M. & Hotový, K. 'Problémy kolem masa', *PH*, XXVI, 7, 1973

Pécsi, K. *Economic Questions of Production Integration within CMEA*, Budapest, 1978

Pelikán, J. 'Cesta vesnice k socialismu', *NM*, IV, 1950

Pešek, J. *Přerod jihočeské vesnice*, České Budějovice, 1985

Piekalkiewicz, J. *Public Opinion Polling in Czechoslovakia 1968–69: Results and Analysis of Surveys Conducted During the Dubcek Era*, New York, 1972

Pivrnec, J. 'Třicet let technického vývoje československých motocyklů Jawa', *Automobil*, III, 1959

Pivrnec, J. & Schulmann, J. 'Situace ve světové výrobě a odbytu jednostopých motorových vozidel', *Automobil*, I, 1957

Planning and Market Relations: International Economic Association Conference 1970, Ekonomický ústav ČSAV, Prague, 1970

Poláček, K. 'K novému pojetí mzdové politiky', *Práce a mzda*, XVI, 1968

'Úkoly automobilového průmyslu ve třetí pětiletce', *Automobil*, V, 1961

'Úspěchy strojírenství v mezinárodní socialistické dělbě práce', *Strojírenství*, XIII, 1963

Portes, R. & Winter, D. 'Disequilibrium estimates for consumption goods markets in centrally planned economies', *Review of Economic Studies*, XLVII, 1980

Pospíšil, M. 'Co ukázala prověrka kolektivních smluv', *HN*, 1967, 40

Potáč, S. 'Plán urychlení intenzifikace ekonomiky', *PH*, XXXV, 1, 1982

'Předmět sporu: VHJ = podnik?' *HN*, 1987, 41

'Přehlídka tvůrčích výsledků práce textiláků a oděvářů', *Textil*, XV, 1960

Problémy nové soustavy plánování a financování československého průmyslu, Prague, 1957

Provazník, J. & Vlasák, F. *Socialistické soutěžení v ČSR*, Prague, 1960

Průša, J. *Ekonomické řízení a mzdové soustavy*, Prague, 1969

Ptáček, J. 'Decentralizovaný model socialistického hospodářství a úloha financí v národním hospodářství', *PE*, XIV, 1966

Půček, Z. 'O pojetí a methodách socialistického plánování', *NM*, IV, 1950

'Za zlepšení metodiky plánování rozvoje národního hospodářství v ČSR', *PH*, V, 4, 1952

Púčik, J. 'O štátnom pláne rozvoja národného hospodárstva ČSR na rok 1954', *PH*, VII, 2, 1954

Rabiška, M. 'Plánování, programování a řešení komplexních inovací', *Podniková organizace*, XXXIX, 1985

Radice, E. A. 'General characteristics of the region', in Kaser, *The Economic*

Reh, M. 'Charakteristické rysy současného investování', *Finance a úvěr*, XIX, 1969

Rendl, V. 'Information on the main features of the proposed economic development in Czechoslovakia, 1966–1970', *Czechoslovak Economic Papers*, IX, 1967

Rett, P. 'Za splnění akčního programu', *Sklář a keramik*, XIII, 1963

Řezníček, J. et al. *Hospodářská politika KSČ*, Prague, 1977

Základy hospodářské politiky KSČ, Prague, 1984

Řezníček, J. & Toman, J. 'Demokratizace hospodářství a postavení podniku', *HN*, 1968, 16, supplement

Romančík, L'. *Ekonomické problémy tvorby kombinátov v priemysle*, Bratislava, 1969

Rosická, H. *Mzdové diferenciační procesy v chozrasčotní sféře*, Ekonomický ústav ČSAV, Prague, 1984

Rosický M. 'Diskuse k analýze nové soustavy řízení ekonomiky', *PE*, XIX, 1971

Organizace výrobní základny a plánovité řízení ekonomiky, Prague, 1983

Společnost hospodářských možností, Prague, 1969

Rothwell, R. 'Innovation in textile machinery: the Czechoslovak experience', *Textile Institute and Industry*, 1977

'The relationship between technical change and economic performance in mechanical engineering: some evidence', in M. Baker (ed.) *Industrial Innovation: Technology, Policy, Diffusion*, London, 1979

Routh, G. *Occupation and Pay in Great Britain 1906–1979*, London, 1980

Rozsypal, K. 'Co je a co není reálné', *HN*, 1964, 9 & 10

Československé národní hospodářství po 2. světové válce, Prague, 1974

'Dvacet let vývoje plánování a řízení československého národního hospodářství', in *Vývoj a cíle národohospodářské politiky ČSSR*, Prague, 1968

'Príspevok k analýze predchádzajúceho úsilia o zdokonaľovanie sústavy riadenia', in Iša, *Revizionizmus*

Úvod do teorie národohospodářského plánování, Prague, 1981

'Rozvoj masného průmyslu do 25. výročí osvobození ČSSR', *Průmysl potravin*, XXI, 1970

Rufert, S. 'Vliv nové techniky na profesní a kvalifikační strukturu a početní stavy pracovníků', *Práce a mzda*, XIV, 1966

RVHP a ČSSR. Štvrťstoročie spolupráce a perspektívy so zameraním na zahraničný obchod, Bratislava, 1974

Rychetník, L. 'The industrial enterprise in Czechoslovakia', in I. Jeffries (ed.) *The Industrial Enterprise in Eastern Europe*, Eastbourne and New York, 1981

'Vývoj inflačního tlaku 1955–66', *PH*, XXI, 9, 1968

SR, see *Statistická ročenka*

Schejbal, D. & Vintera, J. 'K statnímu plánu na roku 1964', *PH*, XVI, 11, 1963

Sedlák, V. et al. *Národohospodářské plánování v ČSSR*, Prague, 1963

Sekerka, B. & Typolt, J. 'The method used in the overall reform of wholesale prices in Czechoslovakia', *Czechoslovak Economic Papers*, X, 1968

Selucký, R. *Czechoslovakia: The Plan that Failed*, London, 1970

Semerák, F. 'Úkoly čs. textilního průmyslu v páté pětiletce', *PH*, XXV, 4, 1972

Ševčovič, R. 'Pohled na potravinářský průmysl v 20. roce osvobození', *Průmysl potravin*, XVI, 1965

'Zpracovatelské kapacity potravinářského průmyslu', *Průmysl potravin*, XV, 1964

Šíba, V. 'Ekonomická reforma a důchodová politika', *PH*, XXII, 2, 1969

Šik, O. 'Cesty k překonání nerovnováhy v našem hospodářství', *NM*, XXI, 8, 1967

The Communist Power System, New York, 1981

Czechoslovakia: The Bureaucratic Economy, New York, 1972

'Demokratické a socialistické tržní hospodářství', in *Systémové Ekonomika, zájmy, politika*, Prague, 1962

Plan and Market under Socialism, Prague, 1967

'Překonat pozůstatky dogmatismu v politické ekonomii', *NM*, XVI, 1963

'Příspěvek k analýze našeho hospodářského vývoje', *PE*, XIV, 1966

'Problémy nové soustavy řízení', *NM*, XVII, 1964

'Socialistické zbožně peněžní vztahy a nová soustava plánovitého řízení', *PE*, XIII, 1965

The Third Way, London, 1976

Šimon, B. et al. 'Cesty k ekonomické rovnováze', *NM*, XXI, 25, 1967

'Nástroje řízení', *NM*, XXI, 26, 1967

'Obsah a cíle', *NM*, XXI, 21, 1967

Šimůnek, O. 'Do 4. roku Gottwaldovy pětiletky', *Chemický průmysl*, II, 1952

X. sjezd Komunistické strany Československa, Prague, 1954

XI. sjezd Komunistické strany Československa 18.6.58, Prague, 1958

XII. sjezd Komunistické strany Československa, Prague, 1962

XIII. sjezd Komunistické strany Československa, Prague, 1967

XIV. sjezd Komunistické strany Československa, Prague, 1971

XX. sjezd KSSS, Prague, 1956

Skilling, H. G. *Czechoslovakia's Interrupted Revolution*, Princeton, 1976

Šlajer, V. 'Úvahy k zamyšlení', *HN*, 1987, 40

Slánský, R. *Za vítězství socialismu: stati a projevy 1925–1951*, 2 vols., Prague, 1951

Slunečko, M. 'Nová metodika plánování v chemických závodech', *Chemický průmysl*, II, 1952

'Směrnice k zabezpečení komplexní přestavby hospodářského mechanismu', *HN*, 1988, 8, supplement

Šmolcnop, V. 'Sociologický a psychologický výzkum odměňování v hornictví', *Práce a mzda*, XVI, 1968

Smrkovský, J. *The Story of the Czechoslovak Invasion of 1968 as Told by an Insider*, Australian Left Review pamphlet, 1976

Sochor, L. *Contribution to the Analysis of the Conservative Features of the Ideology of 'Real Socialism'*, Cologne, 1984

Sokol, M. 'Changes in economic management in Czechoslovakia', *Czechoslovak Economic Papers*, VIII, 1967
'Ekonomická reforma jako problém', *PH*, XXII, 1, 1969
'Existují východiska z těžkostí v hospodářství?', *NM*, XXIII, 1969

Soldaczuk, J. (ed.) *Handel zagraniczny a wzrost krajów RWPG*, Warsaw, 1969

Soška, K. 'Dvě koncepce rozvoje československé ekonomiky', *HN*, 1966, 16

Sousedík, V. 'Budoucí postavení podniku v textilním odvětví', *Textil*, XXIII, 1968

Špaček, P. & Parízek, P. 'Cíl – kurs a směnitelnost', *HN*, 1988, 1

Špaček, P. & Válek, V. 'Sbližování místo autarkie', *HN*, 1988, 7
'Systémové předpoklady', *HN*, 1986, 48

Spáčil, J. 'Některé výsledky kolektivizace na střední a severní Moravě v letech 1952–1953', *Příspěvky k dějinám KSČ*, VII, 6, 1967

Špěváček, V. 'Bilanční metoda v národohospodářském plánování', *PH*, XXIV, 7, 1971

Špindler, M. 'JZD v čele pokroku', *Zemědělský pokrok*, XVII, 1950

Šrein, Z. *Plánovité řízení a efektivnost investiční výstavby*, Prague, 1984

Šrůtka, J. *O rozvoji životní úrovně pracujících za socialismu*, Prague, 1962

Stalin, J. V. *Economic Problems of Socialism in the USSR*, Moscow, 1952

Statisches Jahrbuch der Deutschen Demokratischen Republik, Berlin, 1955

Statistická ročenka Republiky československé, subsequently *Statistická ročenka ČSSR*, Prague, 1957–1986

Štefanský, M. 'Vplyv industrializácie na tempo kolektivizácie poľnohospodárstva v podmienkach Hornej Nitry', in *Kapitoly*

Steinhauser, J. 'Malé strojírenské závody', *HN*, 1966, 2

Strejček, M. 'Účinněji řídit rozestavěnost', *PH*, XXXV, 10, 1982

Štrougal, L. 'O současných ekonomických problémech', *Život strany*, 1967, 23

Strużek, B. *Rolnictwo europskych krajów socjalisticznych*, Warsaw, 1963

Šuba, J. 'Za pravdu v ekonomice', *HN*, 1968, 17

Suchánek, R. 'Proč limity zaměstnanosti?' *PH*, XXIV, 2, 1971

Suchý, Z. 'Změnami struktury ke snížení kvant', *HN*, 1986, 13
'Cesta, kterou jsme zvolili', *HN*, 1986, 51–2

Šujan, I. 'Analýza príčin spomalenia rozvoja čs. ekonomiky v r. 1980–1985', *PE*, XXXV, 1987

Šujan, I. & Viktorínová, B. 'Rovnováha na spotrebiteľskom trhu a jej ovplyvňovanie hodnotovými nástrojmi', *Finance a úvěr*, XXXVI, supplement 4, 1986, and XXXVII, supplement 1, 1987

Sýkora, S. 'Nad licencemi zataženo', *HN*, 1985, 23

Systémové změny, Cologne, 1972

Tesák, P. 'Problémy potravinárskeho priemyslu na Slovensku', *Práce a mzda*, XVIII, 1970

Tesař, J. & Krejcar, B. 'K důchodové politice v nové soustavě řízení', PH, XXI, 4, 1968

Toms, M. & Hájek, M. 'Proces intenzifikace a prognózování růstu souhrnné hospodárnosti čs. ekonomiky', PH, XXX, 1982

Trapl, M., Kraváček, F. & Pospíchal, M. 'Realizácia roľníckej politiky KSČ pri združstevňovaní poľnohospodarskej malovýroby v horských a podhorských oblastiach Českomoravskej vrchoviny (1949–1955)', in Ku vzniku

Třeška, V. 'Úkoly plánu rozvoje zemědělství a výživy v ČSR a roce 1986', PH, XXXIX, 4, 1986

Tupý, I. 'Disproporce podle plánu?' HN, 1987, 26

Turek, O. 'Ceny – klíčový problém nové soustavy řízení', HN, 1966, 3
'Jak dál v nové soustavě řízení?', HN, 1966, 51–2
'Jak dál v nové soustavě řízení?', HN, 1968, 4
O plánu, trhu a hospodářské politice, Prague, 1967
'O plánu, trhu a hospodářské politice', HN, 1967, 43

Typolt, J. 'Hospodářská politika a ceny', NM, XXIII, 1969
'Realizace ekonomické reformy a cenová politika', PH, XXI, 2, 1968

Úloha financí v současné ekonomice Československa, Prague, 1959

United Nations Economic Commission for Europe, Structure and Change in European Industry, New York, 1977

United Nations Economic Survey of Europe in 1953, Geneva, 1954

United Nations Economic Survey of Europe in 1954, Geneva, 1955

United Nations Economic Survey of Europe in 1958, Geneva, 1959

United Nations Economic Survey of Europe in 1985–1986, New York, 1986

United Nations Economic Survey of Europe in 1986–1987, New York, 1987

Urmínsky, J. 'Kvalifikácia z pohľadu riaditeľov v priemysle', Práce a mzda, XX, 1972

Usnesení a dokumenty ÚV KSČ: Od celostátní konference KSČ 1960 do XII. sjezdu KSČ, 2 vols., Prague, 1962

Usnesení a dokumenty ÚV KSČ: Od XI. sjezdu do celostátní konference 1960, Prague, 1960

Usnesení a dokumenty ÚV KSČ: od listopadu 1962 do konce roku 1963, Prague, 1964

'Úspechy čsl. automobilového průmyslu v r. 1948–1958', Automobil, II, 1958

Vaculík, L. 'A co dělníci', Literární listy, 1968, 6

Valenta, F. 'Organizační struktury v intenzívním rozvoji', HN, 1985, 16

Valenta, F. et al. Inovační proces v socialistickém průmyslu, Prague, 1977

Vanko, A. 'Výkup poľnohospodárskych výrobkov v období kolektivizácie v Československu', in Ku vzniku

Váňová, J. 'Co povědí a co ne', HN, 1985, 36

Vejvoda, J. 'Příspěvek k analýze vývoje naší ekonomické teorie v šedesátých letech', PH, XIX, 1971

Vencovský, F. 'Devizová rovnováha je nezbytnou podmínkou rozvoje', HN, 1987, 50
'Sbližování cen', HN, 1987, 32

Vergner, Z. & Soucek, M. Teoretické otázky ekonomického růstu ČSSR, Prague, 1967

Věrtelář, V. 'Osmá pětiletka', HN, 1986, 3

Vesel, J. 'Príprava mládeže na povolanie v Slovenskej socialistickej republike', Práce a mzda, XXVIII, 1980

Veselý Z. 'Čs. výroba a spotřeba energie v mezinárodním srovnání' PH, XXV, 9, 1972

Vintera, J. 'K předpokladům hospodářského vývoje v roce 1967', PH, XX, 7, 1967

Vintrová, R. Národohospodářská bilance: nástroj analýzy reprodukčního procesu v ČSSR, Prague, 1979

Vintrová, R. et al. Reprodukční proces v ČSSR v 80. letech, Prague, 1984

Vitak, R. 'Workers control: the Czechoslovak experience', Socialist Register, 1971

Vlasák F. 'Tendence národního hospodářství', HN, 1968, 43

Vojtěch, M. 'Spolupráce mezi strojírenskými průmysly zemí tábora míru', Automobil, VI, 1962

Volná, A. 'Licence v praxi', HN, 1985, 18

'VI. všeodborový sjezd a odměňování pracujících', Práce a mzda, XV, 1967

Výška, K. '15 let výroby nákladních automobilů v ČSR', Automobil, IV, 1960

'Vývoj národního hospodářství a plnění plánu v roce 1987', HN, 1988, 7, supplement

Wacker, V. et al. Ekonomika zahraničního obchodu ČSSR, Prague, 1968

Ward, B. 'The firm in Illyria: market syndicalism', American Economic Review, XLVIII, 1958

Wiles, P. J. Communist International Economics, Oxford, 1968

Zahálka, V. 'Je nerealizovaná kupní síla problém?' Finance a úvěr, XVI, 1966

Základy první československé pětiletky, Prague, 1948

Zasedání Ústředního výboru Komunistické strany Československa 21.–24. února 1951, Prague, 1951

Žatkuliak, J. 'Činnosť národných výborov na úseku poľnohospodárstva na Slovensku v prvých rokoch výstavby socializmu', in Ku vzniku

Závodný, O. 'Některé problémy obnovy základních fondů v potravinářském průmyslu', Průmysl potravin, XVII, 1966

Zdokonaľovanie plánovitého riadenia národného hospodárstva, Bratislava, 1983

Zdycha, P. 'Úloha kovoroľníkov v prvých rokoch združstevňovania na strednom Slovensku (1949–1953)', in Kapitoly

Zhospodárněním výroby splnit zvýšené úkoly Gottwaldovy pětiletky, Prague, 1951

'Znovu o traktorech', Automobil, V, 1961

'Zpráva o vývoji národního hospodářství v 1. pololetí 1968', HN, 1968, 30

Index

Soviet and East European Studies

Soviet and East European Studies

The following series titles are now out of print:

Soviet and East European Studies

Soviet and East European Studies